Remedies against international organisations

International organisations have become major players on the international scene, whose acts, actions and omissions affect individuals, companies and states. Damage to interests or violation of rights sometimes occurs (such as during peacekeeping operations, for example). Karel Wellens considers what remedies are available to potential claimants such as private contractors, staff members or, indeed, anyone suffering damage as a result of their actions. Can they turn to an ombudsman or national courts, or do they have to rely on support from their own state? Are the remedies provided by international organisations adequate? Wellens' conclusions include suggestions for alternative remedial options in the future.

Karel Wellens is Professor of Public International Law and the Law of International Organisations, at the Catholic University of Nijmegen, the Netherlands. He is also Chairman of the Advisory Committee on International Legal Issues to the Dutch Foreign Ministry and Co-Rapporteur of the International Law Association Committee on Accountability of International Organisations. His other publications include editing *Resolutions and Statements of the UN Security Council (1946–1992): A Thematic Guide* (1993) and *Economic Conflicts and Disputes before the World Court (1922–1995)* (1996).

CAMBRIDGE STUDIES IN INTERNATIONAL AND COMPARATIVE LAW

This series (established in 1946 by Professors Gutteridge, Hersch Lauterpacht and McNair) is a forum of studies of high quality in the fields of public and private international law and comparative law. Although these are distinct legal sub-disciplines, developments since 1946 confirm their interrelation.

Comparative law is increasingly used as a tool in the making of law at national, regional and international levels. Private international law is increasingly affected by international conventions, and the issues faced by classical conflicts rules are increasingly dealt with by substantive harmonisation of law under international auspices. Mixed international arbitrations, especially those involving state economic activity, raise mixed questions of public and private international law. In many fields (such as the protection of human rights and democratic standards, investment guarantees and international criminal law) international and national systems interact. National constitutional arrangements relating to 'foreign affairs', and to the implementation of international norms, are a focus of attention.

Professor Sir Robert Jennings edited the series from 1981. Following his retirement as General Editor, an editorial board has been created and Cambridge University Press has recommitted itself to the series, affirming its broad scope.

The Board welcomes works of a theoretical or interdisciplinary character, and those focusing on new approaches to international or comparative law or conflicts of law. Studies of particular institutions or problems are equally welcome, as are translations of the best work published in other languages.

GENERAL EDITORS

Professor James R. Crawford SC FBA
Whewell Professor of International Law, Faculty of Law and
Director, Lauterpacht Research Centre for International Law
University of Cambridge

Professor John S. Bell FBA
Professor of Law
Faculty of Law
University of Cambridge

EDITORIAL BOARD

Professor Hilary Charlesworth, University of Adelaide
Professor Lori Damrosch, Columbia University Law School
Professor John Dugard, Universiteit Leiden

Professor Mary-Ann Glendon, Harvard Law School
Professor Christopher Greenwood, London School of Economics
Professor David Johnston, University of Edinburgh
Professor Hein Kötz, Max-Planck-Institut, Hamburg
Professor Donald McRae, University of Ottawa
Professor Onuma Yasuaki, University of Tokyo
Professor Reinhard Zimmermann, Universität Regensburg

ADVISORY COMMITTEE
Professor Sir D. W. Bowett QC
Judge Rosalyn Higgins QC
Professor Sir Robert Jennings QC
Professor J. A. Jolowicz QC
Professor Sir Eli Lauterpacht QC
Professor Kurt Lipstein QC
Judge Stephen Schwebel

Remedies against international organisations

Karel Wellens
Catholic University of Nijmegen

CAMBRIDGE UNIVERSITY PRESS
Cambridge, New York, Melbourne, Madrid, Cape Town, Singapore, São Paulo

Cambridge University Press
The Edinburgh Building, Cambridge CB2 2RU, UK

Published in the United States of America by Cambridge University Press, New York

www.cambridge.org
Information on this title: www.cambridge.org/9780521812498

© Karel Wellens 2002

This publication is in copyright. Subject to statutory exception
and to the provisions of relevant collective licensing agreements,
no reproduction of any part may take place without
the written permission of Cambridge University Press.

First published 2002

A catalogue record for this publication is available from the British Library

Library of Congress Cataloguing in Publication data

Wellens, Karel.
Remedies against international organisations / Karel Wellens.
     p.   cm. – (Cambridge studies in international and comparative law; [21])
Includes bibliographical references and index.
ISBN 0 521 81249 6 (hardback)
1. Tort liability of international agencies. I. Title. II. Cambridge studies in inter-
national and comparative law (Cambridge, England: 1996); 21.
K967.5.W45 2002   341.2–dc21   2001043130

ISBN-13 978-0-521-81249-8 hardback
ISBN-10 0-521-81249-6 hardback

Transferred to digital printing 2005

Contents

Acknowledgements	*page* ix
List of abbreviations	xi
Introduction	1

Part I General features of remedies against international organisations

1	The accountability regime for international organisations	7
2	Remedies against international organisations	10
3	The different levels of accountability and the appropriateness of various remedies: scope *ratione materiae*	28
4	Access to remedies	36
5	Remedies against whom: the scope *ratione personae respondentis*	44
6	The potential outcome of remedies: scope *ratione remedii*	54

Part II Procedural aspects of remedial action against international organisations

7	Introduction to procedural aspects of remedial action against international organisations	63
8	Procedural aspects of remedial action by member states	66
9	Procedural aspects of remedial action by staff members	81
10	Procedural aspects of remedial action by private claimants	88

viii   CONTENTS

11 Procedural obstacles for representational non-governmental
organisations   106

12 Procedural obstacles common to remedial action by
non-state claimants   114

**Part III Substantive outcome of remedial action against
international organisations**

13 General features of remedial outcome   135

14 Remedial outcome for staff members   147

15 Remedial outcome for private claimants   156

**Part IV Alternative remedial action against international
organisations and options for the future**

16 Introduction to alternative remedial action against
international organisations and options for the future   169

17 Pre-remedial action   172

18 Non-legal alternative remedial action   177

19 Amendment of existing judicial remedies   198

20 An inevitable role for the International Court of Justice   224

Conclusion   263

Bibliography   271
Index   279

Acknowledgements

My main debt of gratitude goes to Professor James Crawford. As the then ILA Director of Studies he put forward my name as one of the Co-Rapporteurs when the Executive Council decided to establish a new ILA Committee on Accountability of International Organisations. In his capacity as Director of the Lauterpacht Research Centre of International Law he kindly agreed to my stay as a Visiting Fellow at the Centre in the spring of 2000. The publication of this study in the International and Comparative Law Series of which he is one of the general editors would not have been possible without his active involvement at crucial moments of this endeavour.

As regards my stay in Cambridge, particular thanks must go to all staff members and visiting fellows of the Lauterpacht Centre whose presence and friendship was invaluable throughout the process of writing, and to Clare Hall for having provided me with hospitality at West Court.

I should also like to express my gratitude to Miss Lesley Dingle, Foreign and International Law Librarian of the Faculty of Law, University of Cambridge, for her kind assistance.

I also greatly appreciated the support and encouragement of Sir Franklin Berman and Professor Malcolm Shaw, Chairman and Co-Rapporteur of our ILA Committee, and of my fellow Committee members: their dedication in carrying out the mandate given to us has been a constant source of inspiration in the preparation of this study.

Of course, all the errors and mistakes remain my exclusive accountability and the views expressed do not necessarily reflect those of the ILA Committee or of any of its members. I have attempted to render this study up to date as of 30 June 2000. This inevitably implies that important later developments could not be covered.

I am indebted to the anonymous readers who reviewed my draft manuscript for Cambridge University Press; their valuable comments and suggestions, which I have largely followed, helped to improve the book. I am particularly grateful to Finola O'Sullivan and her team for preparing this publication in their well-known efficient and professional way.

On the institutional side I would like to express my gratitude to the Faculty of Law of the Catholic University of Nijmegen: my brief sabbatical period would not have been possible without their financial support.

My sincere admiration goes to Peter Morris for his meticulous English revision of the draft manuscript.

Finally, and most importantly, I would like to thank my wife, Chris, who not only had to endure several months of sabbatical separation, but with kindness and patience took over from my incapable hands the arduous task of ensuring the technical improvement of the final manuscript. This book is dedicated to her.

Abbreviations

AFDI	*Annuaire Français de Droit International*
AJIL	*American Journal of International Law*
ASIL	American Society of International Law
ATCA	Alien Tort Claims Act
BYIL	*British Yearbook of International Law*
CFI	Court of First Instance
CHR	Commission on Human Rights
DPKO	United Nations Department of Peacekeeping Operations
EBRD	European Bank for Reconstruction and Development
EC	European Community/Communities
ECHR	European Court of Human Rights
ECJ	European Court of Justice
ECOSOC	Economic and Social Council
EFTA	European Free Trade Association
EU	European Union
FSIA	Foreign Sovereign Immunities Act
GATT	General Agreement on Tariffs and Trade
IACHR	Inter-American Court of Human Rights
IBRD	International Bank for Reconstruction and Development
ICAO	International Civil Aviation Organisation
ICJ	International Court of Justice
ICLQ	*International and Comparative Law Quarterly*
ICRC	International Committee of the Red Cross
ICTR	International Criminal Tribunal for Rwanda
ICTY	International Criminal Tribunal for the Former Yugoslavia
ILA	International Law Association
ILC	International Law Commission
ILM	*International Legal Materials*

xii LIST OF ABBREVIATIONS

ILO	International Labour Organisation
ILOAT	ILO Administrative Tribunal
ILR	*International Law Reports*
ITLOS	International Tribunal for the Law of the Sea
JAB	Joint Appeals Board
JWTL	*Journal of World Trade Law*
LJIL	*Leiden Journal of International Law*
NATO	North Atlantic Treaty Organisation
NGO	Non-governmental organisation
NILR	*Netherlands International Law Review*
OAS	Organisation of American States
OECD	Organisation for Economic Co-operation and Development
OIOS	Office of Internal Oversight Services
ONUC	Opérations des Nations Unies au Congo
OJ	*Official Journal*
OPCW	Organisation for the Prohibition of Chemical Weapons
PCA	Permanent Court of Arbitration
PCIJ	Permanent Court of International Justice
RBDI	*Revue Belge de Droit International*
RCADI	*Recueil des Cours de l'Académie de Droit International*
SOFA	Status of Forces Agreement
UN	United Nations
UNAMIR	United Nations Assistance Mission for Rwanda
UNAT	United Nations Administrative Tribunal
UNCITRAL	United Nations Commission on International Trade Law
UNCLOS	United Nations Convention on the Law of the Sea
UNDP	United Nations Development Programme
UNEF	United Nations Emergency Force
UNESCO	United Nations Educational, Scientific and Cultural Organisation
UNFICYP	United Nations Peacekeeping Force in Cyprus
UNHCHR	United Nations High Commissioner for Human Rights
UNHCR	United Nations High Commissioner for Refugees
UNICEF	United Nations Children's Fund
UNMIK	United Nations Interim Administration Mission in Kosovo
UNOSOM	United Nations Operation in Somalia
UNPROFOR	United Nations Protection Force
UNRIAA	United Nations Reports of International Arbitral Awards

UNRWA	United Nations Relief and Works Agency for Palestinian Refugees in the Near East
UNSCOM	United Nations Special Commission on Iraq
UNTAC	United Nations Transitional Authority in Cambodia
UNTAES	United Nations Transitional Administration for Eastern Slavonia, Baranja and Western Sirmium
UNTAET	United Nations Transitional Administration in East Timor
UNTEA	United Nations Temporary Executive Authority
US	United States
WHO	World Health Organisation
WIPO	World Intellectual Property Organisation
WTO	World Trade Organisation
ZAÖRV	*Zeitschrift für Ausländisches, Öffentliches Recht und Völkerrecht*

Introduction

During the second half of the twentieth century, international organisations have become important actors on the international scene, alongside states and multinational corporations, as a result of their proliferation and the subsequent unprecedented worldwide expansion of their institutional and operational activities. Whereas the international political and legal order has designed and put in place a comprehensive body of primary rules governing the acts, conduct and omissions of the main actors, coupled with an evolving system of secondary rules on the consequences of state responsibility, nothing similar appears to have occurred with regard to international organisations. Even the international legal framework governing the position of the individual, in both its protective and repressive aspect, seems to be well ahead of an analogous development for international organisations.

Although this picture mainly reflects the general perception and claims to correspond to present-day realities, it has to be qualified in several ways. First, it would be incorrect to assume that the conduct of international organisations escapes the governance of the international political and legal order altogether, even if only in terms of the imperatives flowing from the instrument establishing each international organisation in the first place. As subjects of international law, international organisations have to abide in good faith by the treaties to which they have become parties, they are subject to rules and norms of customary international law to the extent required by their functional powers and they have to observe the general principles of law recognised by civilised nations.

Secondly, the expansion of the activities of international organisations has always been and will continue to be the result of and under the

2 INTRODUCTION

control of the power exercised within every international organisation by its constituent members.

Thirdly, the greater degree of autonomy enjoyed by international organisations in their decision-making and operational activities, especially since the end of the Cold War, has been matched by a growing awareness that they have to account for their acts, actions and omissions. This accountability also covers the way in which they exercise their supervisory and monitoring role towards member states, based upon their constituent instrument, and/or towards all states parties to conventions entrusting them with such a function. International organisations have to comply with the normal requirements of due process of law; as a result, their accountability applies not only to their membership but extends to all actors involved and/or affected by their daily functioning.

This study will look into the implementation of that accountability regime by way of undertaking remedial action against international organisations, and the various difficulties those claiming to be entitled to raise that accountability are facing in their endeavours.[1]

The fundamental question, which deserves the most attention, is whether the mechanisms specifically put in place by international organisations to deal with claims against them or permanent mechanisms serving other purposes as well, and the actual outcome of their utilisation by a variety of potential claimants, have indeed satisfactorily assured the accountability of international organisations.

The analysis of the remedial regime starts at the point in time at which the mere occurrence of the situation that gave rise to the remedial action for organisational liability/responsibility has been established. The problems associated with establishing this organisational responsibility, such as proving that a legal act has caused damage or that an illegal act which can be attributed to an international organisation has been carried out in appropriate cases in circumstances that cannot preclude its wrongfulness – and that will normally constitute the subject-matter of the dispute opposing a claimant to an international

---

[1] The active and passive accountability of international organisations are by their very nature interconnected. An international organisation being able to be a respondent party flows from the internal logic of the ICJ's Advisory Opinion in the *Reparations for Injuries Suffered in the Service of the United Nations* case, although that particular aspect did not fall within the scope of the question submitted by the General Assembly: P. De Visscher, 'Observations sur le fondement et la mise-en-oeuvre du principe de la responsabilité de l'organisation des Nations Unies', *Revue de Droit International et de Droit Comparé* 40 (1963), 165–73, at 167.

organisation – are beyond the scope of this study. The analysis is limited to the implementation of the accountability of international organisations, leaving untouched the existence and scope of primary rules the infringement of which has allegedly caused the accountability to arise. As inter-organisational accountability is currently the subject of a doctoral thesis under my supervision, that problem will not be covered either. This book concentrates on the basic issues: who might be held accountable by whom, in which situations and by what means?

The focus will be on the general features of remedies against international organisations (Part I), the procedural aspects of remedial actions (Part II), the substantive outcome of remedial actions (Part III) and options for alternative remedial action (Part IV).

The purpose of Part I is to lay down the overall framework of the remedial regime from various perspectives. It will not only constitute the necessary basis for the more detailed analysis of the procedural and substantive aspects in Parts II and III, but it will also provide a sound foundation for the discussion of alternative remedial action in Part IV. The implication of member states in the alleged liability or responsibility of international organisations will only be taken into account from the same perspectives.

This study on remedies against international organisations has been written from a constitutional perspective in an attempt to provide and review the secondary rules that should be applicable in the process of the implementation of the primary rules of accountability governing the relationships between the international organisation and its member states, non-member states, staff members and non-state parties dealing with it on a voluntary or incidental basis.[2]

The views expressed in this study, although mostly based on the practice of the United Nations, do apply to other international organisations as well, with an exception being made for the supranational European Community, which is endowed with its own political and judicial, highly institutionalised system of accountability. Its functioning will remain outside the scope of the present study; one of its structural features – that of institutions being answerable for their (wrongful) acts – is far

---

[2] In a functional approach the emphasis is on the operational functioning of the international organisation requiring a large degree of autonomy and independence; a reluctant acceptance of the need for and the modalities of an accountability regime for international organisations being put in place, including its remedial aspects, is frequently inherent in this approach.

4   INTRODUCTION

less evident or indeed not present at all in the constituent instruments of most other international organisations. In order to remedy this structural weakness and in order that these other international organisations are not placed 'virtually' above the law, mechanisms of accountability have to be devised.[3]

[3] J. Usher, *General Principles of EC Law* (London and New York: Longman, 1998), p. 10.

PART I · GENERAL FEATURES OF REMEDIES AGAINST INTERNATIONAL ORGANISATIONS

1 The accountability regime for international organisations

As for remedies against states and individuals – the accountability of the former always having been firmly rooted as one of the cornerstones of the international legal and political order, and the accountability of individuals also having entered into the body of international law[1] – any discussion on the more procedural and consequential issues falling within the scope of redress against international organisations has to be correctly placed against the background of their accountability regime. Albeit in an embryonic form, it has been in place since the establishment of international organisations: such a regime's formulation and adjustment is bound to be a continuous process.

The need for a reasonably comprehensive and consolidated body of applicable rules, recommended practices and guidelines is all the more pressing given the ever-increasing calls from various quarters – states and non-state parties potentially affected in their interests and/or rights by the acts, actions or omissions of international organisations – for appropriate remedies to become available. In further elaborating the body of primary rules, care should be taken not to undermine pre-existing or emerging rules of legal liability or responsibility by inadvertently including them as merely good practice. The codification of principles common to all international organisations, as they have been listed by the ILA Committee on Accountability of International Organisations in its Second Report,[2] could be a first, but crucial, step in establishing a comprehensive accountability regime.

---

[1] *ILA Report of the 68th Conference*, held at Taipei, Taiwan, Republic of China, 24–30 May 1998 (London, 1999), p. 597.

[2] ILA Committee on Accountability of International Organisations, *Second Report*, submitted to the 2000 ILA Conference (London; 2000), pp. 4–8.

8   GENERAL FEATURES OF REMEDIES

Given the overarching character of accountability as a concept, an exclusively legal approach to the problems and issues involved seems to be prevented; this also has a bearing on the category of relevant secondary rules – that is, the remedies against international organisations. To be adequate, remedies for the implementation of accountability of international organisations should correspond to the kind and nature of the complaints addressed to them.

The three components or levels of accountability have been identified in the ILA Committee's First Report as interrelated and mutually supportive. Accountability will always and inevitably be triggered by member states and third parties through the proper functioning of mechanisms to monitor the conduct of international organisations. From a remedial perspective this may result in the international organisation maintaining or adjusting its course of conduct; it may eventually lead to the invocation of non-contractual liability as a consequence of damage caused during operational activities or it may result in full-scale organisational responsibility when rules or norms of international and/or institutional law have been violated.[3]

The different forms of accountability (political, legal, administrative and financial) will be determined by the particular circumstances surrounding the acts, actions or omissions of international organisations, their member states or third parties, and this will have an impact on the question of remedies.[4] However, a precise identification of their corresponding nature in those terms (political, legal, administrative and financial) will not always be possible because of the complexity of the relevant case law. The diverse forms of accountability do, therefore, prevent the situation where only legal interests that have or may have been affected could trigger accountability. Sufficient grounds to raise accountability may also come from political, administrative and financial interests that are not necessarily couched in legal terms.[5]

Furthermore, on the strictly legal level there are a variety of legal layers depending upon the circumstances and matters at issue. This situation reflects the wide range of levels on which international organisations are capable of operating. There is not just the purely international level but also multiple national and regional levels. Contrasting concerns call for greater flexibility because of multilevel operations and for the assertion of control and supervision, including appropriate remedial avenues, from the perspective of the relevant legal order.[6]

---

[3] *ILA Report of the 68th Conference*, pp. 600–1.   [4] *Ibid.*, p. 598.
[5] *Ibid.*, p. 603.   [6]*Ibid.*, pp. 591–2.

THE ACCOUNTABILITY REGIME   9

In contrast to the situation of states there is, generally, no one single comprehensive system governing all relevant questions. The plurality of political and legal guidelines, principles and limitations constraining the exercise of the institutional and operational authority and powers of international organisations[7] is bound to have an impact on the whole question of remedies; that is not surprising as a matter of principle because questions of substantive law cannot be clearly separated from questions of remedies.[8] Fundamental changes in the law of organisational responsibility, such as are currently underway, cannot take place without (judicial) remedies being affected.[9] The degree of development and refinement of the different legal layers and the various branches of law under which international organisations are operating are influencing both the need for and the adequacy of existing or future remedial mechanisms. In addition, the political constellation in which the accountability is being raised should not be ignored. Moreover, a well-functioning accountability regime increases the efficiency of international organisations and is thus also indispensable to them in terms of assisting them to serve their purpose.[10]

The form of accountability at issue will determine the availability of, access to, and selection and successful use of mechanisms of redress. The variety of legal layers providing flexibility for an international organisation when conducting its multilateral operations has to be matched by a comprehensive set of means of redress and remedies so as to leave no loopholes at each individual legal level. The inherent right of an international organisation unilaterally to qualify its activities is not unlimited, but is instead subject to independent review, which will constitute an important element in the implementation of their accountability.

---

[7] *Ibid.*, p. 601.

[8] C. Gray, *Judicial Remedies in International Law* (Oxford: Clarendon Press, 1987), p. 194.

[9] *Ibid.*, p. 224.

[10] As far as the UN is concerned, the establishment of a transparent and effective system of accountability and responsibility is currently underway and is based upon an integrated approach and made operational through a set of procedures aimed at ensuring adequate monitoring and control (A/C.5/49/1 of 5 August 1994, para. 6).

2 Remedies against international organisations

Remedies in international law

Limiting ourselves for a moment to the international legal context within which states, international organisations, non-governmental organisations and individuals are operating, some observations have to be made regarding remedies in international law.

It was commonly understood, sometimes tacitly, that doctrinal writings were neglecting (admittedly to varying degrees) the issue of remedies. Christine Gray was right when she observed, back in 1987, that the question of judicial remedies had generally been regarded as peripheral to the main study of international law; attention had been centred on the substantive rules with little consideration given to the consequences of their violation in general or judicial remedies in particular.[1] The remedies are something to be invented anew in each case.[2] In addition, partly because the statutes of international administrative tribunals govern the appropriate remedies for injuries to officials, these tribunals 'in their generally rather summary discussion of remedies' did not make any substantial theoretical contribution to the general international law on remedies.[3]

Since 1987 not only has the International Law Commission made substantial progress in its work on the draft on state responsibility, but the problem of remedies, not merely the judicial ones, has become the focus of attention, spreading over a wide range of different branches of international law. The creation of the new dispute settlement mechanism within the World Trade Organisation has led to an unprecedented

[1] C. Gray, *Judicial Remedies in International Law* (Oxford: Clarendon Press, 1987), p. 1.
[2] *Ibid.*, p. 108.   [3] *Ibid.*, p. 164.

flow of studies on remedies in international trade law. The highly institutionalised accountability regime of the European Community has always attracted analysis from a remedial perspective but the focus has certainly increased in recent times,[4] complemented by in-depth comparative studies on the level of coherence, or the lack thereof, in the international law of remedies.[5]

The protective function of accountability has perhaps nowhere been more prominent, from the very start, than in the sector of human rights, but it was only recently that an in-depth study on remedies in international human rights was undertaken by Dinah Shelton.[6] The few previous studies were clearly based on a sectoral kind of approach while at the same time they were mostly limited to the category of judicial remedies. However, the coming into being of particular regimes within the overall system of international law, such as in the areas of disarmament and the environment, each entailing tailor-made non-compliance procedures and remedies, unexpectedly led to an institutional dilemma for those considering resorting to these mechanisms; this was aptly demonstrated in the fascinating volume edited by Malcolm Evans.[7]

This briefly described renewed focus and the main conclusions reached in the research that had been undertaken will undoubtedly influence the further development in practical terms of remedies as a crucial counterpart of the ever-increasing refinement of the primary rules addressed to the various categories of actors in present-day international society. The identification of the particular difficulties stemming from the fact that we are dealing with international organisations and the search for possible solutions must take place within the perspective of the developments just referred to. Lessons may be learned and directions drawn from experiences in various sectors of international life in respect of availability, access to and the outcome of non-legal and legal, judicial and non-judicial remedial action and mechanisms *vis-à-vis* international organisations.

[4] J. Lonbay and A. Briondi (eds.), *Remedies for Breach of EC Law* (Chichester: John Wiley and Sons, 1997).

[5] J. Charney, 'Is International Law Threatened by Multiple International Tribunals?', *RCADI* 271 (1998), 101–382, at 137.

[6] D. Shelton, *Remedies in International Human Rights Law* (Oxford: Oxford University Press, 1999).

[7] M. Evans (ed.), *Remedies in International Law: The Institutional Dilemma* (Oxford: Hart Publishing, 1998).

12 GENERAL FEATURES OF REMEDIES

Given the different levels and forms of accountability, this book uses the term 'remedy' as a form of shorthand for an acceptable outcome arrived at by means of the choice of an aggrieved party.[8]

The need for remedies against international organisations

The 'perfect rational desire on the part of governmental officials and international civil servants neither to lose political or administrative control of disputes nor to embarrass other states and organisations'[9] will inevitably have to give way to the need for, and access to, internal and external, impartial, judicial and non-judicial dispute settlement mechanisms for states and non-state entities alike.

The entirely speculative character of the discussion on the responsibility of an international organisation as it was described by Clyde Eagleton half a century ago[10] has clearly been overtaken by events.

It may be useful at this stage to illustrate this development with a few real-life examples.

- Visitors on their way to the headquarters building of an international organisation are injured in an accident involving the car of the chief administrative officer driving at high speed.
- A female staff member is unfairly dismissed after her allegations of sexual harassment by a senior official were not properly dealt with in the course of an internal complaint procedure.
- A commodity organisation is unable to meet the claims of its creditors as a direct result of (unauthorised) speculative market trading by the organisation's buffer stock manager.
- During an armed conflict, international relief organisations decide to withdraw their international staff from a dangerous area, leaving the victims, albeit temporarily, without assistance or protection.
- Refugees or displaced persons do not survive a railway journey operated by a sub-contractor acting on behalf of an international relief organisation.
- A message originating from the head of an observer mission and containing detailed information on an imminent genocide in a

---

[8] *Ibid.*, p. vii. On the lack of uniformity in the terminology of the international law of remedies, see S. Haasdijk, 'The Lack of Uniformity in Terminology of the International Law of Remedies', *LJIL* 5 (1992), 245–63.

[9] M. Janis, 'Individuals and the International Court' in A. Muller, D. Raic and J. Thuransky (eds.), *The International Court of Justice: Its Future Role After Fifty Years* (The Hague, Boston and London: Martinus Nijhoff Publishers, 1997), pp. 205–16, at p. 209.

[10] C. Eagleton, 'International Organisations and the Law of Responsibility', *RCADI* 76 (1950), 323–423, at 386.

country already torn apart by a civil war, is not channelled through headquarters. As a result an executive organ decides to send too small a contingent of peacekeepers with a limited mandate and supported by inadequate resources and equipment.

- An organ monitoring the implementation of economic coercive measures authorised the publication of a report containing detailed but incorrect information about non-compliance by private companies, who, as a result, sustain considerable financial and economic losses.

The questions arising in each of these situations are identical. Who has an interest or a right to bring a claim? Against which entity or person should such a claim be addressed? Before which forum could or should the claim be brought? And finally, what means of redress, what remedies, are open to those who have successfully invoked the applicable rules and norms before the appropriate forum?

The need for the existence of effective, proportional and dissuasive remedies against international organisations cannot only be derived from the expansion of their activities and the ensuing complexity of situations and circumstances in which a plurality of state and non-state entities may find themselves when working closely with international organisations.[11] There are obviously other imperatives and considerations that have to be taken into account when devising or refining mechanisms of redress.

The efficacy of any accountability regime for international organisations depends to a large extent, if not entirely, on the nature of the remedies afforded.

A constitutional obligation

A first and prominent source of obligation and inspiration can be found in conventional requirements aimed at international organisations and

---

[11] More attention should be paid and efforts made to identify different stakeholders in different operational areas of international organisations: S. Schlemmer-Schulte, during a 'Panel on the Accountability of International Organisations and Non-state Actors', *ASIL Proceedings* 92 (1998), 359–73, at 371. In addition one should consider the long-term impact of privatisation on the structure, functioning and thus also the accountability of international organisations operating in particular areas such as postal services, telecommunications, etc. See in this regard G. Burdeau, 'Les Organisations internationales entre gestion publique et gestion privée' in J. Makarczyk (ed.), *Theory of International Law at the Threshold of the 21st Century: Essays in Honour of K. Skubiszewsky* (The Hague, London and Boston: Kluwer Law International, 1996), pp. 611–24. See also L. Ravillon, 'Les Organisations internationales de télécommunications par satellite: vers une privatisation?', *AFDI* 44 (1998), 533–51.

14 GENERAL FEATURES OF REMEDIES

providing for appropriate means of redress and remedies. These may be couched in more general terms such as 'promoting justice' as formulated in a constituent instrument, or in more specific provisions contained in particular conventions concluded by an organisation's member states on its privileges and immunities, or agreements entered into by the international organisation such as headquarters agreements with member states or non-member states.

Such provisions of a constitutional or quasi-constitutional nature should be given due regard whenever remedies against international organisations are considered to be defective, moribund, insufficient or lacking altogether. Derek Bowett succinctly provided the starting point for discussion when he wrote 'in justice, the United Nations could scarcely refuse to meet claims as a defendant'.[12] There is no inherent reason why the well-known ruling of the International Court of Justice – that it would 'hardly be consistent with the expressed aim of the Charter to promote freedom and justice for individuals and with the constant preoccupation of the UN to promote this aim' not to afford 'judicial or arbitral remedy'[13] – should not apply, on the second and third level of a comprehensive accountability regime, to the settlement of any disputes that arise between an international organisation and all other third-party claimants. And there is, as was pointed out by R. H. Harpignies, no aspect of the relationship between an international organisation as such and third parties, be it contractual or otherwise, which is beyond judicial or quasi-judicial settlement.[14]

The human rights protection imperative

A second and certainly equally important reason why international organisations have to provide appropriate remedies for those entities whose interests have been or may have been affected by their acts, actions and omissions emanates from the imperative of the protection of human rights.

The creation of a comprehensive body of primary and secondary rules on human rights protection has taken place in parallel, although at

[12] D. Bowett, *UN Forces: A Legal Study of United Nations Practice* (London: Stevens, 1964), p. 242.

[13] *Effects of Awards of Compensation made by the UN Administrative Tribunal*, Advisory Opinion of 13 July 1954, *ICJ Reports* (1954), p. 47, at p. 57.

[14] R. Harpignies, 'Settlement of Disputes of a Private Law Character to which the United Nations is a Party: A Case in Point: The Arbitral Award of 24 September 1969 in Re Starways Ltd v. United Nations', *RBDI* 7 (1971), 451–68, at 453.

a different pace, to the proliferation and expansion of international organisations. In numerous cases and at various levels either international organisations have been the initiators of such efforts or the process has at least taken place under their auspices. In a number of conventional human rights instruments, international organisations or treaty-based organs have been entrusted with important supervisory and monitoring responsibilities while, not infrequently, themselves designing, servicing or actually providing the appropriate remedies *vis-à-vis* (member) state parties to such Conventions.

The basic imperative of human rights protection underpinning this network of regional and universal instruments and regimes irreversibly permeates almost every single aspect of the way states conduct their internal and external affairs. Its scope of application has extended to non-governmental organisations and multinational corporations, and its impact has been increasingly felt in the way in which international organisations operate, both those organisations of a general political nature and those active in particular financial, economic or technical areas.

Although there has been for years a reluctance by international organisations to acknowledge in explicit terms a legal obligation to comply with human rights, there is certainly a recent trend by these actors to incorporate, admittedly to varying degrees, protection of human rights into their operational guidelines and directives. The pre-existing reluctance was hardly consistent with the expressed aim of the United Nations to promote and encourage respect for human rights and fundamental freedoms. The human rights imperative may have influenced and entered into internal and external primary rules governing the conduct of international organisations, but it is certainly giving rise to rather far-reaching demands in the important area of remedies against them. We may, at present, merely be witnessing the first stages of a development the ultimate outcome of which is impossible to predict.

Ultimately, 'it would be quite ironic to negate the rights of individuals on the assumption that they might be incompatible with the functions of International Organisations'.[15] The functional needs of an international organisation should always be subordinated to basic international human rights standards, such as the right to adequate means of redress in the case of violations of one's rights.[16] However, it should

---

[15] M. Arsanjani, 'Claims against International Organisations: Quis Custodiet Ipsos Custodes?', *Yale Journal of World Public Order* 7 (1980–1), 131–76, at 175, note 172.

[16] A. Muller, *International Organisations and their Host-states: Aspects of their Legal Relationship* (The Hague and London: Kluwer Law International, 1995), p. 282.

16 GENERAL FEATURES OF REMEDIES

also not be forgotten that for 'all its revolutionary advances ... human rights law has yet to develop a coherent theory or consistent practice of remedies for victims of human rights violations'.[17] The fact remains, though, that the guarantee of effective legal protection must be considered a general principle of law, which (increasingly) underlies the common constitutional traditions of the member states of international organisations.[18]

The right to a remedy

A third important element to bear in mind is linked to the previous factor but is also distinct from it. In many countries, based on the rule of law a partial or more fully fledged[19] system has been put in place providing protection for individuals and legal persons in their daily dealings with public authorities. The system of protection has been expanding rapidly and comprises a wide variety of political, administrative and legal remedies available to those whose interests or rights have been or may have been affected.[20] Individuals and groups of individuals are increasingly becoming used to some form of redress towards the state under whose jurisdiction they find or have placed themselves, and they cannot really be expected not to look for similar remedial mechanisms when their interests have or may have been affected by acts, actions or omissions on the part of an international organisation. This becomes more relevant given the frequency with which international organisations, separate from the particular cases of systems of integration, assert or exercise some minor or more pronounced attributes of governmental authority: peacekeeping operations, with their infinite variety of mandates and post-conflict transitory authorities, are examples in point.

If a judicial review of governmental and, sometimes, legislative acts by established courts is possible and 'deemed desirable in a democratic

---

[17] Shelton, *Remedies*, p. 1.

[18] E. Schmidt-Assmann and L. Harrings, 'Access to Justice and Fundamental Rights', *European Review of Public Law* 9 (1997), 529–49, at 530, citing the 1986 judgment of the ECJ in Case 222/84 *Johnstone v. Chief Constable of the RUC* [1986] ECR 1651, at 1682.

[19] Schmidt-Assmann and Harrings rightly stressed that even in countries where there is an absolute guarantee of access to the courts in the constitution not *all* acts of the administration are subject to judicial control: 'Access to Justice', 539.

[20] See, for instance, at the European level (in addition to Article 13 of the European Convention on Human Rights), Principle I of Recommendation R (84) 15 on public liability adopted by the Council of Ministers of the Council of Europe on 18 September 1984 as referred to by Shelton, *Remedies*, p. 22, note 63.

system', Bowett argues, 'the question must be posed: why not in the UN?'[21]

However, as Shelton convincingly stressed, it is not a perfect analogy as the international-level proceedings where the individual victim seeks redress also function as mechanisms to further the treaty regime in the interests of the international community:[22] that certainly applies with the same vigour to the accountability of international organisations, which has to be considered as applying *erga omnes*. Any regime of accountability for international organisations should from its inception be addressing individual and community concerns and carry it through the process of formulating primary rules and secondary remedial ones. One of the consequences of this duality of interests is that even after compliance with a primary rule by an international organisation there is still an interest in pursuing remedial actions in order to establish the basis of liability that the organisation might incur as a result of its default.[23]

The right to a remedy is well established: it is even a norm of customary international law,[24] and therefore also directs international organisations in their dealings with states and non-state entities beyond the first level of accountability; the right would include both the 'procedural right of effective access' and 'the substantive right to a remedy'.[25] From this perspective, a refusal by an international organisation to investigate complaints about its conduct would be a matter for serious

[21] D. Bowett, 'The Court's Role in Relation to International Organisations' in V. Lowe and M. Fitzmaurice (eds.), *Fifty Years of the International Court of Justice: Essays in Honour of Sir Robert Jennings* (New York and Cambridge: Grotius Publications and Cambridge University Press, 1996), pp. 181–92, at p. 190.

[22] Shelton, *Remedies*, p. 3.

[23] As the ECJ ruled with regard to member state responsibility in Case C-361/88 *Commission of the European Communities v. Federal Republic of Germany* [1991] ECR I-2567, at I-2605, para. 1, referred to by Charney, 'Is International Law Threatened?', 248, note 563.

[24] Shelton, *Remedies*, p. 182.

[25] *Ibid.*, pp. 14–15. It should be noted that responsibility of international organisations has been rightly identified as one of the areas where 'customary international law as being generally applicable will govern': C. F. Amerasinghe, *Principles of the Institutional Law of International Organisations* (Cambridge: Cambridge University Press, 1996), p. 19.

The underlying, more fundamental, issue whether international organisations have to observe fundamental customary human rights imperatives is not uncontroversial but it belongs to the sphere of the existence and modalities of primary rules and that is beyond the scope of this study. Exemption from the application of international customary law based upon the argument that operational activities are beyond their reach or that the organisation's functional autonomy would be unduly affected cannot seriously be invoked in the case of the right to a remedy.

18   GENERAL FEATURES OF REMEDIES

concern, given the evidently pivotal role of such a pre-remedial measure for any subsequent action considered by claimants.

Caution is called for as the voluntary submission by private parties to alternative settlement mechanisms has to be assessed against the overall context and background of the fundamental inequality in power between the international organisation and its (contracting) non-state parties. In this sense the ECHR's pronouncement in the *Deweer* case in 1980 that 'a waiver of one's right of access to court frequently encountered in the shape of arbitration clauses in contracts does not *in principle* offend against the Convention'[26] is indeed subject to the particularities of each individual case. Also in the *Waite and Kennedy v. Germany*, and *Beer and Regan v. Germany* cases the ECHR did not go into the concern expressed by the European Commission on Human Rights that the applicants did not receive legal protection within the international organisation that could be regarded as equivalent to the jurisdiction of the competent domestic courts.[27]

In these and similar cases, the prior exhaustion of the available internal remedial mechanisms within the international organisation[28] eventually leading to an inadmissibility ruling would probably compel domestic and international courts to undertake a thorough examination of the equivalent protection requirement instead of assuming that there would be no practical problem. At the same time, such a sequence of procedures would have the additional advantage of underlining the delineation of the respective responsibilities of the different quasi-judicial and judicial actors involved. In doing so, the applicant would still be able to request an international court such as the ECHR to examine whether this degree of access *limited to a preliminary issue* was sufficient to secure the applicant's right of access to a court.[29] The ECHR would

---

[26] *Deweer*, ECHR, 27 February 1980, Series A, No. 35 cited by A. Reinisch, 'Note on the Judgement of the ECHR of 18 February 1999 in *Waite and Kennedy v. Germany*, Application 26083/94 and in *Beer and Regan v. Germany*, Application 28934/95', *AJIL* 93 (1999), 933–8, at 936, note 24 (emphasis added).

[27] *Ibid.*, 938.

[28] As indicated by the ECHR in the *Waite and Kennedy* and *Beer and Regan* cases: 'they could and should have . . .' (*Waite and Kennedy*, para. 69). It should be noted that a failure to have recourse to a remedy which meets the requirements of Article 13 of the European Convention on Human Rights would not necessarily amount to a failure to exhaust domestic remedies in the sense of Article 26: D. Harris, M. O'Boyle and C. Warbrick, *Law of the European Convention on Human Rights* (London: Butterworths, 1995), pp. 445 and 449.

[29] *Waite and Kennedy v. Germany*, Application No. 26083/94, ECHR Judgment, 18 February 1999, para. 59.

then have an opportunity to establish whether the rights guaranteed by the European Convention were theoretical or illusory instead of practical and effective.[30]

Although the impact of this third factor on the question of remedies will probably be less than that of constitutional requirements and the human rights imperative, it is certainly not going to diminish in the future.

Comparing remedies against states with remedies against international organisations

The purpose of the following remarks is not to compare exhaustively the two systems of remedies but merely to highlight some of the specific features to be taken into account when devising and adapting remedies against international organisations. There are certainly common elements between international organisations and states with respect to remedial action against them, but far more relevant here are the main features that distinguish them.

Distinctive features

The *first* distinctive feature is related to the kind of jurisdiction normally exercised by international organisations, in Finn Seyersted's terms 'inherent' and mainly comprising 'jurisdiction over the organs of the international organisation, including officials and member states in their capacity as members of such organs'.[31] Disputes between international organisations and individuals other than officials can only arise 'in those fields where such individuals have been placed under the legislative and/or administrative authority of the organisation' – that is, the

---

[30] *Ibid.*, para. 67. In this particular case an inadmissibility ruling by the organisation's internal Appeals Board would probably have resulted in domestic courts reaching a different conclusion than the one actually reached. The problems caused by these two recent judgments of the ECHR were exacerbated further by the operation of harmless clauses *vis-à-vis* third parties and underwritten by the direct contractors of the international organisation concerned. For international organisations such as financial or commodity organisations, there is the additional concern that in order to protect and maintain their credibility in the marketplace they have to provide appropriate remedies for their partners from both the private and public sector.

[31] F. Seyersted, 'Settlement of Internal Disputes of Intergovernmental Organisations by Internal and External Courts', *ZAÖRV* 24 (1964), 1–121, at 4.

extended jurisdiction.[32] This so-called extended jurisdiction, which is inherent for states, is the exception to the rule for international organisations. As a result, one would expect the issue of remedies against international organisations to be rather limited in scope *ratione personae* and *ratione materiae*. However, the proliferation of their operational activities may have caused that distinction to become less relevant than it used to be. The point had already been made by Wilfred Jenks more than half a century ago when he argued, while discussing trusteeship agreements, that 'it should be possible for the UN ... to be a respondent in such a case in its capacity as administering authority'.[33] In all circumstances in which an international organisation exercises some kind of governmental authority over a particular territory on a temporary basis there is obviously a direct personal jurisdiction. In the *Report of the Commission of Inquiry, established pursuant to Security Council Resolution 885 (1993) to Investigate Armed Attacks on UNOSOM II Personnel which led to Casualties Among Them*, it was observed that the UN has to bear responsibility for at least some of the basic state concerns traditionally appertaining to a government.[34]

When legislative and administrative powers are clearly being conferred upon an international organisation they can be accompanied by judicial powers through the establishment of UN tribunals – as was done by General Assembly resolutions for Libya and Eritrea – 'to decide on the basis of "law" all disputes arising between Italy, the Administering Powers and the government of the territory concerned relating to the interpretation and application of ... economic and financial provisions "although" the Peace Treaty made no mention of judicial powers'.[35] When concluding the Peace Treaty the parties were probably not 'aware that in doing so they also accepted the compulsory judicial power of the UN in disputes arising out of the legislation enacted by the UN pursuant to the Treaty'.[36] Other historic examples of the increasing number of transitory administrations set up by the UN in a post-conflict peacebuilding context include the UN Temporary Executive Authority (UNTEA) established by the General Assembly in its Resolution 1752 (XVII) adopted on 21 September 1962 and administering the territory of West New Guinea (1962–3) and the UN Council for Namibia (1967–90), which was

---

[32] *Ibid.*
[33] C. W. Jenks, 'The Status of International Organisations in Relation to the International Court of Justice', *Transactions Grotius Society* 32 (1946), 1–41, at 28, para. 40.
[34] S/1994/653, para. 253.
[35] Seyersted, 'Settlement of Internal Disputes', 49.   [36] *Ibid.*

established by the General Assembly in its Resolution 2248 (S–V) adopted on 19 May 1967.[37]

Whereas the competences of states are considered to be of a general and comprehensive nature, subject of course to the limitations imposed by international law on their very existence, range, scope and the means of exercising them, the competences of an international organisation are necessarily of a limited, attributed nature: it has to act *intra vires*[38] and, of course, in compliance with international law.

As a result, the content and scope of applicable primary rules is the *second* most obvious element of distinction between international organisations and states. As there is in practice no limit to the potential scope of rules governing state conduct because of their full statehood and attributes of sovereignty, the situation for international organisations in fact starts from the opposite direction. Indeed, norms and rules are becoming applicable to international organisations only to the extent that this has become necessary because of the range of their expanding institutional and operational activities. The kind and scope of remedies that international organisations will have to make available to their partners will inevitably be affected by this difference, which in turn is bound to become increasingly less pronounced.

A further complicating factor is that the body of primary rules governing the activities of international organisations is still far more in a process of development than those governing state conduct. From a systemic point of view, and in spite of reasonable degrees of differential treatment in particular areas, the governance of primary rules over states is, in principle, uniform, whereas the functional variety of international organisations substantially reduces the range and number of guidelines, rules, norms and standards that may be considered commonly applicable. Thus, in contrast with states, the quest for more tailor-made means of redress and remedies beyond the standard minimum

---

[37] Other, current, examples are UNTAET (United Nations Transitional Administration in East Timor) established by Security Council Resolution 1272 (1999) of 22 October 1999 and UNMIK (United Nations Interim Administration Mission in Kosovo) established by Security Council Resolution 1244 (1999) of 10 June 1999. Completed examples include UNTAC (United Nations Transitional Authority in Cambodia) established by Security Council Resolution 745 (1992) of 28 February 1992 and UNTAES (United Nations Transitional Administration for Eastern Slavonia, Baranja and Western Sirmium) established by Security Council Resolution 1037 (1996) of 15 January 1996.

[38] On the strict and broad view of competences of an international organisation see, *inter alia*, M. Singer, 'Jurisdictional Immunity of International Organisations: Human Rights and Functional Necessity Concerns', *Virginia Journal of International Law* 36 (1995), 53–165, at 117–23.

requirements will have to be taken into account in the debate during the coming years.

A *third* major point of difference between states and international organisations has to do with the forum before which their respective accountability can be raised. There is certainly an imbalance in available remedies stemming from the fact that the jurisdictional immunity claimed and enjoyed by states within their own domestic and foreign legal systems is limited and thus affords more protection to affected parties. Although I will have to qualify this later, in principle and at first glance a similar degree of protection is not provided against international organisations because of their far-reaching jurisdictional immunities before domestic courts.

Conversely, states have established and submitted themselves to remedies at the regional and universal level within the context of human rights protection mechanisms. Those regimes do not provide, as things currently stand, for the submission of requests and claims of human rights violations allegedly committed by international organisations.

A *fourth* major element of distinction is connected with the different role and function of states and international organisations within the international political and legal order, and the ensuing different constituencies to which they can be held accountable. Individual state conduct challenged by the international community as represented by its most representative international organisations may face coercive measures, whereas action by international organisations considered by a minority of states to depart from their constitutional objectives cannot be subject to identical responses.

A *fifth* distinctive feature, somewhat linked to the previous one, stems from the different quality as a respondent facing remedies. Except in particular cases where judicial remedies target various states as also being respondents in their capacity as part of a consortium of states (for example, the *Nauru* case), or as member states of an international organisation (for example, the applications by Yugoslavia against NATO member states), in most situations states face challenges to their conduct individually and in their own right. When an international organisation is called to account, a corporate body is being dealt with: remedies will have to adapt to that factor, while at the same time raising the question of the joint or concurrent accountability of the member states. Will that corporate character require adaptation to every single aspect of the remedial regime: availability and access, scope both *ratione personae* and *ratione materiae*, the forum where the remedy can be sought and its potential outcome? That question is addressed below.

A *sixth* factor could be added to this non-exhaustive list. Remedies against states at the inter-state level are necessarily based on potential reciprocity: shaping of remedies has been heavily influenced as a result. This element of reciprocity is certainly lacking when remedies against international organisations are being considered, even, one can assume, at the inter-organisational level. Reciprocity does not operate in the relationship between international organisations and their member states, and *a fortiori* not when the claimant parties are individuals or non-governmental organisations. This lack of reciprocity may not only have an effect on the frequency of resorting to available remedial mechanisms, but it may also have a bearing upon the willingness of international organisations to provide them in the first place or to leave their functioning unchanged, especially as to their potential outcome. It has to be added that member states do have at their disposal a limited range of remedial actions *vis-à-vis* the organisation, which as a rule and as a matter of fact are obviously not being made available to non-state entities.

Common features

There are also, of course, common features between international organisations and states: for present purposes a few of the major ones are indicated below.

A *first* common feature is that both actors claim a certain degree of autonomy in order to adopt the appropriate policies to fulfil their purposes.[39] Although determining the purposes of an international organisation is primarily a task for the organisation itself, acting through and jointly with its member states, the remedial perspective emerges if and when an international organisation claims to be the sole judge of what acts are strictly necessary to achieve its purposes and this without external control becoming available.[40] State conduct aiming at particular objectives does not remain without external scrutiny either.

A *second* common feature of remedial action against international organisations and states may be found in the 'imbalance in respective power and juridical status' between the claimant non-state entities and the respondent parties, and this basic inequality 'affects the procedures

[39] *Ibid.*, 65.   [40] *Ibid.*, 117, note 260.

and the perceived role of the ... institution in affording remedies',[41] as one of the essential features of corrective or remedial justice is that the parties are treated as equal.[42]

Thirdly, in cases of state and organisational responsibility, their global interests are engaged in disputes arising out of the activities of their functionaries.[43] It is the entity whose responsibility has been established who is itself shielding its agent from third-party claims. 'No international procedure exists today for bringing an international civil action against'[44] the individual agent or official who actually adopted the act, took the action or failed to act, thereby giving rise to state or organisational responsibility.

The need for, the availability of, access to and outcome of remedies will finally also be affected by the increasing trend to privatise the operational activities conducted by international organisations, and this to a larger extent than has so far been the case with states. Telecommunications, space activities and energy-related operations are prime examples of activities in which private commercial actors are taking part, sometimes on an equal footing with the organisation's member states. This phenomenon – which must be distinguished from the growing practice of sub-contracting or contracting-out in sectors such as peacekeeping and humanitarian or development assistance, which is also posing complex problems for remedial action – will decisively change the remedy system for other affected parties.[45]

A number of arguments which in the context of remedial measures and mechanisms are normally deduced from or associated with the sovereignty of states – for example, in favour of a restrictive interpretation of the jurisdiction of a tribunal – are not relevant in situations where a complaint is lodged against an international organisation,[46] and this basic fact is bound to permeate the whole discussion of remedies.

---

[41] Shelton, *Remedies*, p. 2.   [42] *Ibid.*, p. 38.

[43] *Difference Relating to Immunity from Legal Process of a Special Rapporteur of the Commission on Human Rights*, Advisory Opinion of 22 April 1999, *ICJ Reports* (1999), Separate Opinion of Judge Weeramantry, p. 94.

[44] Shelton, *Remedies*, p. 2.

[45] See Burdeau, 'Les Organisations internationales' and Ravillon, 'Les Organisations internationales'.

[46] *Judgments of the Administrative Tribunal of the ILO Upon Complaints Made Against the UNESCO*, Advisory Opinion of 23 October 1956, *ICJ Reports* (1956), p. 77, at p. 97. The Court's observation is *mutatis mutandis* of greater application than to cases involving an official and an international organisation.

The mere existence of the main common and distinctive features of states and international organisations from a remedial point of view does not necessarily mean that the more traditional remedies of the international political and legal order would become unavailable, although one can expect access and outcome to be influenced to varying degrees.

Some further observations of a more general nature

In its First Report the ILA Committee on Accountability of International Organisations convincingly pointed out that the model rules envisaged 'will have to keep the balance between preserving the necessary autonomy in decision-making of International Organisations and guaranteeing that the International Organisations will not be able to avoid accountability'.[47] From a remedial point of view it has to be noted that the functional decision-making autonomy of an international organisation is guaranteed, on the one hand, by the mechanism of jurisdictional immunities before domestic courts and, on the other, by the probable absence of a rule of general international law on the basis of which member states are co-responsible for the non-fulfilment by the organisation of its international commitments and obligations *vis-à-vis* third parties.[48] In the sphere of remedies the pre-existing inequality between non-state parties and the international organisation may come into play to adjust the balance by maintaining a reasonable degree of respect for the organisation's continuous well-functioning, while providing adequate redress for the claimants. This balancing act should permeate the debate concerning remedies against international organisations, both in its procedural and substantive aspects.

International organisations should thus have due regard to the unequal position existing between them and the other parties concerned, especially individuals, when they are devising remedial mechanisms to ensure or to enhance their accountability. I submit that the implied powers of an international organisation 'which are essential to the performance of its duties'[49] would currently include not only the power but also the duty to establish appropriate remedial mechanisms to do justice

---

[47] *ILA Report of the 68th Conference*, p. 602.   [48] See below p. 46 and p. 114
[49] *Reparations for Injuries Suffered in the Service of the United Nations*, Advisory Opinion, *ICJ Reports* (1949), p. 174, at p. 182 as referred to by Seyersted, 'Settlement of Internal Disputes', 20.

as between the international organisation and third parties other than officials. In the case of a dispute between a state and an international organisation being brought before international adjudication, the basic principle would be equality of the parties.

Depending on the particular circumstances of a situation, the timing of the use of remedies may be pre-emptive or prospective before a decision on a course of action is reached, by way of injunctive or affirmative order. Remedial measures may also be resorted to during the unfolding of an operational activity. After the action has come to an end, only retrospective remedies will be available. Factors such as an awareness by potentially affected parties of the remedial mechanisms at the appropriate time are therefore crucial in ensuring the effectiveness and dissuasiveness of any remedial action. Hence the importance of pre-remedial efforts and of the provision of alternative, less-damaging means to achieve a particular objective should not be underestimated. The same holds true, for instance, for putting into operation a well-functioning internal oversight service function to monitor, for example, the procurement system. Devising mechanisms to facilitate or enhance subsequent remedial impact are equally important.

By far the most important pre-remedial action is that of the international organisation complying with applicable primary rules. It means, for instance, that 'all agents [of an international organisation], in whatever official capacity they act, must take care not to exceed the scope of their function, and should so comport themselves as to avoid claims against the [organisation] . . .'[50] Indeed, the area of protection accorded to them (that is, the agents) coincides with the limits of the performance of their duties.[51]

Generally speaking, the overarching accountability regime of international organisations presents itself, almost inevitably one would say, as a regime of ever-decreasing circles, each of them belonging to or resulting from a different degree of kinship between those entitled to raise the accountability and the international organisation. That would apply not only to the category and scope of applicable primary rules but also as a consequence in the context of the implementation of that accountability, subject, *inter alia*, to the different layers on which the

---

[50] *Difference Relating to Immunity from Legal Process of a Special Rapporteur of the Commission on Human Rights*, Advisory Opinion of 22 April 1999, *ICJ Reports* (1999), para. 66. The Court's statement was considered 'unnecessary' by Judge Oda in his Separate Opinion, p. 108, para. 26.

[51] *Ibid.*, Judge Weeramantry, Separate Opinion, at p. 98.

organisation has chosen to operate in order to achieve its objectives. These decreasing circles emerge both in connection with the procedural aspects and when the substantive outcome of remedial action is being reviewed.

A vital prerequisite for the optimal functioning of the accountability regime is the further elaboration by the international organisations themselves and by the international community of states of the principal norms and rules guiding their actions. The adoption of a common code of good conduct, derived from and based upon general principles of law, principles common to the domestic systems of their member states and general international law, would not only relatively enhance the predictability of international organisations' action towards the different entities of their constituencies, but it would also provide the necessary preconditions for any serious attempt at remedial action against them. This process of elaboration is clearly well under way within the most important international organisations which are operating on a purely intergovernmental level of co-ordination.

Given the quality and legal status of the main actors involved it comes as no surprise that most of the same questions that arise in the case of human rights violations by states deserve an answer within the accountability regime of international organisations. Who is entitled to remedies? Should a distinction be made between individual cases and collective acts, actions or omissions affecting groups of individuals or states? Should compensation be favoured as a remedy or are non-monetary remedies more important? Does remedial justice demand the prosecution and punishment of those responsible for the violations? In the concluding part of this study and in the light of the following discussion, I will return to these questions.

3 The different levels of accountability and the appropriateness of various remedies: scope *ratione materiae*

Generally speaking, the effectiveness of a remedy has to be tested by using criteria such as the independence of the decision-maker from the respondent authority (institutional effectiveness) and an element of enforceability (remedial effectiveness), thus excluding mere advice to the ultimate decision-making body.[1]

In order to be both effective and dissuasive, remedies of whatever kind have to be appropriate given the interests they are aiming to protect or restore. Accordingly, the scope *ratione materiae* of remedies against international organisations has to match so as to be in harmony with the various components or levels of accountability as they have been described in the ILA Committee's First Report.[2] On the first level, international organisations are subject to forms of internal and external scrutiny and monitoring when they are fulfilling their responsibilities as laid down in their constituent instruments. This monitoring takes place irrespective of potential and subsequent liability and/or responsibility. On the second level, tortious liability for injurious consequences may arise from a variety of acts or omissions. Damage may have been caused without violation of any rule or norm of international and/or institutional law. On the third level, organisational responsibility may arise from acts or omissions in breach of a rule or norm of international and/or institutional law.

A distinction has to be drawn between institutional acts and operational activities because potential claimants, their *locus standi* or lack of it, the applicable law, the mechanisms of redress and the nature of the remedy will necessarily be different. In order to establish

---

[1] D. Harris, M. O'Boyle and C. Warbrick, *Law of the European Convention on Human Rights* (London: Butterworths, 1995), pp. 450 and 455.

[2] *ILA Report of the 68th Conference*, pp. 599–601.

the accountability of an international organisation, administrative, financial, political and legal controls appear to be required for the former category of activities, whereas operational control functions as an additional requirement for the latter category.

As a rule international organisations do not issue decisions that are directly addressed to non-state entities, but this does not prevent individuals and others from having their interests or rights (potentially) affected by such institutional acts. On the other hand, operational activities undertaken by international organisations will in a number of circumstances be specifically addressed to non-state entities such as refugees, victims of armed conflict who will almost by definition and intentionally be affected by it. The need for and the kind of remedies required will vary accordingly.

Because of their membership links, states should demonstrate an attitude towards the international organisation and its agents that is 'at least as constructive as that which characterises diplomatic relations between States',[3] and that should apply to the accountability regime of international organisations at large.

Member states and the first level of accountability

On the first level of accountability – that is, the daily functioning of the international organisation that does not give rise to non-contractual liability or organisational responsibility – the remedies are obviously of a more, although not merely, political/administrative nature. It should be noted that although many of these remedial actions belong to the political/administrative sphere, this does not prevent them from giving rise to legal problems.

Member states have not only an interest in but also a right *vis-à-vis* the secretariat and the organisation's other organs to the actual accomplishment of the organisation's purposes: they have a right to insist that the international organisation remains within the functional limits of its purposes[4] and that it does not adopt decisions that are incompatible with the object and purpose of the constituent treaty. A duty even exists to ensure adequate supervision of the organisation, serving two

---

[3] *Difference Relating to Immunity from Legal Process of a Special Rapporteur of the Commission on Human Rights*, Advisory Opinion of 22 April 1999, *ICJ Reports* (1999), Separate Opinion of Judge Rezek, p. 110.

[4] P. Bekker, *The Legal Position of Intergovernmental Organisations: A Functional Necessity Analysis of their Legal Status and Immunities* (Boston and London: Martinus Nijhoff Publishers, 1994), p. 50.

30 GENERAL FEATURES OF REMEDIES

purposes: to protect the member states' own interests in the effective operation of the international organisation, and to protect third parties' interests in the case of a failure by the international organisation to perform adequately.[5] A norm of international law may be emerging, which requires member states to ensure that non-state entities are not harmed through their collective action.[6]

Dissatisfaction with the line of policy implemented in practice by senior officials within the margin of manoeuvre or independence given to them may ultimately, in the event of prior unsuccessful, sometimes non-public, attempts to effectuate a change of course, lead to member states withholding their reappointment, respectively voting against such a decision. The institutional memory of various international organisations provides sufficient evidence of this political remedy.

Member states always have the possibility to challenge, before a particular organ, any decision which has been taken – for example, the taking note of the reports and working methods of a Special Rapporteur and the extension of his/her mandate if they are of the opinion that words spoken or acts undertaken by the Special Rapporteur, whether or not a national of that state, have gone beyond the mandate given and have fallen outside the course of his/her functions.[7]

In the case of dysfunctioning subsidiary organs the majority of members of a principal organ may decide, or be forced to decide, to restrict,

---

[5] A good example of a representative plenary organ of an international organisation reaffirming its supervisory role may be found in General Assembly Resolution 51/241 on the Strengthening of the United Nations System adopted on 31 July 1997.

[6] Such an overarching norm based on the privileged position of member states mirrors the obligation referred to by the International Court of Justice in the *Cumaraswamy* case that 'all agents of the United Nations, in whatever official capacity they act, must take care not to exceed the scope of their functions, and should comport themselves as to avoid claims against the United Nations': *Difference Relating to Immunity from Legal Process of a Special Rapporteur of the Commission on Human Rights*, Advisory Opinion of 22 April 1999, *ICJ Reports* (1999), p. 62, at p. 89, para. 66. Developments in the law of international organisations since 1993 may thus have overtaken the contrary view expressed by C. Chinkin, *Third Parties in International Law* (Oxford: Clarendon Press, 1993), p. 119.

[7] *Difference Relating to Immunity from Legal Process of a Special Rapporteur of the Commission on Human Rights*, Advisory Opinion of 22 April 1999, *ICJ Reports* (1999), p. 62, at p. 86, para. 55. In the same *Cumaraswamy* case Costa Rica rightly pointed to the fine line separating a formal ratification by an international organisation of the words of one of its experts on mission and a less definite sign of approval consisting of the release of the same statement on the organisation's stationery (CR/98/15, p. 48, para. 13). Malaysia observed that after three reports had been lodged by the Special Rapporteur, the Government of Malaysia 'did not undertake any steps to institute proceedings against the Special Rapporteur' (CR/98/17, p. 42).

suspend or revoke even the delegation of powers that had previously been exercised by the principal organ; it is not necessary for this remedial measure in all cases to entail the termination of the subsidiary organ's existence altogether. A similar political/legal remedy would obviously not be available to members in areas where an irreversible transfer of competences had taken place towards the international organisation or to one of its constituent organs.

On this same direct level between member states and the international organisation, concerns in the area of political/administrative accountability may incite member states to refuse the payment of their contribution under the regular budget, irrespective of the unconstitutional character of such a remedial action. Discontent with the degree of consultation in all stages of the process may convince member states contributing financially or otherwise to an organisation's operational activities to withhold voluntary contributions. In more general terms a member state may decide to suspend several or all areas of active co-operation with the international organisation. The appropriate and dissuasive effect of this kind of temporary remedial action will in any event be limited by a cost-benefit analysis, which would place beneficiary developing member states in a more vulnerable position in comparison with their developed counterparts. This argument will also assist in determining, and may be decisive in making, the choice for temporary withdrawal: the dissuasive effect of temporary withdrawal by the main contributing countries cannot be underestimated, as examples in the not-too-distant past have demonstrated.

Permanent withdrawal, although perceived as the *ultimum remedium*, certainly has the lowest degree of effectiveness given that any dissuasive impact will be lacking unless other influential member states follow suit. Permanent withdrawal is a remedy of a political/legal nature of the first kind, as membership links will be severed, the former member becoming, for all purposes other than the settling of its financial accounts with the organisation, a third party with all the consequences attached to that status in terms of availability and access to remedial action against the international organisation to which it used to belong.

The remedies just indicated are situated at the international level but are still within the internal sphere of the international organisation. Member states could, however, also resort to remedial action on their home-front, within the confines of their own political system, for instance by setting up a parliamentary Commission of Inquiry entrusted with investigating an international organisation's handling of particular

32 GENERAL FEATURES OF REMEDIES

situations of a peacekeeping or humanitarian nature. Conducting such an inquiry may raise difficult procedural problems such as the provision of documents or testimony by the organisation's (former) officials, but its outcome could eventually provide calls for further remedial action and in any case it will provide indications for the international organisation as to its future course of action: a certain degree of injunctive or affirmative effect cannot be denied. National parliaments are one of the most effective natural agents of accountability towards international organisations.

The remedies briefly reviewed so far were all based on the conviction of member states that the daily political and administrative functioning of the international organisation could no longer be supported unreservedly, without this causing significant harm to particular interests or affecting any of the legal rights deriving from their membership links.

The remedies on this first level of accountability generally possess institutional effectiveness given the axiomatic independent position of member states towards intergovernmental international organisations. Their remedial effectiveness may be qualified by the relative position held by a particular member state within the overall membership.

Member states and the second and third level of accountability

Clearly belonging to the sphere of legal remedies is the institution of judicial proceedings against the organisation before international courts or tribunals. This decision implies that the member state is of the opinion that the action or inaction by the international organisation has caused substantial harm, and will eventually also constitute an alleged violation of norms and rules of international and/or institutional law. When a member state, or a non-member state for that matter, protests against the behaviour or a decision of an international organisation while claiming that such behaviour or decision constitutes a tortious act and/or a breach of a treaty, the opposing attitudes of the state and the international organisation may give rise to a dispute, even if the accused organisation does not advance any argument to justify its conduct.[8] From a remedial perspective it is also important to note that the existence of such a difference or dispute does not require

---

[8] *Applicability of the Obligation to Arbitrate under Section 21 of the United Nations Headquarters Agreements of 26 June 1947*, Advisory Opinion, *ICJ Reports* (1988), p. 12, at p. 28, para. 38: *mutatis mutandis.*

'that any contested decision must already have been carried out into effect'.[9]

At the combined international/domestic level (member) states may render the continuance by officials of an international organisation of the functions they had been entrusted with within a particular territory difficult or even impossible because the organisation has allegedly not respected the dignity and honour of the host state: this remedial action may be taken all the way through to the actual expulsion of the officials of the organisation from a state's territory, eventually resulting, in a finally deteriorating scenario, in the termination of the Headquarters Agreement. Such a decision is clearly political in essence and by nature, and at the same time constitutes a legal act entailing legal consequences.

Over a (considerable) period of time members of a particular international organisation may gradually have come to the political conclusion that no useful purposes would be served by continuing to keep in existence the international organisation they once jointly established: developments in the organisation's functional area may have made its further existence redundant to a large extent, or the advantages flowing from membership for major contributors may have been eroded. Dissolution of the international organisation may then be considered and carried out; this is the most drastic political/legal remedial measure that member states of any international organisation could possibly take.

The institutional and remedial effectiveness of actions on the second and third level of accountability seems to be well guaranteed.

Non-member states and non-state third parties

Leaving the membership links and moving into the sphere of relationships between international organisations and states and non-state third parties, it is self-evident that the interests protected by primary rules governing the organisation's conduct, which in the case of negative impact or effect are potentially remedied by the measures and actions referred to earlier, will not now be present.

The global political and legal configuration within which the issue of remedies has to be approached will be completely different: with the change in applicable rules comes the reduction in available effective remedies, the dissuasive potential of which must from the outset and for obvious reasons be considered more marginal, although in normal cases

---

[9] *Ibid.*, para. 42.

when third parties are involved political and legal remedies are almost inevitably more at the forefront to the exclusion of administrative ones.

Non-member states considering membership of an international organisation may resort to a kind of pre-emptive remedial move that preserves their total independence, by postponing their application in order to persuade the international organisation to change its course of policy. The remedial effectiveness and persuasiveness of such an option will greatly depend on the potential significance of the incoming member state for the organisation's future functioning and it will obviously be more appropriate *vis-à-vis* an organisation with a rather limited membership or with a semi-closed nature because of its functions and purposes.

Non-member states may also resort to withholding whatever voluntary contributions they were considering or were expected to make to the organisation's operational activities, whereas host states could eventually be persuaded to terminate the Headquarters Agreement linking it to the organisation.

As proceedings in a court of law do provide an excellent way to ensure the accountability of international organisations,[10] both states and non-state third parties are empowered to commence legal proceedings before, respectively, international and domestic courts in order to remedy any alleged direct or indirect organisational liability or responsibility.

This first and brief overview of the range of remedies available to member states, non-member states and other third parties appears to indicate a reasonable degree of congruence between the different levels of accountability and the kind of effective and dissuasive or persuasive remedies; I deal below with whether this will be confirmed when the other aspects of remedial measures and actions are reviewed.

At the same time it would appear that, at least at first glance, the availability of appropriate remedies would inevitably be greater in the relationship between an international organisation and its member states or its staff members than would normally be the case in relations with a third party. Pre-existing membership links will in most cases provide the member state with a larger selection of available remedies, some of them being offered by the organisation's constitutional framework. Precisely because of the greater availability of membership-connected

---

[10] M. Singer, 'Jurisdictional Immunity of International Organisations: Human Rights and Functional Necessity Concerns', *Virginia Journal of International Law* 36 (1995), 53–165, at 64.

remedies, the aforementioned obligation for international organisations to provide adequate and effective remedies to third parties in all situations where its accountability could be questioned has to be considered a real and an important one.

Finally, it has to be said at this stage that it does not appear that institutional acts or omissions would necessarily call into action other categories of remedies than in situations when operational activities are being challenged; only an analysis of the practice could provide further indications here. Whether the same would apply in terms of standing is dealt with in the next chapter.

4   Access to remedies

Access to remedies: scope *ratione personae* and differential standing

Bearing in mind the frequency with which issues of accountability of international organisations are bound to arise – most such issues being dependent on the kind of situations in which other parties find themselves, of their own free will or unintentionally, facing the political, financial, administrative and legal consequences as regards their interests and the rights of acts, actions or omissions of the international organisation – it is possible, in rather abstract terms, to make the following list, in descending order, of preferential standing for remedial measures or action.

Institutional standing covers all internal aspects, at the different levels of accountability, of the organisation's normal functioning, since member states must be assumed, as observed by Christine Chinkin, to have actual or at least constructive knowledge of an international organisation's action, so that they cannot claim ignorance.[1] The most comprehensive standing, in terms of internal accountability, unsurprisingly, can be claimed by all member states, except when some or all of the privileges and rights attached to membership have been temporarily suspended.

Other international organisations have to be identified as rightfully claiming *preferential treatment in terms of standing*, if only on the basis of the analogous application of good neighbourliness between international organisations.

Privileged institutional standing will normally be reserved for the states having concluded a Headquarters Agreement, the very essence

---

[1] C. Chinkin, *Third Parties in International Law* (Oxford: Clarendon Press, 1993), p. 102.

of it being 'a body of mutual obligations of co-operation and good faith'.[2] Non-member states will here join member states, but only with respect to the remedies provided in the Headquarters Agreement, since membership-linked remedies will additionally continue to be available to member states, although the maxim *expressio unius est exclusio alterius* could become applicable. August Reinisch was correct in pointing out that the host state factor alone is not decisive in explaining the number of cases which have arisen before domestic courts with the international organisation as the defendant party.[3] The high number of cases in the United States and Italy could be explained respectively by lack of determination and an inclination to treat international organisations like states as far as immunity is concerned.[4] Whether rules on the immunity of international organisations are a self-contained regime separate from state immunity is a matter of debate.[5]

What could be called *privileged operational standing* would cover, at the different levels of accountability, both the internal and external aspects of the operational activities of international organisations. In their capacity of, for instance, troop-contributing countries, that category of member states would deserve preferential standing leaving unaffected the same countries' 'external' standing if they were to put forward a claim *vis-à-vis* the international organisation arising in connection with the specific operation they have been contributing to financially or otherwise. The same approach seems to be required with regard to member states hosting or benefiting from an organisation's operational activity. What has been observed with regard to Headquarters Agreements seems to apply here in the case of non-member states as well.

In a potential *combination of institutional and operational standing*, states finding themselves confronted with special economic problems arising from the carrying out of preventive or enforcement measures taken by the UN Security Council do have a preferential standing within or towards the organisation through the Security Council under Article 50 of the UN Charter. The General Assembly recently recommended that the Security Council should facilitate the access of such states to Sanctions Committees and consider the establishment of

---

[2] *Interpretation of the Agreement of 21 March 1951 between the WHO and Egypt*, Advisory Opinion, *ICJ Reports* (1980), p. 73, at p. 93, para. 43.

[3] A. Reinisch, *International Organisations before National Courts* (Cambridge: Cambridge University Press, 2000), p. 18.

[4] *Ibid.*, pp. 18–19.   [5] *Ibid.*, p. 21, note 97.

38 GENERAL FEATURES OF REMEDIES

further mechanisms or procedures for early consultations with such states.[6]

Any preferential or privileged standing for states may also be affected in cases where the breach of a rule of international law by an international organisation may be pursued independently of the identification of a particular state interest when the illegal act results from the breach of an obligation *erga omnes*.[7]

A *combination of institutional and contractual standing* is reserved for staff members of an international organisation, a standing which could be qualified by the exclusive jurisdiction of international administrative tribunals.

The *penultimate ranking* would be for non-member states not finding themselves in one of the situations referred to earlier. Although the absence of membership links clearly limits the range of available remedies, it could at the same time mean that their remedial response will be less hindered by considerations that member states would be likely to take into account before resorting to any of their larger selection of remedial actions. However, non-member states would only be capable of challenging the institutional or operational activities of an international organisation from an international (political) and legal perspective, as the internal legality of these acts and actions cannot become a matter for their alleged concern. All states, however, have the right to monitor whether performance *intra vires* by an international organisation is in conformity with applicable principles of law.

The *lowest ranking* for non-state third-party entities also appears to call for a further distinction. Indeed, a relatively higher quasi-institutional standing could certainly be considered for non-governmental organisations that have, for example through their consultative status, been more directly involved in the international organisation's activities.

Major problems in terms of a total lack of or inadequate standing arise in situations where other non-governmental organisations or private parties are seeking effective and appropriate remedies against an international organisation.

---

[6] General Assembly Resolution 54/107, Implementation of the Provisions of the Charter of the United Nations related to Assistance to Third States affected by the Application of Sanctions, adopted on 9 December 1999, paras. 2 and 1.

[7] There is no inherent reason why Lauterpacht's reasoning within the context of state responsibility should not be transferable to organisational responsibility as well: E. Lauterpacht, *Aspects of the Administration of International Justice* (Cambridge: Grotius Publications, 1991), p. 63.

ACCESS TO REMEDIES   39

This picture of differential standing will have to be adjusted and qualified in the light of a series of ulterior procedural and other obstacles facing the holders of a preferential standing as soon as they actually make a serious attempt to use one of the remedial mechanisms they would normally have access to, a problem which will be dealt with later.

Access to remedies: scope *ratione fori* and differential standing

It is obvious that 'remedies for abuse ought to be found in means internal to the organisation',[8] although organs remain masters of their own procedures. Accordingly, internal disputes between an international organisation and one of its member states 'are usually settled, not judicially but by administrative decision of the deliberative or executive organ where the question arises, or of a superior organ';[9] in principle, the legality of this administrative decision could subsequently be challenged by the member states. The availability of and access to such judicial remedies deserves separate attention.[10]

As far as *political remedial mechanisms* are concerned, the overall picture appears to be rather homogeneous. The different options available to member states and non-member states, both at the domestic and international level, are relatively easily initiated as a result of initiatives and pressure from non-state entities such as national and international non-governmental organisations, groups of individual claimants, natural or legal persons alike.[11] States wishing to resort to political remedial actions can decide to do so whenever they like, unhampered by procedural obstacles on their way to a particular outcome, their action

[8] D. Bowett, 'The Court's Role in Relation to International Organisations' in V. Lowe and M. Fitzmaurice (eds.), *Fifty Years of the International Court of Justice: Essays in Honour of Sir Robert Jennings* (New York and Cambridge: Grotius Publications and Cambridge University Press, 1996), pp. 181–92, at p. 191.

[9] F. Seyersted, 'Settlement of Internal Disputes of Intergovernmental Organisations by Internal and External Courts', *ZAÖRV* 24 (1964), 1–121, at 7.

[10] *Ibid.*, 14–15, note 49 on the 1957 Resolution of the Institut de Droit International. See below, pp. 40 and 198.

[11] General guidelines issued by parliaments for national representatives before international organisations may, as pointed out by Gerster, facilitate earlier interventions for exerting influence than during a public debate at the time of the final decision: R. Gerster, 'Accountability of Executive Directors in the Bretton Woods Institutions', *JWTL* 27 (1993), 87–116, at 96. However, research with regard to accountability in the WTO has shown that, with the exception of the United States, in the majority of cases parliaments do not participate in the development of the negotiating mandate or in the formulation of guidelines: C. Bellmann and R. Gerster, 'Accountability in the World Trade Organisation', *JWTL* 30 (1996), 31–74, at 54.

40   GENERAL FEATURES OF REMEDIES

mainly being limited by the overall framework of the international political and legal order, and by the particular constitutional provisions of the international organisation.[12] The successful outcome will, *inter alia*, be determined by the vital role of a particular state's participation in the organisation's activities.[13] There appears to be no inherent limit to the frequency with which one or more political avenues could be tried over a short or longer period of time, but obviously the effective and dissuasive outcome will eventually suffer.

Turning to the *legal remedial mechanisms* the overall picture is substantially different: indeed, factors emanating from different sources will decisively determine the availability, access and potential outcome of any resort to a legal mechanism, both at domestic and international level. The issue of the outcome will be left untouched here, as that aspect is discussed below.[14]

Amongst the legal remedies, judicial protection occupies a prominent, in most cases ultimate, position. Access to a court based, *inter alia*, on equality of arms and a sufficient scope for judicial review are important elements.[15] Given all the particular features, because of an international organisation's involvement it would seem that for member states, staff members and third parties alike 'a procedure with certain guarantees to be conducted before a legally competent court is indispensable for the stability' of the entire accountability regime.[16] Moreover, the claimant must be able to discern which legal remedy to choose in a particular case.[17] The potential effect of resorting in vain to domestic courts because of the jurisdictional immunity claimed by the international organisation clearly poses the crucial question, to be discussed later, concerning the availability of alternative equivalent mechanisms for legal protection.[18]

As to availability, a *first* distinctive feature of judicial protection certainly exists in the ad hoc, incidental, semi-permanent or permanent

---

[12] Whether the governments of member states can be subject to injunctions from their own domestic courts regarding the modalities of their active participation or non-participation in the institutional and operational activities of the organisation is, of course, a matter for constitutional and other provisions of the relevant municipal system.

[13] H. Schermers and N. Blokker, *International Institutional Law: Unity Within Diversity* (Dordrecht and London: Martinus Nijhoff Publishers, 1995), para. 999.

[14] See below, pp. 54 and 135.

[15] E. Schmidt-Assmann and L. Harrings, 'Access to Justice and Fundamental Rights', *European Review of Public Law* 9 (1997), 529–49, at 531.

[16] *Ibid.*, 533.   [17] *Ibid.*, 537.   [18] See below, p. 169.

character of a particular legal remedial mechanism. Fundamental is the absence of any kind of permanent legal machinery of an administrative nature that is competent and capable to deal with the variety of claims which may be addressed to a particular international organisation because of its contractual or non-contractual liability or its fully fledged responsibility. Suitable forms of effective legal protection by way of 'transnational administrative proceedings'[19] should be developed. To date, the only such permanent arbitral mechanism is that under the 1992 Headquarters Agreement between the OAS and the United States, to which a private claimant may turn for claims amounting to less than $2,000 arising from contractual and non-contractual sources of liability. The case will be decided within a very short period of time after the closing of an oral hearing by a single arbitrator to be chosen by the claimant from a list drawn up by the OAS Secretary-General.[20]

Proposals made in the early days, such as those presented by Wilfred Jenks for the establishment of a permanent administrative tribunal, did not materialise.[21]

The protective function of any remedial action is partly based on a sufficient degree of predictability, irrespective of the chances of a successful outcome. The general picture indicates a correlation between a decreasing degree of predictability and a lower ranking on the list of preferential standing referred to in the previous section. Mainly as a result of the state of affairs just referred to (namely the absence of any kind of permanent judicial machinery), a *second* feature is a plethora of autonomous and quasi-autonomous, non-judicial, quasi-judicial and judicial organs, some of them endowed with competences to deal with either a particular category of claims potentially originating from all kinds of requesters or claimants; others having a more or less open-ended competence to deal with requests or claims which will only be considered if put forward by a rather restricted range of entities or persons. On this particular point, it should be noted that even the most preferential and equal standing for member states *vis-à-vis* the international organisation does not allow them to bring a claim before the

---

[19] Schmidt-Assmann and Harrings, 'Access to Justice', 533.

[20] P. Klein, *La Responsabilité des organisations internationales dans les ordres juridiques internes et en droit des gens* (Brussels: Editions Bruylant and Editions de l'Université Libre de Bruxelles, 1998), p. 253.

[21] C. W. Jenks, 'Some Problems of an International Civil Service', *Public Administration Review* 3(2) (1943), 93–105, at 104.

International Court of Justice as a result of the wording of Article 34(1) of the Court's Statute. Article 34(1) is double-edged because international organisations cannot in principle be brought before the ICJ as respondent, whereas injured international organisations have no *locus standi* as applicant, and neither have individuals nor other non-state entities.

With regard to another category of preferential claimants, it must be observed that the jurisdiction of administrative tribunals is 'compulsory as far as the organisation is concerned, and exclusive as far as the officials are concerned',[22] because of the organisation's immunity before domestic courts. This is an obstacle also facing the least privileged of potential claimants – that is, natural or legal persons who in most cases would be naturally tempted to commence legal proceedings before their own domestic courts; this issue will be analysed in more depth later.[23]

In all these cases there is a high degree of predictability in the negative sense as to availability and access to an international or domestic legal remedy. In contrast with legal remedies against states, similar action addressed to international organisations by any entity on the tentative list of potential requesters/claimants is certainly not faced with an institutional dilemma because of a variety of remedial mechanisms – in fact, quite the reverse. This applies more to claims arising from operational activities than when, for instance, institutional acts are being challenged, for example, by staff members. Conversely, the policy dilemma facing the respondent international organisation in this respect is a relatively simple one in the sense that the alternatives are apparently limited either to providing expanded direct access to existing mechanisms or the establishment of appropriate alternatives along the lines analysed in Part IV of this study.

In brief anticipation of a problem still to be discussed, it is relevant merely to observe the lack of parallelism between states and international organisations as to the existence of internal remedies; this is partly the result of most international organisations lacking any kind of (personal) jurisdiction over non-state entities without the context of a contractual relationship. Constitutional or conventional provisions may require the organisation to provide such remedies, which also leads to the further question of the possible applicability

---

[22] Seyersted, 'Settlement of Internal Disputes', 22.   [23] See below, p. 114.

of the exhaustion of local remedies rule to claims against international organisations.[24]

Finally, legal remedies aiming to provide redress for non-contractual liability or organisational responsibility will normally only operate upon the crucial condition that the respondent international organisation possesses a separate legal personality, at the domestic and/or international level. Access to legal remedies for third parties will thus not only depend on their availability, but will also require prior or simultaneous acceptance of the organisation's legal personality at the appropriate level either explicitly or in an implied way by merely instituting legal proceedings. In this regard it should be recalled that there is no general customary rule obligating non-member states to recognise an international organisation's legal personality within their own domestic system.

---

[24] See below, p. 76. On the rule of exhaustion of local remedies see, *inter alia*, the *Interim Report* by Professor Juliane Kokott in the *First Report of the ILA Committee on Diplomatic Protection of Persons and Property* submitted to the London ILA Conference (2000), pp. 3–27.

5 Remedies against whom: the scope
ratione personae respondentis

The claimant's approach

Except in situations where states have intentionally acted jointly and in concert, legal remedial actions based on claims of state responsibility have in most cases been addressed to one single state allegedly being solely liable or responsible. Requesters or claimants considering similar action *vis-à-vis* an international organisation – irrespective of their ranking on the preferential standing list – face the additional problem that acts, actions or omissions being decided or undertaken by an international organisation are the direct result of political decision-making by the organisation's organs composed of member states, which are, moreover, the suppliers of the organisation's financial resources. In the process of selecting the appropriate forum for a possible legal action it will be particularly relevant for claimants to consider, obviously on a prima facie basis, if, how and under what circumstances (the) member states can be held liable/responsible and to what extent may direct, concurrent or subsidiary recourse be had to (the) member states.

The claimant third party may consider that its chances could be improved if the remedial action could be instigated jointly against the international organisation and its member states, or in any event by taking a subsidiary approach in case the organisation would not be willing or capable to carry out the obligations it had entered into (contractual) or which allegedly arise for it otherwise (non-contractual). In both scenarios the corporate veil erected by the organisation's legal personality – which is essential for its independent functioning – would have to be pierced at either the domestic or international level for such a remedial action to become successful, although in the case of a contractual link 'disregarding' the organisation's personality will be more difficult for quasi-judicial or judicial bodies to accept. This remedial action, concurrently or subsidiarily targeting the international organisation and its member states, is by definition based, rightly or wrongly, upon the assumption that member states are thus liable for the obligations undertaken by the organisation and its action (or inaction as the case may be) can be attributed to them in their capacity as member states. Manfred Wenckstern has persuasively recalled the distinction between organisational responsibility (that is, acts or omissions by the organisation as a matter of principle not being attributable to member states) and member states' liability for the consequences of the organisation's non-compliance with primary obligations towards third parties.[1] Member states may be responsible for individual acts they have committed in (close) connection with those carried out by the international organisation, but that does not need any further elaboration here.

The problem of the 'selection' by potential claimants, both state and non-state entities, of their respondent (that is, the international organisation and the member states or some of them, or only some or all of the member states) has been controversial both in doctrine and in practice.[2]

This question also arises in the post-adjudicatory stage of the implementation of a judgment rendered in a contentious proceeding between one member state and an international organisation.[3] Is there room for

---

[1] M. Wenckstern, 'Die Haftung der Mitgliedstaaten für Internationale Organisationen', *Rabels Zeitschrift* 61(1) (1997), 93–114, at 97 and 104–5.

[2] For the report by Judge Higgins and the ensuing discussion, see R. Higgins, 'The Legal Consequences for Member States of the Non-fulfilment by International Organisations of their Obligations toward Third Parties', *Annuaire de l'Institut de Droit International* 66(1) (1995), 251–469 and 66(2) (1995), 233–320. A draft resolution was submitted in October 1994 (66(1) (1995), 465–9). The final resolution was adopted in September 1995 (66(2) (1995), 445–53). Other leading commentators are Wenckstern, 'Die Haftung'; M. Hartwig, *Die Haftung der Mitgliedstaaten für Internationale Organisationen* (Berlin, Heidelberg and New York: Springer, 1993); M. Hirsch, *The Responsibility of International Organisations Towards Third Parties: Some Basic Principles* (Dordrecht, Boston and London: Martinus Nijhoff Publishers, 1995), in particular pp. 96–172.

[3] P. Couvreur, 'Développements récents concernant l'accès des organisations intergouvernementales à la procédure contentieuse devant la Cour Internationale de Justice' in E. Yakpo and T. Boumedra (eds.), *Liber Amicorum Mohammed Bedjaoui* (The Hague, Boston and London: Kluwer Law International, 1999), pp. 293–323, at p. 303 and I. Seidl-Hohenveldern, 'Access of International Organisations to the International Court of Justice' in A. Muller, D. Raic and J. M. Thuransky (eds.), *The International Court of Justice: Its Future Role After Fifty Years* (The Hague, Boston and London: Kluwer Law International, 1997), pp. 189–216, at p. 201. See also the same concern expressed within the Working Group of the Special Committee on the

46   GENERAL FEATURES OF REMEDIES

a residual secondary liability of member states? Or would such a solution potentially undermine the organisation's independence by some larger contributors?[4] And in such a case of lifting the corporate veil, should not all member states become liable along the lines of reasoning formulated by the International Court of Justice in the *Certain Expenses* case?[5]

The state of the law

The question whether states have concurrent or subsidiary liability for the fulfilment of the international organisation's obligations due solely to their membership is a matter of international law to be determined by reference to the rules of the international organisation.[6]

There is no need within the scope of the present study to reiterate all the arguments put forward in opposing views on the matter and to reopen the debate, or to go over all the comments made on the *Westland Helicopters* and *International Tin Council* cases. Suffice it here to recall the main salient features of the question as they have been reflected in the thorough and well-balanced report presented by Judge Higgins to the Institut de Droit International.

A separate legal personality is a necessary precondition for an international organisation to be liable for its own obligations, but it does not necessarily determine whether member states have a concurrent or residual liability.[7] There is no general concept that member states retain an international legal responsibility for the acts of their international organisation endowed with a separate legal personality;[8] no distinction should be made in this respect between the contractual

---

Charter of the United Nations and on the Strengthening of the Role of the Organisation, during the discussion of Guatemala's proposal on broadening access to the ICJ (see also below, p. 237), A/52/33 of 2 April 1997, para. 111.

[4] Seidl-Hohenveldern, 'Access of International Organisations', p. 202.

[5] *Ibid.* and Reply of Guatemala: A/52/33, para. 114.

[6] Article 4(b) and Article 5(a) of the 1995 Resolution of the Institut de Droit International, in the *Annuaire de l'Institut de Droit International* 66(1) (1995), 444–53. Article 4(b) reads: 'Whether States have concurrent or subsidiary liability for the fulfilment of such obligations due solely to their membership in an international organisation is a matter of international law ...'. Article 5(a) reads: 'The question of the liability of the members of an international organisation for its obligations is determined by reference to the Rules of the Organisation.'

[7] *Annuaire de l'Institut de Droit International* 66(1) (1995), 382, para. 21.

[8] *Ibid.*, at 410, para. 94.

and tortious liability of the international organisation towards third parties.[9]

Although treaties (and contracts) concluded by an international organisation incur no obligation for the member states, as they are not considered to be parties, they may nevertheless not act in such a way as to thwart their execution.[10]

Liability for member states may be incurred either in accordance with a relevant general principle of international law, such as acquiescence or the abuse of rights, or through undertakings by that state or if the international organisation has acted as its agent, in law or in fact.[11] There is no norm of general international law stipulating that member states bear a concurrent or subsidiary liability to third parties for the non-fulfilment by the international organisation of its obligations towards third parties.[12] The existence of non-liability clauses in constituent instruments does not justify a presumption to the contrary in case of silence.[13] Member states may exclude or limit their liability prior to any relevant dealings with third parties: that should be specified in appropriate detail.[14]

[9] Article 7 of the 1995 Resolution of the Institut de Droit International reads: 'Unless the Rules of the Organisation direct otherwise, no distinction is to be made between claims in contract and other claims for purposes of determining whether any liability exists for member States for the obligations of an international organisation.'

[10] *Annuaire de l'Institut de Droit International* 66(1) (1995), 410, para. 93.

[11] Article 5(b) and (c) of the 1995 Resolution of the Institut de Droit International reads as follows:
> '(b) In particular circumstances, members of an international organisation may be liable for its obligations in accordance with a relevant general principle of international law, such as acquiescence or the abuse of rights.
> (c) In addition, a member State may incur liability to a third party:
> (i) through undertakings by the State
> or
> (ii) if the international organisation has acted as the agent of the State, in law or in fact.'

[12] Article 6(a) of the 1995 Resolution of the Institut de Droit International reads as follows: '(a) Save as specified in Article 5, there is no general rule of international law whereby State members are, due solely to their membership, liable, concurrently or subsidiarily, for the obligations of an international organisation of which they are members.'

[13] Article 6(b) of the 1995 Resolution of the Institut de Droit International reads as follows: '(b) No inference of a general rule of international law providing for liability of States is to be deduced from the fact that the Rules of some organisations make specific provision: (i) for the limitation or exclusion of such liability ...'.

[14] Article 9(3) of the 1995 Resolution of the Institut de Droit International reads as follows: 'Member States may, unless prohibited by the Rules of the organisation,

48   GENERAL FEATURES OF REMEDIES

Fault or negligence may engage the liability of member states towards third parties for their own acts, but not for the acts of the international organisation itself.[15]

In its 1995 Resolution the Institut de Droit International declared that there is no reason to change the law in order to place a concurrent or secondary liability upon member states: the Institut actually referred to important considerations of policy which could be advanced against the development of a general and comprehensive rule of liability.[16]

From a pre-remedial point of view, third parties should know exactly with whom they are contracting or dealing, and from whom they can expect compensation in case of breach or failure to perform.[17] International organisations, for their part, should not conduct themselves in such a way as to leave these questions vague or open in their dealings with third parties; there are a variety of measures which could be taken

exclude or limit their liability for the obligations of the organisation, provided that they do so before any relevant dealings with third parties and provided that such limitation or exclusion is specified in appropriate detail in accordance with paragraph 1.'

[15] *Annuaire de l'Institut de Droit International* 66(1) (1995), 414, para. 107.

[16] Article 8 of the Resolution reads as follows: 'Important considerations of policy, including support for the credibility and independent functioning of international organisations and for the establishment of new international organisations, militate against the development of a general and comprehensive rule of liability of member States to third parties for the obligations of international organisations.' See on the developments at the time, *inter alia*, the Provisional Report of Judge Higgins in *Annuaire de l'Institut de Droit International* 66(1) (1995), 408–10. An earlier attempt to provide for the concurrent liability of member states towards third parties in case of treaties concluded by international organisations failed in 1986 (Article 36bis of the Vienna Convention on the Law of Treaties between States and International Organisations or between International Organisations).

[17] Article 9(1) of the 1995 Resolution of the Institut de Droit International reads as follows:

'1. Important considerations of policy entitle third parties to know, so that they may freely choose their course of action, whether, in relation to any particular transaction or to dealings generally with an international organisation, the financial liabilities that may ensue are those of the organisation alone or also of the members jointly or subsidiarily. Accordingly, an international organisation should specify the position regarding liability:
(a) in its Rules and contracts;
(b) in communications made to the third party prior to the event or transaction leading to liability; or
(c) in response to any specific request by any third party for information on the matter.'

On the advantages and disadvantages for both the international organisation and third parties of concurrent, secondary and indirect responsibility see further, *inter alia*, Hirsch, *Responsibility*, pp. 154–8.

(such as insurance or specific ad hoc guarantees from member states) to protect third parties from undue exposure to loss and damage flowing from the acts, conduct or omission of the organisation.[18] The organisation should specify the position, *inter alia*, in its rules and contracts and in communications made to third parties prior to the events or transaction.[19] However, estoppel may displace the presumption of no concurrent or secondary liability in cases where there is evidence that member states, or the international organisation with their approval, gave creditors reason to believe otherwise.[20] Any limitation or exclusion clause for member state liability should be clear and explicit.[21]

The question how the international organisation will cope with the fulfilment of its obligation financially to compensate a successful third-party claimant is an internal matter to be settled between the international organisation and its member states. The financial liability of the member states is not towards third parties, but towards the organisation – that is, to provide it with funds so that it can honour its contracts and meet its liabilities.[22] This obligation should be proportionate to the member's share in the budget or the capital.[23]

From an accountability perspective the approach taken by the Institut de Droit International appears to have struck the necessary balance by preserving the necessary autonomy in the organisation's

---

[18] *Annuaire de l'Institut de Droit International* 66(1) (1995), 419, paras 121–2.

[19] Article 9(1): see above, note 17. See, for instance, Annex IX to UNCLOS: pursuant to Articles 2, 3 and 5, guarantees to third parties have to be provided by way of a declaration specifying the matters in respect of which the international organisation has competence, a declaration that has to be made by an international organisation at the time of signature or accession to UNCLOS. Otherwise there is a presumption that member states are competent and thus potentially responsible. Failure to provide information as to who has responsibility in respect of a specific matter will entail joint and several responsibility (Article 6(2)).

[20] C. F. Amerasinghe, *Principles of the Institutional Law of International Organisations* (Cambridge: Cambridge University Press, 1996), p. 284. And *vice versa* a third party who is aware of an applicable rule of the international organisation might be precluded from asserting later member state responsibility: Hirsch, *Responsibility*, p. 106.

[21] *Annuaire de l'Institut de Droit International* 66(1) (1995), 420, para. 126.

[22] *Ibid.*, para. 124.

[23] Article 9(3), *in fine* of the 1995 Resolution of the Institut de Droit International reads as follows: 'This is without prejudice to the duty of member States at all times to pay their assessed and apportioned contributions, or subscription to capital, as the case may be.' Article 10 of the same Resolution reads as follows: 'If pursuant to its Rules, member States have an obligation to put an international organisation in funds to meet its obligations, their obligation should (unless the Rules make different provision) be proportionate to their contribution to the regular budget or to their subscription to the capital, as the case may be.'

50   GENERAL FEATURES OF REMEDIES

decision-making process (no day-to-day interference by member states because of potential concurrent or secondary liability) and leaving no gaps in the organisation's accountability (protection of third parties by pre- and post-remedial measures), as reflected in the first paragraph of the preamble of its Resolution.

The way the issue has been dealt with by domestic courts is, of course, intimately linked to the approach that they have taken with regard to the claim of jurisdictional immunity made by the international organisation involved.[24] Wenckstern has proposed that a private individual or company would be entitled/allowed to address a private-law claim against its own national state because it has no jurisdictional immunity before its own domestic courts.[25] Attractive as this proposal appears to be at first glance, from the remedial perspective of a non-state third party the potential impact of such a remedial possibility on member states' interference in the daily functioning of the organisation would substantially distort the required balance.

The procedural aspects

The problems reviewed here constitute an additional obstacle facing claimants who are seeking remedies from international organisations on any level. It should be noted that requests for redress or applications for remedies should as a general rule be addressed to the international organisation itself, since it remains fully accountable for the actions and omissions of all of its constituent organs. Danesh Sarooshi rightly pointed out that lawfully established subsidiary organs of the UN are subsidiary organs of the UN as a whole, enjoying privileges and immunities as a result.[26] A degree of conferred personality separate from that of the UN Secretariat[27] does not necessarily mean that the right to waive that immunity no longer belongs to the UN Secretary-General;[28] at the

---

[24] See below, pp. 114 and 208.   [25] Wenckstern, 'Die Haftung', 110.

[26] D. Sarooshi, 'The Legal Framework Governing United Nations Subsidiary Organs', *BYIL* 67 (1996), 413–78, at 414 and note 2. The problem is rather more complicated in cases of autonomous or semi-autonomous agencies: see P. Szasz, 'The Complexification of the United Nations System', *Max Planck Yearbook of UN Law* 3 (1999), 1–57.

[27] Such as provided in the Statute of the UNHCR, para. 8. Extension of UNHCR duties and obligations towards internally displaced persons and in-country protection must be accompanied by according it greater rights and responsibilities: G. Gilbert, 'Rights, Legitimate Expectations, Needs and Responsibilities: UNHCR and the New World Order', *International Journal of Refugee Law* 10 (1998), 349–88, at 365.

[28] *Ibid.*, 354, note 26 (UNHCR).

same time the lines of accountability of such agencies within the UN may not always be reasonably clear.[29]

The same 'corporate approach' holds true for actions brought by third parties against the officials of an international organisation in respect of their official acts.[30]

Finn Seyersted has rightly pointed out that international organisations do have the inherent power to confer jurisdiction upon their internal courts in order to deal with such cases.[31] The practical need for this has become more obvious in recent times, although the international organisations may still consider it 'more appropriate to assume responsibility themselves for acts performed on their behalf'.[32] That may be true but it does not address the argument that there is 'no alternative jurisdiction which could reasonably contest' the acts of the international organisation,[33] in spite of the fact that parties to a dispute may attempt to bring an action in an external court, without the consent of the organisation.[34] Moreover, the 'constitution of the organisation concerned may preclude the national courts of member states from reviewing the validity of acts of the organisation, by providing for another exclusive mode of settlement of disputes in this respect'.[35]

As with regard to disputes between itself and physical or legal persons other than officials, the international organisation is entitled 'to establish courts for the adjudication of such disputes ... The individuals and companies concerned may be given the right to sue the organisation before such internal courts. And if they consent, they may themselves be sued by the organisation or by third parties.'[36] Although this observation was made in connection with the so-called 'extended jurisdiction' of an international organisation on a territorial or personal basis, from an accountability point of view there is

---

[29] Ibid., 356–7.

[30] C. F. Amerasinghe, 'International Court of Justice Cases relating to Employment in International Organisations' in V. Lowe and M. Fitzmaurice (eds.), Fifty Years of the International Court of Justice: Essays in Honour of Sir Robert Jennings (New York and Cambridge: Grotius Publications and Cambridge University Press, 1996), pp. 193–209, at p. 197. Amerasinghe has recalled that international administrative tribunals exercise their jurisdiction not against an individual or the head of the organisation but against the international organisation as such, whereas domestic court proceedings can also be instituted against individual officials, agents or experts of the organisation, but then of course the jurisdictional immunity obstacle will surface.

[31] F. Seyersted, 'Settlement of Internal Disputes of Intergovernmental Organisations by Internal and External Courts', ZAÖRV 24 (1964), 1–121, at 28.

[32] Ibid.   [33] Ibid.   [34] Ibid., 72.   [35] Ibid., 85.   [36] Ibid., 40–1.

52 GENERAL FEATURES OF REMEDIES

every reason to pursue this line of reasoning further, as Seyersted underlined.[37]

Peacekeeping and peace-enforcement operations: a separate category

Peacekeeping operations undertaken by the UN pose additional problems in this regard given that the overall political direction is the purview of the Security Council, the Secretary-General provides executive direction and control while command in the field rests with the Chief of the Mission (Special Representative or the Field Commander). In spite of the command being a conceptual whole and a practical continuum, these distinctions are real and important, avoiding a blurring of functions and responsibilities.[38] Moreover, UN command is not full command and is closer in meaning to the generally recognised military concept of 'operational command' as pointed out by the UN Secretary-General.[39]

In the same report it was rightly observed that in case of forces not under UN command, but co-operating with the UN under Chapter VII of the Charter, issues of accountability and transparency are crucial and new modalities for review by the Security Council have to be devised.[40] The determination of responsibility becomes particularly difficult where forces are provided in support of a UN operation, but not necessarily as an integral part thereof, and where operational command and control is unified or co-ordinated.[41] Consequently, responsibility will be determined in each and every case according to the degree of effective control exercised by either party in the conduct of the operation.[42] Geoff Gilbert correctly recalled that troop-contributing countries remain responsible for alleged violations of the applicable law of armed conflict by their national contingents while the same states are not a respondent party when their nationals working for an international organisation have committed acts on behalf of that international organisation.[43]

---

[37] *Ibid.*, 45.   [38] A/49/681 of 21 November 1994, paras. 4–5.
[39] *Ibid.*, para. 6.   [40] *Ibid.*, para. 23.
[41] A/51/389 of 20 September 1996, para. 17: this was the case with the Quick Reaction Force and the US Rangers in Somalia and the Rapid Reaction Force in the former Yugoslavia.
[42] *Ibid.*, para. 18.   [43] Gilbert, 'Rights, Legitimate Expectations', 353.

As a result of this, separate remedial mechanisms should be made available by states not contributing in an integrated way to a UN peace-keeping operation.

With regard to the Force in Korea under the agreements between the United States and the participating states, claims by third states or their nationals against the governments or nationals of participating states were to be a matter for disposition between the respective governments; the agreements did not delimit respective liability of the parties. Claims were directed against participating states (mainly the United States). In some cases the United States refused to take direct responsibility, but the UN did not assume it.[44]

In separate actions and at various points in time during the armed conflict in the former Yugoslavia, the Federal Republic of Yugoslavia brought applications before the ICJ against the member states of NATO while Bosnia and Herzegovina made public its intention to institute proceedings against the United Kingdom; on 29 April 1999 the Federal Republic of Yugoslavia instituted separate proceedings against Belgium, Canada, France, Germany, the Netherlands, Portugal, Spain, the United Kingdom and the United States.[45]

With regard to the binding settlement of claims against UN Forces, claims commissions having compulsory jurisdiction should have been established by the UN.[46]

---

[44] F. Seyersted, 'United Nations Forces: Some Legal Problems', *BYIL* 37 (1961), 351–475, at 421–3.

[45] On 24 November 1993 the Republic of Bosnia and Herzegovina stated its intention to institute legal proceedings against the United Kingdom for having violated the 1948 Convention on the Prevention and Punishment of the Crime of Genocide, the 1965 Convention on the Elimination of All Forms of Racial Discrimination and the other sources of international law set forth in Article 38 of the Statute of the ICJ. The charge of the alleged imposition and maintenance of an arms embargo was addressed to the United Kingdom in its capacity as a Permanent Member of the United Nations Security Council (A/48/659 and S/26806). The intention was never carried out. On 16 March 1994 the Federal Republic of Yugoslavia presented an application against the member states of NATO for having breached Articles 2(4) and 53(1) of the UN Charter, basing the Court's jurisdiction on Article 38(5) of the Rules of the Court. The Application was not entered in the Court's General List (Press Communiqué 94/11 of 21 March 1994).

[46] See below, p. 103.

6 The potential outcome of remedies: scope *ratione remedii*

With regard to the potential outcome of remedies, there generally seems to be an obvious connection between the identity of the party seeking redress, the kind of accountability involved, and the forum before which a remedial action has been brought. Although remedies available to states within the internal system of an international organisation are not designed to afford redress to the individual, they may produce indirect remedial effect to groups of individuals potentially affected by the organisation's act or omissions.

Judicial remedies

The potential outcome of non-judicial legal remedies will be analysed shortly, but with regard to judicial remedies the following aspects are of particular relevance, both to proceedings before the International Court of Justice and before arbitral tribunals.

- Express guidance on declaratory judgments, specific performance or injunctive relief cannot be found in Article 36 of the Statute of the ICJ, which in the remedial sphere has applied general principles of procedural law.[1]
- The remedial function of declaratory judgments has perhaps too often been underestimated and regarded as a separate category. Ian Brownlie has identified, *inter alia*, the following 'remedial forms sheltering under the umbrella of the declaratory judgment':[2] the finding of liability could provide an impetus for negotiations as an appropriate solution to the dispute; the ruling as a matter of

---

[1] I. Brownlie, *The Rule of Law in International Affairs at the Fiftieth Anniversary of the United Nations* (The Hague and London: Martinus Nijhoff Publishers, 1998), p. 122.
[2] *Ibid.*, p. 126.

THE POTENTIAL OUTCOME OF REMEDIES 55

principle that certain conduct is not in conformity with international law; that specific performance is required as the *consequence* of the decision on entitlement.[3]

- There is no reason why the same remedial potential could not be found in declaratory judgments concerning disputes involving international organisations. Moreover, in such cases the Court may use its discretion and request the international organisation's observations after having consulted the Chief Administrative Officer of the organisation.[4]
- Remedial potential also occurs in the intermediate form of Advisory Opinions on, for example, the legality of acts, conduct or course of action by international organisations, which are binding upon the parties to the dispute, or the difference as is currently provided for in particular conventional arrangements. Emil Zaslawski states, rightly, that there is little difference between a declaratory judgment and an Advisory Opinion.[5] They both have the advantage of not being hostile litigation, whereas the remedial effect for member states – given their privileged institutional standing in being able to submit their point of view in the course of advisory proceedings before the ICJ – is obvious.
- Finally, claims for damages and *restitutio in integrum* should not be considered as a separate category from declaratory judgments since they are both 'contingent upon the declaration of a legal entitlement of some kind'.[6]

As pointed out by Elihu Lauterpacht, there is no problem of an international organisation being a contentious party in proceedings before any international tribunal 'that is not affected by a provision similar to Article 34 of the Statute of the International Court of Justice'.[7] Shabtai Rosenne observed that it does not follow from Article 34 that a construction of the legal position of a state with regard to a non-state entity would not be within the Court's competence.[8] Although I would be inclined to agree from a remedial point of view, it is questionable whether the Court in such circumstances would not invoke the (analogous) application of the rule in the *Monetary Gold* case. Such an approach by the ICJ can be contrasted with a decision of the IACHR to decline to

[3] *Ibid.*, pp. 126–9.

[4] S. Rosenne, *The Law and Practice of the International Court 1920–1996* (The Hague, Boston and London: Martinus Nijhoff Publishers, 1997), p. 647. See also Article 69 of the Rules of the Court.

[5] *Transactions Grotius Society* 36 (1951), 42.   [6] Brownlie, *Rule of Law*, p. 131.

[7] E. Lauterpacht, *Aspects of the Administration of International Justice* (Cambridge: Grotius Publications, 1991), p. 61, referring as an example to Article 187 of UNCLOS and Annex VI to the Convention, ITLOS Statute, Article 20.

[8] Rosenne, *Law and Practice*, p. 607.

56   GENERAL FEATURES OF REMEDIES

hear a request for an Advisory Opinion 'because it directly addressed the interests of a victim and therefore denied him the opportunity to participate'.[9]

On the other hand, Advisory Opinions requested under Headquarters Agreements and under the General Convention on Privileges and Immunities, in which the UN Secretary-General is a direct party in a dispute with a member state, are procedurally treated like any other Advisory Opinion, although the Court's procedure does not envisage that type of Advisory Opinion.[10]

Furthermore, as international organisations 'have an *amicus curiae* function and responsibility in cases relating to their activities'[11] in the situations contemplated under Article 34(2) and (3) of the ICJ's Statute, they could be indirectly involved in an inter-state dispute where a decision of the organisation is implicated or constitutes one of the aspects of the case. The questions of the potential application by the Court of Article 34(2) to the UN itself and how the UN should deal with any request for information under that provision are left open, since they might not arise.[12] The degree of the organisation's involvement or implication in the actual case will obviously co-determine the remedial effect that the settlement of the dispute may entail *vis-à-vis* the international organisation.

Given both the different standing of the various potential claimants and the particular position of the respondent international organisation, the full remedial potential of incidental proceedings such as intervention and interim measures of protection[13] should not be underestimated either.

For instance, a court might conclude that interim measures of protection are justified on the basis of allegations that are uncontested by the respondent international organisation.[14] John Merrills rightly observed that if an effective order is secured, the requesting party has obtained a

---

[9] Inter-American Court of Human Rights, *Other Treaties Subject to the Advisory Jurisdiction of the Court (Art. 64 American Convention on Human Rights)*, Advisory Opinion OC-1/82, Series A, No. 1 referred to by J. Charney, 'Is International Law Threatened by Multiple International Tribunals?', *RCADI* 271 (1998), 101–382, at 165, note 187.

[10] Rosenne, *Law and Practice,* p. 1750.

[11] C. W. Jenks, 'The Status of International Organisations in Relation to the International Court of Justice', *Transactions Grotius Society* 32 (1946), 1–41, at 38, para. 54.

[12] Rosenne, *Law and Practice*, p. 650.   [13] Brownlie, *Rule of Law*, pp. 123–4.

[14] R. Plender, 'Procedure in the European Courts: Comparisons and Prospects', *RCADI* 267 (1997), 1–343, at 121.

useful, albeit temporary, remedy.[15] The remedial value derives from the promptness of their indication by the ICJ and the evidence supporting the request, which is likely to be reflected in the Court's order, even if not respected.[16] Even an unsuccessful request for the indication of interim measures of protection can perform a remedial function.[17]

As to intervention, in a case involving a number of closely related issues, the remedial value consists first in the requester being able to present its views, which also happens in cases of unsuccessful requests to intervene. Furthermore, the intervener may be allowed to go beyond the prescribed limits of its intervention.[18] On the other hand, intervention under Article 62 of the Court's Statute cannot be regarded as an appropriate mechanism for protecting community values, as the rights of the intervener are limited to what is necessary to protect its interests.[19]

The foregoing observations, although formulated with regard to the International Court of Justice, may claim more general application to other international quasi-judicial and judicial bodies and organs to which potential claimants may resort.

First-level remedies

What about the remedies targeting the first component of accountability? The Recommended Rules and Practices as formulated by the Co-Rapporteurs, Professor Malcolm Shaw and myself, in the ILA Committee on Accountability of International Organisations' Second Report,[20] cover a wide range of areas of concern at this first level. The following observations could be made when reviewing some of these rules and practices from the perspective of the type of remedy in question. Mechanisms of political accountability cannot operate in a legal framework. As a result, remedies on that level are different, but they may have an impact on legal remedies later, because they may just provide

---

[15] J. Merrills, 'Reflections on the Incidental Jurisdiction of the International Court of Justice' in M. Evans (ed.), *Remedies in International Law: The Institutional Dilemma* (Oxford: Hart Publishing, 1998), pp. 51–70, at p. 52.

[16] *Ibid.*, p. 55.   [17] *Ibid.*, p. 56.   [18] *Ibid.*, p. 60.

[19] P. Okawa, 'Environmental Dispute Settlement: Some Reflections on Recent Developments' in M. Evans (ed.), *Remedies in International Law: The Institutional Dilemma* (Oxford: Hart Publishing, 1998), pp. 157–72, at p. 165.

[20] ILA Committee on Accountability of International Organisations, *Second Report*, submitted to the 2000 ILA Conference, London, pp. 10–19.

the necessary prerequisite background material or evidence for putting legal remedial opportunities into operation.

The individual or collective element of the transparency in both the decision-making process and the implementation stage of operational decisions could incite interested parties to look for an affirmative action to obtain timely notification of projects envisaged by an international organisation, or to obtain full access to information in the case of a failure to so provide arising in which the entitlement to that information is undisputed under the organisation's applicable rules.

On a more general level, an affirmative action could become available – for example, to minority members in the case of an organisation not complying with its obligation to carry out its functions. Third parties could look for a similar course of action so that member states exercise adequate supervision over the international organisation to ensure that by operating responsibly it does protect their interests.

Injunctive relief could be sought by (potentially) affected parties in the case of impending unauthorised disclosure of external, commercial or technological information which is otherwise confidential, whereas corrective measures would be appropriate in the case of information distributed by an international organisation allegedly containing incorrect data having a negative impact on interested parties. The situation is different when studies of whatever nature have been prepared by outside consultants and the organisation disclaims responsibility for their content. The disclaimer may only be overturned when the international organisation, for example, not only takes note of the report but makes it its own.[21] Corrective remedial action may also consist in a primary organ, upon request, (a) overruling any decision by a secondary organ if the decision is, even on a prima facie basis, allegedly contrary to the organisation's general interest because it was manifestly mistaken or based on erroneous conclusions or information – except, of course, if the organ concerned is exercising a judicial function – or (b) restoring the right to a fair hearing, fair procedure and fair treatment, or (c) after a complaint, clearly setting out the principal issues of law and fact upon which a decision of an individual nature was based. The process of reporting and evaluation is situated at the crucial juncture of the governing primary rules and the implementation of accountability. With regard to operational activities a combination of remedies seems appropriate. The retrospective evaluation and assessment of such an operation should

---

[21] M. Arsanjani, 'Claims against International Organisations: Quis Custodiet Ipsos Custodes?', *Yale Journal of World Public Order* 7 (1980–1), 131–76, at 140.

take place in the light of the information available to the international organisation at the relevant time. A useful prospective remedy could consist in the functioning of an Operational Lessons-Learned Unit.

The first level of accountability provides a wide-ranging variety of potential remedial actions to which particular categories of interested and/or affected parties could resort. Although the three levels of accountability will obviously require separate and particular remedies, it is also true that in most situations involving member states the different forms of accountability (political, administrative, financial and legal) will call for a combination of corresponding kinds of remedies in order to achieve a maximum degree of implementation of the organisation's accountability.

PART II · PROCEDURAL ASPECTS OF REMEDIAL ACTION AGAINST INTERNATIONAL ORGANISATIONS

7 Introduction to procedural aspects of remedial action against international organisations

This second part reviews in more detail the procedural aspects facing the different categories of potential claimants when they attempt to resort to quasi-judicial or judicial remedial mechanisms against an international organisation.[1] As procedural justice is an essential precondition for substantive justice,[2] access to mechanisms that can redress harm and impose accountability is vital.[3] Procedure and substance can often not be separated, and the outcome of a procedural dispute is likely to influence the substantive issue.[4]

The inequality between the parties to a dispute may result in non-state claimants leaving the negotiating mechanism and seeking confrontation if and when the international organisation does not make a reasonable attempt to accommodate conflicting interests.[5] Resort to quasi-judicial or judicial remedial mechanisms does not, of course, prevent the parties from reaching a negotiated settlement pending the proceedings. Once the hurdles of availability of and access to mechanisms have been

---

[1] The following pages are, *inter alia*, based upon working papers submitted within the ILA Committee by P. Szasz, 'Main Strategies within the UN Family for the Handling of Damages by Insurance, Exoneration Clauses in Contracts and Otherwise' (15 April 1999, 15 pages), and by D. Ruzié, 'Denial of Justice in International Administrative Law (International Civil Service Law)', Working Paper No. 1 and Working Paper No. 2: these working papers are on file with the author.

[2] H. Nehl, *Principles of Administrative Procedure in EC Law* (Oxford: Hart Publishing, 1999), p. 24, note 39.

[3] James N. Paul, 'Law and Development in the 1990s: Using International Law to Impose Accountability to People on International Development Actors', *Third World Legal Studies* (1992), 1–16, at 7.

[4] Benedetto Conforti as cited by Y. Blum, *Eroding the Charter* (Dordrecht and London: Martinus Nijhoff Publishers, 1993), p. 18.

[5] D. Anderson, 'Negotiation and Dispute Settlement' in M. Evans (ed.), *Remedies in International Law: The Institutional Dilemma* (Oxford: Hart Publishing, 1998), pp. 111–21, at p. 112.

64 PROCEDURAL ASPECTS OF REMEDIAL ACTION

overcome, claimants may then face problems deriving from the internal law of the organisation, such as compliance with the principle of loyalty and discretion or difficulties resulting from the applicable statutes of competent international organs such as international administrative tribunals.

Alleged contractual and non-contractual liability and organisational responsibility trigger the mechanisms envisaged here; we are thus moving away from the first level of accountability. The potential interaction between political and legal remedies should not be underestimated from an accountability point of view. This aspect is returned to in Part IV of this study. An overview of the substantive outcome of these remedial actions will follow in Part III.

Irrespective of the kind of claim addressed to an international organisation and of the identity, quality or standing of the claimant, an international organisation is 'under an obligation to interpret and evaluate the substance of the complaint with all the care that a large and well-equipped organisation owes to those having dealings with it . . .'.[6] The principle of good governance demands that an explicit and reasoned reply to the complaint be given, irrespective of the availability of a subsequent review as to legality by an external body. This requires as a bare minimum, and as a first step only, that the international organisation determines whether the particular claimant has submitted a prima facie case: a relationship must exist between the international organisation and the claimant that is based on a contract or tortious liability and damage must allegedly have arisen during the course of that relationship.[7]

The so-called pre-litigation procedures have an important role to play, particularly on the first level of accountability, although they are capable of performing, and designed to perform, both fact-finding and conciliatory functions at all levels.

Procedural aspects present themselves differently according to in which legal sphere the remedial action is envisaged to take place

---

[6] Advocate-General Thesauru in the *del Amo Martinez* case before the European Court of Justice (Case 133/88, *Casto del Amo Martinez v. Parliament*, judgment of 14 March 1989 [1989] ECR 689 (referring to the judgment in Case 54/77, *Herpels* [1978] ECR 585)) as cited by C. De Cooker, 'Pre-litigation Procedures in International Organisations' in C. De Cooker (ed.), *International Administration: Law and Management in International Organisations* (looseleaf publication) (The Hague: Kluwer Law International), contribution VI, pp. 1–23, at p. 3.

[7] R. Harpignies, 'Settlement of Disputes of a Private Law Character to which the United Nations is a Party: A Case in Point: The Arbitral Award of 24 September 1969 in Re Starways Ltd v. United Nations', *RBDI* 7 (1971), 451–68, at 454.

(internal law of the organisation, domestic law, international law). The absence of a proper, general tort or contract law of international organisations is a fact which has nothing to do with the procedural issues of remedies against international organisations. The question of the applicable law and of the appropriate mechanisms to enforce it should, as always, be clearly distinguished.

The first obligation for international organisations is to conduct their activities in accordance with the primary and secondary rules of their own internal law. Non-compliance in their institutional or operational activities may trigger remedial action the procedural aspects of which will vary amongst the potential initiators. Member states, for instance, may be required to utilise particular remedial mechanisms to the exclusion of others, while in (most) other cases they may face the absence of any opportunity of quasi-judicial or judicial review.

In the case of organisational responsibility for alleged violations of international legal norms and rules, a state can only resort to appropriate remedial action upon the traditional condition of being either directly – or indirectly in the case of diplomatic protection – an injured state. This condition obviously does not apply as such to pre-remedial efforts such as the setting up of an internal or international Commission of Inquiry. From the perspective of potential victims, such a measure would accommodate the right to know the exact sequence of events.[8] One must at this point also recall that grounds for invoking illegality will not be substantially different from those forming the subject-matter of similar remedial action within domestic legal systems, although there appears to be a widespread, judicially supported presumption in favour of the legality of acts of international organisations.

First, the procedural aspects which could be considered to be specific to each separate category of claimants (chapters 8 to 11) are reviewed, before turning to a procedural obstacle that is common to all non-state claimants, namely the jurisdictional immunity of international organisations before domestic courts (chapter 12).

---

[8] D. Shelton, *Remedies in International Human Rights Law* (Oxford: Oxford University Press, 1999), p. 19 referring to Theo van Boven.

8 Procedural aspects of remedial action by member states

Exhaustion of internal remedies

The first forum to which member states would turn in order to challenge, even prior to its adoption, the legality of a particular decision, is the organ that is considering its adoption. That will eventually also be the first remedial level for staff members but without the same preventive effect. The importance of this possibility for member states is increased in the absence of a proper system of judicial review and in spite of the principle *nemo judex in causa sua* being seriously damaged. As is common in other cases such as the international financial institutions, special remedial mechanisms have been put in place.

Given the absence in most international organisations of a system of judicial review for the legality of institutional acts and operational activities, the question of the applicability of the rule of exhaustion of internal remedies does not even arise with regard to member states, except of course when it has been (explicitly) provided for in particular categories of agreements: in such cases the clause 'other mechanisms of settlement' could imply this first form of remedial action. The *Lockerbie* cases clearly demonstrate that, within the context of contentious judicial proceedings between two member states, a form of indirect remedial action could result from either of them challenging, in their application or in an incidental way, the legal validity – under, respectively, the internal law of the organisation and/or international law at large – of institutional acts or operational activities belonging to the overall legal context of the dispute between them.

When states take up the claim of their nationals, be they staff members or third parties, and unless it has been waived by the organisation, the exhaustion rule applies to all available administrative, quasi-judicial and judicial remedial mechanisms established by the organisation on a permanent or an ad hoc basis. There is also a recent tendency in the UN to move away from routine reference to some standing arbitral institution and to look towards provisions for ad hoc arbitration,[1] in the absence of a successful outcome of prior conciliation under UNCITRAL Conciliation Rules.

There is good reason to rely in this regard on the ECHR's pronouncement that this generally recognised rule of international law on the exhaustion of local remedies should be applied 'with some degree of flexibility and without excessive formalism' and with a realistic assessment of the general and political context in which the remedies operate and the personal circumstances of the applicant.[2] Peacekeeping operations, for instance, would constitute a prime category for such an approach. It also has to be observed, however, that within the context of an attempt to reach a satisfactory settlement for a claim against an international organisation it 'does not seem appropriate to regard the Legal Department ... as a "local remedy"'.[3]

A total lack of internal remedies would clearly amount to a complete denial of justice, giving rise to a separate ground for organisational responsibility.[4]

One of the corollaries of the impartiality of an international adjudicatory body is the judicial equality between the parties in their capacity as litigants,[5] which is strictly observed in case of inter-state disputes. Given the fundamental difference in configuration in the pre-litigation stage,

---

[1] P. Szasz, Working Paper No. 1, ILA Committee, p. 4: on file with the author.

[2] *Akdivar v. Turkey*, judgment of 16 September 1996, *Reports of Judgments and Decisions* 4 (1996), 1210 as cited by D. Shelton, *Remedies in International Human Rights Law* (Oxford: Oxford University Press, 1999) p. 25.

[3] C. Eagleton, 'International Organisations and the Law of Responsibility', *RCADI* 76 (1950), 323–423, at 412.

[4] There is, of course, the separate issue of the accountability of these (quasi-)judicial organs themselves for the way they administer domestic and international justice. With due regard to the particular characteristics of the exercise of the judicial function, one could also mention transparency and access to information such as, for example, the availability of the *travaux préparatoires* of the applicable rules of procedure to potential litigants, who are entitled to act on the basis that these rules are being interpreted according to the *travaux préparatoires*. See further, *inter alia*, P. Szasz, 'The Complexification of the United Nations System', *Max Planck Yearbook of UN Law* 3 (1999), 1–57, at 4, note 9, and at 14–15. See for instance the report on the operation of the ICTY presented by its President on behalf of the Judges of the Tribunal to the UN Secretary-General on 12 May 2000 in response to the reports of the Experts Group responsible for evaluating the effectiveness of the institution pursuant to General Assembly Resolution 53/212 of 18 December 1998.

[5] R. Martha, 'Representation of Parties in World Trade Disputes', *JWTL* 31 (1997), 84–96, at 94–5 referring to Bin Cheng.

68   PROCEDURAL ASPECTS OF REMEDIAL ACTION

there is every need to call for strict observance of this principle in disputes or differences between international organisations and non-state claimants.

Disputes over Headquarters Agreements between the host state and the international organisation and differences over the interpretation or application of the General Convention on Privileges and Immunities are of a special nature because of the vital importance of this kind of agreement for the proper functioning of every international organisation, resulting in a preference for negotiations to solve such disputes.

The purpose of provisions in Headquarters Agreements such as section 21 of the Headquarters Agreement between the UN and the United States 'is precisely the settlement without any prior recourse to municipal courts and it would be against both the letter and the spirit of the Agreement for the implementation of that procedure to be subjected to such prior recourse'.[6] The ICJ left no room for doubt when it added that such a provision 'cannot require the exhaustion of local remedies as a condition for its implementation'.[7]

Differences over privileges and immunities

If a difference arising between a state and an international organisation over the interpretation and/or application of the General Convention on Privileges and Immunities or of the Special Convention on the Privileges and Immunities of Specialised Agencies cannot be resolved in some

---

[6] *Applicability of the Obligation to Arbitrate under Section 21 of the United Nations Headquarters Agreement of 26 June 1947*, Advisory Opinion, *ICJ Reports* (1988), p. 12, at p. 29, para. 41. Section 21 reads as follows:

'(a) Any dispute between the United Nations and the United States concerning the interpretation or application of this agreement or of any supplemental agreement, which is not settled by negotiation or any other mode of settlement, shall be referred for final decision to a tribunal of three arbitrators, one to be named by the Secretary-General, one to be named by the Secretary of State of the United States, and the third to be chosen by the two, or, if they should fail to agree upon a third, then by the President of the International Court of Justice.

(b) The Secretary-General or the United States may ask the General Assembly to request of the International Court of Justice an advisory opinion on any legal question arising in the course of such proceedings. Pending the receipt of the opinion of the Court, an interim decision of the arbitral tribunal shall be observed by both parties. Thereafter, the arbitral tribunal shall render a final decision, having regard to the opinion of the Court.'

[7] *Ibid.*

MEMBER STATES 69

other way, it has to be settled upon the request of either party by a binding Advisory Opinion of the ICJ under sections 30 or 32 respectively of the two Conventions. This alternative judicial method of settlement does not necessarily operate in the same way on the atmosphere of the claim and the state's willingness to settle by negotiation as Mahnoush Arsanjani assumes it does when mere private parties are involved.[8] Attempts to reach an out-of-court settlement are not always success-ful, as became clear in the *Cumaraswamy* case.[9] By taking the initiative to start this procedure the international organisation itself creates a unique opportunity to have the decision or act challenged, tested and eventually upheld by the ICJ.

States hold varying views on the question of the exclusive authority of the UN Secretary-General to determine whether words spoken or acts performed by UN officials, agents or experts – and being challenged by a (member) state – actually took place in the course of a mission for the UN. The UN Legal Counsel, defending the exclusiveness of the Secretary-General's authority and stressing that such matters cannot be determined or adjudicated by domestic courts,[10] recalled the propriety, reasonableness or good faith of the Secretary-General's determination and stated that the assertion of immunity could be challenged by any member state under Article VIII of the General Convention.[11] The Court in its Advisory Opinion acknowledged the 'pivotal' role of the Secretary-General in this respect,[12] affirming that his findings were only to be set aside by domestic courts for the most compelling reasons.[13] The Court ruled that the Secretary-General's determination was correct,[14] without addressing the argument put forward by counsel for Malaysia that the General Convention does not contain a provision on the question of who has to take such a decision.[15]

In underlining the primary responsibility of the Secretary-General of the UN in safeguarding the interests of the organisation, which may require assertion of immunity for an expert on mission,[16] the Court

---

[8] See below, p. 94.

[9] *Difference Relating to Immunity from Legal Process of a Special Rapporteur of the Commission on Human Rights*, Advisory Opinion of 22 April 1999, *ICJ Reports* (1999), p. 62, at pp. 71–2, paras. 14–15.

[10] *Ibid.*, p. 80, para. 33.   [11] CR/98/15, p. 29, para. 58.

[12] *Difference Relating to Immunity from Legal Process of a Special Rapporteur of the Commission on Human Rights*, Advisory Opinion of 22 April 1999, *ICJ Reports* (1999), p. 62, at pp. 84–5, para. 50.

[13] *Ibid.*, p. 87, para. 61.   [14] *Ibid.*, p. 86, para. 56.   [15] CR/98/16, p. 30, para. 14.

[16] *Difference Relating to Immunity from Legal Process of a Special Rapporteur of the Commission on

70   PROCEDURAL ASPECTS OF REMEDIAL ACTION

implicitly recognised that these interests may, in the Secretary-General's view, be paramount over the obligation not to impede the course of justice. The UN Legal Counsel argued that maintaining the Special Rapporteur's immunity would not impede the course of justice, as appropriate modes of settlement are provided for.[17]

The holding-harmless clause

States, whether or not they have membership links with the international organisation concerned, hosting or benefiting from a particular operational activity undertaken by the organisation on their territory such as the provision of technical assistance or the holding of a conference will normally conclude a special agreement containing a holding-harmless clause in favour of the international organisation: the responsibility for dealing with claims resulting from the operation and which are brought by third parties against the international organisation or its agents, employees or experts is taken over by the state. This transfer will not operate, however, with regard to claims involving gross negligence or wilful misconduct on the part of the organisation or its agents, experts or officials. Wilfred Jenks considers the holding-harmless clause to be a legitimate condition of assistance by international organisations to governments, particularly in order to prevent the international organisation from becoming the target of irresponsible claims from all over the world given the substantial financial resources involved in its operation.[18] However, this does not prevent the clause from constituting the price to be paid by all beneficiary states for any kind of assistance by international organisations: this is further corroborated by, for instance, the Model Agreement for the provision of operational, executive and administrative personnel, paragraph 6 of which reads: 'The assistance rendered ... is in the exclusive interest and for the exclusive benefit of the people and Government of ... *In recognition thereof ...* '[19]

Paul Szasz, amongst others, put forward as one of the main reasons for the use of such clauses that the international organisation may not

---

Human Rights, Advisory Opinion of 22 April 1999, *ICJ Reports* (1999), p. 62, at p. 87, para. 60.

[17] CR/98/15, p. 19, para. 30.

[18] C. W. Jenks, *International Immunities* (London and New York: Stevens & Sons and Oceana Publications, 1961), pp. 79–80.

[19] *Yearbook International Law Commission* (1967), vol. II, p. 218, para. 48.

MEMBER STATES 71

be fully in control of all the aspects of the activity undertaken, which mirrors perfectly the grounds underlying the acceptance of liability in peacekeeping operations. The other reason Szasz advanced is that private claimants 'will receive any compensation due to them under local law'.[20] This second reason appears only partially convincing as it only addresses the actual outcome of the claim, whereas the actual discontent with the activity being organised does not come within the purview of the local remedies, and this has to be regretted from an accountability point of view. The fact that the holding-harmless clause not only covers claims but also 'other demands' does not close the gaps here.[21] At the very least, there should, as a primary rule, be a corollary duty incumbent upon the international organisation to conduct its operations with due regard to their effect on the conditions in the territory concerned.[22]

Attempts to delineate more precisely the respective role and responsibility of the parties involved can be found in, for example, the UNHCR's Model Co-operation Agreement with governments, according to which the UNHCR provides protection, with the host state remaining responsible, de jure, for those in refugee camps. Assistance will be co-ordinated by the UNHCR, while local authorities will carry out the day-to-day running of the camp, but in effect the lands on which the camps lie are no longer de facto under the control of the host state.[23]

The holding-harmless clause and peacekeeping operations

The reversed holding-harmless clause operates to the benefit of participating states contributing resources to UN peacekeeping operations as contained in Article 9 of the Model Memorandum of Understanding.[24]

---

[20] Working Paper No. 1, ILA Committee, p. 11: on file with the author.

[21] See, for example, Article X of the Model Conference Agreement as cited by Szasz, Working Paper No. 1, ILA Committee, p. 12, note 20: on file with the author.

[22] That would be analogous to Article I of the Articles of Agreement of the IBRD as amended in 1989.

[23] G. Gilbert, 'Rights, Legitimate Expectations, Needs and Responsibilities: UNHCR and the New World Order', *International Journal of Refugee Law* 10 (1998), 349–88, at 360.

[24] A/51/967 of 27 August 1997. In a recent report on the procedures to calculate the amount of reimbursement to member states for contingent-owned equipment, the Office of Internal Oversight Services reaffirmed the need for these claims to be processed promptly and in an efficacious way; the existing procedure should be substantially improved. At the time of the audit, 185 claims for reimbursement amounting to a total of $463 million and representing 36 per cent of the overall amount of the claims were still pending. As a pre-remedial measure the OIOS also

72 PROCEDURAL ASPECTS OF REMEDIAL ACTION

With regard to peacekeeping operations, the UN will normally be responsible for dealing with any claim by third parties for loss, damage, death or injury caused by the personnel or equipment provided by the government in the performance of services, activities or operations.[25] The UN may seek recovery from a troop-contributing state if damage has occurred as a result of gross negligence or wilful misconduct on the part of a member of its contingent or if the damage has entailed the troop member's international criminal responsibility.[26] The recovery system has been included in the Memorandum of Understanding between the UN and states contributing resources to peacekeeping operations.[27] Pending the conclusion of an agreement, the UN shall apply the customary principles and practices which are embodied in the Model Status of Forces Agreement (SOFA).[28] Article 13 of the Model Agreement provides for negotiations within the mission, at the level of the Under-Secretary-General for peacekeeping operations, a mutually agreed conciliator or mediator, and eventually provides for arbitration. Under Article 51 of the Model SOFA, both the host country and the UN participate on an equal footing before the standing claims commission. Difficulties between the host government and the UN may occur as a result of the delays in the settlement of claims by the local claims review board because of the increasing number and complexity of claims.[29]

    stressed the need for the procedures to negotiate the revision of Memoranda of Understanding: A/54/765 of 23 February 2000, paras. 22 and 10. The Special Committee on Peacekeeping Operations once again called for the current delays to be resolved: A/54/839 of 20 March 2000, para. 149.

[25] A/50/995 of 9 July 1996, para. 9, Art. 9.

[26] A/50/389 of 20 September 1996, paras. 42–4. In a follow-up report on management irregularities causing financial losses to the organisation, the UN Secretary-General rightly observed that a 'definition of gross negligence that can be automatically applied without interpretation to any particular situation is practically impossible to formulate'. The Secretary-General then made reference to a legal opinion dated 30 June 1981 from the Office of Legal Affairs to the Assistant Secretary-General, Office on Financial Services, which had defined gross negligence as 'negligence of a very high degree involving wilfulness, recklessness or drunkenness and, in consequence, manifest disregard for the safety of life and property'. In Judgment No. 742, in the *Manson* case (1995), the UNAT held that 'gross negligence involves an extreme and reckless failure to act as a reasonable person would with respect to a reasonably foreseeable risk. Thus, to establish gross negligence, a far more aggravated failure to observe the "reasonable person" standard of care must be shown than in the case of ordinary negligence': A/54/793 of 13 March 2000, paras. 3 and 4. 'It has been the policy of the Organisation since 1969 that proof of negligence or wilful misconduct is required to justify a staff member being held accountable for losses to the organisation': *ibid.*, para. 5.

[27] A/50/995, Annex, para. 9.   [28] A/46/185 of 23 May 1991, para. 6.

[29] A/51/389, para. 26.

MEMBER STATES 73

Under the Model SOFA any appeal that both the UN peacekeeping operation and the government agree under paragraph 51, or any other dispute between them, shall be submitted to an arbitral tribunal unless otherwise agreed by the parties.[30] If the difference between the UN and the government arising out of the (Model) SOFA involves a question of principle concerning the General Convention on Privileges and Immunities, it shall be dealt with in accordance with the procedure of section 30 of that Convention.[31] Special mechanisms have been established to deal with claims submitted by contributing states on behalf of their nationals for compensation for death or injury attributable to service with a UN peacekeeping operation, as these claims are not regarded as 'private-law' claims.[32]

With regard to claims submitted by nationals of member states for personal injuries and/or property loss or damages arising from operations of the UN in the Congo, special compensation arrangements were established with several member states.[33] With regard to other peacekeeping operations, for instance the UNFICYP and UNEF, agreements provided for resort to a claims commission.

Diplomatic protection vis-à-vis the international organisation

When, after a peacekeeping operation, lump-sum agreements settling all claims have been concluded with the international organisation, member states concerned may still face legal proceedings before their own domestic courts initiated by private claimants against the state for not having properly defended their interests.[34] This is unless, of course (even in the absence of a particular provision in the national law of *approbation* of the accord aimed at preventing private claimants from instituting proceedings against the UN), the agreement between

---

[30] A/45/594 of 9 October 1990, para. 53. [31] *Ibid.*, para. 54.

[32] A/C.5/49/65 of 24 April 1995, p. 13, note 9. For figures over the backlog of such claims for death and disability benefits see, for example, A/C.5/54/47 of 28 January 2000. The Special Committee on Peacekeeping Operations urged 'the Secretariat to accelerate the verification and claims payment process': A/54/839, para. 154. 'Claims for compensation in the event of death, injuries or illness attributable to the performance of official duties, in respect of which the Advisory Board on Compensation Claims ... makes recommendations' are excluded from the competence of the (normal) appellate bodies: A/55/57, *Report of the Joint Inspection Unit on the Administration of Justice at the United Nations* of 2 March 2000, para. 75(b).

[33] A/C.5/49/65, p. 14, note 15.

[34] See further M. Arsanjani, 'Claims against International Organisations: Quis Custodiet Ipsos Custodes?', *Yale Journal of World Public Order* 7 (1980–1), 131–76, at 150–1.

the international organisation and the state exercising diplomatic protection explicitly refers to the settlement as final and binding upon the parties.[35] Conversely, the prior question could arise as to whether, by analogous application of the Calvo clause, a state could argue that its rights to 'protect its nationals cannot be taken away from it by any agreement which its national might sign binding him to the procedures of settlement stated in the contract and denying him the right of diplomatic protection'.[36]

In his First Report dated 7 March 2000, the new ILC Special Rapporteur on Diplomatic Protection has rightly stated that until the 'individual acquires comprehensive procedural rights under international law, it would be a setback for human rights to abandon diplomatic protection'.[37] The Special Rapporteur, however, does not seem to consider at this stage the possibility of diplomatic protection by states *vis-à-vis* international organisations when he writes that diplomatic protection is 'only available to protect individuals against a foreign Government'.[38]

Almost four decades ago Jean-Pierre Ritter observed that the exercise of diplomatic protection by a state *vis-à-vis* an international organisation on behalf of one of its nationals was one of the least explored areas of public international law.[39] His observation is still valid today as state practice is rare and case law has not yet explicitly addressed the point of such an exercise being practicable.[40] If existing procedures do not result in damage being compensated or if there are no remedial mechanisms available to individuals, then diplomatic protection can be exercised by the state.[41]

The slow but gradual putting into place by international organisations – by way of 'secondary legislation' not directly derived from or based upon the organisation's constituent instrument – of primary rules on their contractual and tortious liability towards third-party claimants – thus not being staff members – directly confers substantive and procedural rights on individuals, although not on the state of which they are nationals.

Ritter sharply pointed to the problem caused by this state of affairs, stressing that the ICJ in the *Effect of Awards* case did not address the

---

[35] See also *ILR* 45 (1972), 446–55 (*Menderlier* case).
[36] Eagleton, 'International Organisations', 393.
[37] A/CN.4/506, para. 29.   [38] *Ibid.*, para. 31.
[39] J. P. Ritter, 'La Protection diplomatique à l'égard d'une organisation internationale', *AFDI* 8 (1962), 427–56, at 427.
[40] *Ibid.*, 428.   [41] *Ibid.*, 455.

question of whether in appropriate circumstances any violation by the UN would be a violation of principles and rules of UN law or rather of public international law.[42] Member states can only intervene using their diplomatic protection if the contractual relationship between the international organisation and the individual can be directly founded on a Conventional rule imposing upon the international organisation an obligation to comply with its own internal rules such as in the case of staff contracts.[43] That is a correct presentation of the traditional view that international organisations are only directly accountable to the member states that created them and according to which non-state actors should not be able to hold the organisation directly accountable unless they have a direct relationship with the organisation, such as through a contract.[44] That perception of organisational accountability is being called into question, as will become clear throughout this study. At first it would seem that – given the absence of applicable Conventional rules whose application by the international organisations would, because of being states parties to such a Convention, automatically be a legitimate concern for (member) states, even if their nationals would be the main or only beneficiaries of those clauses – only the elaboration of a comprehensive set of primary rules on accountability of international organisations and their adoption by both international organisations and (member) states could remedy this fundamental obstacle towards the exercise of diplomatic protection by (member) states towards the international organisation. However, the lack of adequate internal remedial mechanisms could at present already give rise to a 'denial of justice'.[45]

Within the scope of this exercise of diplomatic protection *vis-à-vis* an international organisation on behalf of one of its nationals, a state enjoys the traditional discretion whether or not to use this power; consequently, the choice of an appropriate remedial mechanism lies within the same area of discretion. Here both the interest and the capacity to act are determining factors. However, as the holding-harmless clause operates 'both at an international level and in terms of national law',[46] it thus prevents the exercise of diplomatic protection for claims arising under the operational activity envisaged. Peter Bekker has rightly observed that, rather than relying on their state's discretion, the interests

---

[42] *Ibid.*, 451.   [43] *Ibid.*, 452–3.

[44] D. Bradlow, during the 'Panel on Accountability of International Organisations Towards Non-state Actors', *ASIL Proceedings* 92 (1998), 359.

[45] Ritter, 'La Protection diplomatique', 455.

[46] *Yearbook International Law Commission,* (1967) vol. II, p. 217, para. 45.

76 PROCEDURAL ASPECTS OF REMEDIAL ACTION

of private parties would be better served by the further development of procedures to which they have direct access,[47] a point which will be dealt with in Part IV of this study.

The obligation for international organisations to provide alternative dispute settlement procedures should be distinguished from the actual availability of such procedures, as individuals cannot normally rely on the relevant provisions in Headquarters Agreements or similar treaties.[48] It will thus be for the potential claimant's national state to demand, at the international level, on the claimant's behalf and in its own right, that the international organisation should comply with such an obligation.

Diplomatic protection and the exhaustion of internal remedies

A further question briefly touched upon earlier is whether a government is only allowed to exercise its diplomatic protection against an international organisation after the exhaustion of the organisation's internal remedies; or will it only take up a claim of one of its nationals when the exhaustion of the internal remedies through the organisation's own procedures has resulted in a denial of justice?[49]

Chittharanjan Amerasinghe has pointed to the absence of judicial decisions or agreed or accepted practice in the area of relations between an international organisation and states as regards the question of whether the exhaustion of internal remedies rule applies or is even applicable at all,[50] unless of course the obligation has been disposed of by a particular provision, such as in a Headquarters Agreement.[51]

The argument against the application of the rule based upon the impossibility or impracticality for international organisations to provide local or internal remedies[52] has gradually been countered by the putting into place under the influence, *inter alia*, of the human rights

---

[47] P. Bekker, *The Legal Position of Intergovernmental Organisations: A Functional Necessity Analysis of their Legal Status and Immunities* (Boston and London: Martinus Nijhoff Publishers, 1994), p. 206.

[48] A. Reinisch, *International Organisations before National Courts* (Cambridge: Cambridge University Press, 2000), p. 277.

[49] D. Bowett, *UN Forces: A Legal Study of United Nations Practice* (London: Stevens, 1964), pp. 247–8.

[50] C. F. Amerasinghe, *Local Remedies in International Law* (Cambridge: Grotius Publications, 1990), p. 367.

[51] *Applicability of the Obligation to Arbitrate under Section 21 of the United Nations Headquarters Agreement of 26 June 1947*, Advisory Opinion, *ICJ Reports* (1988), p. 12, at p. 29, para. 41.

[52] Amerasinghe, *Local Remedies*, p. 374.

imperatives (and to varying degrees, admittedly) of such mechanisms by international organisations.

The lack of a jurisdictional connection between the individual and the international organisation – the existence of such a connection being one of the basic requirements of the rule – becomes vital both with regard to the subsequential exercise of diplomatic protection by an individual's national state and within the context of resorting to, for example, regional or universal quasi-judicial or judicial organs and bodies entrusted with monitoring the right of access to a court.

Two observations can be made. First and foremost, this lack of jurisdictional connection, although it is clearly demonstrated here, constitutes a fundamental problem for the overall accountability regime of international organisations. Various mechanisms have been put in place in order to 'remedy' this, and these are discussed in Part IV of this study. Secondly, the lack of jurisdictional connection arises in 'ordinary circumstances',[53] whereas most of the tort claims will arise from activities which are out of the ordinary, such as peacekeeping operations. It is precisely in the latter circumstances that the establishment of the claims review commissions is being guaranteed by particular provisions in the SOFA with the host country, which by entering into the agreement accepts the jurisdiction of that body, thus giving rise to the duty of private claimants to exhaust those remedies first.[54] These special rules would take precedence over general, procedural rules in the field of international legal responsibility.[55] But Jean Salmon rightly observed that in the case of private claims against the UN for damages caused during the course of the ONUC operation, the decision by both parties (namely the UN and Belgium) to opt for a diplomatic solution was taken in circumstances having 'le caractère flou', thus preventing any conclusion in this case on the application of the rule of exhaustion of internal remedies.[56] The UN implicitly waived this obligation when the Belgian Government endorsed the claims of its nationals.[57]

[53] *Ibid.*

[54] Thus fulfilling one of the conditions set forth in the 1971 Resolution of the Institut de Droit International, *Annuaire de l'Institut de Droit International* 54(2) (1971), 469–70.

[55] Ritter, 'La Protection diplomatique', 433.

[56] J. Salmon, 'Les Accords Spaak–U Thant du 20 février 1965', *AFDI* 11 (1965), 469–97, at 486.

[57] P. Klein, *La Responsabilité des organisations internationales dans les ordres juridiques internes et en droit des gens* (Brussels: Editions Bruylant and Editions de l'Université Libre de Bruxelles, 1998), p. 540.

78   PROCEDURAL ASPECTS OF REMEDIAL ACTION

Apart from explicit provisions designed to ensure adequate procedural opportunities for claimants to present evidence and to defend their interests,[58] the common understanding seems to be that there is no general principle that the exhaustion of local remedies rule is automatically applicable[59] to third-party individual claimants *vis-à-vis* international organisations.

It is worth adding that Antonio Cançado Trinidade's in-depth study of experiments in the first half of the twentieth century supported the view that there is nothing sacrosanct about the rule of exhaustion of local remedies and that it 'is not a requirement of inflexible or mechanic application, and [that it] is not necessarily inherent in every international experiment granting procedural status to individuals'.[60]

Disputes involving staff members

In disputes between individual staff members and an international organisation no states as such are involved and a staff member's national state does not exercise diplomatic protection when he or she brings an action against the international organisation.[61] As far as the diplomatic protection of UN officials is concerned, the concern expressed by the ICJ about potential damage to the official's independence contrary to Article 100 of the UN Charter[62] is fully justified, but in my

---

[58] According to a GATT Panel in the case of US Anti-Dumping Duties on Gray Portland Cement and Cement Clinker from Mexico, GATT Doc. No. ADP/82, at p. 161, para. 5.10 as referred to by J. Charney, 'Is International Law Threatened by Multiple International Tribunals?', *RCADI* 271 (1998), 101–382, at 299.

[59] Amerasinghe, *Local Remedies*, p. 376. The Draft Article 3 proposed by the new ILC Special Rapporteur on Diplomatic Protection 'does not preclude a possibility of a claim being pursued by the individual on the international plane – *where there is a remedy available.* At the same time it places no restraint on the State of nationality to intervene itself' (emphasis in the original). But '[in] practice a State will no doubt refrain from asserting its right of diplomatic protection while the injured national pursues his international remedy': A/CN.4/506, at p. 26, paras. 70 and 73.

[60] A.Cançado Trinidade, 'Exhaustion of Local Remedies in International Law Experiments Granting Procedural Status to Individuals in the First Half of the Twentieth Century', *NILR* 57 (1977), 373–92, at 380 and 391.

[61] Amerasinghe, *Local Remedies*, p. 377.

[62] *Reparations for Injuries Suffered in the Service of the United Nations*, Advisory Opinion, *ICJ Reports* (1949), p. 174, at p. 183: 'In order that the agent may perform his duties satisfactorily, he must feel that this protection is assured to him by the Organization, and that he may count on it. To ensure the independence of the agent, and consequently, the independent action of the Organization itself, it is essential that in performing his duties he need not have to rely on any other protection than that of

view is not applicable when the addressee of the claim put forward in the exercise of diplomatic protection would be the international organisation itself; otherwise a substantial lack of protection might occur. Although with regard to staff members there is no general principle of law that they must exhaust internal remedies first, the written internal laws of international organisations make provision for this[63] while at the same time making it clear that lobbying of member states by individual staff members against positions taken by the Secretary-General is not permitted.[64]

For a period of forty years (1955–95) member states also had the procedural opportunity to submit a request to the Committee on Applications for Review of Administrative Judgments, as could the applicants themselves. However, this possibility was only used once, by the United States, which led to the ICJ judgment in the 1982 *Mortished* case.

In the case of unsuccessful candidates for employment with an international organisation the situation is different, of course, as far as the applicable legal rules are concerned: if their national state, should it wish to do so, were to discuss the problem directly with the executive head of the organisation, Article 100 of the UN Charter and similar provisions would render such a representation highly debatable. The candidates themselves would not have *locus standi* before, for example, the UNAT and ILOAT, and would thus be deprived of remedial opportunities.[65]

From the general perspective of remedial state action against international organisations there is no reason why the range of remedies could not include, *inter alia*, declaratory judgments and injunctions both of a prohibitive and affirmative nature, as well as damages for tort and for contractual liability. Indeed, factors which *vis-à-vis* states could lead to hesitation or restrictive approaches are arguably not present in claims towards international organisations, if only because of the initial inequality between the parties.

The 'general interest' part of accountability has to fit in with the 'individual interest' of claimants in the overall remedial system *vis-à-vis*

---

the Organization (save of course for the more direct and immediate protection due from the State in whose territory he may be). In particular, he should not have to rely on the protection of his own State. If he had to rely on that State, his independence might well be compromised, contrary to the principle applied by Article 100 of the Charter.'

[63] Amerasinghe, *Local Remedies*, p. 379.   [64] A/52/488 of 17 October 1997, p. 43.

[65] See below, p. 84.

international organisations. Accordingly, Dinah Shelton's observation in the field of human rights violations by states is very appropriate in this context: remedies that provide redress for the individual victim are serving the rule of law at all levels of society because they also serve the community interest.[66] Consequently, redress for the individual claimant is the key, and that issue will be discussed in the following chapters of Part II.

[66] Shelton, *Remedies*, p. 358.

9 Procedural aspects of remedial action by staff members

The present system of protection

In its Resolution 47/226, adopted on 8 April 1993, the UN General Assembly stressed the importance of a just, transparent, simple, impartial and efficient system of internal justice at the Secretariat and requested the Secretary-General to undertake a comprehensive review of the UN system for the administration of justice. A task-force not only proposed a complete reform of the administrative review system, but also called for measures to encourage settlement through informal channels, such as through the office of an ombudsman.[1] This issue is dealt with in Part IV of this study.

Given their special position under the internal law of the organisation, and also because of their contractual relationship with the organisation, it is not surprising that staff members have submitted, and will certainly continue to submit, the largest majority of claims against international organisations originating from private parties.[2] Although most of these claims are of a contractual nature, there is no reason to exclude tortious liability as a matter of principle or otherwise. The challenge to the legality of decisions may be based on incompetence, procedural irregularity, abuse of power or violation of applicable statutes or institutionalised rules, as in most domestic forms of administrative review.

One of the reasons why international organisations establish their own settlement machinery to deal with employment-related disputes

---

[1] A/C.5/49/1 of 5 August 1994, para. 94.

[2] A substantial number of cases before domestic courts have arisen because of the alleged applicability of the respective local labour law to persons rendering services to international organisations on the basis of contracts but without becoming staff members: A. Reinisch, *International Organisations before National Courts* (Cambridge: Cambridge University Press, 2000), p. 25.

between the organisation and staff members is that otherwise 'national courts could be induced to assume jurisdiction in such cases'.[3] The remedial system established by international organisations especially to deal with this category of claimants and claims is well known and is (sometimes) considered by domestic courts to be able to grant judicial relief more appropriately than a national court.[4] This 'advantage' also partly stems from the non-invocability of Staff Regulations before domestic jurisdictions as they are internal statutes of the international organisation concerned and are therefore not within their jurisdiction *ratione materiae*.[5] On the other hand, it should be noted that a number of international organisations exist whose staff members are deprived of any form of judicial remedies towards their organisation.[6]

With regard to internal recourse procedures, suffice it to recall that after discussion with superiors a quasi-judicial stage follows, which results in non-binding recommendations, adopted by the specially constituted Joint Appeals Board of mixed composition and addressed to the Executive Head who was the addressee of the complaint. This procedure conducted within the organisation – which in some cases has taken six years to complete[7] – may be followed by resort to a judicial organ, namely an international administrative tribunal, provided the internal remedies have been exhausted. The quasi-judicial procedure may be dispensed with by agreement of both parties in a case where the dispute is of a purely legal nature, such as the interpretation of a Staff Regulation, and in such a case the matter goes immediately before the international administrative tribunal.[8]

---

[3] C. F. Amerasinghe, as cited by M. Singer, 'Jurisdictional Immunity of International Organisations: Human Rights and Functional Necessity Concerns', *Virginia Journal of International Law* 36 (1995), 53–165, at 99.

[4] *Martin Broadbent et al. v. OAS*, US Court of Appeals for the District of Columbia Circuit, 8 January 1980, *ILM* 19 (1980), 208–18, rejecting the entitlement of former officials to sue the OAS.

[5] D. Ruzié, Working Paper No.1, ILA Committee, p. 3, paras. 16–21: on file with the author.

[6] *Ibid.*, p. 1, para. 2. For the list of thirty-seven organisations that, as of March 2000, had recognised the competence of the ILOAT see A/55/57, *Report on the Administration of Justice at the United Nations presented by the Joint Inspection Unit in March 2000*, Annex III.

[7] See UNAT Judgment No. 784, reviewed by D. Ruzié, 'Jurisprudence du Tribunal Administratif des Nations Unies', *AFDI* 43 (1997), 430–44, at 430.

[8] P. Szasz, 'Adjudicating IGO Staff Challenges to Legislative Decisions' in G. Hafner et al. (eds.), *Liber Amicorum Professor Ignaz Seidl-Hohenveldern in Honour of his 80th Birthday* (The Hague and London: Kluwer Law International, 1998), pp. 699–720, at p. 703.

These 'preliminary administrative proceedings'[9] or 'pre-litigation procedures'[10] can effectively unburden judicial protection, but they must not degenerate into factual obstacles to access to the courts.[11] Although their aim is always to review and eventually rectify administrative acts, Chris De Cooker rightly pointed out that 'the absence of a [subsequent] external judicial body ... transforms the pre-litigation procedure into a *de facto* process of legal judgment'.[12] In the other cases they do have a conciliatory function.[13]

The link between the pre-litigation and litigation procedures is clear: the issue and the relief sought are the same,[14] and there is a high rate of settlement under the former mechanism.[15] As an example, the average length of both the pre-litigation and litigation procedure before the ILO Administrative Tribunal is three years.[16]

From the perspective of providing adequate alternative dispute settlement mechanisms, the following should be added regarding international administrative tribunals. The appointment of their members by the political organs of an international organisation for limited terms may raise concern over the degree of their independence.[17] As to the adequacy of the procedures from a judicial point of view, the almost complete refusal by the UNAT and ILOAT to have oral hearings provides reasons for serious concern.[18] On the other hand, it is interesting to note that in order to avoid a denial of justice the UNAT and ILOAT have in some cases extended their jurisdiction to an aggrieved employee who would have no other recourse against the organisation.[19] This remedial mechanism is not normally available to, for instance, consultants who have special service agreements, although Article II(4) of the ILOAT Statute provides access for this category: ad hoc arbitration may

[9] E. Schmidt-Assmann and L. Harrings, 'Access to Justice and Fundamental Rights', *European Review of Public Law* 9 (1997), 529–49, at 543.

[10] C. De Cooker, 'Pre-litigation Procedures in International Organisations' in C. De Cooker (ed.), *International Administration: Law and Management in International Organisations* (looseleaf publication) (The Hague: Kluwer Law International), contribution VI, pp. 1–21.

[11] Schmidt-Assmann and Harrings, 'Access to Justice', 543.

[12] De Cooker, 'Pre-litigation Procedures', p. 1.

[13] *Ibid.*, p. 8.   [14] *Ibid.*, p. 2.

[15] According to a study by the International Civil Service Commission referred to in *ibid.*, p. 4.

[16] D. Ruzié, 'Jurisprudence du Tribunal Administratif de l'Organisation Internationale du Travail', *AFDI* 43 (1997), 445–61, at 447, note 17.

[17] Singer, 'Jurisdictional Immunity', 155.   [18] *Ibid.*, 156–7.

[19] Reinisch, *National Courts*, pp. 272–4 and the cases cited there.

be offered to them in cases in which negotiations have proved to be unsuccessful.[20]

The possession of staff member status is the prime condition for *locus standi* before an international administrative tribunal. This implies that those applying for employment within an international organisation are ultimately unable to contest any unsuccessful application before an administrative tribunal except when an offer for employment had already been made.[21] The UN's policy is not to enter into any litigation or arbitration but to reply in a reasoned manner to such individuals; in the Secretary-General's opinion, using public funds to do otherwise would be inappropriate.[22] This contrasts sharply with the liberal interpretation followed by the ECJ and a similar, admittedly more cautious, approach taken by the administrative tribunals of the European Co-ordinated International Organisations comprising, *inter alia*, the Council of Europe, OECD and NATO,[23] where apparently the argument that the applicants are not yet part of the international civil service has not been upheld.

As to service-incurred injuries, the Advisory Board for Compensation Claims, a quasi-judicial body, advises the UN Secretary-General on the qualification of the injury and the amount of appropriate compensation. The UNAT is competent to deal with appeals against the relevant decisions of the Secretary-General. Under the Model SOFA the Special Representative/Force Commander shall establish administrative procedures to deal with claims submitted by locally recruited personnel.[24]

Challenging legislative decisions

The relationship between staff members and an international organisation is of a special nature. Therefore, challenges before international administrative tribunals not only to individual decisions but also to legislative decisions of general applicability are almost inevitable. There is no obstacle of inadmissibility to such challenges as the jurisdiction of such tribunals has not excluded them.[25] Although the number of such challenges has been increasing, in most cases the legislative acts are

---

[20] P. Szasz, Working Paper No. 1, ILA Committee, p. 14: on file with the author.
[21] UNAT Judgments Nos. 96 and 106, ILOAT Judgment Nos. 339 and 621: D. Ruzié, Working Paper No. 1, ILA Committee, p. 2, para. 7: on file with the author.
[22] A/C.5/49/65 of 24 April 1995, p. 10, para. 24.
[23] D. Ruzié, Working Paper No. 1, ILA Committee, p. 2, paras. 8–11: on file with the author.
[24] A/45/594 of 9 October 1990, para. 52.
[25] Szasz, 'Adjudicating IGO Staff Challenges', pp. 704–5.

upheld, according to Paul Szasz, because of the thoroughness of the legal preparation prior to the issuance of those decisions by rule-making organs.[26] These actions are brought either against the Executive Head (UNAT) or against the organisation itself (ILOAT).[27]

From a procedural point of view it is obvious that the validity of the legislative decision will normally only be open to challenge by way of an exception of illegality raised with regard to its application in a particular individual case. However, Szasz recently pointed out that the procedure of the UN Common System Tribunals is not adequate to deal with these kinds of cases. Therefore on 23 December 1993 the UN General Assembly adopted Resolution 48/224 to require that the International Civil Service Commission and the UN Joint Staff Pension Board should be informed and be given an opportunity to intervene in proceedings during which their recommendations or decisions are being challenged. The same procedural mechanism would be applied in favour of any international organisation that is not the respondent but which might also be affected by the outcome of the proceedings.[28] The General Assembly requested the ILOAT to take a similar kind of approach.[29] These new procedures have not as yet been incorporated in new rules of procedure of the Tribunal, but they have so far developed as a matter of practice.[30] The form and modalities of such 'intervention' – ranging from giving advice to the respondent organisation to complementing independent submissions – will partly depend on the particular circumstances of the case.[31]

The danger of incompatible case law between the two common-system tribunals as regards challenged legislative decisions is a further complicating factor, in addition to the absence of a *stare decisis* rule applicable to each of the tribunals' own decisions.[32] The problem has so far been kept within manageable bounds by the tribunals taking account of each other's decisions and the Executive Heads of the international organisations belonging to the common system conceding challenge in one tribunal following rejection by the other.[33] As a result of this, a limited extent of forum shopping is possible.[34] The basic problem of

---

[26] *Ibid.*, p. 705.

[27] *Ibid.*, p. 706. This competence of the international administrative tribunals constitutes one of the procedures for the settlement of differences as provided for in the relevant conventions on privileges and immunities of international organisations: *ibid.*, p. 701.

[28] Resolution 48/224 of 23 December 1994, Part IV.

[29] Resolution 49/223 of 23 December 1994, Part X.

[30] Szasz, 'Adjudicating IGO Staff Challenges', p. 709.   [31] *Ibid.*   [32] *Ibid.*, pp. 711–12.

[33] *Ibid.*, pp. 712–13.   [34] *Ibid.*, p. 713.

86   PROCEDURAL ASPECTS OF REMEDIAL ACTION

divergent judicial decisions with regard to the interpretation and application of a common legal norm has also arisen between the administrative tribunals of the European Co-ordinated International Organisations.[35]

The review system

After the General Assembly decided in its Resolution 50/54 on 29 January 1996 to eliminate the appeal review procedure against judgments of the UNAT at the ICJ, only a limited review possibility remains with regard to the ILOAT, to be instituted exclusively by the international organisation concerned.[36] The underlying, protective rationale for the establishment of the review system by the ICJ was not so much to protect the staff members, which from an accountability point of view should have been the prime concern, but to enhance the UNAT's position *vis-à-vis* the UN General Assembly. By restoring the pre-1955 situation the General Assembly would have less difficulty in departing from judgments rendered by the UNAT, particularly when compliance would involve substantial financial resources: but that in turn would presuppose a larger degree of judicial activism by the UNAT than it has demonstrated in recent years. One of the other reasons put forward in favour of restoration – that the Article XI procedure offered only an illusionary guarantee to staff members – appears to be rather unconvincing as the review possibility was kept intact for the ILOAT. The elimination of the ICJ review did not affect, of course, the authority of the General Assembly 'to request an advisory opinion on these matters on a case-by-case basis'.[37]

Attempts to solicit Advisory Opinions from UN common-system tribunals on the legality of a proposed decision have failed because both tribunals considered that it was not within their competence to render such an opinion.[38] For a number of rule-making organs considering legislative decisions affecting the entire category of staff members there remains the option of using the possibility of Article 96 of the UN Charter and to request an Advisory Opinion from the ICJ, although as

[35] D. Ruzié, Working Paper No. 1, ILA Committee, pp. 4–5, paras. 23–7; on file with the author.
[36] D. Ruzié, 'Jurisprudence du Tribunal Administratif de l'Organisation Internationale du Travail', *AFDI* 43 (1997), 445–61, at 461.
[37] J. Charney, 'Is International Law Threatened by Multiple International Tribunals?', *RCADI* 271 (1998), 101–382, at 122, note 27.
[38] Szasz, 'Adjudicating IGO Staff Challenges', p. 718.

a matter of principle Szasz was probably right in pointing out that the Court 'does not really have the expertise in international administrative law to enable it to make a useful contribution to the resolution of these often technically complex cases'.[39] The ICJ is probably not looking favourably at any proposals that would restore, albeit in a different way, its involvement in the UNAT's judicial decisions, the termination of which it did not deplore in 1996.

[39] *Ibid.*, p. 720.

10 Procedural aspects of remedial action by private claimants

Section 29(a)–(b) of the General Convention on the Privileges and Immunities of the UN and the corresponding section 31(a)–(b) of the Convention on the Privileges and Immunities of Specialised Agencies require these international organisations to make provision for appropriate means of settlement. Pierre Klein rightly observed that given the rationale of this obligation, namely to respect the fundamental rights of the individual and to ensure a due process of law, it does impose itself on every international organisation even without special provisions.[1] If by way of the holding-harmless clause the private claimant is directed towards the domestic legal system of the host state, then this implies the potential for additional, different procedural obstacles arising from that system's particular structure, for example with regard to the individual's judicial protection *vis-à-vis* national administrative authorities.[2]

As has already been made clear above, member states do have access to a number of mechanisms to submit claims based on political or policy-related grievances against the UN, usually made in connection with actions or decisions taken by the Security Council or the General Assembly. When similar claims – often seeking substantial monetary compensation – are made by third parties, the UN is not willing to engage in litigation or arbitration because in the Secretary-General's view utilising public funds would be inappropriate to submit to any form of litigation.[3] The question could be raised as to whether the principle of sound financial management could be successfully invoked in circumstances where the accountability regime requires appropriate mechanisms to deal with such claims or requests. Such mechanisms obviously

---

[1] P. Klein, *La Responsabilité des organisations internationales dans les ordres juridiques internes et en droit des gens* (Brussels: Editions Bruylant and Editions de l'Université Libre de Bruxelles, 1998), p. 248.
[2] *Ibid.*, p. 251.   [3] A/C.5/49/65 of 24 April 1995, para. 23.

do not have to be of a litigious nature and the claims arising could be based on situations in which the claimant has not necessarily sustained financial losses; that is a matter that is discussed in Part IV, below.

When private claimants are raising claims of contractual or tortious liability against one of the officials of an international organisation for acts performed in the course of official functions, they are faced with the obstacle of the jurisdictional immunities enjoyed by these officials. In the absence of a waiver by the Secretary-General, Article VIII, section 29(b) of the General Convention applies, but it does not provide for a specific mechanism to settle this kind of dispute, although Article V, section 21 requires the UN to co-operate with the appropriate authorities of members to facilitate the proper administration of justice. In most cases, which are generally of a domestic nature, immunity is waived, while traffic accidents are dealt with by the insurance company.[4]

Although the context within which private claimants would normally be led to consider remedial action against an international organisation in most cases originates from contractual or tortious acts and actions, the temporary exercise of governmental or quasi-governmental authority by an international organisation over private persons and enterprises within a particular territorial scope beyond district head-quarters may also give rise to claims that the acts performed by the organisation under that authority are illegal. However, the lack of an appropriate remedial mechanism within the international organisation to carry out the legality test, let alone upon a private individual's request, leaves him or her without direct means of protection. Exceptions of illegality against the organisation's institutional or operational acts provide an indirect remedy. They can be raised before a domestic court or arbitral tribunal seised with a dispute between, for instance, other private or state entities and involving the controversial act. Such exceptions can also be raised during legal proceedings instituted by the international organisation against a private company for allegedly having violated a norm issued by the organisation.

Contractual liability claims

The overall picture

Public- or private-law commercial enterprises, and private individuals who are not officials of the international organisation, may enter into

---

[4] *Ibid.*, p. 12, paras. 31–2.

a variety of contractual relationships with an organisation. The variety of subject-matter of the contract may involve the supply of office equipment (all international organisations), commodities (commodity organisations), military equipment (peacekeeping operations) or the construction of buildings or transport of goods.[5]

One of the major characteristics of a contract with an international organisation is the superiority of concerns of an international public interest over the binding force of the contractual link,[6] although one must recall that the traditional distinction between contracts of a private/public law nature as well as between contracts *iure gestionis/iure imperii* is inoperable;[7] the more reason therefore, from an accountability perspective, to devise measures correcting the initial inequality between the contracting partners. When deciding upon the tender – and, by their very nature, not in cases of immediate operational requirement procedures or letters of assist – the UN, in addition to checking that the normal necessary qualifications are fulfilled, also takes into account the company's financial position in order to gauge its willingness to grant grace of payment,[8] but this does not contribute to the contractant's perception on remedial action it might eventually consider. This is, of course, the consequence of the fact that 'le marché onusien attise suffisamment les convoitises pour les rendre moins exigeantes envers l'Organisation, plus disposées à prendre le risque de contrats inégalitaires résultant de l'insertion des clauses générales'.[9] These general clauses putting in place a system of control and surveillance for the benefit of the organisation are, in practical terms, not subject to negotiation.[10] The frequently changing nature of both the mandate and the circumstances of, for instance, peacekeeping operations underscores the importance of leaving the international organisation with the option of terminating the contract *unilaterally.*[11]

This overall context of subordination is, moreover, guaranteed by the organisation's determination to place the contract under the governance of its own internal law – domestic law is only occasionally applicable.[12]

---

[5] See A. Reinisch, *International Organisations before National Courts* (Cambridge: Cambridge University Press, 2000), p. 26 and notes 115–17 referring to relevant case law. We have already referred to international organisations themselves rendering services to particular countries in view of the organisation's technical or development expertise.

[6] J. P. Colin, 'Les Relations contractuelles des organisations internationales avec les personnes privées', *Revue de Droit International et de Droit Comparé* (1992), 6–43, at 20 as cited by D. Meyer, 'Les Contrats de fournitures de biens et de services dans le cadre des opérations de maintien de la paix', *AFDI* 42 (1996) 79–119, at 97.

[7] Meyer, 'Contrats de fournitures', 86.

[8] *Ibid.*, 101.   [9] *Ibid.*, 106.   [10] *Ibid.*, 107.   [11] *Ibid.*   [12] *Ibid.*, 112.

PRIVATE CLAIMANTS 91

In contrast with normal contractual liability between private parties, the resort to domestic courts is an ineffective remedy because of the jurisdictional immunity of the organisation. In addition, UN officials are shielded by contractual provisions from claims directed against them personally. As a consequence private contractors cannot expect to be successful in any attempt to commence judicial proceedings before domestic courts, for example because the international organisation has allegedly violated the principle of non-discrimination. The functional limitation of legal personality within domestic legal systems should not entail the international organisation being released from its contractual obligations towards private contractors which are lying beyond those limits, as that would run counter to the principle of good faith.[13] One of the approaches to defining more precisely how much jurisdictional immunity should be stripped away as regards contractual claims would consist of reversing the clauses so that an explicit clause would be required for a dispute concerning a contractual provision to escape from domestic court jurisdiction.[14]

The absence of an arbitration clause or the fact that a private party is unwilling to arbitrate could lead to legal proceedings before a domestic court but this time initiated by the international organisation, which would thereby waive its jurisdictional immunity and open the possibility for the private party to submit a counterclaim.[15] The possibility of being exposed to counterclaims is normally not mentioned in treaty immunity provisions. Sometimes it is regarded as a customary law-based exception to the principle of immunity.[16] An exceptional but limited example did occur in 1992 when the International Civil Aviation Organisation applied to a Canadian court for a declaratory judgment with regard to its jurisdictional immunity *vis-à-vis* the arbitral tribunal that had been constituted according to a compromissory clause in a contract with a private company. The application was met by an exception of inadmissibility, which was upheld by the Canadian judge.[17]

---

[13] T. Rensmann, 'Internationale Organisationen im Privatrechtsverkehr', *Archiv des Völkerrechts* 36 (1998), 305–44, at 308.

[14] M. Singer, 'Jurisdictional Immunity of International Organisations: Human Rights and Functional Necessity Concerns', *Virginia Journal of International Law* 36 (1995), 53–165, at 144 and 146.

[15] P. Szasz, Working Paper, ILA Committee, p. 6; on file with the author.

[16] Reinisch, *National Courts*, pp. 204–5 referring to C. Dominice in note 192.

[17] *ICAO v. Tripol Systems Pty Ltd*, Supreme Court of Québec, 9 September 1994, *Recueil de Jurisprudence du Québec* (1994), 2560 as referred to by Klein, *La Responsabilité*, pp. 259–60.

92 PROCEDURAL ASPECTS OF REMEDIAL ACTION

As a pre-remedial mechanism in peacekeeping operations (which have recently been responsible for a significant increase in procurement contracts), the resident auditor could play a relevant role. Moreover, contractors should be aware that the implicit or explicit functional contractual capacity of a peacekeeping operation does not imply a separate legal personality[18] entailing all the possible consequences for any kind of judicial remedial action that might have been envisaged.

Sub-contracting

In situations of sub-contracting – that is, when activities of any operational kind are carried out by private contractors – it may very well be the case that the organisation's immunity is partly extended to such contractors, but as a rule the providers of services do not become officials or staff members.[19] Sub-contracting the clearance of the Suez Canal was an external operation of an entirely civilian nature carried out by civilian employees of the private firms involved: the clearing was implemented under the instructions, directions and control of the UN Secretary-General, the civilians enjoying the status of UN personnel *vis-à-vis* Egypt.[20]

Whether a claim against an international organisation before a domestic court based on fault under the domestic law of the (sub-)contractor must fail – in the absence of jurisdictional immunity – because the organisation does not itself execute the contract or project is a matter for debate. Although not directly engaged in the action affecting the complainant, the organisation might nevertheless be in a position to compel its (sub-)contractor to take precautionary or remedial measures in order to prevent further damage from occurring.[21]

The problem of the derivative immunity of a sub-contractor operating for and on behalf of an international organisation, 'calling for close study and great caution',[22] has recently been dealt with, *inter alia*, by the

---

[18] Meyer, 'Contrats de fournitures', 87 and 88.   [19] *Ibid.*, 94.

[20] F. Seyersted, 'United Nations Forces: Some Legal Problems', *BYIL* 37 (1961), 351–475, at 355.

[21] See *contra*, S. Schlemmer-Schulte, 'The World Bank Inspection Panel: Its Creation, Functioning, Case Record and its Two Reviews', *Zeitschrift für Europarechtliche Studien* 1 (1998), 347–70, at 369.

[22] C. W. Jenks, *International Immunities* (London and New York: Stevens & Sons and Oceana Publications, 1961), pp. 142–3.

US Court of Appeals for the District of Columbia Circuit, which held that the immunity provision concerning the IBRD's operations could not be read to include within its scope activities conducted by any other entity such as independent contractors, as nothing in the Articles of Agreement had indicated that the signatories had contemplated that the Bank would retain independent contractors to perform its lending operations. In order for derivative immunity to become possible, the connection between the international organisation and its (sub-)contractor must be so close that the two cannot realistically be viewed as separate entities: close control by the organisation over the terms of the contract and the way it is being performed does not therefore transform the contractor into an instrument of the organisation.[23]

From an accountability perspective the US court's reasoning, once transferred into the area of sub-contracting in peacekeeping operations, humanitarian assistance or development co-operation, could result in those non-state sub-contractors becoming vulnerable to all but contractual liability claims by private parties because of damage sustained as a result of actions and operations conducted by these sub-contractors when under close control and monitoring by the international organisation. It is interesting in this respect to compare ECHR case law, according to which a state can be held responsible for a violation of human rights in spite of delegation to private entities.[24]

Arbitration

Standard arbitration clauses for use in all commercial contracts and purchase agreements as well as lease agreements have been prepared by the Office of Legal Affairs of the UN.[25] These clauses are normally followed by a provision which clarifies that neither the contractual agreement nor its arbitration clause constitutes a waiver of the organisation's jurisdictional immunity.[26]

Mahnoush Arsanjani observed that the mere provision of some alternative judicial method of dispute settlement 'makes some difference in the atmosphere of settling the claim and may be an incentive to

---

[23] US Court of Appeals for the District of Columbia Circuit, *IBRD v. District of Columbia*, *ILM* 38 (1999), 819–26.

[24] *Costello-Roberts v. UK*, ECHR, Series A, vol. 247 C, 25 March 1993, p. 57, para. 26 referred to by J. Charney, 'Is International Law Threatened by Multiple International Tribunals?', *RCADI* 271 (1998), 101–382, at 242.

[25] A/C.5/49/65, p. 2. [26] *Ibid.*, p. 3.

94   PROCEDURAL ASPECTS OF REMEDIAL ACTION

settle by negotiations'.[27] Whether this incentive works in a completely neutral way when individual claimants are involved is certainly a matter for further debate, especially given the particular preference of international organisations for this method of settlement. A further question that may arise before domestic courts, namely as to whether all the appropriate means of settlement provided offer substantially equivalent protection, will be dealt with later. Given the pivotal role of a well-functioning procurement system in peacekeeping operations, ensuing claims are dealt with in essentially the same manner as non-peacekeeping-related commercial agreements: the vast majority of claims are settled by direct negotiations, which means that few cases lead to arbitration.[28]

As in the case of states, there is a noticeable recent tendency within the UN to move away from reference to standing arbitration and towards the provision for ad hoc arbitration[29] in the absence of a successful outcome of prior conciliation under UNCITRAL Conciliation rules. This leaves untouched the 'internal mechanism evolved by the Office of Legal Affairs for negotiated settlement of claims'.[30]

Although international organisations normally have no difficulty in complying with any arbitral awards, the United Nations General Assembly in its Resolution 53/217, adopted on 7 April 1999, has expressed deep concern about the increase in pending procurement-related claims instituted against the organisation and has asked the Secretary-General to prepare a report.[31]

---

[27] M. Arsanjani, 'Claims against International Organisations: Quis Custodiet Ipsos Custodes?', *Yale Journal of World Public Order* 7 (1980–1), 131–76, at 139.

[28] A/C.5/49/65, p. 8, para. 21. See, *inter alia*, Arsanjani referring (in 'Quis Custodiet', 145–6) to the *Starways Limited* case of 24 September 1969, *ILR* 44 (1972), 433–7. Although the parties reached a settlement before arbitration, it was unique in the sense that the UN had been willing to allow the arbitrator to decide whether the UN had been in breach of duty of care (*ibid.*).

[29] P. Szasz, Working Paper ILA Committee, p. 4: on file with the author.

[30] Memorandum of the Director of the Office of Legal Affairs, A/C.5/51/9 of 18 October 1996, at p. 12, para. 47.

[31] Pursuant to paragraph 2 of the Resolution the Report should cover, *inter alia*, the reasons for arbitration cases, the roles and mandates of various Secretariat structures and negotiating teams in arbitration and settlement processes, the sources of funding for arbitration awards, and settlement payments, pending arbitration cases and measures taken or proposed to prevent or reduce contract disputes, which may lead to arbitration in the future. In his Report submitted on 14 October 1999 the UN Secretary-General pointed out that given 'the risks and costs associated with arbitration, every effort is made, consistent with the interests of the Organisation, to reach negotiated settlements of contract claims with contractors. This has proved

PRIVATE CLAIMANTS 95

Arbitration does not have to be the natural choice as, for instance, the ILO 'generally makes use of Article II(4) of the Statute of its Administrative Tribunal, which makes the latter competent to hear disputes arising out of contracts to which ILO is a party and that contains a compromissory clause to that effect'.[32] Apparently only one case has so far been decided, although it was on the borderline of an employment-related and services-providing dispute.[33] According to Wilfred Jenks, one of the difficulties in explaining this state of affairs could very well be that the ILOAT may be perceived by a third party 'as a body subject to [the organisation's] influence rather than an impartial court'.[34] Since the exercise of the contractual jurisdiction of the ILOAT did not become a reality, the question of *exequatur* of its judgments did not arise.[35]

In 1957 the Institut de Droit International demanded that for every decision of an international organ or organisation that affects private rights or interests, appropriate procedures should be provided in order to settle, by judicial or arbitral methods, any juridical differences that might arise from such a decision.[36] At its 1977 Oslo Session the Institut adopted a further resolution,[37] Article 7 of which provided for the settlement by an independent body of disputes arising out of contracts concluded with private persons by international organisations. According to Article 8 such an independent body could be an arbitration body set up in accordance with the rules of a permanent institution or in pursuance of ad hoc clauses; it could be a tribunal set up by an international organisation, if conferring such jurisdiction is compatible with the rules of the organisation, or a national judicial body, if this is compatible with the status and functions of the organisation.

successful with the overwhelming majority of claims' (A/54/458, para. 12). Once the contractor has handed the dispute to its lawyers, the Office of Legal Affairs usually takes over the negotiations (*ibid.*, para. 11). Once a dispute proceeds to arbitration 'the validity of available obligated funds in approved peacekeeping missions budgets for non-governmental liabilities is extended and maintained to cover the potential liability' (*ibid.*, para. 14). The Report also dealt with the selection of outside legal counsel (*ibid.*, paras. 15–20). Part III of this study returns to the other aspects of procurement-related arbitrations.

[32] P. Szasz, Working Paper ILA Committee, p. 7: on file with the author.

[33] *Rebek v. WHO*, ILOAT judgment no. 77, 1 December 1964 referred to by Reinisch, *National Courts*, p. 269, note 85.

[34] Jenks, *International Immunities*, p. 44.

[35] C. W. Jenks, *The Proper Law of International Organisations* (London and New York: Stevens and Oceana, 1962), p. 117.

[36] *Annuaire de l'Institut de Droit International* 47(2) (1957), 488.

[37] *Annuaire de l'Institut de Droit International* 57(2) (1977), 336.

Tort liability claims

Insurance and self-insurance

During his 1950 Hague Academy lectures, Clyde Eagleton gave the following example of potential tortious liability: an international organisation may, in developing the economic life of a country, cause economic loss to another country, even if the advice is given by the international organisation, while the action is taken by the state.[38] August Reinisch has succinctly listed the variety of torts that have occurred as a result of acts or decisions by international organisations, namely: infringement of the personal property rights of private persons; accusations of libel or slander; and false imprisonment.[39]

Although the UN has set up an insurance mechanism against third-party liability in accordance with General Assembly Resolution 22 E (I) of 13 February 1946, it has no general scope of application, as it is limited to accidents involving UN motor vehicles. Suppliers of aircraft or ships for use by the UN in peacekeeping operations require the UN to secure third-party liability insurance, while conversely the UN requires charterers to obtain insurance under which the UN is jointly insured.[40]

Fluctuation in premium rates has influenced UN policy towards liability insurance with regard to its several headquarters and other seats.[41]

Out-of-court settlement by the insurer can be negotiated directly with the claimant. However, in a case of litigation before domestic courts, immunity-based defences cannot be invoked by the insurer either with respect to the international organisation or to one of its agents.[42] It is fair to say that an 'international organisation obtains liability insurance coverage to remedy any injustice that its jurisdictional immunity would impose on parties whom it might damage'.[43]

The alternative model of self-insurance by the UN – other international organisations do not make use of such a system – involves direct contact between the claimant and the organisation. An internal Tort Claims Board, comprising five members of the Secretariat, reviews claims that are not settled by the Office of Legal Affairs because they exceed a ceiling of US$5,000 and in respect of which the UN is not insured. The Board can make a recommendation to the Controller as to the maximum

---

[38] C. Eagleton, 'International Organisations and the Law of Responsibility', *RCADI* 76 (1950), 323–423, at 390.

[39] Reinisch, *National Courts*, p. 28 and accompanying footnote for relevant case law.

[40] P. Szasz, Working Paper, ILA Committee, p. 7: on file with the author.

[41] *Ibid.*   [42] *Ibid.*, pp. 7–8.   [43] Singer, 'Jurisdictional Immunity', 80.

amount that can be offered to the claimant. In the absence of an amicable settlement by negotiation, recourse to arbitration has been provided for by a Secretary-General's Bulletin.[44]

Operational activities

As already indicated in the previous section, there is no standing remedial mechanism available to private claimants, which substantially adds to the degree of unpredictability once international organisations become engaged in operational activities that are bound to result in some kind of damage to non-state entities that find themselves temporarily or permanently under the jurisdiction of the host or beneficiary state. Moreover, international organisations are not very inclined to allow even temporary arbitral mechanisms to 'interfere' (albeit only subsequently) with the proper conducting of their legitimate operational activities of whatever kind, except when the hazardous nature of these activities (such as space or nuclear activities) has from the outset led to the establishment of particular liability regimes.

As a result of the normal holding-harmless clause inserted into the agreement between the international organisation and the host state, private claimants who have allegedly sustained damages as a direct result of the operation are inevitably obliged to bring their claims before the government that exercises territorial jurisdiction over the operational zone. Only in cases of gross negligence or wilful misconduct will it be possible for them to address their claim directly to the organisation.

Considerations of fairness towards both the beneficiary state and private claimants (of whatever nationality) bring into question whether, from an accountability perspective, the continued insertion and application of these holding-harmless clauses can be maintained.

Peacekeeping operations as a separate category: the ONUC case

The situation changes drastically when the organisation is involved in a particular category of operational activities, namely that of peacekeeping and peace-enforcing operations. Writing back in 1981, Arsanjani pointed out that some responsibility for unjustifiable injury to states and individuals had been recognised in bilateral agreements between the UN and host states, albeit in 'general and vague provisions'.[45] In

[44] A/C.5/49/65, p. 5, para 12.   [45] Arsanjani, 'Quis Custodiet?', 141.

98 PROCEDURAL ASPECTS OF REMEDIAL ACTION

the case of the Opérations des Nations Unies au Congo, disputes could be settled by negotiation, or by any other method agreed between the parties, or by arbitration upon unilateral request. In contrast, a claims commission would settle similar claims in the case of UNFICYP and UNEF;[46] moreover, it should be noted that no such mixed claims commissions have so far been established. Arsanjani considers the absence of complex and lengthy legal procedures and the predominance of the principles of common sense and fairness as the major advantages of mixed claims commissions over other forms of settlement:[47] that may be so, provided they are not prevented from coming into existence in the first place by a mere unilateral refusal to establish them on behalf of the UN.[48] The compromissory clause inserted into Article 46 of the ONUC Status Agreement of 27 November 1961, which provides for arbitration, was confined to disputes between the UN and the government concerning the interpretation and application of this Agreement. In contrast with, for example, UNEF, there was no provision for the settlement of claims of a private-law nature between the UN and the host state.

The reason for this paucity of settlement procedures may, according to Derek Bowett, very well have been that because the operation was heavily committed to the financial support of the Congo, 'there was little point in providing for lengthy procedures for settlement which would in the result mean little more than a book-keeping exercise with the figures showing what financial assistance had been provided to the Congo'.[49]

With regard to claims between Congolese civilians and the UN, Article 10(b) of the Status Agreement provided for negotiations, and eventually arbitration, concerning disputes regarding loss or damage caused by an act performed by a member of the Force or an official in the course of his official duties. The Secretary-General was authorised to arrange for the necessary arbitral procedure, or to establish a claims commission. 'The jurisdiction of the Congolese courts was not to be exercised until after all these procedures had been exhausted.'[50] Apparently, therefore, the claims mechanisms were not put in place because the Force was enjoying immunity before the domestic courts, and the exhaustion of these remedies had to precede any resort to Congolese domestic courts. However,

---

[46] For a brief description of the system for UNEF see, *inter alia*, D. Bowett, *UN Forces: A Legal Study of United Nations Practice* (London: Stevens, 1964), pp. 149–51.

[47] Arsanjani, 'Quis Custodiet?', 175.

[48] As reported by Klein with regard to UNAMIR, *La Responsabilité*, p. 264.

[49] Bowett, *UN Forces*, p. 243.   [50] *Ibid.*, p. 244.

the claims commissions that operated over several months were not of a mixed nature, as they had been created unilaterally by the UN within its own administration: this was, in fact, in line with Article 34(d) of the ONUC Regulations and in accordance with the Status Agreement, which only provided for arbitration for disputes of a private-law nature.[51] These purely internal claims commissions had to formulate recommendations as to the follow-up to be given to claims addressed to ONUC. Given the steady increase in the number of claims, the system was abandoned in favour of the well-known lump-sum agreements between the UN and various countries.

For claims between Congolese civilians and members of the Force involving non-official acts, the UN, pursuant to Article 10(c), should have used its good offices to assist the parties to arrive at a settlement, with arbitration eventually becoming available.[52]

Claims between the UN and non-Congolese civilians were not dealt with in the Status Agreement; established UN practice – that is, arbitration – would thereby apply.[53]

As Jean Salmon convincingly argued, one is led to believe that the UN was unwilling to establish a mechanism of a judicial nature before which the different claims could have been brought. Apart from the costs involved and the delay in the settlement of claims, the international organisation had nothing to gain from a public procedure unveiling the details of inevitable but less fortunate aspects of its activities in the Congo.[54] Considerations of non-accountability were probably among those which prevented the establishment of appropriate remedial mechanisms.

The conditions of control and command

Apart from claims arising from commercial agreements,[55] tort claims related to UN peacekeeping operations consist of third-party claims for compensation for personal injury/death or property loss/damage. The types of damage most commonly encountered in the practice of UN operations are non-consensual use and occupation of premises, personal injury, property loss or damage arising from the ordinary operations of the Force, and such injury and damage as result from combat

---

[51] Klein, *La Responsabilité*, p. 263.   [52] Bowett, *UN Forces*, p. 244.   [53] *Ibid.*
[54] J. Salmon, 'Les Accords Spaak–U Thant du 20 février 1965', *AFDI* 11 (1965), 469–97, at 485.
[55] See above, p. 89.

operations.[56] The liability covers injuries resulting from wrongful actions by the peacekeepers on condition that they can be attributed to the international organisation, a condition that presupposes exclusive UN control and command. It should be added that, pursuant to Article 47(3) of the UN Charter, the Military Staff Committee 'shall be responsible under the Council for the strategic direction of any armed forces placed at the disposal of the Security Council'. Exclusive responsibility on the part of the UN for the peacekeeping or peace-enforcement operations would, however, require a degree of internationalisation of the forces involved which as yet has not been achieved.[57]

The control exercised by an international organisation over its agents provides a sound basis for the organisation's responsibility for acts carried out by its agents.[58] The actual amount of freedom from external control or, conversely, the actual amount of control left to the respondent entity will have to be ascertained in each separate case to discover the liability/responsibility.[59]

The crucial importance of operational command becomes clear, of course, in dramatic circumstances such as evacuation from a particular area as a result of a UN decision (Srebrenica, Dutchbat operation), which contrasts with an evacuation of a national contingent from a host country as a result of a decision by the troop-contributing country (Rwanda and Operation Silver Back, Belgium). Writing before the publication of the Report of the Secretary-General on Srebrenica,[60] a leading authority on peacekeeping operations had

---

[56] A/51/389 of 20 September 1996, para. 3.

[57] P. De Visscher, 'Observations sur le fondement et la mise-en-oeuvre du principe de la responsabilité de l'organisation des Nations Unies', *Revue de Droit International et de Droit Comparé* 40 (1963), 165–73, at 169. But see the House of Lords decision in *Attorney-General v. Nissan* ([1969] 1 All ER 629, HL), where it was held that the United Kingdom was liable for damages caused to a British subject by British troops not only before the troops joined UNFICYP, but even afterwards (see further BYIL 44 (1968–9), 217–26). On these issues see, *inter alia*, D. Sarooshi, *The UN and the Development of Collective Security: The Delegation by the UN Security Council of its Chapter VII Powers* (Oxford: Clarendon Press, 1999), pp. 141–67, at pp. 164–5. On the control and command issue with regard to the Forces in Korea and on the ensuing respective responsibility see Seyersted, 'United Nations Forces', 362–70 and 430–4. In 'military and operational terms, control was firmly in the hands of the US. However, the parties involved clearly regarded the US as the agent of the UN and the action in which they were engaged as a UN action': R. Higgins, *UN Peacekeeping 1946–1967: Documents and Commentary*, vol. II, *Asia* (London: Oxford University Press, 1970), p. 197. On the operational control in UNEF and ONUC: Seyersted, 'United Nations Forces', 406–10.

[58] Eagleton, 'International Organisations', 358.   [59] *Ibid.*, 358.

[60] See below, pp. 193–7.

already convincingly argued that because the UN command structure remained intact and the Netherlands did not issue orders in contravention of it,[61] the Netherlands could not be held legally responsible for the actions of Dutchbat in relation to the events in and around Srebrenica, and that consequently the UN could not pass its responsibility in the matter on to the Netherlands.[62] Following the same line of argument it was quite unsurprising that in the spring of 2000 the ICTY Prosecutor labelled as 'complete nonsense' a formal complaint against the former Dutch Defence Secretary and the Dutchbat Commander in Srebrenica. In his capacity as 'commander-in-chief' of UN operations, the Secretary-General may issue instructions and regulations to members of UN Forces through the Secretary-General's Bulletins, which are binding on members of these Forces.[63] On the other hand, and in other cases such as UNSCOM, the responsibility for operational oversight may lie with the Security Council rather than with the Secretary-General.

Even more delicate issues of respective responsibility can arise in other areas of operational activities such as in cases of (in)voluntary repatriation by a government and the obligation incumbent upon the UNHCR to protect refugees.[64] Although in different situations a division of responsibilities between the UNHCR and the International Committee of the Red Cross could be informal, and based on institutional expertise and location on the ground,[65] this could result in their respective accountability becoming blurred.

As rightly pointed out by Geoff Gilbert, if the UNHCR incorrectly declares a source state safe for return, closes a refugee camp and facilitates the repatriation of the refugee population which suffers persecution on return, there is 'no obvious mechanism by which UNHCR might be held accountable, although a State might defend itself before the Human Rights Committee or other supervisory organ, and argue that any breach of its human rights obligations was due to UNHCR'.[66]

---

[61] R. Siekmann, 'The Fall of Srebrenica and the Attitude of Dutchbat from an International Legal Perspective', *Yearbook of International Humanitarian Law* 1 (1998), 301–12, at 303 and 305.

[62] *Ibid.*

[63] D. Shraga, 'UN Peacekeeping Operations: Applicability of International Humanitarian Law and Responsibility for Operations-related Damage', *AJIL* 94 (2000), 406–12, at 409.

[64] G. Gilbert, 'Rights, Legitimate Expectations, Needs and Responsibilities: UNHCR and the New World Order', *International Journal of Refugee Law* 10 (1998), 349–88, at 380–1.

[65] *Ibid.*, 383, note 221.

[66] *Ibid.*, 382. This indirect remedy against an international organisation or one of its

Limitation of third-party liability

Given the fact that because of their inherent complexity and the variety of actors involved peacekeeping operations are likely to give rise to a large number of claims, the General Assembly adopted Resolution 52/247 on 'Third-party liability: temporal and financial limitations'. Claims generally have to be submitted within six months of the occurrence of the damage or after its discovery, but in any case within one year after the termination of the peacekeeping operation.[67] In contrast with the Model Agreement between the UN and member states contributing personnel and equipment to UN peacekeeping operations,[68] the claims settlement mechanism under paragraph 51 of the Model SOFA[69] would remain in force until the settlement of all claims arising prior to the termination of the Agreement and submitted prior to or within three months of such termination.[70] Such a time-limit does not apply to the envisaged arbitral tribunal.[71] The time-limit placed upon the liability of the UN reflects a balance of interests between the organisation (no unknown and possibly large financial liabilities for past operations, restricted ability to investigate the claim and defend itself after withdrawing from the area) and the claimant (no undue deprivation of his or her right to seek compensation).[72]

As far as combat-related activities are concerned, if the damage was caused in violation of any particular rule of international humanitarian law or the laws of war and could not be justified on grounds of military necessity, third-party liability could arise,[73] 'subject to the exception of' operational necessity 'that is where damage results from necessary actions taken by a peacekeeping force in the course of carrying out its operation in pursuance of its mandates'.[74] The two concepts derive from different sources, 'operational necessity' having been developed during the practice of UN operations, 'military necessity' being governed by the laws of war and limited to combat operations. They both serve as an

---

organs has some (albeit remote) resemblance to the exception of illegality invoked by staff members before international administrative tribunals (see below, p. 148).

[67] Resolution 52/247 of 26 June 1996, para. 8. See below, p. 163.

[68] Model Agreement between the UN and Member States contributing Personnel and Equipment to UN Peacekeeping Operations, A/46/185 of 23 May 1991, para. 32.

[69] It is important to note that the Secretary-General explicitly mentioned that the Model SOFA would *mutatis mutandis* also serve as the basis for an agreement with a host country in operations where no UN military personnel are deployed: A/45/594 of 9 October 1990, para. 2.

[70] A/45/594, para. 60.   [71] *Ibid.*   [72] A/51/903 of 21 May 1997, para. 15.

[73] A/51/389 of 20 September 1996, para. 16.   [74] *Ibid.*, para. 13.

PRIVATE CLAIMANTS   103

exemption from liability, as a legitimisation of an act that would otherwise be considered unlawful.[75] The decision concerning what constitutes 'operational necessity' remains within the discretionary power of the Force Commander.[76]

The unilateral qualification – although guided by indications contained in the Secretary-General's Report[77] – may be challenged by both the individual claimant and its national state within the context of negotiations. Observations made earlier as to the inequality of the parties also apply here. Acts or activities undertaken by international organisations and intentionally causing death, personal injury, or damage to or loss of property within the forum, in the absence of adequate alternative dispute settlement mechanisms, would not require jurisdictional immunity from domestic courts.[78]

In order to establish the organisation's liability, the causal link with an act performed in the course of official duties must exist: while an official's independent 'acts in an individual capacity' do not result in the organisation being responsible, it *is* liable for acts associated with 'the performance of official duties'.[79]

The claims review boards

'[For] any damages incurred as a result of acts performed by the UN or by its agents acting in their official capacity' in cases where their immunity has not been waived by the Secretary-General,[80] appropriate means of settlement provided for by the UN pursuant to the applicable provisions of the General Convention on Privileges and Immunities should be used to claim compensation. The standing claims commission as envisaged under the Model SOFA has in fact never been established, perhaps as a result of a lack of political interest on the part of host states, or because the procedure of local claims review boards has

---

[75] *Ibid.*, note 5.   [76] *Ibid.*, para. 14.

[77] A/51/389, para. 14: good-faith conviction of the Force Commander, operational need not merely convenient or expedient, part of an operational plan and proportional damage.

[78] Singer, 'Jurisdictional Immunity', 151.

[79] I. Scobbie, 'International Organisations and International Relations' in R. J. Dupuy (ed.), *A Handbook of International Organisations* (The Hague, London and Boston: Kluwer Law International, 1998), pp. 831–96, at p. 890. Thus there are obviously limits to the exclusion of attribution on the basis of functionalism: *ibid.*, p. 889.

[80] *Difference Relating to Immunity from Legal Process of a Special Rapporteur of the Commission on Human Rights*, Advisory Opinion of 22 April 1999, *ICJ Reports* (1999), p. 62, at p. 89, para. 66.

104   PROCEDURAL ASPECTS OF REMEDIAL ACTION

been considered as expeditious, impartial and generally satisfactory.[81] The Secretary-General's view that the mechanism of the standing claims commission provides for a tripartite procedure for the settlement of disputes, in which both the organisation and the claimant are treated on a par,[82] appears at present to be unsubstantiated because, as the Secretary-General himself admits, there is no acquired operational experience against which the effectiveness or ineffectiveness of such a procedure can be judged.[83]

In situations of peace-enforcement not only would the establishment of a standing claims commission be problematic, but also the nature of the claims would become different.[84]

In the absence of a standing claims commission, an internal local claims review board is established for each peacekeeping mission to deal with private claims on condition that the loss or injury and damage is attributable to acts performed in connection with official duties by civilian or military personnel of the mission;[85] for claims exceeding the financial limit authorised by the Controller, referral is made to UN headquarters. Once a recommended settlement amount has been approved, it is offered to the claimant.[86]

The local claims review boards are composed exclusively of UN staff members, which raises concerns over the boards' independence and the objectivity of their rulings, which are the two elements in assessing any kind of claims settlement procedure as an adequate alternative system for protection. Also, the lack of any obligation to make their decisions public contributes to the assessment that they do not function properly. The Secretary-General himself also pointed to the possible perception of the UN acting as a judge in its own case;[87] accordingly he proposed the retention in the Model SOFA text of a procedure involving a neutral third party as an option for potential claimants.[88]

Delays in the settlement of claims by the local claims review boards as a result of the increasing number and complexity of claims can be unfair to the claimant.[89] Two modifications could remedy this

---

[81] A/51/903, para. 8.

[82] *Ibid.*, para. 10.   [83] *Ibid.*, para. 8.   [84] A/C.5/49/65, paras. 17 and 20.

[85] *Ibid.*, para. 17.   [86] *Ibid.*, para. 19.   [87] A/51/903, para. 10.

[88] *Ibid.* Although it is not very clear, the Secretary-General seems to see the standing claims commission as a neutral third party, when he proposes to delete the appeal to a tribunal against the standing commission's award: A/51/903, note 2.

[89] A/51/389, para. 26. In a report on the liquidation of peacekeeping operations, the Office of Internal Oversight Services pointed to the fact that some missions 'did not promptly process claims during the operating stage of the mission, resulting in an

disadvantage. The financial authority of the local claims review board could be changed and a division of work could be organised along the specific areas of personal injury or property damage claims.[90] The Special Committee on Peacekeeping Operations has urged the Secretary-General to give high priority to the processing of pending claims, including those for troops and equipment provided by member states to operations whose mandates have been terminated.[91]

Although the peacekeeping operation enjoys wide immunity as provided for in the Model SOFA, the absence of a duty requiring prior exhaustion of local remedies is quite reasonable given the difficult circumstances under which peacekeeping operations normally take place. Local courts will be called upon to hear claims related to the peacekeeping operation, but only where the damage cannot be attributed to the UN.

additional burden during liquidation when other tasks should have been given priority': A/54/394 of 23 September 1999, para. 63.

[90] A/51/389, paras. 31–2.   [91] *Ibid.*, para. 82.

11   Procedural obstacles for representational non-governmental organisations

Non-governmental organisations and international organisations: an ambivalent relationship

Most agencies, funds and programmes of the UN system would agree that non-governmental organisations provide the following assets: local accountability, independent assessment of issues and problems, expertise and advice, important constituencies, provision and dissemination of information, and awareness-raising.[1] The role and influence of civil society and of non-governmental organisations, in particular, consists, *inter alia*, of spurring the UN system towards greater transparency and accountability.[2] This chapter focuses on the availability to representational non-governmental organisations, which can assume an important role as representational agents of accountability, of mechanisms to ensure that accountability.

When considering remedial action to ensure accountability of international organisations, representational NGOs find themselves on familiar ground. The identity and quality of the respondent, be it a state or an international organisation, does not seem to influence the procedural obstacles they are facing.

The range of relationships between international organisations and non-governmental organisations is as broad as the functional areas covered by the international organisations themselves, ranging from arrangements in which the NGO has a constitutional role (such as trade unions in the ILO) to relatively less-developed links with international organisations, such as those of a military nature. The appropriateness of available remedies will vary accordingly.

---

[1] A/53/170 of 10 July 1998, para. 33.   [2] A/51/950 of 14 July 1997, para. 71.

106

When non-governmental organisations are acting as an instrument of the policy of an international organisation – for example, as implementing partners for agencies of organisations in the areas of development or humanitarian assistance – appropriate, possibly separate, means of redress and remedial mechanisms will have to be designed for issues of shared or concurrent accountability. In the case of the delegation of administrative powers by public authorities to private associations, a general condition accepted in any society founded on the rule of law is complete legal protection against the measures adopted by these associations, in addition to a significant degree of control.[3]

Lack of *locus standi* for representational non-governmental organisations

When remedial action undertaken by representational non-state entities is directed against states or commercial enterprises, this usually takes place outside established, institutionalised settlement-of-disputes mechanisms, and the non-governmental organisations thereby claim that they are acting in the exercise of an international mandate conferred upon them.[4] One of the reasons for such an approach obviously has to do with limited *locus standi* for collective action before the courts[5] in most domestic legal systems, perhaps slightly tempered before quasi-judicial bodies.

The main purpose of the Convention of the Council of Europe on the recognition of legal personality of international non-governmental organisations is precisely to facilitate the NGOs' work within the various domestic legal systems;[6] this then enables them to bring a claim before the domestic courts against international organisations for tortious liability or organisational responsibility. That approach obviously does not address the lack of international legal personality of this category of international actors. In the Swiss domestic legal system,

---

[3] Advocate-General Romer in ECJ Case 9/56, *Meroni v. High Authority* [1958] ECR 177 at 190 as cited by D. Sarooshi, *The UN and the Development of Collective Security: The Delegation by the UN Security Council of its Chapter VII Powers* (Oxford: Clarendon Press, 1999), at p. 37, note 145.

[4] S. Hobe, 'Der Rechtsstatus der Nichtregierungsorganisationen nach Gegenwärtigen Völkerrecht', *Archiv des Völkerrechts* 37 (1999) 152–76, at 156.

[5] On the different models along these lines see, *inter alia*, E. Schmidt-Assmann and L. Harrings, 'Access to Justice and Fundamental Rights', *European Review of Public Law* 9 (1997), 529–49, at 539–40.

[6] Hobe, 'Der Rechtsstatus', 160.

108   PROCEDURAL ASPECTS OF REMEDIAL ACTION

both its judiciary and its executive authorities have been at the forefront in recognising their character as 'quasi-governmental' international organisations by way of conferring certain privileges and immunities on non-governmental organisations. Similar examples have recently been occurring in the Philippines.[7]

Within the UN system non-governmental organisations do participate – to varying degrees according to their consultative status and in an ever-increasing way – in the process of norm-setting by international organisations. There are, however, from a procedural point of view, almost no corresponding remedial possibilities and mechanisms for these same non-governmental organisations to present, in their representational capacity, claims against international organisations. This is a general picture that can be confirmed from looking at practice evidence; the prospects of such non-governmental organisations having *locus standi* at the domestic and international level are practically non-existent under present conditions.

This lack of standing for representational non-governmental organisations is a significant obstacle in the establishment and further development of a comprehensive accountability regime for international organisations. Christine Gray has expressed it succinctly when she wrote that 'the idea of a general right to secure the observance of international law is not established'.[8] As a result, problems that 'affect the international community as a whole cannot be dealt with by means of bilateral claims for a declaratory judgement'.[9]

Representational non-governmental organisations presenting their views before international courts and tribunals

At the international level, the hope formulated by Wilfred Jenks in 1946 that the ICJ would, under Article 67 of its Statute and having due regard to Article 71 of the UN Charter, provide non-governmental organisations with an opportunity to express their views in the course of advisory proceedings before it[10] unfortunately did not materialise. The question whether the expression 'any ... International Organisation' in

---

[7] A. Reinisch, *International Organisations before National Courts* (Cambridge: Cambridge University Press, 2000), p. 171, note 9.

[8] C. Gray, *Judicial Remedies in International Law* (Oxford: Clarendon Press, 1987), p. 211.

[9] *Ibid.*, p. 214.

[10] C. W. Jenks, 'The Status of International Organisations in Relation to the International Court of Justice', *Transactions Grotius Society* 32 (1946), 1–41, at 5.

PROCEDURAL OBSTACLES FOR REPRESENTATIONAL NGOs   109

Article 66(2) of the Statute 'may also refer to non-governmental organisations is still a subject of controversy'.[11]

Relevant practice is regarded by Shabtai Rosenne as 'ambivalent'. He recalls the case of the former officials of the Governing Commission of the Saar Territory, where the League of Nations renounced its right pursuant to Article 66 of the Statute 'if the same possibility cannot be given to the petitioners, since it does not wish to have greater opportunities of furnishing information to the Court than the petitioners themselves'.[12] In the 1950 South West Africa advisory proceedings, the ICJ permitted the International League for the Rights of Man to submit information,[13] while in the *Asylum* case the difference in wording in the Statute between Article 66 governing advisory opinions and Article 34 on contentious proceedings was relied upon by the Registrar to reject its request for participation.[14]

An intermediate 'solution' was found in the *Legality of Nuclear Weapons* case where an *amicus* brief from a non-governmental organisation had been received, was not admitted as part of the record, but was available to members of the Court in their library.[15] Judge Higgins has pointed to the potential problem that 'a judge may be influenced by something which those actually making written or oral statements may not know about and have no opportunity to challenge'.[16]

In the *Namibia* case the Registrar had informed an individual that the ICJ would be unwilling to accept a document on the legality and

---

[11] President Bedjaoui in his address to the General Assembly's Sixth Committee in 1994, *ICJ Yearbook* 49 (1994–5), p. 222, para. 23.

[12] Cited by S. Rosenne, *The Law and Practice of the International Court 1920–1996* (The Hague, Boston and London: Martinus Nijhoff Publishers, 1997), p. 1742.

[13] D. Shelton, 'The Participation of Non-governmental Organisations in International Judicial Proceedings', *AJIL* 88 (1994), 611–42, at 623. The advantages and disadvantages of the *amicus curiae* position have been clearly listed by Shelton, at 611–12. They are: (advantages) the focus on costs, time, the binding nature of the decision, freedom to raise an issue, threshold of interest; (disadvantages) no control of the action, not served with documents in the case, no possibility to offer evidence or to examine witness, no compensation or costs and no right to be heard without special leave of the Court.

[14] Shelton, 'Participation', 623. (*Asylum* case (Colombia/Peru) Judgment, *ICJ Reports* (1950), p. 266.)

[15] Rosenne, *Law and Practice*, p. 1731. (*Namibia* case: Legal Consequences for States of the continued presence of South Africa in Namibia (South-west Africa) notwithstanding Security Council Resolution 276 (1970). Advisory Opinion, *ICJ Reports* (1971), p. 16.)

[16] R. Higgins, 'Remedies and the International Court of Justice: An Introduction' in M. Evans (ed.), *Remedies in International Law: The Institutional Dilemma* (Oxford: Hart Publishing, 1998), pp. 1–10, at p. 2.

110 PROCEDURAL ASPECTS OF REMEDIAL ACTION

admissibility of international *amicus curiae* briefs.[17] All international tribunals except the ICJ have developed procedures to enable third parties to submit statements or written observations on the case.[18]

Rutsel Martha has recalled that with regard to adjudicatory organs before which states appear, such as the ICJ, no attempt has been made in their Statutes to regulate the way in which a party shall be represented. Parties have taken the liberty of including in their delegation both governmental officials and private practitioners.[19] There seems to be no reason deriving from the propriety of judicial proceedings as to why non-governmental organisations and private claimants in general should be prevented from forming part of an official delegation in a dispute settlement mechanism without, however, being able directly to present their views before the court or tribunal.

As rightly observed by Rosenne, '[From] the point of view of the procedure in contentious cases, [non-governmental organisations] are regarded as individuals.'[20]

Even in international organisations of an integrationist type endowed with a fully fledged system of judicial protection, because of the jurisdictional connection between the organisation and non-state private claimants, there is no specific associational standing for non-governmental organisations, the rules on third-party intervention being strict and the ECJ not welcoming public interest action.[21] It is interesting to note that part of the reason why Greenpeace was not granted a *locus standi* before the ECJ was because it could bring proceedings in domestic courts which could then request the ECJ for a preliminary ruling,[22] an argument that obviously does not apply in the relationship between non-governmental organisations and other international organisations. Recently, the Inter-American Court of Human Rights went further and declined 'to hear a request for an advisory opinion because it directly

---

[17] Rosenne, *Law and Practice*, p. 1745.

[18] Shelton, 'Participation', 641–2. On the practice of the ECJ, ECHR and IACHR see *ibid.*, 628–40.

[19] R. Martha, 'Representation of Parties in World Trade Disputes', *JWTL* 31 (1997), 84–96, at 88–9.

[20] Rosenne, *Law and Practice*, p. 653.

[21] C. Harlow, 'Access to Justice as a Human Right: The European Court of Justice and the European Union' in P. Alston (ed.), *The European Union and Human Rights* (Oxford: Oxford University Press, 2000), pp. 187–213, at pp. 194 and 199.

[22] Case C-321/95P, *Stichting Greenpeace Council (Greenpeace International) and Others v. Commission of the European Communities* [1998] ECR I-1651.

addressed the interests of a victim and therefore denied him an opportunity to participate'.[23]

Whereas in 1996 Article 13(2) of the WTO Dispute Settlement Understanding was described as 'theoretically' allowing for the technical contribution of non-governmental organisations upon the request of the panels,[24] the actual submissions by non-governmental organisations under Article 13 of the WTO Understanding are regarded by some as controversial,[25] while others are of the opinion that recourse to this type of contribution should be made compulsory.[26] The controversy surrounding third-party rights in general and over granting civil-society representatives the right to submit their views to panels on their own initiative continues under the present review of the Dispute Settlement Understanding.

The procedural incapacity non-governmental organisations are facing is to a large extent identical to that with which ordinary private claimants have to deal when they want to raise either the contractual or tortious liability of an international organisation. The additional difficulty stems from their representational feature and the potentially far-reaching consequences flowing from that for the international organisations, both in terms of the institutional adequacy of existing quasi-judicial and judicial mechanisms – assuming for a moment that there is not an issue of their jurisdiction *ratione personae* – and in terms of the large-scale impact of a successful collective remedial action. The derivative international legal position for particular categories of non-governmental organisations based upon Article 71 of the UN Charter and ensuing ECOSOC Resolution 1296 (XLIV) and the latter's implicit recognition of these non-governmental organisations' potential with regard to settlement of disputes[27] is incapable of providing a solution to this basic procedural problem.

---

[23] Advisory Opinion OC-12/91, 6 December 1991 referred to by J. Charney, 'Is International Law Threatened by Multiple International Tribunals?', *RCADI* 271 (1998), 101–382, at 165, note 187.

[24] C. Bellmann and R. Gerster, 'Accountability in the World Trade Organisation', *JWTL* 30 (1996), 31–74, at 36.

[25] A. Qureshi, 'Extraterritorial Shrimps, Non-governmental Organisations and the WTO Appellate Body', *ICLQ* 48 (1999), 199–206, at 205–6 discussing the *US-Import Prohibition of Certain Shrimp and Shrimp Products* case (Report of the WTO Appellate Body, WT/DS58/AB/R).

[26] Bellmann and Gerster, 'Accountability', 37.

[27] Hobe, 'Der Rechtsstatus', 162 and 161.

The slow but constant and welcome trend within the context of human rights protection to accord improved legal standing before regional quasi-judicial and judicial bodies to relevant non-governmental organisations in line with their pre-existing position under the Statute of the ILO is limited (although not by necessity) to claims addressed against states. Also worth mentioning is the increase in direct involvement by non-governmental organisations possessing relevant expertise and knowledge in the enforcement of other inter-state agreements such as environmental protection treaties, where their role in the non-compliance procedure system has increasingly been acknowledged.

A still embryonic, fragile and perhaps almost accidental development may be discerned in the indirect involvement of non-governmental organisations in international judicial proceedings in a role as *amicus curiae*. The indications are that an extension of some kind of international procedural standing outside the field of human rights protection has indeed been limited to some kind of indirect participation in a small number of particular cases lending themselves relatively easily to these innovative steps. The potential of this cautious development for the future role of major international non-governmental organisations as an 'Agent of the Interests of the International Community'[28] is briefly reviewed in Part IV of this study. A state claimant may omit certain issues from international proceedings against an international organisation for a variety of reasons, in spite of those issues being of broad public interest.[29] A role for non-governmental organisations as *amici curiae* would be particularly appropriate where obligations *erga omnes* are at issue.[30]

The proper administration of justice should be the guiding principle for courts and tribunals when deciding whether to use their discretionary power to permit such *amicus curiae* participation.[31] One argument put forward in favour of the (wider) acceptance by the ICJ of *amicus* briefs from representational non-governmental organisations – limited to those having Consultative Status with the UN, as that would guarantee a broad representation of interests[32] – is particularly relevant to the accountability regime of international organisations: as 'the ICJ

---

[28] *Ibid.*, 172.   [29] Shelton, 'Participation', 615.   [30] *Ibid.*, 627.
[31] *Ibid.*, 618.   [32] *Ibid.*, 625.

moves into new areas of global public concern, it is crucial that the Court hear from all relevant interests'.[33]

The crucial issue in this debate has been succinctly and aptly formulated by Stephan Hobe when he wrote: 'Die Frage einer Kompatibilisierung der über Staaten hinausgreifenden Aktivitäten und Interessen der Zivilgesellschaft durch Akteure der Gesellschaftwelt, repräsentiert durch die Nichtregierungsorganisationen, mit der Kategorie des Völkerrechtssubjekts macht gewisse Grenzen der definitorischen Erfassbarkeit solcher Aktivitäten und Interessen deutlich.'[34]

[33] *Ibid.*, 641.   [34] Hobe, 'Der Rechtsstatus', 173.

12 Procedural obstacles common to remedial action by non-state claimants

The jurisdictional immunity of international organisations before domestic courts

Every category of non-state claimants is faced with procedural obstacles deriving from or connected with their own distinctive features. Additionally, all non-state claimants are confronted with a common procedural obstacle flowing from and inevitably linked to the quality and the status of the respondent entity they all want to hold liable and/or responsible: international organisations traditionally enjoy, under both conventional and customary international law, jurisdictional immunity before the domestic courts of their member states.

It hardly needs to be emphasised that in the overall framework of implementation of accountability of international organisations this jurisdictional immunity has always constituted a decisive barrier to remedial action for non-state claimants. This state of affairs continues, almost irrespective of the availability and the degree of adequacy of alternative remedial protection for staff members, contractors and private individuals suffering damages by organisational acts, actions or omissions.

The absence of adequate alternative internal remedies within an international organisation could, if combined with a successful claim for jurisdictional immunity before domestic courts, easily amount to a denial of justice.

In 1964 Finn Seyersted put it succinctly as follows: '[n]ot even the risk of denial of justice could induce the national courts ... to assume jurisdiction, inasmuch as they declined jurisdiction, even in those cases where the organisation itself had no internal tribunal which could settle the dispute judicially'.[1] This section discusses whether the attitudes of domestic courts remain unchanged today.

One of the leading authorities on immunities of international organisations aptly described international immunities as 'the legal device through which international action escapes national control', immediately adding that the 'remedy for . . . abuses is the development of appropriate forms of international control'.[2] It is precisely the adequacy of the international control put in place that is controversial.

Domestic court proceedings concerning contractual or tortious liability can also be instituted by private claimants against individual officials, agents or experts of an international organisation. Domestic courts, however, cannot review an organisation's decision not to waive immunity in a given case.[3] The use of this discretion may be justified in order to protect officials from vexatious suits, but it would be undesirable and unnecessary to use it when in normal times the relations with the authorities are good.[4] It should be duly noted that the immunity of the international organisation, if granted, also protects the staff member involved in a particular action; conversely, the granting of immunity to staff members also protects the international organisation concerned: that is the reciprocal protective function of these immunities.

The ICJ affirmed that it is a generally recognised principle of procedural law that questions of immunity should be expeditiously decided *in limine litis*.[5] 'The question of the legal personality of International Organisations precedes that of jurisdictional immunity, even in Member States, but in domestic legal proceedings it is *generally* not disputed.'[6]

---

[1] F. Seyersted, 'Settlement of Internal Disputes of Intergovernmental Organisations by Internal and External Courts', *ZAÖRV* 24 (1964), 1–121, at 79.

[2] C. W. Jenks, *International Immunities* (London and New York: Stevens & Sons and Oceana Publications, 1961), p. 18.

[3] I. Scobbie, 'International Organisations and International Relations' in R. J. Dupuy (ed.), *A Handbook of International Organisations* (The Hague, London and Boston: Kluwer Law International, 1998), pp. 833–67, at p. 856.

[4] Jenks, *International Immunities*, p. 119.

[5] *Difference Relating to Immunity from Legal Process of a Special Rapporteur of the Commission on Human Rights*, Advisory Opinion of 22 April 1999, *ICJ Reports* (1999), p. 62, at p. 88, para. 63.

[6] M. Singer, 'Jurisdictional Immunity of International Organisations: Human Rights and Functional Necessity Concerns', *Virginia Journal of International Law* 36 (1995), 53–165, at 67: emphasis added. See further A. Reinisch, *International Organisations before National Courts* (Cambridge: Cambridge University Press, 2000).

116   PROCEDURAL ASPECTS OF REMEDIAL ACTION

The focus in this section is on the way this procedural obstacle to remedial action against international organisations has been maintained or, alternatively, (partially) lifted by the domestic courts. This is done against the background of the human rights perspective indicated earlier[7] and keeping in mind the balance to be found between respect for the necessary degree of independent functioning by the international organisation and the need to provide redress for those claiming that the organisation is liable and/or responsible. This section is not confined to domestic court proceedings involving the UN and international organisations of the UN system; the importance of the issue stretches well beyond them and towards providing indications for future developments to be dealt with in Part IV of this study.

International organisations before domestic courts

In his recently published, comprehensive book, which provides plenty of documentation, on *International Organisations before National Courts*, August Reinisch has investigated under what circumstances domestic courts exercise their adjudicatory jurisdiction or refrain from doing so, what the justifications are for their particular approach and whether there are any trends to move away from the currently predominant party-focused immunity.[8] The findings of his extensive research are particularly instructive and relevant for present purposes, as the answers provided by Reinisch are important tools in devising a well-functioning

---

[7] The UN legal counsel's argument in the *Cumaraswamy* case that the adjudication of privileges and immunities in a national court would not 'only operate against the interests of the UN generally' but also against 'the human rights mechanisms of the UN system specifically' (CR/98/15, at p. 25, para. 51) is unconvincing as it gives the impression of being based on the assumption that adjudication by domestic courts would in general provide less adequate protection than the human rights mechanisms. Although that may be the case with regard to several domestic systems, the generalisation underlying the argument is certainly unwarranted. Moreover, the question whether or not remedial mechanisms 'within the UN system' itself provide adequate protection is not beyond controversy, as this study demonstrates.

[8] Reinisch, *National Courts*, p. 2. Given the remedial perspective of the present volume, it does not go into the substantive law aspect covered by the privileges of the international organisations, *i.e.* the non-application of areas of national law to international organisations (dealt with in Reinisch, *National Courts*, p. 14); the potential pre-remedial effect of such exemptions could be substantially reduced unless appropriate remedial mechanisms are simultaneously provided. In fact, only issues of a purely internal nature or explicit provisions could provide exceptions to the general rule that international organisations are subject to the applicable domestic law (*ibid.*, p. 15).

accountability regime for international organisations. The imperatives that are part and parcel of any accountability system[9] in fact inevitably affect and radically change the self-contained character of the regime of the immunities of international organisations as it was referred to by the ILA Committee on State Immunity in its final 1994 Report.[10]

The further question of whether national courts do in fact provide an appropriate forum for disputes involving international organisations will be dealt with separately in Part IV of this study.

In the descriptive analytical part of his monograph, Reinisch reviews in a surgical way the techniques used by domestic courts to avoid becoming involved in a case implicating or against an international organisation and, conversely, the strategies developed by domestic courts in order to make their involvement possible.[11] The second part of his book is devoted to the policy issues of the rationales for judicial abstention and the strategies and reasons for asserting jurisdiction.[12] Both the techniques and rationales for judicial abstention and the strategies and reasons for judicial involvement are derived from and connected with considerations the relevance of which goes beyond their role within the sphere of domestic judicial remedies and well into the overall remedial approach towards international organisations. Several of the rationales explicitly referred to by domestic courts clearly also underpin some attitudes towards the general features and other procedural aspects reviewed in Parts I and II of the present study.

Judicial abstention by domestic courts

Although according immunity has been the main technique used by domestic courts in order not to have to exercise adjudicatory jurisdiction over cases involving international organisations, the other techniques identified by Reinisch are ample proof of the creativeness of national judges in this regard. Suffice it merely to list them here: non-recognition as a legal person under domestic law, non-recognition of a particular

---

[9] See above, pp. 13–19

[10] *ILA Report of the 66th Conference* held at Buenos Aires, Argentina, 14–20 August 1994 (Buenos Aires, 1994), p. 474. Moreover, the same Committee pointed to the functional approach as a possible solution: immunity would not apply in cases of tortious conduct or even flagrant human rights violations, as they are not covered by the function of an international organisation; *ibid.*, p. 476. On the functional approach see below, p. 215.

[11] Reinisch, *National Courts*, pp. 35–168 and pp. 169–229 respectively.

[12] *Ibid.*, pp. 233–51 and pp. 252–313 respectively.

118   PROCEDURAL ASPECTS OF REMEDIAL ACTION

act of an international organisation (*ultra vires* and non-attributability), prudential judicial abstention through doctrines of act of state, political question and non-justiciability, lack of adjudicative power of domestic courts, no case or controversy and judicial discretion to prevent harassing lawsuits and mock trials.[13]

It is relevant to look into the reasons why national judges have resorted to these techniques and what doctrinal arguments have been put forward for the same purpose: some of them have also been advanced in the larger context of the debate over remedies against international organisations and on their accountability in general. This is certainly the case for the paramount rationale for granting jurisdictional immunity: to secure the independence and to guarantee the functioning of the respondent.[14] It is generally undisputed that their independence should be protected from undue interference; the crux of the question lies in the precise delineation of the point beyond which influence and interference become undue.

Reinisch rightly questions whether the threat of unwarranted lawsuits alone, as part of a hostile domestic environment argument, is a proper reason to deny the possibility of bringing any suits: speedy administration might weigh less than the right of access to a court.[15] Michael Singer has rightly observed that if an international organisation should be enabled to conduct its affairs without undue interference this does not entail the privilege of never having to defend a lawsuit.[16]

A second factor that could produce undesirable effects on the functioning of the organisation has to do with the alleged lack of familiarity amongst national judges with the issues lying at the heart of the dispute before them. The argument may have its merits in connection with internal disputes of a constitutional character and with staff disputes, but, according to Reinisch, certainly does not in disputes over contractual or tortious liability where a particular domestic law provides the governing legal rules.[17] The fact that the costs of lawsuits may have an harassment aspect for international organisations should also not be exaggerated, because most jurisdictions do allow for the recovery of legal costs from the losing party.[18]

The argument that international organisations should be granted absolute immunity because of their relative weakness compared to states

---

[13] *Ibid.*, pp. 35–127.   [14] *Ibid.*, p. 233.
[15] *Ibid.*, p. 236.   [16] Singer, 'Jurisdictional Immunity', 128.
[17] Reinisch, *National Courts*, pp. 236–7.   [18] *Ibid.*, pp. 237–8.

OBSTACLES COMMON TO NON-STATE CLAIMANTS 119

has to be posited against the initial imbalance in power and the resulting inequality between non-state claimants and international organisations, referred to earlier.[19]

Part I, above, briefly reviewed the remedial action to which member states can resort on the first level of accountability in order to compel the international organisation to continue or to change its course of action, decisions and general policy. Although the exercise of adjudicatory jurisdiction by domestic courts cannot be considered to constitute a legitimate, additional, external channel of influence over the international organisation, its non-exercise for that particular reason, for granting immunity, should not lead it to serve as a complete shield from domestic adjudication.[20] Sometimes the argument has also been complemented by the equality of member states preventing an indirectly more influential position for the forum state.[21] The fact that many domestic cases against international organisations are employment-related disputes clearly demonstrates that this issue is governed by the organisation's staff regulations and applicable general principles of labour law, so securing uniformity in dispute settlement as an argument against judicial involvement does not in fact address the uniformity of the applicable law. Different national courts should be able to apply identical legal rules.[22]

The possession of international legal personality by international organisations constitutes the paramount precondition for the establishment of any liability or responsibility on their part. It is thus not surprising, although unconvincing, that jurisdictional immunity has sometimes been considered, both by domestic courts and in doctrine, as an inherent quality of that same international legal personality.[23]

As an international organisation has no power to grant immunity to other entities and it does not incorporate an internal judicial organ enjoying compulsory jurisdiction over such entities, there is a lack of any concern over reciprocal immunity that could act as an incentive to international organisations to restrict their own jurisdictional immunity.[24] Furthermore, claims of immunity cannot be backed up by any threat of retaliation.[25]

---

[19] See also Reinisch, *National Courts*, p. 238.
[20] Reinisch, *National Courts*, pp. 239–40.   [21] *Ibid.*, pp. 241–2.
[22] *Ibid.*, pp. 243–5.   [23] *Ibid.*, pp. 246–8.
[24] Singer, 'Jurisdictional Immunity', 54–5.   [25] *Ibid.*, 54, note 6.

Precedent and prestige are not only amongst the dominant purposes of according privileges and immunities to international organisations:[26] they also seem to operate as the underlying but forceful counter-factor in the laborious endeavour to set up a comprehensive accountability regime. In this context it is important to recall 'that no international tribunal has compulsory jurisdiction over international organisations'.[27]

Immunity of an international organisation is a double-edged instrument. Denying it in a particular case may entail the forum state's international responsibility[28] while providing the claimant with a remedial action. Conversely, granting the immunity may be in compliance with both international and domestic legal rules, but at the price of a potential denial of justice *vis-à-vis* the claimants if no adequate alternative remedial mechanisms are available or open to them. Issues concerning the immunity of international organisations are primarily matters of international law, as stressed by the UN on several occasions,[29] but the decision as to its scope normally rests solely with the forum state; domestic courts do not appear to feel bound to follow the view of representatives of an organisation in that respect.[30] Disputes concerning the scope of the immunity are regarded as issues of public international law, as clearly demonstrated by, *inter alia*, the INPDAI affair and its aftermath[31] and the *Cumaraswamy* case before the ICJ.[32]

From the procedural point of view it is important to note that under many national legal systems domestic courts have to respect the immunity of an international organisation *ex officio*, thus even when it has not been invoked by the respondent party;[33] in some national legal systems a failure to appear in court in order to claim immunity could result in the loss of such immunity.[34]

The right of the UN to invoke its immunity under the provisions of the 1946 General Convention could be based in an alternative or cumulative way on its being a mere beneficiary or a party to that Convention.[35] Given the silence of most treaty provisions on an obligation to invoke immunity, most international organisations communicate

---

[26] Reinisch, *National Courts*, p. 251.   [27] Singer, 'Jurisdictional Immunity', 64.

[28] Reinisch, *National Courts*, p. 127.   [29] *Ibid.*, p. 127, note 481.

[30] *Ibid.*, pp. 129–30.   [31] *Ibid.*, pp. 132–4.

[32] *Difference Relating to Immunity from Legal Process of a Special Rapporteur of the Commission on Human Rights*, Advisory Opinion of 22 April 1999, *ICJ Reports* (1999), p. 62.

[33] Reinisch, *National Courts*, p. 137.

[34] Argentina, as referred to by Reinisch, *National Courts*, p. 137, note 531.

[35] *Ibid.*, pp. 143–4.

their legal point of view on this issue to the courts, either directly or indirectly.[36]

The extent of the immunities ranges – at least according to constituent instruments – from absolute 'functional' immunity under the formula used in Article 105 of the UN Charter to clauses that in principle allow suits against the international organisation and codify certain exceptions, such as for international financial institutions.

The generally broad interpretation by international organisations of their immunity as covering protection from every form of legal process, thus including every type of legal proceedings before national authorities,[37] should be noted. It is complemented and strengthened even by wide interpretations of applicable restrictive immunity provisions.[38]

Judicial activism by domestic courts

As is the case with their counterparts trying to *avoid* becoming involved in disputes between private claimants and international organisations, national judges looking for ways to *exercise* their adjudicatory jurisdiction over that category of disputes have been creative in developing strategies to achieve that objective. In his descriptive analysis Reinisch has identified the following approaches: non-qualification as an international organisation, no delegation of immunity, no recognition of an international organisation as a legal person under domestic law, denying immunity, restricting the scope of immunity and a broad interpretation of a waiver.[39]

Domestic courts have attempted to achieve a denial of immunity. For example, they may deny either the international applicability of immunity instruments altogether or the domestic direct applicability of relevant international law – because of their dualistic system and the absence of domestic implementing legislation – or deny the potential existence of a customary rule in the absence of conventional immunity provisions.[40]

Domestic courts have developed two main strategies in order to become judicially involved: restriction of the scope of the immunity and a wide interpretation of applicable waivers.

The first strategy may be used in different modalities; the trend in this direction had already been indicated by Mahnoush Arsanjani

---

[36] *Ibid.*, pp. 138–9, and in particular notes 535–7.   [37] *Ibid.*, p. 158.
[38] *Ibid.*, pp. 163–7.   [39] *Ibid.*, pp. 169–229.   [40] *Ibid.*, pp. 177–85.

122   PROCEDURAL ASPECTS OF REMEDIAL ACTION

in 1981.[41] In the face of absolute immunity clauses or in the absence of an express domestic or international norm containing limitations,[42] domestic courts may actually apply a standard of restrictive immunity similar to the one used with regard to states. In the process of doing so, they may in fact incorporate functional immunity considerations when they qualify commercial acts of an international organisation as having a *iure imperii* character provided these acts are instrumental (or even essential) for the organisation's functioning.[43]

In the absence of an international or domestic immunity regime, national courts may prefer to invoke a customary restrictive state immunity standard by applying the *acta iure imperii/acta iure gestionis* distinction to international organisations.[44]

A domestic International Organisations Immunity Act may provide for the same absolute immunity as the one enjoyed by foreign governments. Substantial judicial and doctrinal debate may follow later developments in practice towards restrictive state immunity, while the UN's absolute immunity clause from the 1946 General Convention still supersedes that domestic law.[45]

The US courts qualified most employment-related cases as internal administrative matters of the organisation,[46] while in tort cases the action of the organisation was sometimes considered to be a governmental activity and on other occasions the act was seen as not coming within the FSIA discretionary-functions exception to the tort exemption from immunity.[47]

It is also obvious that under the domestic laws that are of potential relevance to the tortious liability of international organisations (such as the US Alien Tort Claims Act), the nature of the immunity granted and the relationship of the potential defendant to the organisation must be determined before a complaint under the ATCA is filed against anyone associated with an international organisation.[48]

As to the scope and content of the functional immunity of international organisations, it is particularly relevant to note from an accountability perspective the UN's view that functional immunity

---

[41] M. Arsanjani, 'Claims against International Organisations: Quis Custodiet Ipsos Custodes?', *Yale Journal of World Public Order* 7 (1980–1), 131–76, at 169 and 172.

[42] Reinisch, *National Courts*, pp. 185–91.   [43] *Ibid.*, p. 192.   [44] *Ibid.*, pp. 194–7.

[45] *Ibid.*, pp. 198–203: an attempt to reduce the international organisation's immunity on the occasion of and along the lines of the FSIA failed; *ibid.*, p. 199, note 154.

[46] *Ibid.*, p. 199.   [47] *Ibid.*, pp. 202–3.

[48] B. Stephens and M. Ratner, *International Human Rights Litigation in US Courts* (Irvington-on-Hudson and New York: Transnational Publishers, 1996), p. 135.

requires complete protection from national jurisdiction[49] and that it would not be in the organisation's interest when dealing with the functional immunity of its officials to be bound by a definition of 'official capacity', 'which may fail to take into account the many and varied activities of UN officials'.[50]

The first argument – namely that functional immunity requires complete protection from national jurisdiction – seems hardly compatible with a restrictive view based upon a literal reading of Article 105 of the UN Charter:[51] indeed, the principle *ne impediatur officia* does not necessarily imply that an international organisation must in every case be granted total immunity from legal process.[52]

Domestic courts sometimes equate functional immunity with *iure imperii* acts, in other cases they widen the scope of functional immunity,[53] while in a number of further cases employment and lease disputes have been regarded as being covered by functional immunity.[54]

Domestic courts may, by qualifying the activities of an international organisation as lying outside the scope of its functional immunity, assert jurisdiction by laying down a stringent requirement that the actions must be inherent or essential for the organisation's institutional purposes.[55] This may eventually lead to a judicial pronouncement, admittedly as an *obiter dictum*, that the allegedly tortious interference and destruction of the claimant's property by UN Forces (for example) cannot be included within the purposes of the international organisation.[56] It has to be acknowledged, however, that the more controversial an international organisation's functions are in order to fulfil its purposes, the greater the claim to jurisdictional immunity will normally be.[57] The reversed argument holds with regard to such an organisation's accountability: the perception of the need for accountability may be influenced by such factors, but so are the provision and selection of remedial action.

---

[49] As stated in its *amicus curiae* brief in *Marvin R. Broadbent et al. v. Organization of American States et al.*, US Court of Appeals DC Cir., 8 January 1980, ILR 63 (1982), 337–46, as reproduced by Reinisch, *National Courts*, p. 205, note 197.

[50] Extract from a Letter of the Office of Legal Affairs reproduced by Reinisch, *National Courts*, p. 206, note 199.

[51] *Ibid.*, pp. 253–4.

[52] As pointed out by the Austrian delegation before the 44th General Assembly, referred to in *ibid.*, p. 54, note 12.

[53] *Ibid.*, p. 206.   [54] *Ibid.*, pp. 206–12.   [55] *Ibid.*, p. 212.   [56] *Ibid.*, p. 214.

[57] P. Bekker, *The Legal Position of Intergovernmental Organisations: A Functional Necessity Analysis of their Legal Status and Immunities* (Boston and London: Martinus Nijhoff Publishers, 1994), p. 116.

124 PROCEDURAL ASPECTS OF REMEDIAL ACTION

The alternative route for domestic courts to assert jurisdiction, apart from applying restrictive immunity, is to put forward a broad interpretation of a waiver. In fact, not much discretion is normally left to them, whether the waiver is ad hoc or in advance by contractual stipulation,[58] and in practice international organisations waive their immunity only infrequently. As the US Court of Appeals for the District of Columbia Circuit stated in *Mendoza v. World Bank*, 'it is likely that most organisations would be unwilling to relinquish their immunity without receiving a corresponding benefit which would further the organisation's goals'.[59] The General Convention appears to provide only for ad hoc waivers and this interpretation seems to be supported by the Convention's *travaux préparatoires*.[60] From an accountability perspective, however, the general policy considerations demanding a high level of protection for international organisations may be questioned: an evenly arguable interpretation clause would allow advance contractual waivers as they would be invoked in a particular case.[61] The urge on the part of international organisations for a narrow definition of waiver of immunity is indeed hardly reconcilable with reasonable and legitimate expectations of parties that deal with them.[62] On the other hand, a domestic court's determination of whether the organisation has in fact waived its immunity should be made regardless of whether this would benefit the organisation.[63] As to constitutive waivers, other concerns may have led member states to formulate narrower immunities in the relevant provision of the organisation's constituent instrument.[64]

In the absence of relevant provisions, the possibility of a waiver could be considered to be part of an organisation's inherent power,[65] a power for the UN to be exercised by the Secretary-General as the organisation's chief administrative officer.[66]

Similarly, as with regard to the reasons for judicial abstention, the considerations leading domestic courts to assert jurisdiction are relevant to the extent that they can be linked to the overall accountability

---

[58] Reinisch, *National Courts*, pp. 214–15.

[59] As cited by the US Court of Appeals for the District of Columbia Circuit in *Janet Atkinson v. The Inter-American Development Bank*, 8 October 1998, ILM 38 (1999), 92–9, at 94.

[60] Reinisch, *National Courts*, pp. 217–18. However, Singer convincingly argued that there is no need to resort to the *travaux préparatoires*: 'Jurisdictional Immunity', 75.

[61] Reinisch, *National Courts*, pp. 218–19. See also Singer, 'Jurisdictional Immunity', 74–9.

[62] Singer, 'Jurisdictional Immunity', 73.   [63] *Ibid.*, 80.   [64] *Ibid.*, 82.

[65] Reinisch, *National Courts*, p. 220.

[66] *Ibid.*, p. 222, note 283. It was upon Iraq's proposal, but without further debate, that 'in his opinion' was inserted into the draft of the General Convention to make it clearer.

regime. Limited immunity may in fact have two diverging effects. The self-interest aspect becomes apparent when the creditworthiness of the organisation is enhanced and the willingness of private parties to do business with it will increase, enabling the organisation to function well.[67] Reinisch rightly pointed out that a reduction in immunity could result in private contractors not adding potential costs in the final price for the services rendered or goods delivered because of the organisation escaping liability.[68]

Allowing claims brought against international organisations to be litigated would not only contribute to another public perception of international organisations,[69] but also certainly substantially improve their accountability regime.

The principle of fairness towards parties dealing with international organisations and to other third parties affected by their activities calls for limited immunity, in the same way as that principle operated with regard to state immunity,[70] although this time the immunity does not follow the *iure imperii/iure gestionis* dichotomy. The view that the unjustifiable privileged position of international organisations might even lead to a denial of justice where there is no adequate alternative remedial mechanism provided for[71] seems to be beyond any real dispute from an accountability perspective. The obligation to establish such a (judicial) remedial system for the settlement of conflicts or disputes in which international organisations may become involved[72] does not disappear when immunity is restrictive, rather than absolute.

The burden of proof and evidence

The second procedural obstacle that is common to the category of non-state claimants is the burden of proof and evidence, which is eventually required at both the international and domestic level once the jurisdictional immunity of the international organisation has been waived or has not been granted. It should be recalled that issues of accountability may arise both in the pre-litigation stage and during adjudicatory proceedings. The degree of access to information to be achieved by way of redress will be determined accordingly: access will be less than full in the pre-litigation phase (that is, the non-adjudicative stage, which is

---

[67] Reinisch, *National Courts*, pp. 256 and 257.   [68] *Ibid.*, p. 257.   [69] *Ibid.*
[70] *Ibid.*, pp. 261–2.   [71] *Ibid.*, p. 264.
[72] ILC Special Rapporteur on relations between states and international organisations referred to by Reinisch, *National Courts*, p. 270.

126 PROCEDURAL ASPECTS OF REMEDIAL ACTION

of an administrative or inquisitorial nature).[73] However, the administrative right of access to information, which is derived from procedural fairness,[74] is increasingly being recognised as an autonomous procedural right.[75]

Hersch Lauterpacht rightly pointed out that, with regard to evidence and proof, the importance of interests at stake in international proceedings precludes excessive or decisive reliance upon formal and technical rules.[76] The absence of sovereign equality between the parties involved in proceedings against international organisations would, however, require flexibility: the causality requirement and thus the standard of proof imposed upon the claimant should not be unduly or utterly stringent in cases of tort brought by third parties. Staff members and private contractors are probably in a better position to comply with standards of proof on the link of causality, given their pre-existing contractual links with the international organisation. Moreover, the burden of proof should be fairly allocated so that claimants are not subject to discriminatory limitations.[77]

Disclosure of information and documents

As far as the disclosure of information and documents by international organisations is concerned, they have a clear duty to facilitate the administration of justice by both internal and external, domestic and international quasi-judicial and judicial bodies. On the other hand, they should take care not to prejudice legitimate interests by disclosing information at their disposal.[78] Protecting the organisation from curiosity and external inquisitorial behaviour, which Paul Reuter was willing to accept back in 1956,[79] may come up for reconsideration from a remedial and accountability point of view. Any third-party dispute settlement procedure derives its legitimacy from its impartiality, which requires

---

[73] H. Nehl, *Principles of Administrative Procedure in EC Law* (Oxford: Hart Publishing, 1999), p. 31, note 69.

[74] *Ibid.*, p. 60.   [75] *Ibid.*, p. 49.

[76] As referred to by C. Gray, *Judicial Remedies in International Law* (Oxford: Clarendon Press, 1987), p. 19.

[77] James N. Paul, 'Law and Development in the 1990s: Using International Law to Impose Accountability to People on International Development Actors', *Third World Legal Studies* (1992), 1–16, at 15.

[78] P. Reuter, 'Le Droit au secret et les institutions internationales', *AFDI* 2 (1956), 46–65, at 51.

[79] *Ibid.*

that parties should not be obstructed when presenting their arguments and submitting evidence.[80]

A tribunal will take notice of any refusal by an international organisation to disclose information or documents, but it is not always certain that such an attitude will lead to an unfavourable presumption.[81] Failure to provide full access to information directly held by an international organisation could be remedied by granting an affirmative order following a request by interested parties entitled to have access under applicable rules. Such a limitation would not apply when archives are involved because, as Dinah Shelton has stated in general terms, the right to know also encompasses the preservation of and access to archives.[82] The rule of inviolability of archives was designed to protect the internal information of the international organisation, but an authorisation for access may be granted by the organisation in appropriate circumstances, such as when required for the proper administration of justice.[83]

Reuter rightly pointed out that the problems associated with the right to secrecy present themselves on the level of international law, the applicable texts referring to 'professional secret' or 'duty of discretion', without, however, determining their nature or regime.[84] General principles of law, particularly those derived from internal law, could be relied upon.[85] It is worth noting that Reuter admits that only interests of a hierarchically higher group could lead to the mitigation of the secrecy.[86] The way in which the Commission of Inquiry into the events in Rwanda was able to carry out its mandate could be a good example of this precedence.

Reuter has convincingly argued that only an accusatorial procedure would require total disclosure but his view that in an inquisitorial approach the judge may keep the content of the information divulged by the organisation to himself during the judicial decision-making

---

[80] R. Martha, 'Representation of Parties in World Trade Disputes', *JWTL* 31 (1997), 84–96, at 91.

[81] Reuter, 'Le Droit au secret', 48–9, and note 7.

[82] D. Shelton, *Remedies in International Human Rights Law* (Oxford: Oxford University Press, 1999), p. 321.

[83] A. Muller, *International Organisations and their Host-states: Aspects of their Legal Relationship* (The Hague and London: Kluwer Law International, 1995), pp. 212 and 205.

[84] Reuter, 'Le Droit au secret', 57–8. See, for instance, the ILOAT *Anglion* case, no. 1030, in which the Tribunal ruled that, given the nature of a document that was addressed to the Secretary-General and because it was intended for internal Secretariat use, it should accordingly not be brought to the notice of a third party. In a letter dated 14 March 2000, D. Ruzié drew my attention to this case: on file with the author.

[85] Reuter, 'Le Droit au secret', 58.   [86] *Ibid.*, 61.

128 PROCEDURAL ASPECTS OF REMEDIAL ACTION

process[87] has to be placed under the caveat formulated by Judge Higgins,[88] as the judge may also decide to exclude documents as evidence and not to take them properly into account in reaching a decision on the ground that their confidential character had made them inaccessible to certain parties.[89] In non-contentious proceedings fact-finding is inquisitorial rather than accusatorial, while in contentious cases against international organisations there is unlimited jurisdiction to evaluate the facts.[90]

A judicial review of acts of international organisations could be prevented if documents relating to the organisation's internal working would be privileged from disclosure, but courts might be prepared to recognise a limited degree of protection for confidential information located in internal communications if required for the organisation's proper functioning or for the protection of the rights of third parties in cases in which the confidential information had been obtained from the third parties.[91] An alternative approach has been followed by the ICJ Rules of Court, where only parts of a document that has not been published and has not been freely available will form part of the record of the case, while a copy of the whole document is in the possession of the Registry.[92] A tribunal's statute can, of course, also provide an obligation for a respondent international organisation to transmit all documents irrespective of any order from the court.[93] A refusal to disclose on grounds of alleged irrelevance could be remedied by requesting the court to grant a positive injunction.[94]

Chittharanjan Amerasinghe has noted that the possibility for international organisations to withhold documents for reasons of confidentiality has been significantly limited by international administrative tribunals.[95]

Recent changes are to be noted in the practice of domestic courts no longer upholding the international organisations' absolute exemption from a duty to produce and disclose evidence and information in their

---

[87] *Ibid.*, 62.   [88] See above, p. 109.

[89] *Jurisdiction of the Oder Commission case, (1929) PCIJ*, Series C, No. 17-II, at 25–31 as referred to by R. Plender, 'Procedure in the European Courts: Comparisons and Prospects', *RCADI* 267 (1997), 1–343, at 164.

[90] Plender, 'Procedure in European Courts', 144–5.   [91] *Ibid.*, 175.

[92] *Ibid.*, 117, referring to Article 50(1) and (2) of the Rules of the Court.

[93] *Ibid.*, 117–18, citing the example of Article 23 of the EFTA Court Statute.

[94] *Ibid.*, citing Article 24 of the EFTA Court Statute.

[95] C. F. Amerasinghe, 'Evidence Before Administrative Tribunals' in R. Lillich (ed.), *Fact-finding Before International Tribunals, Eleventh Sokol Colloquium* (Ardsley-on-Hudson and New York: Transnational Publishers, 1992), pp. 205–33, at pp. 232–3.

possession.[96] The UN General Convention's provision on inviolability of archives and documents precludes issuing an order addressed to (former) employees of an international organisation to produce evidence. An obligation for the organisation to comply with national procedural law and a court order to produce documents cannot be implied by a waiver of immunity from legal process.[97] However, the organisation's general obligation to co-operate with host and other states in the proper administration of justice may require a shift of the burden upon the organisation to present imperative reasons relating to the need to avoid intolerable interference with its functioning and independence, thus even going beyond the ECJ ruling in the *J. J. Zwartveld* case.[98]

Proof and evidence before international criminal tribunals

With regard to international criminal tribunals a combination of 'interests of a hierarchically higher group' and the accusatorial character of the procedure occurs. This (potentially) gives rise to difficulties surrounding requests made in the course of these proceedings for access to information and documents held by an international organisation – or by a unique international non-governmental organisation with limited international legal personality such as the ICRC in the *Simic* case[99] of the ICTY – or motions for testimony by (former) Force Commanders or other officials who have participated in peacekeeping operations.

In such cases where the accountability of the international organisation and/or of the international civil servants is potentially involved, even in an indirect way, the question could be raised as to whether the obligation to contribute to the proper administration of justice would not require the international organisation temporarily to release (former) individual staff members or experts from the observation of the principles of loyalty and discretion. Danesh Sarooshi has convincingly argued that the immunities of UN officials do not operate towards UN organs that are an integral part of the organisation, and that consequently the international criminal tribunals have the power to require them to give evidence, even without an authorisation from the UN Secretary-General because there is no need for such authorisation.

---

[96] Reinisch, *National Courts,* pp. 158–9 and the case law reviewed in notes 655 and 656.
[97] Muller, *International Organisations and their Host-states,* p. 205.
[98] Case 2/88, *J. J. Zwartveld and Others,* 13 July 1990 [1990] ECR I-3365 as cited by Muller, *International Organisations and their Host-states,* pp. 206–7 and by Reinisch, *National Courts,* p. 340.
[99] *Prosecutor v. Simic et al.,* Case IT-95-5-PT.

130   PROCEDURAL ASPECTS OF REMEDIAL ACTION

The issue of confidentiality cannot in itself constitute a reason for withholding evidence from a tribunal.[100]

The Rules of Procedure of an international criminal tribunal may allow an international organisation or one of its officials to give confidential information to the prosecutor so that further evidence may be uncovered, and may also preserve the anonymity of the witness from the accused.[101] The Rules may also restrict the right to demand additional information beyond that which has been agreed upon, but this is counterbalanced by the right to a fair trial: the prosecutor has to disclose evidence beneficial to the accused irrespective of the source.[102]

UN Secretariat co-operation with the international criminal tribunals 'to the maximum extent possible' is clearly subject to three categories of safeguards. The protection of the organisation's essential interests is the first safeguard that could be invoked to reduce or limit co-operation; this is, apparently, distinct from the second safeguard, which is the protection of confidential information. Finally, the personal safety of mission personnel could also be raised.[103]

Although from a human rights perspective, too, the personal safety of mission personnel should certainly occupy a prominent place in the organisation's weighing-up of the degree of its co-operation, the protection of the organisation's essential interests and of confidential

---

[100] D. Sarooshi, 'The Powers of the United Nations International Criminal Tribunals', *Max Planck Yearbook of UN Law* 2 (1999), 141–67, at 166.

[101] Rules 70 and 75 of the ICTR. On 8 June 2000, Trial Chambers I and III of the ICTR decided that a three-page internal and confidential memorandum – dealing with the circumstances of the shooting down on 6 April 1994 of the aircraft carrying President Juvenal Habyarama of Rwanda and President Cyprien Ntaryamire of Burundi – that had been written for the Office of Internal Oversight Services might be relevant and that a copy of it should be served on the defence; a copy would also become available to the prosecution. The document had been transmitted by the UN Secretary-General to the President of the ICTR 'so that if this matter is raised before the Tribunal, the appropriate Trial Chamber could decide if the document is relevant for the defense of any of the cases on which the attorneys are working and, if so, determine under what circumstances and conditions the document can be released'. The memorandum had been located at the request of a number of defence attorneys working at the ICTR (Case ICTR-95-IA-T, *The Prosecutor v. Ignace Bagilishema*, Decision of 8 June 2000 on the request of the defence for an order of seizure of a UN memorandum prepared by Michael Hourigan, former ICTR investigator; and Cases ICTR-97-34-I and ICTR-97-30-I, *The Prosecutor v. Kaibiligi and Ntabakuze*, Decision of 8 June 2000 on the request of the defence for an order of service of a UN memorandum, prepared by Michael Hourigan).

[102] Rules 70 and 68 of the ICTY. G. Gilbert, 'Rights, Legitimate Expectations, Needs and Responsibilities: UNHCR and the New World Order', *International Journal of Refugee Law* 10 (1998), 349–88, at 386–7.

[103] A/AC.121/43 of 23 February 1999, para. 19.

information are to be considered as far less or hardly compatible with both the general imperatives of an accountability regime and the particular duty of international organisations to contribute to the proper administration of justice.

Apparently the UN Secretariat does not share Sarooshi's view, as it is pursuing 'a policy of waiving the immunity from legal process enjoyed by Force Commanders and other peacekeeping personnel to the extent necessary to permit them to answer questions that seek to establish the existence of any of the elements of any of the crimes set out in the statutes of the international tribunals, or that might establish the existence, in respect of any individual, of circumstances of an exculpatory or mitigatory nature'.[104] The waivers are made conditional upon testimony in closed session and a prohibition by the International Criminal Tribunal on disclosing information of a sensitive or confidential nature to third parties (that is, those not the parties to the case and their advisers). Further additional protective measures may eventually be required.[105]

The waivers are not only conditional, but also limited in scope *ratione materiae*, as disclosure of information relating to internal decision-making by the UN or troop-contributing countries is excluded: such information is 'not only strictly confidential, but also irrelevant to establishing the elements of any of the crimes that fall within the jurisdiction of the two international tribunals'.[106] The successive orders in the *Simic* case have clearly demonstrated that the position held by the UN Secretariat would not necessarily be upheld by the international criminal tribunals for the reasons the Trial and Appeals Chamber have indicated with regard to the unique position of the ICRC.[107]

As member states will be confronted with the problems arising from requests addressed to former UN peacekeeping personnel to give testimony to the international criminal tribunals, the Secretariat will develop comprehensive guidelines on this topic.[108]

[104] *Ibid.*, para. 20.   [105] *Ibid.*   [106] *Ibid.*, para. 21.
[107] *Simic et al.* (Case IT-95-9-PT) 'Bosanksi Samac':
  Decision, 7 June 2000: denying request for assistance in securing documents and witnesses from the International Committee of the Red Cross.
  Decision, 28 February 2000: on (1) Application by Stevan Todorovic to reopen the Decision of 27 July 1999; (2) Motion by ICRC to reopen Scheduling Order of 18 November 1999 and (3) Conditions for Access to Material.
  Scheduling Order of 18 November 1999.
  Decision (*ex parte* confidential) on the Prosecution Motion under rule 73 for a ruling concerning the testimony of a witness, 27 July 1999.
[108] A/AC.121/43 of 20 March 2000, para. 19. The Secretariat has continued to pursue a

132 PROCEDURAL ASPECTS OF REMEDIAL ACTION

According to one authority there is, by the very nature of international administrative law, to some extent a virtual presumption that the excessive powers of international organisations and their administrations are being exercised in a manner that is acceptable and without question.[109] To prove wrongdoing on the part of international organisations is thus more difficult and there is a tendency to hold that they are within their rights in acting as they do.[110] This could eventually also apply to the ICJ if the suggestion by some commentators is correct, namely that when the authority of an international organisation is in question, the ICJ is guided by the rule of effectiveness.[111] This near-presumption is dealt with in the conclusion of this study.

> policy of close co-operation (A/54/670 of 6 January 2000, para. 25). The Special Committee on Peacekeeping Operations reiterated its request 'that the Secretariat keep Member States continuously apprised of all developments' with regard to the provision of testimony by peacekeeping personnel: A/54/839, para. 79.

[109] C. F. Amerasinghe, 'The Future of International Administrative Law', *ICLQ* 45 (1996), 773–95, at 783.

[110] *Ibid.*

[111] J. Charney, 'Is International Law Threatened by Multiple International Tribunals?', *RCADI* 271 (1998), 101–382, at 140–1.

PART III · SUBSTANTIVE OUTCOME OF REMEDIAL ACTION AGAINST INTERNATIONAL ORGANISATIONS

13 General features of remedial outcome

The general features of remedies against international organisations have been described in Part I of this study. Once claimants are considering taking remedial action against an international organisation their different status *vis-à-vis* the organisation will have important consequences on the procedural level; that was the focus of Part II. Part III is devoted to a general picture of the substantive outcome of remedial action undertaken by non-state claimants.

The relationship between the specific features of member states and the various levels of accountability has been analysed in the first two sections of chapter 3 in Part I. There is no reason to believe that there are additional, membership-linked features of remedial outcome other than the ones described in this current chapter. As to representational non-governmental organisations, there is no remedial outcome as remedial mechanisms are not open to them. Accordingly, neither category of claimants is included here.

The substantive outcome portrayed in Part III is not specific to remedial action against international organisations, as demonstrated by claims against states under secondary rules of liability/responsibility. That the range of available remedial outcomes is almost identical is not surprising because the situations giving rise to organisational liability/responsibility do not substantially differ merely because of the identity of the actors involved. The surrounding circumstances and the modalities of the alleged harm/violation may vary, but that will not necessarily limit the availability or selection of the remedial outcome. The implementation of the remedies by international organisations may be different because of their corporate structure, but this does not detract from the prominent place the issue of remedial outcome occupies within the overall accountability regime for international organisations.

135

It should be noted in the first place that no other international organisation has as yet lodged a claim against the UN, and international claims against the UN by states are rare but have occurred.

Christine Gray has noted that the relationship between remedies for illegal acts and those for legal acts demands consideration.[1] Given the fragmented and embryonic state of any remedial regime *vis-à-vis* international organisations (an exception being made for international administrative law), it is hardly surprising that this question, too, has received almost no attention at all. On the other hand, one may wonder whether both private (law of torts and contracts) and public (protection against acts and conduct of administrative authorities) domestic law could not be, with all due caution, the inspiration for the development of any consistent remedy regime towards international organisations.

The possible outcome of a successful use of judicial remedies based upon the illegality of an institutional act would constitute an example of a *legal restitutio in integrum* such as an order for the repeal or alteration of measures[2] taken by the respondent international organisation, but it may also present itself in other forms such as non-opposability, nullity or the declared non-existence of the act in question, although the latter two consequences can only be achieved if the judicial forum called upon to deliver such a decision had been explicitly attributed with such a competence in its constituent instrument or by way of ad hoc conventional arrangements.

Alternatively, or in addition to these consequences, the illegality of an institutional act of an international organisation could in principle also entail the reparation of the damages caused by its prior application to all categories of addressees, such as member states, staff members and, occasionally, third parties (for example private individuals and enterprises). That would be an example of a *material restitutio in integrum*.[3]

Pierre Klein has rightly observed that when confronted with an institutional act it considers to be illegal, a member state of an international organisation, not of the integrationist type, could always unilaterally, at its own discretion, refuse its further application from the very outset.[4]

Dinah Shelton's assessment of the development of legal remedies – that it 'should be governed by the desire for consistent redress, but more

---

[1] C. Gray, *Judicial Remedies in International Law* (Oxford: Clarendon Press, 1987), p. 10.

[2] *Ibid.*, p. 13.   [3] *Ibid.*

[4] P. Klein, *La Responsabilité des organisations internationales dans les ordres juridiques internes et en droit des gens* (Brussels: Editions Bruylant and Editions de l'Université Libre de Bruxelles, 1998), pp. 88–9.

often is determined by administrative feasibility, institutional functions and relationships, and too often, by government's desire not to be held accountable[5] – equally applies to international organisations which, at present, are not genuinely in favour of the fundamentals of the accountability regime applicable to them. The selection or combination of different kinds of remedies may vary in general terms between the categories of legal responsibility, contractual and non-contractual liability, subject, of course, to aggravating (gross negligence or wilful misconduct) or mitigating (contributory conduct by the claimant) circumstances.

During international judicial proceedings, states have under the law of state responsibility requested restitution, damages, specific performance, satisfaction and injunctive relief.[6] There is no inherent reason why the same remedies should not become available under the law of organisational responsibility.

The remaining part of this chapter is devoted to the substantive outcome of remedial action against an international organisation because of damage caused in the normal course of its institutional or operational activities, the legality of which is uncontested. In assessing the outcome of remedial action concerning contractual or tortious liability vested in the organisation, due notice should be taken of the fact rightly referred to by Klein that for the former category of cases international organisations have been willing to confer that competence on external organs, whereas preference has been given to internal mechanisms for non-contractual liability, because of the importance of questions of principle and general policy that frequently arise in this category of claims.[7] It is no coincidence that the accountability concern is most likely to be prominent here.

Orders for specific performance

It was indicated above that adequate redress for the claimants has to be found while ensuring the preservation of a reasonable degree of respect for the organisation's continuous well functioning; relatively non-intrusive remedies include declaratory judgments and damages.[8]

---

[5] D. Shelton, *Remedies in International Human Rights Law* (Oxford: Oxford University Press, 1999), p. 90.

[6] *Ibid.*, p. 95.   [7] Klein, *La Responsabilité*, p. 147.

[8] Shelton, *Remedies*, p. 55. A number of reservations made by Shelton with regard to violations of human rights by states are particularly relevant to the accountability regime of international organisations.

138   SUBSTANTIVE OUTCOME OF REMEDIAL ACTION

Furthermore, a merely interest-balancing approach[9] may additionally be overstretched by, for instance, the underlying, sometimes explicit, assumption in favour of the adequacy of the decisions and actions undertaken by the respondent international organisation. It is only when the common-law remedies are inadequate, and also when it would not lead to injustice in common-law systems, that the remedy of specific performance will be awarded as an exceptional and equitable remedy.[10] Given the inherent distinctive features of the overall accountability regime of international organisations recalled earlier, remedial orders for specific performance may constitute a more appropriate and arguably more comprehensive remedy than compensation to individual claimants,[11] but this could – although not necessarily in all cases – presuppose some form of class or collective action such as the one allowed to be filed on behalf of all victims in the Inter-American system for the protection of human rights.

The reasons given by Shelton as to why non-monetary remedies such as negative or positive injunctions may be more appropriate or necessary are also to be found when international organisations are their potential addressees: that is, when they have not responded to less intrusive measures, such as an award of damages, and/or it is impossible to estimate such damages.[12] The degree of intrusiveness into the organisation's functioning – in other words, invoking the concept of functional necessity – should not operate as a bar at the cost of the claimant's rights[13] as it so predominantly does as far as their jurisdictional immunity before domestic courts is concerned.

Irrespective of the power to award non-pecuniary remedies being inherent and/or treaty-based, both restraint and activism are to be found in international judicial practice dealing with human rights violations by states.[14]

Further judicial developments since 1987 in the sector of human rights protection *vis-à-vis* states may lead to a reconsideration of Gray's recommendation that in the absence of an express provision to that effect the ICJ should adopt the presumption of other courts that an order is not a suitable remedy against a state.[15] International administrative tribunals have resorted to reparative orders such as requiring the respondent international organisation to restore the claimant to its

---

[9] *Ibid.*, p. 53.   [10] Gray, *Judicial Remedies*, p. 8.   [11] Shelton, *Remedies*, p. 79.
[12] *Ibid.*, p. 293.   [13] *Ibid.*   [14] *Ibid.*, pp. 294–302.
[15] Gray, *Judicial Remedies*, pp. 159–60.

GENERAL FEATURES OF REMEDIAL OUTCOME 139

pre-existing entitlement, but preventive orders do not come within the purview of their competence *ratione remedii*.

As a matter of principle, 'structural injunctions' 'that attempt to remodel an existing social or political institution to bring it into conformity with legal requirements'[16] should not be ruled out from the start, especially as they may be additionally driven by 'conceptions of good management, financial resources, control',[17] considerations that fit well in the overall accountability regime of international organisations.

With regard to all non-monetary remedies it is obviously important that the judicial organ issuing them should have the administrative capability to supervise their compliance or that there is a related political organ, such as the UN General Assembly, which is capable of following up and enforcing compliance, if necessary.[18]

The argument that the availability of sufficient financial resources may undermine the deterrent functions of financial compensation if not accompanied by an order requiring remedial action[19] obviously does not have the same value with regard to international organisations, but it does not detract from the possible need for non-financial remedial action from an overall accountability perspective. Ultimately, Gray convincingly pointed out that the disagreement over the suitability of orders of specific performance emanates more from differences on policy than from interpretations of the existing law.[20]

The internalisation of the costs of damages awarded[21] within the international organisation by way of the normal or extra-budgetary settlement between its member states will certainly contribute to the dissuasive effects envisaged by the provision of such a remedy, even if the organisation has a special Working Capital Fund and schemes of insurance.

The 'complex interplay and mutual influence of national and international law, both public and private' as underscored by Shelton with regard to remedies for violations of human rights[22] will only gradually evolve in the accountability regime for international organisations, this inertia being mainly the result of the jurisdictional immunity that prevents a body of domestic case law from developing. This study has already pointed to the imperatives emanating from remedial action in domestic systems against public administrative authorities and available to both civil servants and ordinary citizens alike; the imperatives

---

[16] Shelton, *Remedies*, p. 302.   [17] *Ibid.*, p. 53.   [18] *Ibid.*, p. 305.   [19] *Ibid.*, p. 359.
[20] Gray, *Judicial Remedies*, p. 17.   [21] Shelton, *Remedies*, p. 54.   [22] *Ibid.*, p. 57.

140   SUBSTANTIVE OUTCOME OF REMEDIAL ACTION

may also provide successful inspiration in identifying common principles of the law of remedies. This will remain particularly relevant as long as international organisations have not developed a comprehensive and transparent remedial regime. Explicit provisions securing remedial rights should be included in the constitutive instruments of any international organisation as a first step in the right direction.

Declaratory judgments

Declaratory judgments have become the most common type of award granted by the ICJ,[23] but their effectiveness and importance as a remedy for breaches has been limited by the strict approach of the Court.[24] This contrasts with the ECJ, which is willing to render such judgments even when there is no longer a dispute or where it will not have any immediate practical effect:[25] claimants against an international organisation may only wish to have a declaration that it had violated applicable legal rules.[26] On the other hand, declaratory judgments may contain detailed guidance for international organisations as regards their future conduct, much in the same way as Advisory Opinions do.[27]

The importance of a determination that an international organisation has violated internal, domestic or international legal rules should not be underestimated.[28] In politically sensitive cases the court or tribunal 'may grant declaratory relief though it chooses not to issue an injunction'.[29]

Further domestic proceedings against international organisations for damages or other reparations are unlikely to succeed because of their jurisdictional immunities: hence, a consequential determination of the nature and scope of redress is preferable, 'to avoid the possibility that the victim will be without adequate remedies and thus deprived of compensatory justice',[30] meeting the concerns of both individual and societal interests. That is even more relevant when operational activities form the subject-matter of the claim rather than institutional acts such as resolutions and regulations. So, generally speaking, 'a declaratory

---

[23] Gray, *Judicial Remedies*, p. 96.   [24] *Ibid.*, p. 102.   [25] *Ibid.*, p. 128.
[26] *Ibid.*   [27] *Ibid.*, pp. 100–1.
[28] See also Shelton in the context of human rights violations by states: *Remedies*, p. 200.
[29] *Powell v. McCormack*, 395 US 486 at 499 (1969), US Supreme Court as cited by Shelton, *Remedies*, p. 200, note 4.
[30] *Ibid.*, p. 201.

GENERAL FEATURES OF REMEDIAL OUTCOME 141

judgment will not in and of itself be an adequate remedy ... It is the beginning of remedies, not the end.[31]

Pecuniary remedies

Shelton rightly recalled the importance of an accurate assessment of the amount of damages due for the remedy to achieve its adequate level of dissuasive force.[32] Protection of the international societal interests (that is, the fact that the accountability regime of international organisations has an *erga omnes* character) may require, as in the sector of human rights violations, higher levels of damages than the protection of the individual interests of the claimant would seem to require[33] when corporate/institutional responsibility is also taken into account.[34]

The actual amount of compensation paid directly by the international organisation to private claimants is certainly, but to varying degrees, influenced by the *lex loci*. The actual payment of financial compensation by an international organisation once it has been ordered to do so by a final and binding judgment, or as a result of a negotiated settlement, normally does not pose any particular problem – exceptions such as the *International Tin Council* case are rare – and drastically reduces the practical importance of the functional protection provided to international organisations by the enjoyment of immunity of execution before domestic courts.

There is, of course, the question of who is the actual debtor of the obligation to remedy the failure of compliance by the international organisation or by one of its agents, either with contractual obligations or with the general obligation not to cause damage in the carrying out of legitimate activities. The different mechanisms present a variety of possible alternatives for the international organisations to obtain reimbursement of, for example, financial compensation from the host state and/or the insurance company and/or the agent in cases of gross negligence or wilful misconduct. The way in which any financial settlement is subsequently dealt with between the various actors themselves is a matter that does not concern us here.

Damages for injury to reputation are commonplace in municipal systems, but are exceptional in international arbitral practice.[35] They can be granted by international administrative tribunals to staff members,

---

[31] *Ibid.*, p. 213.   [32] *Ibid.*, p. 41.   [33] *Ibid.*, p. 43.   [34] *Ibid.*, p. 35.
[35] Gray, *Judicial Remedies*, p. 34.

142   SUBSTANTIVE OUTCOME OF REMEDIAL ACTION

and third parties such as traders may also claim this remedy in cases where their reputation has allegedly been damaged by the publication of a report by or under the auspices of an international organisation which has explicitly identified them as having violated economic coercive measures.[36]

Ex gratia payments

Ex gratia payments by an international organisation are normally a mechanism designed to accommodate the legitimate concerns of private claimants without there being a legally sound basis – by way of admitting unilaterally or accepting the outcome of a judicial or quasi-judicial remedy – for contractual or non-contractual liability or organisational responsibility. From a remedial point of view, these kinds of payments should not necessarily be considered as inappropriate alternatives in spite of the financial outcome being evidently of a substantially lesser amount, unless, of course, the *ex gratia* payment is instrumental in the organisation's refusal to acknowledge liability or responsibility once this has been clearly and objectively established.[37] In this respect there is no difference from situations in which states make similar payments.

Private claimants may settle for the *ex gratia* payment either because otherwise they would face the mounting costs of a hearing, or because they acknowledge perhaps that their claim was a weak one anyway, which would not have any real chance before a quasi-judicial or judicial mechanism. In a different situation they may call upon their national state to contest both the principle and the amount of the *ex gratia* payment offered by the organisation. There is no general pattern that can be laid down here.

Non-pecuniary remedies

Satisfaction could, for instance, redress 'moral, immaterial, or non-pecuniary damage caused by a state, including disrespect and impairing a state's dignity and honour'.[38] Apologies expressed by the Executive

---

[36] *Report of the Panel of Experts established by the UN Security Council pursuant to Resolution 1237 (1999) on Violations of Security Council Sanctions against UNITA*, annexed to the letter dated 10 March 2000 by the Chairman of the Security Council Committee established pursuant to Resolution 864 (1993) concerning the situation in Angola, addressed to the President of the Security Council.

[37] See further Klein, *La Responsabilité*, pp. 612–15 and the examples cited there.

[38] Shelton, *Remedies*, p. 46.

Head on behalf of the organisation can be an appropriate mode of satisfaction, following the results of an independent inquiry into events preceding and during the course of a peacekeeping operation such as in Rwanda and in Srebrenica. This mode of reparation can be complemented, if need be, by disciplinary measures taken by the UN upon request or on its own initiative *vis-à-vis* staff members or agents for serious misconduct or negligence in the performance of their duties and by the troop-contributing states towards members of their national contingent on similar grounds. Formal apologies solemnly expressed also have the potential to affect the assessment of moral damages.[39]

There is no reason why after the occurrence of the most serious failure by an international organisation to take preventive or corrective action, rituals, commemorations and the construction of a monument on the *lex loci commissi* should not constitute an appropriate form of satisfaction;[40] in addition, the temporary preferential treatment of the country and the population that fell victim to such a preventive failure could constitute an appropriate special remedial measure.[41] This, of course, does not detract from the fact that, because of the enormous scale of the consequences of the mistakes made, *inter alia*, by the international organisations, no remedy or means of redress will ever be adequate or proportional.

The foregoing observations are particularly relevant in circumstances where individuals or groups of individuals had no indication whatsoever that they could not legitimately expect the international organisation in its operational activities to provide for their safety and wellbeing, particularly in protected areas.[42] In accordance with the pronouncements in the *Janes* case, reasonable and substantial redress for the mistrust and lack of safety resulting from the international organisation's attitude seems to be required.[43] Guarantees of non-repetition of such inaction could be provided in a set of operational guidelines for the future, eventually following a resolution by one principal organ of the organisation, such as the General Assembly, condemning inaction by another principal

---

[39] *Ibid.*, p. 118.   [40] *Ibid.*, pp. 46 and 51.

[41] *Report of the Independent Inquiry into the Actions of the United Nations during the 1994 Genocide in Rwanda*, 15 December 1999, Recommendations 13 and 14 (hereinafter cited as *Report of the Rwanda Inquiry*).

[42] *Report of the Rwanda Inquiry*, C. 19. A/54/549 of 15 November 1999, *Report of the Secretary-General pursuant to General Assembly Resolution 53/35, The Fall of Srebrenica*, para. 468 (hereinafter cited as *Srebrenica Report*).

[43] *Janes* case *(US v. Mexico)*, 1923, UNRIAA 4(1926), 82 as cited by Gray, *Judicial Remedies*, p. 21. See also Shelton, *Remedies*, pp. 114–15.

144   SUBSTANTIVE OUTCOME OF REMEDIAL ACTION

organ. Such a condemning resolution could constitute 'punishment by disgrace'[44] at the same time as recommending to the whole membership remedial action towards the victim state or population.

Satisfaction may also consist of a judicial declaration coupled with a recommendation or an order calling upon the organisation to change its laws or conduct so as to conform with the primary rules governing all such organisations.[45] Increasingly, judicial and arbitral organs are prepared to consider moulding such appropriate remedies as may be required by the particular circumstances of the case before them. This could include considering the initial imbalance of power between the parties as falling within their inherent jurisdiction, although the organs may still consider that their function does not extend to addressing an order to an international organisation to take disciplinary measures against staff members when serious personal misconduct has caused the harm.[46]

Punitive damages

The primary rule not only of due diligence but of utmost care inevitably has a counterpart on the level of remedies against international

---

[44] Gray, *Judicial Remedies*, p. 215.

[45] Of course, there is a sharp contrast between the practice of almost every international organisation where judicial decisions only play a small part, if any, in controlling the activities of the organs of the organisation and the system applied within the European Community: Gray, *Judicial Remedies*, p. 120.

[46] It is 'the responsibility of the head of mission to ensure that personnel under his or her command behave in accordance with United Nations codes of conduct' (A/54/670 of 6 January 2000, para. 16). The UN Secretariat's ultimate recourse in dealing with misconduct during peacekeeping operations and involving military personnel contributed by member states is repatriation. It is then up to the government concerned to take legal and disciplinary measures (A/AC.121/43 of 23 February 1999, p. 6, para. 45). The Special Committee on Peacekeeping Operations emphasised the need for consultation with the member state concerned and requested the Secretariat to develop a set of guidelines governing the action to be taken in such instances: A/54/839 of 20 March 2000, paras. 65–6. With regard to civilian personnel employed by the UN, direct disciplinary measures do apply (*ibid.*, para. 46).

As of November 1998, '11 civilian staff in peacekeeping missions were found, after the completion of relevant administrative proceedings, to have committed acts of misconduct' (*ibid.*, para. 47).

During 1998, forty-two military personnel were placed under investigation on grounds of alleged misconduct. They were immediately repatriated and relevant permanent missions were requested to submit information about follow-up action at the national level. Seven cases have been resolved, disciplinary action being taken by national authorities in four cases (*ibid.*, para. 48).

organisations. The persistent refusal by international organisations even to consider punitive damages when drafting compromissory clauses cannot be maintained, given the necessary perception that remedies also serve societal interests.

Clyde Eagleton's argument in favour of the possibility of exemplary damages, which was drawn from the need 'to maintain proper observance of international law',[47] also works with regard to claims against international organisations. The attitude of international organisations may, however, be explained by the reluctance of tribunals under the law of state responsibility to award punitive or exemplary damages, in spite of states often having demanded them in diplomatic claims.[48]

Punitive or exemplary damages increase the severity of punishment already present in a declaratory judgment, but the compensatory and deterrent elements in remedial awards are difficult to measure in combination.[49] Shelton's observation that the total award should be higher and that the ratio of the punitive to the compensatory component in the total award should be larger in the case of a high probability that the wrongdoers would not be held accountable[50] certainly applies to international organisations for the reasons stated earlier. Moreover, punitive damages could be useful in encouraging member states to take an active role in overseeing the organisation's activities and in choosing its officers and policy, as is the case with corporate liability.[51] With regard to human rights violations by states, the credibility and effectiveness of the accountability regime requires that the more severe violations be dealt with more severely;[52] there is no reason to hold otherwise when the respondent is an international organisation.

In considering the possibility of punitive damages, international law policy considerations will be crucial, which in turn depend on one's conception of the role of an international judicial forum.[53]

Costs and attorneys' fees

Given the initial imbalance of power between non-state claimants and international organisations, non-monetary remedies such as restitution

---

[47] C. Eagleton, 'International Organisations and the Law of Responsibility', *RCADI* 76 (1950), 323–423, at 380.

[48] Shelton, *Remedies*, pp. 131–2.   [49] *Ibid.*, pp. 280–1.   [50] *Ibid.*, p. 282.

[51] *Ibid.*, p. 284.   [52] *Ibid.*, p. 290.   [53] Gray, *Judicial Remedies*, p. 28.

146   SUBSTANTIVE OUTCOME OF REMEDIAL ACTION

and defraying costs of litigation should complement the compensation of actual harm.[54]

Shelton rightly recalled that there is no issue on which international tribunals have been as divided 'as on the award of costs and attorneys' fees'. International administrative tribunals, for instance, are split 'with some awarding costs and fees while others deny them or hide them in large damage awards'.[55] She welcomed the convergence of the Inter-American and European Courts on awards of fees and costs, because victims need their own attorney before international tribunals, as this may be required for due process.[56] She convincingly added that victims will only be vindicated if they have access to legal assistance and this can only be assured if such assistance is compensated. Consequently, international tribunals should liberalise their views on attorneys' fees and costs to ensure *restitutio in integrum*.[57] The entity causing the wrong should have to bear the costs of the procedures necessary to achieve a remedy, otherwise claimants could find themselves unable to sue, and this could undermine[58] the effectiveness of the accountability regime of international organisations.

The interconnection between the procedural aspects of remedial actions and their outcome becomes particularly poignant because of the limits on litigation flowing from jurisdictional immunities raised before domestic courts, when and to the extent that this major procedural obstacle has either not been adequately removed or counterbalanced by the provision of alternative equivalent forms of remedial protection. This calls into serious question the integrity of the accountability regime of international organisations and of the rule of law.[59] Part IV of this study deals with this issue.

[54] Shelton, *Remedies*, p. 43.   [55] *Ibid.*, p. 307.   [56] *Ibid.*, p. 318.
[57] *Ibid.*, p. 319.   [58] *Ibid.*   [59] *Ibid.*, p. 52.

14   Remedial outcome for staff members

General picture

It is hardly surprising that the outcome of disputes involving staff members provide most of the relevant data for this Part of the study, given the confidentiality surrounding the resolution of differences and disputes between an international organisation and third-party claimants concerning contractual and non-contractual liability: relevant case law is difficult to find, and barely accessible, if at all.

Claims submitted by staff members can be satisfactorily settled in a pre-litigation procedure, and most complaints are settled in that way. If the difference or the dispute persists then international administrative tribunals, because of their attribution of jurisdiction, are competent, within the exercise of a legality control, to annul administrative decisions, but not to replace or adjust them. Nor, indeed, can the tribunals maintain, 'because of a more equitable interpretation', a kind of compromise solution between the position of the claimant staff member and the respondent international organisation.[1] Neither the promotion of justice nor the implementation of accountability of international organisations can be considered to gain from such a manifest *excès de pouvoir*.[2]

The substantive remedial outcome is determined not only by the subject-matter of the claim – which could include a plea for damages and a request for costs and fees – but evidently also by the way international administrative tribunals interpret the scope of their jurisdiction *ratione personae* and *ratione materiae* and by the views that they hold regarding the sources of law applicable to the case before them. An example of

---

[1] D. Ruzié, Working Paper No. 1, ILA Committee, p. 6, paras. 30–1: on file with the author.
[2] *Ibid.*

147

148   SUBSTANTIVE OUTCOME OF REMEDIAL ACTION

the former problem may occur when a quasi-judicial body refuses to pronounce on the right to compensation for damages linked to the irregularity of a refusal to seise a Consultative Committee, and arrives at this conclusion by 'hiding' behind staff statute provisions, which clearly results in a denial of justice.[3] It has to be noted that judgments delivered by international administrative tribunals may also be based on grounds which have not been advanced by one of the parties at all.

The latter problem is particularly poignant when the exception of illegality has been invoked.[4] Administrative tribunals have consistently declared themselves incompetent *ratione materiae* to conduct a legality review of the resolutions of the General Assembly of the UN, acts of a general regulatory nature or the policy followed by the International Commission of the Civil Service.[5]

Staff members have tried to justify acts that were, under the secondary rules of the organisation, undoubtedly illegal by invoking the argument that these acts were, however, in perfect harmony with the organisation's constituent instrument. The fact that the law of an international organisation does not contain a provision comparable to clauses in domestic constitutions that can be directly invoked before the forum state's courts does not necessarily entail the conclusion that international administrative tribunals should or could not recognise the constituent instrument's precedence by way of forming part of general principles.[6]

The case law of international administrative tribunals does not seem to have completely excluded the possibility that in appropriate circumstances justifications drawn from the organisation's objects and purposes, or from ethical considerations, could be accepted.[7]

It has to be recalled that if a legislative decision has been successfully challenged before the UNAT, all other international organisations subject

---

[3] *Ibid.*, pp. 6–7, paras. 34–6 discussing the Appeals Board of ESA: on file with the author.

[4] See in particular UNAT cases 693, 588 and 642, referred to by Ruzié, *ibid.*, p. 1, para. 4: on file with the author.

[5] Other cases resulting in a declaration of incompetence include complaints of alleged wrongs committed by senior officials or a request to waive the immunity of an international organisation's President, respectively ILOAT cases 825–31, 61 and 899, 1713 and 1265, 1535 and 1543. The author gratefully acknowledges Professor David Ruzié for having pointed out these cases in an exchange of letters, on file with the author.

[6] I. Seidl-Hohenveldern, 'Les Organisations internationales et les actes illicites des fonctionnaires' in his *Collected Essays on International Investment and on International Organisations* (The Hague and London: Kluwer Law International, 1998), pp. 37–44, at p. 41.

[7] *Ibid.*, p. 43, referring to the *Duberg* (ILOAT Judgment No. 7 (1955)) and *Andreski* (ILOAT Judgment No. 63 (1962)) cases.

to the Tribunal's jurisdiction are most likely to apply the decision of the Tribunal as well.[8]

Divergence in the case law of international administrative tribunals that belong to the same common system of international organisations provides some reason for concern – the more so when the divergence relates to basic legal concepts such as, for instance, the protection of 'acquired rights'. Past service is the criterion for such rights according to the UNAT, but a basic connection to the contract of employment provides the parameter for the ILOAT.[9]

Apart from one case during the League of Nations period, payments in compliance with challenged judgments of the UNAT and ILOAT were only made after the ICJ, under the then existing review procedure, had upheld the tribunal's jurisdiction.[10]

Statistically, and although estimates do vary, it may be safely assumed that the percentage of cases decided by the UNAT and ILOAT in favour of staff members do not exceed one-third. One could add that there are probably no reasons to believe that, in staff member cases, considerations underpinning out-of-court settlements and factors determining litigation strategy would be substantially different from cases initiated by third parties.

A variety of remedies

With regard to two of the most important international administrative tribunals, namely the UNAT and ILOAT, the following picture of remedial outcome seems to emerge, although it has to be said that extracting any general principles applicable to all tribunals and which would underlie the granting of particular remedies is difficult.[11] As a result of the different statutes, there is no uniformity of approach to the issue of

---

[8] P. Szasz, 'Adjudicating IGO Staff Challenges to Legislative Decisions' in G. Hafner et al. (eds.), *Liber Amicorum Professor Ignaz Seidl-Hohenveldern in Honour of his 80th Birthday* (The Hague and London: Kluwer Law International, 1998), pp. 699–720, at p. 708. Reference could be made to the Geneva-based international organisations deciding in favour of a substantial and retroactive increase in the remuneration of General Service Staff following the ILOAT judgment in the *Berlioz v. WIPO* case referred to by Szasz, *ibid.*, p. 708, note 33.

[9] According to P. Szasz in a written exchange of views with Prof. D. Ruzié: on file with the author.

[10] *Effect of Awards of Compensation Made by the UN Administrative Tribunal*, Advisory Opinion of 13 July 1954, *ICJ Reports* (1954), p. 47.

[11] C. F. Amerasinghe, *The Law of the International Civil Service: As Applied by International Administrative Tribunals* (Oxford: Clarendon Press, 2 vols., 2nd revised edn, 1994), vol. I, p. 446.

150 SUBSTANTIVE OUTCOME OF REMEDIAL ACTION

remedies and each tribunal takes its decisions 'in the light of a certain judicial expediency and discretion'; hence, to use them as an illustration of principles relating to remedies that may be applicable by other tribunals is not always possible.[12]

Although the UNAT's powers freely to grant remedies are more limited by its Statute because the choice between rescission or compensation belongs to the respondent organisation, both the UNAT and ILOAT have sometimes awarded remedies in a manner or in circumstances not explicitly provided for in their Statutes.[13] Often when the decision was not found to be invalid, compensation has been awarded by the UNAT without ordering rescission or specific performance; in a few cases in which the complaint as a whole was not well founded and rescission or specific performance was not appropriate, the ILOAT has granted compensation.[14] Both of these tribunals have considered these powers to be inherent, and have liberally construed the provisions on remedies while recognising the express limitations placed on them by their respective Statutes and not exceeding their powers beyond what is clearly and unequivocally circumscribed in the Statute.[15] Annulment may be granted, rescission may be ordered and, even when a decision has not been tainted by the application of an illegal procedure, specific performance may be ordered.[16]

Specific performance has also been ordered by both tribunals when the decision was regarded as being invalid but had not been specifically annulled because the tribunal considered the order of specific performance, without substitute compensation, to provide the applicant with an adequate remedy.[17] The dissatisfaction of an organisation when a particular international administrative tribunal had been given the competence to order specific performance may eventually lead it to reconsider its submission to that tribunal's jurisdiction in favour of another tribunal that lacks that particular judicial power.

From a remedial point of view it should be noted that procedural irregularities must reach a minimum threshold of seriousness for an act to become eligible for invalidation.[18] However, 'it can be argued that all procedural violations should be compensated because the purpose of the procedural right is to ensure feelings of just treatment as well as to minimise the risk of mistake in the outcome. In a proper case persons

---

[12] *Ibid.*, p. 447.   [13] *Ibid.*, p. 480 and at pp. 444–5.   [14] *Ibid.*, pp. 444–5.
[15] *Ibid.*, pp. 480 and 445.   [16] *Ibid.*, p. 447.   [17] *Ibid.*, pp. 485 and 461.
[18] C. F. Amerasinghe, *Principles of the Institutional Law of International Organisations* (Cambridge: Cambridge University Press, 1996), p. 181.

might recover damages for mental and emotional distress caused by the denial of procedural due process.'[19]

Before or after the merits of the case have been judged, or even examined, remand is possible. Although the choice is not to be justified by purely legal considerations,[20] it is in the interests of justice and fairness that the respondent be given another opportunity to take a decision, sometimes provided with some guidelines offered by the tribunal;[21] in this latter scenario, remand comes close to an order of specific performance.

Compensation

Compensation may be awarded as an alternative to annulment, rescission or specific performance. In some cases the UNAT has assessed the compensation, but in numerous cases it did not, in case the respondent chose not to carry out the order.[22] In many cases the ILOAT, after quashing the administrative decision, decided to award compensation as an alternative to rescission or reinstatement, although this was not always a very reasoned decision.[23] In all cases where the ILOAT annulled and rescinded the decision and offered the respondent the option of providing compensation, the dispute concerned the applicant's termination of service in one way or another.[24]

In cases where the respondent's wrongful act is considered to have caused additional damage to the claimant, compensation may operate as an additional remedy.

Compensation may even function as the sole remedy in circumstances in which, for a variety of reasons, other remedies are inappropriate or impossible.[25] This may, for instance, be the case when the decision taken by the respondent is valid but where there has been conduct that may be construed as a breach of some subsidiary obligation[26] or that may have given rise to subsidiary irregularities or improprieties committed by the respondent in connection with the actual decision, but without invalidating it.[27]

In other cases involving an invalid decision, restoration of the *status quo ante* may be impossible or the applicant may not have requested it, or

---

[19] D. Shelton, *Remedies in International Human Rights Law* (Oxford: Oxford University Press, 1999), p. 91.

[20] Amerasinghe, *Law of the International Civil Service*, p. 486.

[21] *Ibid.*, p. 462.   [22] *Ibid.*, pp. 482–3.   [23] *Ibid.*, p. 464.   [24] *Ibid.*, p. 458.

[25] *Ibid.*, p. 448.   [26] *Ibid.*, p. 467 (ILOAT).   [27] *Ibid.*, p. 491 (UNAT).

152   SUBSTANTIVE OUTCOME OF REMEDIAL ACTION

the circumstances of the case may merely indicate that other remedies are in fact appropriate or practical.[28]

Compensation may also be awarded either without an annulment or, conversely, without the tribunal characterising the decision as valid.[29]

In cases of non-renewal of fixed-term contracts, UNAT has never ordered a renewal of the contract, but has awarded compensation instead.[30]

Undue hardship suffered by the applicant may be compensated in unusual circumstances even when the conduct of the respondent was legally correct.[31]

The quantum of the compensation may be calculated either in terms of the salary earned or by way of a lump sum, whatever the injury.[32]

Although the compensation covers material damage and moral injury in appropriate cases, it is difficult to deduce principles applicable to the calculation of these separate headings as it is not always clear whether the award of compensation includes one or both.[33] The problem, of course, does not present itself in cases where the tribunal limits itself to confirming that the compensation offered by the respondent was adequate.[34]

In cases where moral injury can in fact be identified, compensation is generally reasonably modest.[35] It seems inevitable that the internal valuation scale of each tribunal will influence the calculation of moral injury,[36] but a larger degree of judicial reasoning would be welcome for reasons of both fairness and judicial accountability. In this respect the ILOAT's case law is more elaborate. Starting from the implicit obligation that the administrative authority must respect the dignity and reputation of staff members, grave injury or serious and unnecessary personal distress are required for moral injury to become eligible for compensation in cases of unlawful conduct by the respondent international organisation; the injury to dignity and reputation must be especially serious, and the unnecessary personal distress must be of a heinous nature when the conduct concerned is lawful.[37]

The ILOAT's performance as regards stating the reasoning behind the calculation of compensation is variable.[38] The UNAT has mentioned and applied certain general principles while maintaining a large element of judicial appreciation and discretion.[39] The principles include: *ne ultra petitum* but not in an absolute way; the scope of the commitments made and the conditions of their non-execution; the

---

[28] *Ibid.*, pp. 488 and 490.   [29] *Ibid.*, p. 466 (ILOAT).   [30] *Ibid.*, p. 487.   [31] *Ibid.*, p. 448.
[32] *Ibid.*, p. 449.   [33] *Ibid.*, pp. 449–50.   [34] *Ibid.*, p. 468 (ILOAT).   [35] *Ibid.*, p. 449.
[36] *Ibid.*, p. 451.   [37] *Ibid.*, p. 476.   [38] *Ibid.*, pp. 468–9.   [39] *Ibid.*, p. 494.

damage must not be too remote or indirect; and only actual loss will be compensated.[40]

It certainly cannot be said that in the decisions by the UNAT and ILOAT to award damages the most significant factors are the character of the applicant, the unanimity of the court and the procedural or substantive nature of the right violated.[41] On the other hand, the UNAT and ILOAT's case law apparently does not show that routine and non-controversial substantive violations or a pattern of non-compliance with procedural norms are more likely to give rise to damages.

International administrative tribunals have frequently had to consider the compatibility of administrative acts with the constitutional law of the international organisation or with the UN Charter itself. According to Ralph Zacklin, the tribunals have thus contributed to maintaining the organisations' responsibility as far as their duties in the international legal order are concerned.[42] On several occasions, however, claims presented to the UNAT under the Universal Declaration on Human Rights have generally been rejected as insubstantial.[43]

In a very small number of cases, particularly when there has been no material damage, the UNAT judgment itself was an adequate remedy for the moral injury when it resulted from some irregularity or impropriety committed by the respondent international organisation in connection with a decision whose validity could not be questioned.[44] In other cases the UNAT has awarded compensation because the administration had failed in its duties towards the applicant, whether or not there was a connection with the administrative decision – for example by unduly prolonging a dispute.[45]

Although the option of deciding between rescission and compensation lies within its powers and there is no ceiling for compensation provided in its Statute, the ILOAT generally follows a policy of restraint in awarding compensation.[46] The UNAT, for its part, has in exceptional cases and not without giving reasons exceeded the ceiling of two years' salary.[47]

---

[40] *Ibid.*, pp. 496–7.　　[41] ECHR case law as evaluated by Shelton, *Remedies*, p. 209.

[42] R. Zacklin, 'Responsabilité des Organisations internationales' in Société Française de Droit International: Colloque du Mans, *La Responsabilité dans le système international* (Paris: Pedone, 1990), pp. 91–100, at p. 93.

[43] J. Charney, 'Is International Law Threatened by Multiple International Tribunals?', *RCADI* 271 (1998), 101–382, at 221.

[44] Amerasinghe, *Law of the International Civil Service*, p. 493.

[45] *Ibid.*, pp. 492–3.　　[46] *Ibid.*, pp. 443 and 455.　　[47] *Ibid.*, pp. 443 and 480.

The problem of costs

Recently the problem of costs has been aptly described as a structural problem for the access to justice as a whole.[48] Thus it is not surprising that international administrative tribunals, too, have been confronted with this problem, although almost every international organisation reimburses the travel and subsistence expenses of the staff member and/or counsel when attending the hearing during the pre-litigation procedure.[49]

The Statutes of the UNAT and ILOAT contain no provisions explicitly authorising them to award costs. In a departure from the general principle in contentious proceedings before international tribunals that each party should bear its own costs, the UNAT and ILOAT have been exercising their inherent powers to meet such costs – they have a general policy covering this issue, and do not necessarily give detailed reasons in every single case.[50] They have both awarded costs in certain circumstances to unsuccessful applicants on grounds of equity, stressing their exceptional nature.[51] The maxim *ne ultra petitum* has not been applied in all cases, as the ILOAT has awarded costs even when the applicant has not requested them.[52]

While the ILOAT's competence to award costs has never been questioned by the international organisations accepting its jurisdiction,[53] the UN in 1950 did contest the UNAT's similar competence, which led to a UNAT statement of policy on 14 December 1950.[54] As a general rule, the simplicity of the proceedings before the tribunals results in no costs being awarded to successful applicants and thus *a fortiori* none to unsuccessful applicants either.[55] In practical terms the UNAT often awards costs to successful applicants but at a reduced level because of the potential representation by a member of the UN Panel of Counsel, and only if costs have been claimed.[56]

---

[48] E. Schmidt-Assmann and L. Harrings, 'Access to Justice and Fundamental Rights', *European Review of Public Law* 9 (1997), 529–49, at 544.

[49] C. De Cooker, 'Pre-litigation Procedures in International Organisations' in C. De Cooker (ed.), *International Administration: Law and Management in International Organisations* (looseleaf publication) (The Hague: Kluwer Law International), contribution VI, pp. 1–23, at p. 8.

[50] Amerasinghe, *Law of the International Civil Service*, pp. 452–4.

[51] *Ibid.*, pp. 551 and 454. [52] *Ibid.*, p. 545.

[53] *Ibid.*, p. 547. [54] *Ibid.*, p. 553. [55] *Ibid.*, p. 557.

[56] *Ibid.*, p. 554. 'Panels of counsel in disciplinary and appeals cases are composed of "*current and retired staff members*" from the United Nations Secretariat, UNDP, UNICEF and UNHCR and they provide "*information, advice and, where appropriate, representation*

Under the ILOAT's general policy as deduced from the *Lamardie* case,[57] successful applicants are entitled to costs to the extent warranted by the circumstances of the case, even if they have not expressly requested them or if they have not been assisted by counsel.[58] In one case a successful applicant was not awarded costs because he had unduly criticised the international organisation and its high officials.[59] The ILOAT has been generous in the way it awards costs, although, in general, international organisations coming within the scope of its jurisdiction do not make available to their staff members any mechanism similar to free legal assistance by the UN Panel of Counsel.[60]

Given the immunity normally granted to international organisations by domestic courts the question arises whether international administrative tribunals provide an adequate alternative remedial protection mechanism. August Reinisch supports the view that they generally satisfy the requirements imposed by due process, the rule of law and similar principles.[61] In his view, the danger that international organisations might actually be judges in their own matter and the inherent risk of bias or even a denial of justice seem to be unfounded in practice,[62] although this assessment is certainly not beyond controversy, as indicated earlier.[63]

> before the JAB, the JDC, the Administrative Tribunal and elsewhere"': A/55/57 of 7 March 2000, para. 46.

[57] *Lamardie*, ILOAT Judgment No. 262 (1975).

[58] Amerasinghe, *Law of the International Civil Service*, p. 547.   [59] *Ibid.*, p. 552.

[60] *Ibid.*, p. 547. In comparison, the Inter-American Court of Human Rights started only recently in part to award costs and fees, while the European Court of Human Rights awards costs and fees if they have been actually and necessarily incurred, and are reasonable as to their amount: Shelton, *Remedies*, pp. 158 and 173.

[61] A. Reinisch, *International Organisations before National Courts* (Cambridge: Cambridge University Press, 2000), p. 274.

[62] *Ibid.*, p. 269.

[63] See above, p. 83, and P. Klein, *La Responsabilité des organisations internationales dans les ordres juridiques internes et en droit des gens* (Brussels: Editions Bruylant and Editions de l'Université Libre de Bruxelles, 1998), p. 272.

15 Remedial outcome for private claimants

Contractual liability claims

The substantive outcome of remedial action based on a contractual liability claim is decisively determined by the UN applying its own internal law to its contractual activity, in most cases to the exclusion of any domestic law. Non-compliance with the terms of a contract between an international organisation and a private party may result in either party unilaterally invoking the resiliation clause and eventually applying for judicial enforcement, provided access to such a forum has been granted.

In most instances, problems arising under commercial agreements are resolved by means of direct negotiations between the parties.[1] Claims are reviewed 'on the basis of the contract terms, which we interpret in light of the proper law of the contract, the internal legal rules of the organisation where these have been referred to expressly or by implication in the contract and by application of the general principles of law and commercial practice and usage applicable to the transaction'.[2] As to arbitration, given the almost total absence of reference by the contracting parties to a particular law, and in accordance with Article 33 of the UNCITRAL Rules, the Arbitral Tribunal applies the law determined by the conflict of laws rules, which eventually leads to the application of the *lex mercatoria* and general principles of law, while still having due regard to the terms of the contract and the usages of the trade applicable to the transaction. Dorothée Meyer rightly pointed out that resort to UNCITRAL Rules offers 'un cadre plus favorable à la prise en compte

---

[1] A/C.5/49/65 of 24 April 1995, p. 3.

[2] Unpublished memorandum dated 5 February 1988 as cited by D. Meyer, 'Les Contrats de fournitures de biens et de services dans le cadre des opérations de maintien de la paix', *AFDI* 42 (1996) 79–119, at 116.

156

des intérêts onusiens en cas d'arbitrage'.[3] Under the applicable standard dispute settlement clause in the UN General Conditions of Contract, the Arbitral Tribunal has no authority to award punitive damages or to award interest.[4]

It has been a constant element of concern for those studying contractual claims by private contractors against the UN that even the information on the number of arbitration cases, be it only as regards their outcome, has been guarded with utmost discretion by the organisation.[5] In 1995 the UN Secretary-General merely reported that the UN has 'had recourse to arbitral proceedings in only a number of cases to date'.[6] His expectation that the number of arbitration proceedings might increase as a result of the expansion of UN peacekeeping operations[7] did in fact materialise between 1995 and 1998.[8] Pursuant to paragraph 2 of UN General Assembly Resolution 53/217 of 21 April 1999 the Secretary-General should report to the General Assembly any pending arbitration cases, while member states should be kept duly informed of all arbitration and settlement cases (paragraph 3 of the same Resolution).

Procurement-related arbitration cases

The Fifth Committee of the UN General Assembly has demanded more transparency with regard to the primary rules governing the procurement system, and it has welcomed the publication of the *Procurement Manual*.[9]

Both the original claims and the outcome of the remedial action in a number of procurement-related arbitration cases have been highlighted in the Report of the Office of Internal Oversight Services just referred to. Between 1995 and September 1998 legal action had been

---

[3] Meyer, 'Contrats de fournitures', 116.

[4] As referred to by P. Szasz, Working Paper, ILA Committee, p. 4: on file with the author.

[5] Estimates range from three (M. Hirsch, *The Responsibility of International Organisations Towards Third Parties: Some Basic Principles* (Dordrecht, Boston and London: Martinus Nijhoff Publishers, 1995), p. 126, note 161) to twelve cases (Meyer, 'Contrats de fournitures', 81, note 4).

[6] A/C.5/49/65, p. 3. [7] *Ibid.*, p. 4.

[8] *Report of the Office of Internal Oversight Services on the Review of Procurement-related Arbitration Cases*, of 1 March 1999, presented in response to General Assembly Resolution 52/226 A of 31 March 1998, A/53/843, para. 3. The UN was facing an unprecedented challenge in selecting reliable contractors while preparing contracts and subsequently overseeing their implementation because of the rapid deployment of often volatile peacekeeping operations (A/53/843, para. 4).

[9] A/54/511 of 27 October 1999.

158 SUBSTANTIVE OUTCOME OF REMEDIAL ACTION

initiated against the UN in twelve cases. Three cases with claims totalling (US) $40.7 million had been resolved through arbitration, three cases totalling $32.3 million were in arbitration or negotiations, one case involving a claim of $590,000 was withdrawn by the contractor, and one case, for an amount of $11.2 million, was awaiting arbitration proceedings. Two lawsuits with claims totalling $190.7 million were dismissed, but appeal and arbitration were likely.[10] The arbitration claims submitted by contractors amounted to $96.7 million, or 16 per cent of the total expenditure in the relevant areas. Arbitration awards and settlements had cost the organisation $26.7 million. Legal and arbitration fees amounted to $2.3 million, and interest on delayed payments totalled $4.8 million.[11]

In a case of supplying rations and drinking water to Mission A, an interlocutory award determined the validity of a settlement agreement conditionally entered into by the UN. Before the hearings on the merits, an offer of a lump-sum payment of $10.5 million by the organisation (the claim being $29.6 million) was rejected by the contractor. In the final award the contractor was awarded $14 million, the Tribunal rejecting his claims ($7.5 million) for punitive damages, lost profits, attorneys' fees and arbitration costs.[12] Part of the UN's counterclaim was also rejected.[13]

In another case of fuel storage and transportation services to Mission A, the contractor claimed a total amount of $2,730,146 before the Arbitral Tribunal. The Tribunal awarded the highest disputed amount to the contractor. The UN's counterclaim was partly rejected and it was ordered to pay all arbitration costs and 85 per cent of the contractor's legal costs.[14]

In the case of supplying rations to Mission B, the Arbitral Tribunal awarded $326,404 plus interest,[15] as demanded by the contractor. In the same cases with regard to Mission C $188,764 was awarded by the Tribunal to the claimant without interest and another $219,000 for gains in foreign exchange due to the strengthening of the US dollar against the German mark during the dispute.[16]

Another case involved a claim of $23.3 million for damages allegedly resulting from the UN's failure to adhere to its commercial agreements. The Tribunal awarded $4,688,808 and rejected the claim for legal fees and related costs. The Tribunal was also asked to rule on the transparency and objectivity of the organisation's procurement system, but

---

[10] A/53/843, para. 3.   [11] Ibid., para. 5.   [12] Ibid., paras. 26 and 27.
[13] Ibid., para. 29.   [14] Ibid., paras. 42 and 44–6.   [15] Ibid., para. 49.
[16] Ibid., paras. 54–5.

declared itself incompetent to rule on internal matters and dismissed the claim.[17]

In its Report, the Office of Internal Oversight Services identified unclear contractual terms that were subject to different interpretations, non-compliance with procurement rules and procedures by the mission procurement staff and inadequate contract administration in the field as major factors that had contributed to the substantial additional costs incurred by the organisation as a result of settlement agreements and arbitration cases. One of the main reasons for arbitration cases and legal action against the organisation has been the failure to pay undisputed invoices promptly in accordance with contract terms.[18]

In its comment on the OIOS Report the UN Department for Peacekeeping Operations suggested that an internal mechanism be developed to resolve commercial disputes in a more timely and cost-effective manner rather than resorting to arbitration proceedings.[19] The disadvantages for third parties of comprehensively internalising the mechanism are obvious from a remedial point of view and need no further elaboration here.

In Resolution 53/217, adopted on 7 April 1999, the General Assembly expressed its deep concern about the increase in pending procurement-related arbitration claims instituted against the UN, totalling $56 million as of 19 March 1999. The General Assembly requested that member states should be kept duly informed, *inter alia* by the Secretary-General clearly identifying arbitration and settlement cases as separate items in corresponding financial performance reports (paragraph 3).

On 14 October 1999 the Secretary-General submitted his report on procurement-related arbitration, pursuant to the request of the General Assembly in paragraph 2 of its Resolution 53/217. Out of the twelve arbitration cases that had been initiated against the UN between 1995 and September 1998, eleven related to peacekeeping activities while the twelfth case related to construction activities carried out by the UNDP; eight cases have been completed through either withdrawal, arbitral decision or settlement, leaving only four cases pending, amounting to a total of $14.95 million.[20] The main reasons for the arbitration

---

[17] *Ibid.*, paras. 57–8.   [18] *Ibid.*, para. 62 and A/54/393 of 23 September 1999, para. 66.
[19] A/54/393, para. 63.
[20] A/54/458 of 14 October 1999, paras. 4 and 25. The four pending cases are listed in an Annex to the Report, on p. 9. The claims in the eight other cases totalled $121.65 million, while the total amount the UN was obliged to pay under awards or in the

160 SUBSTANTIVE OUTCOME OF REMEDIAL ACTION

cases, identified by the Secretary-General, were the exponential growth in peacekeeping activities, the use of commercial vendors instead of traditional reliance on member state governments for the provision of a wide range of support services, an unwillingness on the part of the vendors to settle a claim amicably, claims considered to be unreasonable by the organisation, or the organisation having a strong legal case.[21] The number of cases could be reduced by addressing the major causes that had been identified by the OIOS in its Report: 'measures have been taken to ensure that contracts are clearly written and sound', 'a more proactive, preventive and streamlined approach for the handling of commercial contract issues, both before and after they reach the level of a dispute' will be identified; reviews of arbitral judgments 'aim to improve procurement processes, contract management as well as claims and dispute settlement and the process of arbitration', and the Secretariat is considering 'whether it is in the interests of the Organisation to have greater recourse to conciliation'.[22]

Tort liability claims

The law of the territorial jurisdiction where alleged damage has occurred, the *lex loci delicti commissi*, will govern the merits of a tort liability claim against an international organisation. This by definition entails an infinite variety of potential outcome in these cases[23] and, by the same token, constitutes a major, substantive obstacle in the extension of the existing international administrative tribunals' jurisdiction to include tort claims by private claimants.

In a departure from this scenario the UN General Assembly on 11 December 1986 decided to limit its tort liability by way of Headquarters Regulation No. 4 enacted in Resolution 41/220 covering all the premises included in the Headquarters Agreement with the United States. The

settlement of cases was $26.7 million. In one case the arbitration panel ruled in favour of the UN, rejecting all of the approximately $50 million in claims by the contractor: *ibid.*, para. 26. The Secretary-General also pointed out that while 'the total value of United Nations procurement since 1991 has been over $3 billion, the total value of procurement-related claims brought to arbitration during that period has been less than $140 million': *ibid.*, p. 8, note 2.

[21] *Ibid.*, paras. 5–6.   [22] *Ibid.*, paras. 8, 28, 32 and 34.

[23] In contrast, the remedy for non-contractual liability of the European Community is not only guaranteed and preserved by its judicial mechanism, but the system is, moreover, based on general principles common to the law of the member states. See further T. Heukels and A. McDonnell (eds.), *The Action for Damages in Community Law* (The Hague and London: Kluwer Law International, 1997).

General Assembly placed a limit on both economic and non-economic damages, at the same time excluding punitive or moral damages. The Regulation applies equally to both state and non-state entities falling within its territorial scope.

It should be noted that the limitation only applies to claims directed towards the UN itself or against one of its agents (for example, a staff member or a contractor) whom the UN is obliged to indemnify.[24] The Resolution and Regulation constitute an express waiver of jurisdictional immunity at least up to the monetary limit declared.[25] August Reinisch rightly stressed that the UN is not trying to hide behind the shield of immunity and that the relevant provisions of the Headquarters Agreement remain applicable.[26]

If it is determined that there is no liability on the part of the UN in respect of a particular claim arising from accidents involving vehicles operated by UN personnel for official purposes, and as a result no compensation is payable under its world-wide insurance policy, the organisation may decide to make an *ex gratia* payment depending on the circumstances of the particular case.[27]

A recent and prime example of civil tort claims for slander and libel brought before domestic courts against an expert on mission for the UN for words he had spoken in an interview gave rise to the dispute between the UN and Malaysia in the *Cumaraswamy* case.[28] The International Court of Justice unequivocally ruled that the issue of compensation for any damages incurred as a result of acts performed by the UN or by its agents acting in their official capacity should be settled in accordance with appropriate methods of settlement, for which the UN shall make provision.[29]

---

[24] A/C.5/49/65, para. 11.

[25] M. Singer, 'Jurisdictional Immunity of International Organisations: Human Rights and Functional Necessity Concerns', *Virginia Journal of International Law* 36 (1995), 53–165, at 86, note 144.

[26] A. Reinisch, *International Organisations before National Courts* (Cambridge: Cambridge University Press, 2000), p. 16, note 69.

[27] A/C.5/49/65, para. 14.

[28] *Difference Relating to Immunity from Legal Process of a Special Rapporteur of the Commission on Human Rights*, Advisory Opinion of 22 April 1999, *ICJ Reports* (1999): two commercial companies filed suit against the Special Rapporteur for damages amounting to approximately $12 million each, including exemplary damages for slander (para. 5). Another lawsuit was filed against the Special Rapporteur by a lawyer claiming damages amounting to $24 million (para. 11). New plaintiffs filed a third and a fourth lawsuit against the Special Rapporteur for $40 million and $24 million respectively (para. 12).

[29] *Ibid.*, p. 89, para. 66.

Counterclaims

The UN may have counterclaims against the claimant party arising from the same situation; if they have arisen from a different situation they are labelled 'set-offs'.[30] Particularly in the context of a lump-sum agreement between the UN and a government acting on behalf of its nationals the latter claims can be deducted, thus contributing to the lump-sum settlement constituting a finite limit to the financial responsibility of the organisation.[31]

The mechanism was used in the aftermath of ONUC in separate lump-sum agreements, with the governments of Belgium, Greece, Italy, Luxembourg and Switzerland providing for financial compensation of physical, material and moral damage based on estimates made unilaterally by the UN Legal Office. The amounts varied between the various member states but they largely did not correspond to an adequate level of financial compensation, the diplomatic efforts of the states concerned only having convinced the organisation to increase its initial offer slightly. In some cases victims have themselves been considered to have contributed to the occurrence of the acts which had caused the damage that gave rise to the claims.

In the Belgian case the UN accepted 581 out of 1,400 claims as being entitled to compensation. A lump-sum agreement amounting to $1.5 million was agreed as a final settlement of that matter. At the same time, a number of financial questions still outstanding between the UN and Belgium were settled. Payment was effected by offsetting the amount of $1.5 million against unpaid ONUC assessments amounting to approximately $3.2 million.[32] The compensation was apportioned among the private claimants based upon appreciations made by the UN.

The mechanism of lump-sum agreements has now been formally incorporated into the claim-settlement mechanism provided for in peacekeeping operations.

Peacekeeping operations

Given their complexity, both in terms of surrounding circumstances and the variety of actors involved, peacekeeping operations are likely to continue to give rise to a large number of claims. In order to reduce this number, general limitations and exclusions have been adopted in

---

[30] A/51/389 of 20 September 1996, para. 41.   [31] *Ibid.*, para. 35.   [32] *Ibid.*, note 8.

General Assembly Resolution 52/247 of 26 June 1998.[33] In addition to the procedural limitations and the exclusion imposed,[34] the UN's tortious liability has also been limited in the following way: compensation is limited to $50,000, the actual amount to be determined by reference to local compensation standards. No financial limitations are applicable to claims arising from gross negligence or wilful misconduct; the UN would assume liability to compensate a third party, retaining the right to seek recovery from the individual or the troop-contributing state concerned.[35]

Non-economic losses such as pain and suffering, moral anguish, indirect damages or those impossible to verify are excluded, as are punitive damages. Specified formulae will govern the calculation of damages to premises whereas reasonable costs of repair or replacement operate as limitations for the compensation of damages to property. In contrast to, for instance, ECHR's case law, the Resolution does not recognise 'that circumstances within a country may make it difficult if not impossible to adduce the evidence necessary to prove specific values for pecuniary harm'.[36]

As an observation of a more general nature, one could question whether the restriction imposed by the public policy of the organisation on the remedies available is not going beyond the minimum which, according to E. Rabel as cited by Christine Gray,[37] should ensure that as

---

[33] What triggered the call to limit UN liability was an undocumented joint claim submitted by Bosnia and Herzegovina against the UN in the amount of $70 million, of which $64 million was for damages caused in the normal use of roads, bridges and parking places by UN vehicles. In receiving notice of the claim, the Advisory Committee on Administrative and Budgetary Questions noted 'This sort of information is, in the view of the Committee, compelling evidence of the need for the United Nations to develop, as quickly as possible, effective measures which could limit its liability': as cited by D. Shraga, 'UN Peacekeeping Operations: Applicability of International Humanitarian Law and Responsibility for Operations-related Damage', *AJIL* 94 (2000), 406–12, at 410, note 24.

[34] See above, p. 102

[35] A/51/903 of 21 May 1997, para. 14. According to the UN Secretary-General 'the statutory basis for imposing financial liability for gross negligence is staff rule 112.3', a view that is supported by both the UN General Assembly and the UNAT. In the follow-up report on management irregularities causing financial losses to the organisation, the Secretary-General outlined the procedures he is developing for determining gross negligence and for the effective implementation of staff rule 112.3 for financial recovery. In doing so, the due process rights of staff members will be respected: A/54/793 of 13 March 2000, paras. 8, 10 and 11. Cases may be referred to the Joint Disciplinary Committee and/or the Local Property Survey Board, the decisions of which may be appealed to the Joint Appeals Board: *ibid.*, paras. 14 and 15.

[36] As referred to by D. Shelton, *Remedies in International Human Rights Law* (Oxford: Oxford University Press, 1999), p. 235.

[37] C. Gray, *Judicial Remedies in International Law* (Oxford: Clarendon Press, 1987), p. 10.

far as possible the extent of the compensation and the nature of the remedy should be governed by the *lex causae*.

The financial and temporal limitations derogate from the general principles of liability in tort. They have to be consistent with relevant practice in other fields of international law, where limited liability is recognised,[38] and from an accountability point of view it is important to strike a balance 'between considerations of justice and fairness to potential claimants, and the interests of the Organisation'.[39] The financial limitations are applicable to both state and non-state claimants.

Although Paul Szasz is right in pointing out that the legal validity of these limitations will be ensured within the territory of the state concerned through their inclusion in SOFAs,[40] it certainly does not follow that the territorial state is thereby barred from contesting, on behalf of one of its nationals, the actual application of these limitations and their financial outcome. The financial and temporal limitations would also be binding upon a potential claimant who chose to institute proceedings before the local claims review board, because such limitations would be included in their terms of reference.[41]

As far as members of national contingents of peacekeeping operations are concerned, the aforementioned service-incurred damages system[42] has over the years been gradually made applicable to them in their capacity as agents of the organisation. By way of reimbursement to the troop-contributing state of any compensation it has already paid out, a maximum of $40,000 has been fixed by the UN in the case of death.[43]

In the vast majority of cases the offer of an amount for the settlement of third-party claims for compensation for personal injury/death or property loss/damage related to UN peacekeeping operations is accepted.[44]

In the case of peacekeeping forces not financed under the regular UN budget but partly funded by the troop-contributing states, the remedial outcome for the settlement of any claims that are not settled by the troop-contributing countries or the host country has been determined 'within the limits of available voluntary contributions'.[45]

---

[38] Shraga, 'UN Peacekeeping Operations', 410.   [39] *Ibid.*

[40] General Assembly Resolution 52/247, para. 12. See also P. Szasz, Working Paper, ILA Committee, p. 11: on file with the author.

[41] General Assembly Resolution 52/247, para. 13 and A/51/903, para. 41.

[42] See above, p. 73.

[43] It should be noted that the UN, before the occurrence of such events, pays $1,000 per month and per member of a contingent to the troop-contributing country.

[44] A/C.5/49/65, para. 19.   [45] For example, UNFICYP Regulations, para. 16.

When UN peacekeeping operations are followed by, for example, an Implementation Force and later by a Stabilisation Force, the compensation regime for damages caused again becomes national, providing, however, for larger involvement of the host state.[46]

It is worth recalling that the Belgian League for the Defence of Human Rights in its 1963 Report suggested that the UN should establish a Guarantee Fund based on voluntary contributions from member states. The Fund's intervention for the compensation of victims in cases of damages caused by acts performed in the lawful exercise of hostilities during peacekeeping operations would depend entirely on the relationship between damage and UN action being proven. The Fund never came into existence, however.[47]

The exceptions and limitations to the liability of the UN in peacekeeping operations are mainly justified because the funds from which third-party claims are paid are public funds contributed by the member states for the purpose of financing the activities of the organisation as mandated by those member states; any additional compensation should, in the Secretary-General's opinion, come from the host government as the 'beneficiary' of the operation.[48] In the absence of a general or particular norm obliging host states to provide such additional compensation, claimants may be left without a remedial outcome for damage in excess of the UN's limited liability.

Under the claims-settlement mechanism currently provided for peacekeeping operations, only financial compensation is available as a remedy to claimants. In the Model SOFA it has been provided that the Special Representative/Force Commander or the UN Secretary-General shall use their best endeavours to ensure compliance with a final and binding award if rendered against a member of the peacekeeping operation.[49]

Ex gratia *payments*

In its Report, the Commission of Inquiry that was established pursuant to UN Security Council Resolution 885 (1993) to investigate armed attacks on UNOSOM II personnel that led to casualties among

---

[46] See, for instance, M. Guillaume, 'La Réparation des dommages causés par les contingents français en Ex-Yougoslavie et en Albanie', AFDI 43 (1997), 151–66.

[47] P. Klein, La Responsabilité des organisations internationales dans les ordres juridiques internes et en droit des gens (Brussels: Editions Bruylant and Editions de l'Université Libre de Bruxelles, 1998), p. 112. The Inter-American Court of Human Rights has established a Trust Fund for victims: Shelton, Remedies, p. 290.

[48] A/51/903, para. 12.   [49] A/45/594, para. 51.

166 SUBSTANTIVE OUTCOME OF REMEDIAL ACTION

them recommended that without prejudice to who bears legal liability, *ex gratia* payments should be considered for those innocent Somali civilians who suffered injury as a consequence of UNOSOM II's implementation of Security Council Resolution 837 (1993). The Commission of Inquiry added that it might be convenient to set up a mechanism under the UN to determine the criteria for granting such payments.[50] *Ex gratia* payments had been made with regard to earlier peacekeeping operations such as ONUC, where the exact degree of responsibility on the part of the UN itself would probably never be precisely determined, neither in law nor in fact.[51]

Judicial bodies called upon to settle a dispute as to tortious liability or organisational responsibility may eventually recommend such *ex gratia* payments based on considerations of equity, 'particularly in cases in which one of the litigants is at a marked disadvantage in relation to the other'.[52]

Increasing reliance by international organisations on *ex gratia* payments may in fact also be caused by the lack of adequate and equivalent legal protection mechanisms. Whatever the decisive reason prompting international organisations to make *ex gratia* payments, their very occurrence would certainly maintain if not increase the inequality between the parties that would exist were more traditional remedies to be chosen.

---

[50] S/1994/653, *Report of the Commission of Inquiry established Pursuant to Security Council 885 (1993) to Investigate Armed Attacks on UNOSOM II Personnel which led to Casualties among them*, of 1 June 1994, paras. 264–5.

[51] P. De Visscher, 'Observations sur le fondement et la mise-en-oeuvre du principe de la responsabilité de l'organisation des Nations Unies', *Revue de Droit International et de Droit Comparé* 40 (1963), 165–73, at 172.

[52] C. W. Jenks, *The Proper Law of International Organisations* (London and New York: Stevens and Oceana, 1962), p. 110.

PART IV · ALTERNATIVE REMEDIAL ACTION AGAINST INTERNATIONAL ORGANISATIONS AND OPTIONS FOR THE FUTURE

16 Introduction to alternative remedial action against international organisations and options for the future

In Part I of this study, remedies against international organisations were placed within the context of the overall accountability regime for these actors, against the background of the more general problem of remedies in international law and in comparison with remedies normally available against states. The various remedies have to be appropriate for the different levels of accountability and entail different standing for potential claimants.

Part II was devoted to procedural aspects of remedial action envisaged by the various categories of claimants, with non-state claimants facing the common procedural obstacle of the jurisdictional immunity of international organisations before domestic courts.

The different substantive outcome of remedial action undertaken by staff members and private claimants was reviewed in Part III.

Based upon the analysis made so far, this fourth and final Part looks at alternative remedial action and some options for the future. Attention will be paid to pre-remedial action (chapter 17), to non-legal alternative remedial action (chapter 18), to amending existing judicial remedies (chapter 19) and to the inevitable role for the International Court of Justice (chapter 20), so that they can fit in with the unusual status of international organisations.[1]

A few more general observations are appropriate at this stage.

The existence of a legal obligation incumbent upon international organisations to provide remedial mechanisms to states and non-state entities whose interests, legal or otherwise, have been or are likely to be affected by acts, actions or omissions of international organisations

---

[1] C. Eagleton, 'International Organisations and the Law of Responsibility', *RCADI* 76 (1950), 323–423, at 402.

cannot seriously be doubted. The capacity of an international organisation to provide appropriate remedies of course does not have to depend on this remedial action serving the pursuance of the organisation's objectives as laid down in its constituent instrument. Jean-Pierre Ritter argued convincingly that the ICJ's ruling in the *Reparations* case, that 'the rights and *duties* of an entity such as the Organisation must depend upon its purposes and functions', should not, given the context, be interpreted literally.[2] This is further corroborated by Judge Krylov when, in his Dissenting Opinion, he referred to 'the situation in which the said State may find it desirable and necessary to protect the agent against the acts of the Organisation itself'.[3]

Given the proliferation of their activities and the ensuing variety of disputes involving international organisations as a respondent party, it would be unwise and unrealistic to attempt and to expect to accommodate adequately the diversity of claims by providing one single, comprehensive, all-encompassing remedial mechanism. As became clear in Part I, the remedies have to be tailor-made for the level of accountability at stake, the category of claimant and thus also for the interests that are in need of remedial protection. To maximise accountability a combination of remedial mechanisms seems inevitable. In some areas the institution of an ombudsman may be appropriate, while other areas may call for the establishment of an Inspection Panel or a Commission of Inquiry, followed by resorting to quasi-judicial or judicial organs possessing the power to issue binding decisions addressed to the respondent international organisation or official. The choice or consecutive utilisation of these various mechanisms will be determined by the particular context of the claim being put forward, the standing of the claimant and the expected remedial outcome. In the latter respect, it should be recalled that issuing an injunction or a declaration may provide little comfort to individuals who have suffered considerable losses, and retrospective remedies such as the award of damages are inadequate when public-interest claims have been brought.[4]

---

[2] J.-P. Ritter, 'La Protection diplomatique à l'égard d'une organisation internationale', *AFDI* 8 (1962), 427–56, at 430, note 12 (emphasis added by Ritter).

[3] *Reparations for Injuries Suffered in the Service of the United Nations*, Advisory Opinion, *ICJ Reports* (1949), p. 174, Dissenting Opinion by Judge Krylov, at p. 219.

[4] S. Prechal, 'EC Requirements for an Effective Remedy' in J. Lonbay and A. Briondi (eds.), *Remedies for Breach of EC Law* (Chichester: John Wiley and Sons, 1997), pp. 3–13, at p. 11, and C. Gray, *Judicial Remedies in International Law* (Oxford: Clarendon Press, 1987), pp. 64–6.

The tendency in practice in particular areas of the relationship between an international organisation and potential claimants is to settle issues of accountability in a pragmatic way rather than through formal mechanisms and this may be perceived by either or both parties to the dispute as being appropriate. This study has, however, already pointed out the compelling need to take into account the inherent imbalance of power between international organisations and non-state claimants in order to bring the remedial action within the parameters of adequate alternative settlement mechanisms. From that perspective, informal channels of settlement should be looked upon with all due caution.

Both traditional and alternative remedial mechanisms have to comply with the principle of effectiveness, which plays a pivotal role in any accountability regime: the principle permeates all the different stages of the remedial action – pre-remedial through the obligation to provide reasons for a particular decision taken, the procedural issue of access and standing and the remedial outcome.[5] An effective remedy has to produce the desired result, and it has to be proportional and dissuasive.[6] The fact remains, however, that a remedy's effectiveness will be assessed differently from the point of view of an individual claimant compared with the approach taken, for instance, by a representational non-governmental organisation claiming to further the wider general interest;[7] this dichotomy is inherent because of the particular features of the accountability regime of international organisations, of which remedial action is an integral part.

[5] Prechal, 'EC Requirements', p. 4.   [6] *Ibid.*, pp. 9–10.   [7] *Ibid.*, p. 12.

17 Pre-remedial action

It is hard to overestimate the importance of pre-remedial action because of its prospective nature and thus its preventive potential; several aspects deserve to be mentioned here.

Pre-remedial efforts by international organisations with regard to operational activities should include mechanisms early on as part of the planning process, enabling those put at risk – for instance, by a proposed development project – to protest at the adequacy or opportunity of the undertaking or to demand alternative, less damaging means of implementing the goals sought.[1] More generally, the entitlement of an individual to be heard prior to an administrative authority taking a decision that affects him/her in his/her interests or rights is a central standard of administrative justice[2] with a large pre-remedial effect.

A prerequisite for an effective accountability regime of international organisations, apart from their willingness to implement it, is the existence of a clear and well-defined set of rules: the viability of remedial mechanisms depends in the first place on the existence of a coherent body of substantive rules, norms and practices governing the decisions, acts and operational conduct of international organisations. The responsibility for establishing such a comprehensive framework is not made easy by the variety of political and legal levels on which international organisations function; this responsibility can thus only be a joint one, shared by the international community, national legislators, member

---

[1] James N. Paul, 'Law and Development in the 1990s: Using International Law to Impose Accountability to People on International Development Actors', *Third World Legal Studies* (1992), 1–16, at 3 (actually referring to the possibility of contesting the legality of the endeavour).

[2] H. Nehl, *Principles of Administrative Procedure in EC Law* (Oxford: Hart Publishing, 1999), pp. 70–1.

states and the organisations themselves: they all have a distinct role to play in providing the yardsticks that are pre-conditional for the proper functioning of any remedial mechanism.

Peter Bekker has drafted a proposal for a basic provision concerning official activities for inclusion in the constituent instruments of international organisations, which should be elaborated in internal operative rules, including administrative circulars, instructions, guidelines and regulations.[3] Such a body of constitutional and secondary internal law could then be used as parameters in an objective assessment in a dispute settlement mechanism as to whether acts, actions or omissions of the international organisation, and ensuing tort, have arisen in the course of official functions: the inherent right of an international organisation to qualify its activities unilaterally is not unlimited and, from an accountability point of view, has to be subject to external review.

With regard to the first level of accountability, a set of recommended rules and practices may be emerging that are (or will be) commonly applicable to all international organisations, in addition and complementary to specific primary rules laid down in each organisation's constituent instrument. Those rules and recommended practices, such as the ones listed in the ILA Committee's Second Report,[4] are derived from the principles of good faith, constitutionality, institutional balance, supervision and control, and from the principles of stating the reasons, proportionality, procedural regularity, objectivity and impartiality, due diligence and promoting justice.

Contractual and non-contractual liability are governed by a combination of domestic law and elements of the internal law of the international organisation. Both domestic legislators and international organisations have to ensure that the system of applicable norms is coherent, avoiding duplication and lacunae while maintaining the essential balance between respecting the autonomous decision-making power of the organisation and ensuring that the accountability regime does

---

[3] P. Bekker, *The Legal Position of Intergovernmental Organisations: A Functional Necessity Analysis of their Legal Status and Immunities* (Boston and London: Martinus Nijhoff Publishers, 1994), p. 178: 'The official activities of the organisation shall, for the purposes of this Protocol/convention, etc. . . . be such as are strictly necessary for the (administrative/technical/etc.) operation of the organisation in the exercise of its functions and the fulfilment of its purposes, such to be determined ultimately and conclusively and in good faith by the organisation itself, acting through its chief administrative officer (or other person or body).'

[4] ILA Committee on Accountability of International Organisations, *Second Report*, submitted to the 69th ILA Conference (London, 2000), pp. 10–18.

not leave any gaps. The publication of Manual Handbooks setting out the framework for areas such as contracts with non-state third parties and a body of tort law with regard to operational activities appears to be a minimal requirement for the international organisations.

Mention could be made in this regard of the 1963 proposal formulated by the Belgian Human Rights League, which was aimed at the UN elaborating a body of civil responsibility law internal to the organisation, which was to be based on general principles of law recognised by civilised nations, its territorial scope extending to the Headquarters District and damages arising from activities undertaken by the organisation on the territories of its member states.[5] Implementation of the proposal – if coupled with a corresponding adequate remedial mechanism, either through the extension of the jurisdiction of international administrative tribunals[6] or an expanded role for domestic courts[7] – could have provided substantially greater predictability and guarantees to potential non-state claimants *vis-à-vis* international organisations than is currently the case.

At the level of organisational responsibility, the *institutional* relationship between the organisation and member states is governed by the constituent instrument, Headquarters Agreements and Agreements on Privileges and Immunities, supplemented by general international law to the extent called for by the functional limits of the organisation's objectives and powers and, beyond that, by fundamental human rights law. In addition, *operational* responsibility will arise under agreements with troop-contributing countries and host states. The elaboration of model agreements has been a major step forward, contributing to the coherence of the applicable normative framework. The remedial potential might be affected by the high degree of flexibility necessitated by the particularities of each case or situation.

The establishment of a comprehensive set of norms governing the relationship between an international organisation and states, both inside and outside membership links, is, of course, a continuing process.[8] In elaborating primary rules for state conduct, more attention should be paid by states and expert organs to the potential application of these

---

[5] Cited and referred to by P. Klein, *La Responsabilité des organisations internationales dans les ordres juridiques internes et en droit des gens* (Brussels: Editions Bruylant and Editions de l'Université Libre de Bruxelles, 1998), pp. 111–12.

[6] See below, p. 202.   [7] See below, p. 208.

[8] P. Bekker, 'The Work of the International Law Commission on Relations between States and International Organisations Discontinued: An Assessment', *LJIL* 6 (1993), 3–16.

state-oriented rules to international organisations as the other main actors on the international scene.

It is equally important from a pre-remedial point of view that all the actors involved, and certainly the organisation concerned, should take the necessary measures to disseminate – on a wide scale and through appropriate channels of communication – the information on the availability and potential outcome of remedial mechanisms on the three levels of accountability. The need for adequate publicity on claims procedures, including specific information on the filing period and on the organisation's office to be notified, was also underlined by the UN Advisory Committee on Administrative and Budgetary Questions[9] and requires no further elaboration here. The adequacy of the existing mechanism is a separate issue, which should not prevent this pre-remedial action from being taken.

The pre-remedial potential of such an exercise to consolidate a recognisable body of generally accepted principles, rules and norms would result in a measure of uniformity and predictability in a way that would command the confidence of all the parties concerned.[10] The 'Code of Conduct' proposed by the UN Secretary-General in October 1997 was 'part of the establishment of a transparent and effective system of accountability'.[11] It consisted of four parts: provisions of the Charter and of the General Convention on Privileges and Immunities; the status of UN staff; core values to be expected, and basic rights and obligations; and expected performance and ensuring performance. Additionally, pursuant to paragraph 9 of General Assembly Resolution 52/252 adopted on 8 September 1998, the Secretary-General submitted appropriate regulations and rules governing the status, basic rights and duties of the Secretary-General, officials other than Secretariat officials and experts on mission.[12]

Member states do have the competence and the obligation to monitor and supervise the decisions and actions of international organisations. As a pre-remedial effort and as indicated earlier, they are able to invoke concerns of both a political and legal nature during the decision-making process when they consider the probable outcome of that process to be inappropriate, inadequate or illegal even under any of the applicable

---

[9] A/52/410 of 1 October 1997, p. 4, para. 15.

[10] C. W. Jenks, *The Proper Law of International Organisations* (London and New York: Stevens and Oceana, 1962), pp. 113–14.

[11] A/52/488 of 17 October 1997, para. 1.

[12] Respectively in A/54/710 of 24 February 2000 and A/54/695 of 29 December 1999.

legal layers – acting either on their own initiative or on behalf of their citizens.[13] The role of their national parliaments, however, is such that one cannot envisage them being involved in the day-to-day business of formulating specific instructions for national delegations.[14]

A major element in the pre-remedial action is to be found, of course, in compliance by the organisations and their officials, agents and experts with the applicable norms and rules, whatever the legal and political context: incorporation of existing principles, rules and norms by international organisations in their internal operational guidelines and directives is a basic requirement of good governance, while at the same time constituting a vital precondition for successfully resorting to both non-legal and legal remedial mechanisms. Internal monitoring of compliance takes place through offices of internal oversight and control and inspection units, and this is followed, if need be, by disciplinary measures against officials and agents for (gross) negligence or wilful misconduct. It goes without saying that international organisations have to conduct themselves in such a way as to avoid needless harm or injury to other parties and thus claims against the organisation.[15]

---

[13] Bekker, *Legal Position*, p. 177.

[14] R. Gerster, 'Accountability of Executive Directors in the Bretton Woods Institutions', *JWTL* 27 (1993), 87–116, at 94.

[15] *Difference Relating to Immunity from Legal Process of a Special Rapporteur of the Commission on Human Rights*, Advisory Opinion of 22 April 1999, *ICJ Reports* (1999), p. 62, at p. 89, para. 66.

18   Non-legal alternative remedial action

The potential sequence of and interaction between political and legal remedies has been referred to earlier and is a natural consequence of the inter-linkage between the administrative, financial, political and legal forms of accountability. Based upon the analysis in the previous Parts of this study and taking into account the deficiencies, inadequacies and the insufficient degree of remedial potential (in terms of availability, procedural access and substantive outcome) in existing mechanisms for the various categories of potential claimants, this chapter now reviews non-legal alternative remedial actions. The extent to which the instruments considered here are able to fulfil a remedial purpose may vary, but they certainly should not be considered as mutually exclusive alternatives, quite the contrary: together with the amendment of existing judicial remedies, which will be dealt with in the next chapter, they present converging remedial opportunities *vis-à-vis* international organisations.

Suffice it to recall that non-legal remedial mechanisms address situations where the non-performance of non-legal obligations results in mere interests potentially or actually being affected, harm being caused but without there being any form of liability or responsibility on the part of the international organisation. As already seen, in such situations, because of the absence of any kind of legal relationship between the non-state entity and the organisation involved, no accountability is provided towards non-state actors. Non-legal remedies could provide suitable alternatives to the lack or insufficiency of mechanisms of redress by granting private parties direct access to a particular mechanism or office, eventually in combination with or followed by diplomatic protection by the national state *vis-à-vis* the organisation.

Whereas the first two alternative remedial mechanisms (ombudsman and inspection panel) are basically open to individual claimants or

177

178 ALTERNATIVE REMEDIAL ACTION AND FUTURE OPTIONS

requesters, the establishment and use of an independent Commission of Inquiry is mostly bound to fulfil a remedial function having a collective nature, although this does not necessarily always have to be the case. Resorting to these non-legal alternatives answers the grave objections raised by Wilfred Jenks on general grounds of public policy against attempts to establish *actio popularis* by way of real litigation; indeed, these non-legal alternative remedial actions could be instituted at 'the instance of private interests which, without being in a position to claim that a legally vested right has been violated, may be adversely affected'[1] by a decision or a course of action of an international organisation.

The ombudsman model

The ombudsman is a complaint-handling mechanism that attempts to improve the accountability of public bodies and authorities; turning to it could constitute one of the non-legal alternative remedial actions against international organisations. According to one leading authority, the essential conditions for its effective operation, and thus remedial impact, are independence, an impartial stance and broad powers of investigation.[2] Speed, informality and accessibility are considered to be some of the advantages of the ombudsman. Conversely, the ombudsman normally lacks the power to make binding decisions, but uses persuasion to obtain changes in the conduct of the public body or authority through the implementation of recommendations issued by the office.[3] The first level of accountability seems to require exactly this kind of non-legal remedial outcome.

The establishment of ombudsman offices has been rapidly proliferating and offices are now in existence in more than ninety countries. Particularly relevant here is the establishment of the European Ombudsman[4] to act in an extra-judicial capacity alongside the traditional role of the courts,[5] as an intermediary between the European

---

[1] C. W. Jenks, *International Immunities* (London and New York: Stevens & Sons and Oceana Publications, 1961), p. 164.

[2] R. Linda (ed.), *The International Ombudsman Anthology: Selected Writings from the International Ombudsman Institute* (The Hague, London and Boston: Kluwer Law International, 1999), p. xxiii.

[3] *Ibid.*

[4] Under the Maastricht Treaty on European Union and consolidated in the Amsterdam Treaty: Articles 21 and 195.

[5] H. Nehl, *Principles of Administrative Procedure in EC Law* (Oxford: Hart Publishing, 1999), p. 19.

NON-LEGAL ALTERNATIVE REMEDIAL ACTION 179

citizen and the European Institutions. A fact that should therefore be duly noted is that here an international organisation of an 'integrationist' type (namely the European Community) in which direct jurisdictional links between the organs of the organisation and private individuals exist, coupled with a fully fledged system of judicial protection, has none the less considered it necessary and appropriate to establish an ombudsman as an additional alternative non-legal remedial mechanism.

For present purposes it is sufficient to indicate the following elements from the Statute of the Ombudsman as it has been adopted by the European Parliament.[6] All residents of member states and companies registered in a member state are able to submit, even confidentially, a complaint on maladministration in the activities emanating from Community institutions or bodies, except for the judicial role of the ECJ and the CFI. 'Maladministration occurs when a public body fails to act in accordance with the rule or principle which is binding upon it.'[7] Complaints concerning political matters are inadmissible, as are complaints on matters that are or have been the subject of legal proceedings. In conducting inquiries for which he finds grounds, the Ombudsman has access to the necessary information except when considerations of secrecy, to be interpreted narrowly, are being invoked. The Community institution or body concerned, when informed about the complaint, may decide to settle the case of maladministration to the satisfaction of the complainant, after which the case is closed. Alternatively, instances of maladministration having general implications or where maladministration has not been eliminated may lead to the drafting of non-binding recommendations addressed to the institution concerned.

Petitions may since 1987 be addressed to the Committee on Petitions of the European Parliament, which is competent to hear complaints concerning both political and administrative matters. Only new evidence may lead the Ombudsman to open an inquiry into a complaint that has already been dealt with by the Committee on Petitions.

From a remedial point of view there seems to be sufficient reason to argue in favour of other international organisations following the example of the European Communities and of the European Union and to set up an ombudsman's office along the same lines of admissibility of

---

[6] Decision of the European Parliament of 9 March 1994 on the regulations and general conditions governing the performance of the Ombudsman's duties [1994] OJ L113/15, 4 May 1994.

[7] *Annual Report of the Ombudsman* 1997, p. 21.

180 ALTERNATIVE REMEDIAL ACTION AND FUTURE OPTIONS

complaints and competences; the need for such an alternative non-legal mechanism and its way of operating are not decisively determined by the particular integrationist features of the European Community. The adaptation of the ombudsman model so far found in some international organisations is limited to the informal settlement of employment disputes (as in the WHO, UNICEF, ICAO, IBRD and EBRD).[8] A combination with the right of petition also seems perfectly plausible in order to cover both the administrative and political aspects of the first level of accountability: additionally, the proper exercise of discretionary powers by the administration – that is, whether it has been exercised within the established limits – would come under scrutiny, although the prerogative powers themselves are non-justiciable. Judicial review and supervision by an ombudsman could thus be considered complementary remedial mechanisms, which would maximise accountability.

Compared with the non-legal alternative mechanism to be considered in the next section there is no need to be 'a party' to the issue in order to complain, in the sense of

[having to demonstrate] that its rights or interests have been or are likely to be directly affected by an action or omission [of the Bank] as a result of a failure [of the Bank] to follow its operational policies and procedures with respect to the design, appraisal and/or implementation of a project [financed by the Bank] (including situations where the Bank is alleged to have failed in its follow-up on the borrower's obligations under loan agreements with respect to such policies and procedures) provided in all cases that such failure has had, or threatens to have, a material adverse effect.[9]

The remedial potential is open to an unlimited group of non-state claimants, although under the European model all internal claims possibilities must first have been exhausted in cases of complaints regarding employment relations: this is a reasonable condition of admissibility for other international organisations as well.[10]

---

[8] UNDP, UNICEF and the UNCHR have established their own ombudsman systems: A/55/57 of 7 March 2000, paras. 27–33. The Joint Inspection Unit recommended 'the establishment of a full-time Ombudsman function responsible for settling all types of staff-management disputes through informal conciliation, mediation or negotiation procedures designed to eschew the institution of adversary procedures': *ibid.*, para. 149.

[9] Resolution establishing the World Bank Inspection Panel adopted on 22 September 1993 by the Executive Directors of the IBRD, para. 12, *ILM* 34 (1995), p. 521.

[10] *Contra*: C. De Cooker, 'Pre-litigation Procedures in International Organisations' in C. De Cooker (ed.), *International Administration: Law and Management in International Organisations* (looseleaf publication) (The Hague: Kluwer Law International),

As a non-legal alternative remedial mechanism the functioning and reports of an ombudsman could, in spite of the non-binding nature of its recommendations, lead member states of an international organisation to resort more efficiently to political remedies (such as those indicated in Part I) because they would be better informed.

The distinct, remedial role of an ombudsman within the accountability regime of international organisations becomes more important as its complementary character is so low given the limited availability of other non-legal or legal remedial opportunities and mechanisms. In the UN, for instance, an ombudsman would be complementary to other non-legal mechanisms of accountability such as the Joint Inspection Unit and the Office of Internal Oversight Services. In the light of the analysis conducted in the previous Parts of this study it is clear that the procedural review by an organ such as an ombudsman could not compensate for the absence of a substantive judicial review.

It is interesting to note that among the lessons learnt from recent peacekeeping operations under the heading 'relations with local populations', the designation of an ombudsman to consider the grievances of the local population against the mission or its staff has been suggested. Erskine Childers and Brian Urquhart had a more far-reaching function in mind as the ombudsman they envisaged would monitor the peacekeeping force's compliance with human rights standards. The function was needed 'as much to protect the organisation from false or inflated charges of Human Rights abuses as to ensure that if these occur they are properly investigated and reported'.[11]

The inspection panel model[12]

For reasons indicated earlier, individuals and other non-state entities are unlikely to be successful in bringing claims against an international organisation, when such claims are based on liability under domestic law, due to jurisdictional immunity being upheld. They are unlikely to be successful either with claims for organisational responsibility under

contribution VI, pp. 1–23, at p. 15 because he considers them to be outside the formal framework of pre-litigation procedures.

[11] E. Childers and B. Urquhart, *Renewing the UN System* (Uppsala, Sweden: D. Hammarskjold Foundation, 1994), p. 111.

[12] I acknowledge the contribution of the working papers submitted in the years 1997–2000 during the Leyden LL.M. course on the accountability of international organisations, particularly those of Hans Wassgren and Alexander Orakhelashvili.

182 ALTERNATIVE REMEDIAL ACTION AND FUTURE OPTIONS

international law because of a lack of *locus standi*. Is that a convincing reason to look for alternative remedial mechanisms along the lines of independent inspection panels or are these designed to serve different purposes?

The World Bank Inspection Panel

The first initiative to establish an Inspection Panel was taken by the World Bank in 1993,[13] followed later by the Inter-American Development Bank and the Asian Development Bank. Recently one of the leading authorities on the matter has succinctly and aptly described the Panel in the following terms. It is:

an independent investigatory body receiving and investigating complaints of people in the territory of a borrower whose rights or interests are adversely affected by the Bank's failure to comply with its policies and procedures in the design, appraisal and implementation of Bank-financed projects. To that end, the Panel has a mandate to investigate, upon authorisation by the Bank's Board of Executive Directors, the complaints brought before it, in its reports on the investigation providing the Board with an independent review of controversial Bank-financed projects and an assessment to what extent the Bank actually lives up to the standards it has set for itself in its operations.[14]

The functioning and procedures of the World Bank Inspection Panel mechanism and its case record are well known and have been comprehensively commented upon in doctrinal writings;[15] from a remedial perspective the following elements appear to be particularly relevant.

In the first stage of the procedure the Bank's management is given an opportunity to respond to the concerns expressed in the request. This is a common feature of other non-legal remedial mechanisms such as the ombudsman model and the pre-litigation procedures for staff members, and is an expression of the very purpose of the rule of exhaustion of internal remedies.

[13] On the history of the World Bank Inspection Panel, see I. Shihata, *The World Bank Inspection Panel* (Oxford: Oxford University Press, 1994), and more recently by the same author *The World Bank Inspection Panel in Practice* (Washington, DC: Oxford University Press, 2nd edn, 2000).

[14] S. Schlemmer-Schulte, 'Introductory Note to the Conclusions of the Second Review of the World Bank Inspection Panel', *ILM* 39 (2000), 243–8, at 243.

[15] See, *inter alia*: D. Bradlow and S. Schlemmer-Schulte, 'The World Bank's New Inspection Panel: A Constructive Step in the Transformation of the International Legal Order', *ZAÖRV* 54 (1994), 392–415, and S. Schlemmer-Schulte, 'The World Bank's Experience with its Inspection Panel', *ZAÖRV* 58 (1998), 353–88.

The eligibility threshold *ratione materiae* is relatively low as also 'likely' material and harm to rights or interests would meet the requirement, limited by the application of the *de minimis* rule to the violation of operational policies and procedures allegedly causing that harm.

The case law of the Inspection Panel has demonstrated that a request for investigation in respect of the violation of non-material rights or interests is admissible when such violation directly resulted from the material harm. Although the requesters have to demonstrate a causal link between the Bank's actions or omissions and the adverse effect, the Resolution establishing the Panel does not require additional proof of fault. There is no presumption of fault on the part of the Bank either – there is, rather, a prima facie presumption *by member states* that the Bank's projects do meet their own internal standards – but management has to provide evidence to the Panel that it has complied with the applicable operational policies and procedures.

The eligibility threshold *ratione personae* requires, *inter alia*, a community of persons such as an organisation, association, society or other grouping of individuals, in the territory of the borrower; an affected party may be represented by a local representative.

In fact, any two or more people sharing some common interests or concerns would fulfil that requirement under the 1996 Clarifications. The limitation not to allow a single individual to submit a request does not deny the rights and interests of individuals as such. It has been rightly observed that this contrasts with the more formalistic approach of the UN when it recognises the international status of certain non-governmental organisations by granting them the opportunity to participate[16] in the organisation's activities.

The decision actually to conduct an investigation is, in contrast to the ombudsman approach, and like the Commissions of Inquiry to be discussed in the next section, not to be taken independently by the Inspection Panel, as an authorisation has to be granted to the Panel by the Bank's executive authorities, whose accountability under the Articles of Agreement has not been reduced or modified by the Panel's establishment. In conducting its investigation the Inspection Panel has, similar to the investigative powers of an ombudsman and of a Commission of Inquiry, access to relevant Bank records, it can interview staff members of the Bank and other individuals, and it can eventually carry out an investigation in the territory concerned, if the borrower country consents.

---

[16] R. Bissell in a 'Panel on the Accountability of International Organisations to Non-state Actors', *ASIL Proceedings* 92 (1998), 365.

184 ALTERNATIVE REMEDIAL ACTION AND FUTURE OPTIONS

With regard to the scope *ratione remedii*, unlike the ombudsman but not always different from Commissions of Inquiry, the result of the Panel's investigation are its findings on the existence of the alleged violations, whereas the actual remedial action has to be taken by the organisation's executive authorities. The remedial action does not even have to be based upon recommendations formulated in that respect by the Panel.

The World Bank's 1996 Clarifications and the 1999 Conclusions

This general picture of the Inspection Panel's mandate and functioning has to be adjusted in the light of two consecutive reviews of the 1993 Resolution resulting in the 1996 Clarifications and the 1999 Conclusions. Three major points have to be identified in this respect.[17]

The unbalanced focus on assessing harm to the requesters in the first stage, which emerged in practice and was then legitimised in the 1996 Clarifications, created the erroneous impression that remedial action in response to harm was at the heart of the process. This imbalance was redressed so that an assessment of the Bank's failures to comply with its operational policies and procedures should precede an assessment of harm, both eligibility criteria retaining a prima facie character.

Sabine Schlemmer-Schulte's conclusion on this first point reads: 'the renewed focus on the Bank's compliance with its policies and procedures *reaffirms* the qualification of the Inspection Panel as an accountability mechanism as opposed to a remedies mechanism'.[18] Remedial measures eventually taken by the Bank's executive authorities on the occasion of a request to the Panel are based on their own discretionary powers to perform their duties of business and are not taken in response to a claimant's right to remedial measures.[19] I recall the view expressed throughout this study that both access to remedial mechanisms and provision of an appropriate outcome are essential to any accountability regime for international organisations.

By prohibiting the submission of remedial action plans by the Bank's management before the Board of Executive Directors has considered the Panel's recommendation to authorise an investigation, the 1999 Conclusions not only reversed a trend in practice, but prevented further

---

[17] Schlemmer-Schulte, 'Introductory Note', 243–8, preceding the text of the 1999 Conclusions of the Board's Second Review of the Inspection Panel, reproduced at 249 *et seq.*

[18] *Ibid.*, 245; emphasis added. [19] *Ibid.*

subversion of the Panel's process by the Bank's management through the use of its general business powers vested in them under the Bank's Articles of Agreement.[20] Consequently, a Panel recommendation for an investigation should normally and automatically result in an authorisation by the Bank's Board of Executive Directors to conduct one.[21]

Any remedial action now has to be postponed until after the findings of the Panel's investigation have become available and has to originate from the Bank's management and executive directors. The 'interim measures protection' effect no longer occurs, which eventually leads to the sustaining of an irreversible harm during the period of investigation conducted by the Panel and the time needed for executive decisions based on its findings. On the other hand, the overall remedial potential flowing from the Inspection Panel's functioning could in the long run be enhanced, as ultimate remedial measures taken by the Bank's management or Board 'on the occasion' of the request could turn out to be more effective and comprehensive as the measures would now be completely based, of course, on the findings of an investigation prior to the exercise of those discretionary powers.

Thirdly, in the past these remedial action plans primarily included actions to be taken by the borrowers, whereas the Panel process was only originally meant to address the Bank's failures. The 1999 Conclusions make it mandatory for both the Inspection Panel and the Bank's management to distinguish between failures exclusively attributable to the Bank or the borrower and those attributable to both. Only the Bank's failures should be focused upon in the Panel's recommendation and in the management response. Remedial action plans agreed between the borrower and the Bank will eventually be taken into account when the Bank's management takes its final decision, acting upon the results of the Panel's investigation.[22]

The World Bank Inspection Panel as an accountability mechanism

From an overall accountability point of view – the investigatory component of the Panel's functioning comprises political, administrative and legal forms of accountability – the mandatory distinction between the failures of the Bank to comply with its own operational procedures and policies and the failures of the other parties involved to comply with the contractual terms agreed upon with the Bank is in line with the

---

[20] *Ibid.*, 245–6.   [21] *Ibid.*, 246.   [22] *Ibid.*

approach followed by Commissions of Inquiry. This should be supported and welcomed, provided, of course, that the other parties involved in the action or omission constituting the subject-matter of the claim or request do not bar, at the admissibility stage, separate but complementary claims/requests to be handled by different remedial mechanisms. The complexity of operational activities currently being undertaken by international organisations only underlines the compelling need for such distinctions to be drawn and maintained, both at the stage of elaborating the primary rules governing any joint action and also, of course, when remedial mechanisms, measures and action are being established or resorted to.

In the light of this, one can fully agree with Schlemmer-Schulte's concluding assessment of the 1999 Conclusions when she wrote that they 'consolidate the concept of the Inspection Panel as an efficiently functioning mechanism the Bank has set up to be held accountable for its own operational failures by the ultimate beneficiaries of the projects it finances'.[23]

From the remedial perspective, and having due regard to the investigatory powers of the Inspection Panel, the following quasi-judicial features can be identified. At the root of the request there is certainly a dispute in the legal sense between the affected party and the Bank, thus providing the adversarial element in the Panel's functioning. Elements of due process can be found in the time-limits built into the Resolution and the Panel's Operating Procedures (for example, management has to respond to the allegations within a certain period of time) and in the fact that the Panel conducts its investigation both within the Bank and in the borrower state. The requirement that at the start of the process the Panel has to rule on the eligibility of the request, while the Panel's findings are final in the sense that they cannot be reconsidered through a political process, point in the same direction. And, last but not least, of course, the Panel is empowered to determine whether the Bank has acted in compliance with its own operational guidelines and procedures.

The recent changes made by the 1999 Conclusions have in substance not affected the quasi-judicial elements that were brought into existence by the Panel's enabling Resolution, in spite of the flaws in

---

[23] *Ibid.* The Bank Board's unwillingness, expressed on the occasion of the 1996 Clarifications, 'to enlarge any of the Panel's powers and functions that would turn it into an independent adjudicatory body' (Schlemmer-Schulte, 'The World Bank's Experience', 384) has certainly remained unaffected during the 1999 Review.

procedural fairness (such as no direct right for the requesters to participate in the Panel's proceedings) and equality of the parties (no right either for the requesters to react or respond to the Panel's findings), which certainly cannot be ignored either. As such, the Inspection Panel 'might be viewed as a logical extension of the rights of the employees of international organisations to redress (through, for example, ombudsmen), to the provision of similar rights to specific categories of the general public'.[24] There is no difficulty in continuing to regard the Inspection Panel as 'the prototype of a mechanism realising the concept of accountability of international organisations towards non-state actors with whom the Bank has neither a contractual nor a factual direct relationship'.[25] The 1999 Conclusions do not detract from the fact that the decision to establish the Panel in the first place 'implicitly acknowledges that international organisations have a legally-significant, non-contractual relationship with private parties that is independent of either the organisation's or the private party's relationship with the state'.[26]

The innovative aspect is to be found in non-state third parties – without the consent or participation of a state, and throughout the contractual relationship from the stage of design to appraisal and actual implementation – indirectly interposing themselves between the international organisation and its contractual partner in order to compel the organisation to comply with its own internal procedures and guidelines. There is no way in which the borrower (state) can prevent third parties from using the direct access available to them under the Panel's enabling Resolution; in that sense the Panel is essentially not an internal mechanism, as it can hear complaints from third parties.

The World Bank Inspection Panel as a model

Does the World Bank Inspection Panel constitute a precedent? Can it be used as a model? International organisations have to establish a comprehensive set of internal operational procedures and guidelines, also incorporating existing legal rules and norms drawn from different sources and layers. Such internal guidelines and directives do have an inherent external effect through the organisation's commitment to

---

[24] I. Shihata, referred to by R. Bissell, 'Recent Practice of the Inspection Panel of the World Bank', *AJIL* 91 (1997), 741–4, at 741.

[25] Schlemmer-Schulte, 'Introductory Note', 243.

[26] Bradlow and Schlemmer-Schulte, 'The World Bank's New Inspection Panel', 395.

observe them when dealing with external actors, creating a duty for the international organisations' staff members to exert their best efforts to comply. This can be reflected and incorporated in, for example, Status of Forces Agreements and agreements with host countries for the delivery of humanitarian or development assistance. The inspection panel model could be used once this pre-condition has been fulfilled. The usefulness of the inspection panel model may be considered to be particularly noticeable as it is operational during the course of the execution of a project, and thus lacks the traditional retrospective character of other mechanisms such as, for instance, the Bank's Operations Evaluation Department and Lessons-Learned Units in other international organisations.

The utilisation of the model as an accountability mechanism should be along the same lines as the World Bank Inspection Panel's eligibility criteria, substantive competences and potential outcome for non-state actors, complementary to the remedial means and measures available to them under the aforementioned category of agreements.

The embodiment in the guidelines and procedures of (international) legal standards applicable to the international organisation, while not affecting the non-legal character of an investigation conducted by an inspection panel or the nature of the requests or claims put forward by those affected, would, however, considerably increase the possibilities of the third level of accountability becoming operational in its remedial aspect. As no panel can examine the operational procedures and guidelines in complete isolation from general international law relating to international organisations, their constituent instruments and relevant municipal law, the panel's fact-finding investigation could become instrumental in subsequent legal proceedings before domestic courts. The establishment of the inspection panel could be considered a de facto waiver, in the sense that an organisation would normally plead jurisdictional immunity before domestic courts in similar cases. Conversely a domestic court may, by granting jurisdictional immunity, defer to the inspection panel any case falling within the panel's competence.[27]

An inspection panel's findings could also open the door for member states to exercise diplomatic protection in espousing the now-substantiated claim of the affected party, of course limited to the extent that the internal guidelines and procedures coincide with contemporary

---

[27] M. Singer, 'Jurisdictional Immunity of International Organisations: Human Rights and Functional Necessity Concerns', *Virginia Journal of International Law* 36 (1995), 53–165, at 147.

international law. Resorting to the panel would meet the requirement of the exhaustion of the organisation's internal remedies.

Alternatively, in the absence of remedial mechanisms or when there are doubts surrounding the adequacy of existing mechanisms, the inspection panel model could be used for operational activities with its pre-1999 focus on remedial action. Because presently such a panel cannot offer direct relief to affected parties, it could be endowed with recommendatory powers as to the remedial measures it considers to be required by the outcome of the independent exercise of its investigatory powers. Remedial action has to come from the organisation's authorities and may consist of corrective measures concerning the project and/or damages or equitable relief.

The most far-reaching but unrealistic alternative would, of course, consist of a model under which the decision to conduct an investigation would no longer be subject to prior authorisation from an organisation's executive authorities. Similar suggestions made by non-governmental organisations on the occasion of the World Bank Inspection Panel first review in 1996 were not successful.[28]

One should also not exclude the possibility that the process of an inspection panel can be set in motion not only by the potentially affected third party but, in appropriate circumstances, by a representative organisation as distinct from that same *locus standi* granted to individuals[29] because, as analysis of the European case law in the field of human rights has shown, there are 'uncertain and shifting boundaries between those directly affected by a particular measure and those remotely affected'.[30] Because of their institutional links with the organisation, member states do not have to prove any kind of additional particular interest and they may, of course, also resort to such a non-legal remedial mechanism.

One should immediately add, however, that different kinds of operational activities do require different kinds of accountability mechanisms; therefore, doubts have been raised as to whether the inspection panel model would make any sense when transposed to the context of

---

[28] Schlemmer-Schulte, 'The World Bank's Experience', 375.

[29] D. Wirth during the 'Panel on Accountability of International Organisations towards Non-state Actors', *ASIL Proceedings* 92 (1998), 365.

[30] D. Harris, M. O'Boyle and C. Warbrick, *Law of the European Convention on Human Rights* (London: Butterworths, 1995), p. 633 as cited by C. Harlow, 'Access to Justice as a Human Right: The European Court of Justice and the European Union' in P. Alston (ed.), *The European Union and Human Rights* (Oxford: Oxford University Press, 2000), pp. 187–213, at p. 193, note 24.

security,[31] if only because its stakeholders would not be located in one particular country, but would have regional or even world-wide origins.

From a remedial point of view the fundamental *acquis* flowing from the establishment of the World Bank Inspection Panel is certainly found in the acknowledgement 'that international organisations whose actions directly affect individuals, need to establish a forum in which individuals may bring claims on their own behalf'.[32] The argument that the help of non-state actors' vigilance in concrete cases and in general is called upon to improve the quality of the organisation's own performance[33] could be persuasively directed towards all international organisations in order to convince them to establish similar remedial mechanisms.

Commissions of Inquiry

The potential remedial effect of Commissions of Inquiry

Independent expert investigation such as that conducted by an international Commission of Inquiry provides us with a third form of non-legal alternative remedial action against international organisations. To request an inquiry is one of the means available to member states, as was recalled by the ICJ in the *Reparations* case with respect to the active side of organisational responsibility.[34]

The potential remedial effect of a Commission of Inquiry can be found at different levels. The fact-finding and the reconstruction of the chronological unfolding of events may accommodate the right to know on the part of the victims. At the same time, a Commission's findings meet the need for establishing separate and individual responsibility on the part of all the actors involved, as was thoroughly done in the Report on the events in Rwanda. The declaratory effect of the findings could later be confirmed by an international court or tribunal in a declaratory judgment.

---

[31] D. Bradlow during the 1998 'Panel on Accountability of International Organisations towards Non-state Actors', *ASIL Proceedings* 92 (1998), 367.

[32] Bradlow and Schlemmer-Schulte, 'The World Bank's New Inspection Panel', 402.

[33] S. Schlemmer-Schulte, 'The World Bank, its Operations and its Inspection Panel', *Recht der Internationale Wirtschaft* 45 (1999), 175–81, at 179.

[34] *Reparations for Injuries Suffered in the Service of the United Nations*, Advisory Opinion, *ICJ Reports* (1949), p. 174, at p. 177. Among the customary methods recognised by international law for the establishment, the presentation and the settlement of claims, the Court mentioned 'protest, request for an enquiry, negotiation, and request for submission to an arbitral tribunal or to the Court in so far as this may be authorised by the Statute'.

Fact-finding by a Commission of Inquiry also may be crucial in the implementation of the organisation's liability and responsibility for damages caused to private civilians in the course of peacekeeping operations.[35]

The formulation of recommendations by a Commission of Inquiry may very well correspond to the preventive, persuasive and prospective functions of remedial action. Normally the punitive element of remedial action is not included in the terms of reference of a Commission of Inquiry; it is left to domestic and international criminal tribunals, although the Commission may clearly mention this aspect.

The work of a Commission of Inquiry also meets the 'satisfaction' aspect by explicitly calling upon the main actors, individually and collectively, to express remorse and regret, eventually calling upon them, as in the case of Rwanda, to redesign their relationship with the population affected by the events.[36]

It must be added that the reports of Commissions of Inquiry normally clearly encompass the three levels and the four forms of accountability of international organisations.

Recent examples have demonstrated that Commissions of Inquiry have gone well beyond merely affording an opportunity for the ventilation of general dissatisfaction, although they are not designed to grant redress for specific grievances arising from the violation of legal rights or equitable expectations, which are in the nature of legal rights.[37]

Within the context of assessing the accountability of international organisations, issues of judgment are more difficult to identify than obvious breaches of conduct, as guidelines do not exist on 'whether to commit troops or aid personnel to a given area ... whether to suspend operations in response to one provocation or another ... When the lives of international personnel are lost, it may be unclear whether the issue was a failure of individual or organisational judgement, an absence of co-ordinated international strategies, a lack of respect for human values by local parties, bad luck, or some combination of these and other factors.'[38]

---

[35] P. Klein, *La Responsabilité des organisations internationales dans les ordres juridiques internes et en droit des gens* (Brussels: Editions Bruylant and Editions de l'Université Libre de Bruxelles, 1998), p. 547.

[36] Report of the *Independent Inquiry into the Actions of the United Nations during the 1994 Genocide in Rwanda*, 15 December 1999, Part IV, Recommendation 14.

[37] C. W. Jenks, *The Proper Law of International Organisations* (London and New York: Stevens and Oceana, 1962), p. 115.

[38] L. Minear, 'Introduction to Case-studies' in N. Azimi (ed.), *Humanitarian Action and*

192   ALTERNATIVE REMEDIAL ACTION AND FUTURE OPTIONS

If a Commission of Inquiry determines that there has been a failure by an organ of an international organisation to authorise a sufficient number of troops or to formulate clear terms of reference for a particular peacekeeping operation and/or a failure by another organ of the organisation to appropriate sufficient financial resources for the mission, this might subsequently be regarded by a judicial organ as proving culpability and establishing responsibility.[39]

The remedial potential of fact-finding, however, has to be approached somewhat differently depending on where the initiative originated. The findings of a Commission of Inquiry which has been established and which has been conducting its activities outside the context of judicial proceedings could be useful for determining facts that became public knowledge, but not as evidence for judicial purposes. On the other hand, when an international court or tribunal decides to order a preparatory inquiry as the inquisitorial aspect of the judicial proceedings,[40] its outcome will occupy a different role in the further proceedings in accordance with that court's rules. Inquiries such as those into the fall of Srebrenica and the events in Rwanda could thus, for instance, very well have been ordered by the ICJ within the context of relevant pending cases.

The Report on the fall of Srebrenica was made by the UN Secretary-General, while the events in Rwanda were the subject-matter of the Report of the Commission of Inquiry set up by the Secretary-General with the support of the Security Council. A decision by the Security Council itself to conduct an investigation would undoubtedly have fallen within the terms of paragraph 4 of the San Francisco Declaration, making possible the use of the power of the veto.

The issue of the evidential value of the findings of Commissions of Inquiry obviously has to be distinguished from the separate question of, for instance, the ICJ's handling of information, documents and testimony originating from international organisations that are not parties to the proceedings before it and also from the question of organisations providing information to the ICJ.[41]

Peacekeeping Operations: Debriefing and Lessons, Report of the 1997 Singapore Conference (The Hague: Kluwer Law International, 1997), pp. 43–66, at p. 61.

[39] C. Eagleton, 'International Organisations and the Law of Responsibility', *RCADI* 76 (1950), 323–423, at 400 on the possibility of this happening.

[40] R. Plender, 'Procedure in the European Courts: Comparisons and Prospects', *RCADI* 267 (1997), 1–343, at 146.

[41] See below, p. 227.

Two recent examples: the reports on Srebrenica and on Rwanda

The reports on the fall of Srebrenica and on the actions of the UN during the 1994 genocide in Rwanda, which had both been prompted by continuous public controversy and were both published in 1999, deserve separate attention from a remedial point of view. Having due regard to the different status of these reports because of the identity of their authors, the terms of reference under which they were drafted and the kind of conclusions and recommendations contained therein, a few common features may be highlighted.

The overall assessment found in both reports has been made in compliance with the principle that it should be carried out without the benefit of hindsight, in the light of the information available to the international organisation and the other actors involved at the relevant time.

An attempt was made in both reports, although to different degrees, to analyse the respective responsibility, in the ordinary sense of the word, of the different actors involved, in a very systematic, almost surgical, way, including the role played by individual national contingents of troop-contributing countries, similar to the way this had been done in the previous report on UNOSOM II.[42]

Dutchbat was criticised for not having reported more fully the scenes unfolding around them following the fall,[43] whereas in the case of Rwanda Belgium was criticised for its unilateral decision to withdraw its troops after the killing of ten of its peacekeepers, bringing UNAMIR near the brink of disintegration.[44] The failure to protect civilians and to protect political leaders seems to be attributable to a lack of direction from UNAMIR Headquarters, in the latter situation, though also the peacekeepers themselves were blamed in the report.[45] Responsibility rests in particular on the Special Representative for having failed to protect national staff.[46] The countries participating in Operation Turquoise were blamed for not having put these resources at the disposal of UNAMIR II.[47] Responsibility for the logistical problems faced by UNAMIR rested with both the Department of Peacekeeping Operations and with individual troop contributors.

---

[42] S/1994/653, *Note Dated 1 June 1994, Transmitting the Report of the Commission of Inquiry established Pursuant to Security Council Resolution 885 (1993) to Investigate Armed Attacks on UNOSOM Personnel which led to Casualties among Them.* The Report was dated 24 February 1994.

[43] A/54/549, *Srebrenica Report*, para. 474.

[44] *Report of the Rwanda Inquiry*, Conclusion 5.   [45] *Ibid.*, Conclusions 11 and 12.

[46] *Ibid.*, Conclusion 13.   [47] *Ibid.*, Conclusion 17.

194   ALTERNATIVE REMEDIAL ACTION AND FUTURE OPTIONS

The UN Secretary-General, his senior advisers and the Force Commander were wrong to declare repeatedly that they did not want to use
NATO air power against the Bosnian Serbs.[48] In Rwanda the UN strategy
to use the threat of withdrawing UNAMIR as a form of leverage in the
peace process probably had a counterproductive effect.[49]

The way in which the international community, acting through the
Security Council, responded to the war in Bosnia and Herzegovina was
more of a half-measure and a substitute as a result of the lack of political will 'to confront the menace defying it'.[50] Neither the provision
of humanitarian aid nor the deployment of a peacekeeping force was a
coherent response.[51] In Rwanda there was 'a lack of will to take on the
commitment which would have been necessary to prevent or to stop the
genocide'.[52]

Human and institutional failings, at many levels, did account for the
way the Serbs were not prevented from overrunning Srebrenica;[53] the
Rwanda Inquiry identified, inter alia, the lack of co-ordination on the part
of the UN organs concerned (CHR and DPKO), a lack of clarity regarding
which rules of engagement were in force and severe problems of command and control.[54]

In Srebrenica there was the failure fully to comprehend the Serb war
aims and the resulting provision by the UN Secretariat of incomplete and
inaccurate information to the Security Council, creating the impression
that the situation was under control.[55] In Rwanda the mission's mandate
was based on an erroneous analysis of the peace process which was
never corrected,[56] not even when the genocide started. This was a costly
error of judgment by the Secretariat, the leadership of UNAMIR and the
members of the Security Council.[57]

In the case of Srebrenica the UN, relying on member states for intelli-
gence, had no advance knowledge of the Serb offensive.[58] In Rwanda the
reconnaissance mission was unaware of disturbing reports published by
the Special Rapporteur of the Commission on Human Rights,[59] and later
on vital information coming from the Field Commander did not reach either the Secretary-General or the Security Council.[60] Also, member states

---

[48] A/54/549, *Srebrenica Report*, para. 483.   [49] *Report of the Rwanda Inquiry*, Conclusion 3.
[50] A/54/549, *Srebrenica Report*, para. 490.   [51] *Ibid.*, paras. 491–2.
[52] *Report of the Rwanda Inquiry*, Conclusion 1.   [53] A/54/549, *Srebrenica Report*, para. 485.
[54] *Report of the Rwanda Inquiry*, Conclusions 2, 4 and 5.
[55] A/54/549, *Srebrenica Report*, para. 496.
[56] *Report of the Rwanda Inquiry*, Conclusion 1.   [57] *Ibid.*, Conclusion 8.
[58] A/54/549, *Srebrenica Report*, para. 486.   [59] *Report of the Rwanda Inquiry*, Conclusion 2.
[60] *Ibid.*, Conclusion 3.

with an in-depth knowledge of the situation could have done more to share it with the Secretariat.[61]

One of the major operational constraints for all peacekeeping operations is the combined effect of the absence of an intelligence-gathering capacity and the reluctance of member states to share sensitive information with the UN,[62] as well as the institutional weakness apparent in the UN's capacity for political analysis, the responsibility for which falls primarily on the Secretariat under the leadership of the Secretary-General.[63]

The flexibility and ability to adapt mandates to the reality on the ground is of crucial importance, and was lacking in UNPROFOR and UNAMIR.[64] In the case of UNAMIR the responsibility for the limitations of the original mandate was explicitly placed with the Secretariat, the Secretary-General, responsible officials within the Department for Peacekeeping Operations (for mistaken analysis), member states (for exercising pressure to limit the number of troops) and the Security Council (for having limited the mandate).[65]

With regard to the situation in Bosnia and Herzegovina, UNPROFOR's decision to deny the access of the Bosnian forces to some of their weapons was described as particularly ill advised[66] and fundamental mistakes were made with regard to the establishment of the safe areas.[67] In the case of Rwanda the Secretary-General could have done more to argue the case for UNAMIR's reinforcement in the Security Council, whose decision to reduce it is difficult to justify. He could also have been more effective or powerful in influencing Council decision-making.[68] The delay in identifying the events in Rwanda as genocide was a failure by the Security Council.[69]

In both cases, concerns for the safety of the mission seem to have occupied a role of fundamental if not decisive importance in the interpretation and application of the mission's terms of reference, the international organisation considering that to be a special kind of accountability towards troop-contributing countries. That the execution of the mandate was secondary to the security of UN personnel had

---

[61] *Ibid.*, Conclusion 14.   [62] A/54/549, *Srebrenica Report*, para. 486.

[63] *Report of the Rwanda Inquiry*, Conclusion 9.

[64] A/54/549, *Srebrenica Report*, para. 493 and *Report of the Rwanda Inquiry*, Conclusions 1 and 3.

[65] *Report of the Rwanda Inquiry*, Conclusion 2.

[66] A/54/549, *Srebrenica Report*, para. 477.   [67] *Ibid.*, para. 499.

[68] *Report of the Rwanda Inquiry*, Conclusions 5 and 15.

[69] *Ibid.*, Conclusion 5.

already been observed before the publication of the Srebrenica Report.[70] This, of course, raises important issues of accountability as, during an operational activity, the pre-remedial differential standing of the main actors involved (namely the UN, the host country and its population) is reversed, which, in fairness and as a policy issue, should have an impact not only on the host country's standing on the remedial stage, but also on the remedial outcome itself.

In the Report on Srebrenica the ultimate responsibility 'for allowing this course of events by its prolonged refusal to use force in the early stages of the war'[71] is one to be shared between the international community as a whole, the UN Security Council, the Contact Group and other governments, as well as by the UN Secretariat and the mission in the field.[72]

In the Report on Rwanda '[the] responsibility for the failings of the UN to prevent and stop the genocide in Rwanda lies with a number of different actors, in particular the Secretary-General, the Secretariat, the Security Council, UNAMIR and the broader membership of the United Nations'.[73] The international community at large, the international organisations as such, and individual member states did not adequately respond to the clear signals coming from the early-warning system.

In the Report on Srebrenica, the UN Secretary-General expressed the UN's 'deepest regret and remorse when reviewing relevant actions and decisions and recognised error, misjudgement and an inability to recognise the scope of the evil confronting' the UN.[74]

The Independent Commission of Inquiry on the events in Rwanda stated that the responsibility it had established 'warrants a clear apology by the Organisation and by Member States concerned to the Rwandese people'.[75] On the day of the report's publication, the Secretary-General on behalf of the UN acknowledged the organisation's failure and expressed his deep remorse. During a visit to Rwanda in April 2000, the Belgian Prime Minister conveyed apologies on behalf of the Belgian government.

---

[70] R. Siekmann, 'The Fall of Srebrenica and the Attitude of Dutchbat from an International Legal Perspective', *Yearbook of International Humanitarian Law* 1 (1998), 301–12, at 306.

[71] A/54/549, *Srebrenica Report*, para. 501.   [72] *Ibid.*

[73] *Report of the Rwanda Inquiry*, Conclusions, first paragraph. Geoff Gilbert rightly observed that the UNHCR could hardly be liable for the consequences of international inaction, *i.e.* the Security Council's failure to send adequate troops: G. Gilbert, 'Rights, Legitimate Expectations, Needs and Responsibilities: UNHCR and the New World Order', *International Journal of Refugee Law* 10 (1998), 349–88, at 385.

[74] A/54/549, *Srebrenica Report*, para. 503.

[75] *Report of the Rwanda Inquiry*, Conclusions, first paragraph.

Because of their non-legal character, the reports of international Commissions of Inquiry, commissioned in order to meet the right to discover the truth, do in fact provide an alternative and corrective mechanism to the applicable provisions on the inviolability of archives and documents of international organisations, and ultimately also support the views of domestic supreme courts that 'society's interest in ensuring that the truth comes to light in legal proceedings is so strong that it is impossible to accept so broad and far-reaching an exception [*i.e.* the inviolability of archives and documents of an international organisation]'.[76] Converging strands of opinion and practice with regard to disclosure of information and the production of documents could substantially contribute to the effectiveness of the implementation of accountability of international organisations.

[76] The Dutch Supreme Court on 22 December 1989, *ILR* 96 (1994), 353, at 355, in *Algemene Bank Nederland v. Kf and Others* allowed the release of confidential information relating to the operation of the International Tin Council as cited by A. Reinisch, *International Organisations before National Courts* (Cambridge: Cambridge University Press, 2000), p. 158, note 655.

19   Amendment of existing judicial remedies

The non-legal alternative remedial mechanisms that are reviewed in the preceding chapter not only provide remedial opportunities at the first level of accountability, but they may also trigger mechanisms at the second and third levels as a result of their findings. The Ombudsman and the Inspection Panel are in fact available to (small groups of) individual claimants or requesters – the adverse material effect of acts or omissions of the organisation is not an eligibility requirement for access to an ombudsman who, moreover, may also be resorted to by staff members, either in their personal claims or in their capacity as whistleblowers in cases of maladministration in the public interest. Although individual grievances could be at the root of Commissions of Inquiry, it is more likely that they will normally only be set up in the case of events and actions occurring on a larger scale – for example, within the context of complex operational activities – and the initiative would most likely come from the organisation's Executive Head in close consultation with one of its principal organs or from these organs themselves: pressure from member states and from civil society at large does (potentially) play an important role in this respect.

The analysis as to the second and third levels of accountability carried out in the previous Parts of this study has brought to light various deficiencies from a remedial point of view as far as the different categories of state and non-state entities filing a claim against an international organisation are concerned. A solution to the problems identified earlier can be found by amending existing judicial remedial mechanisms, bearing in mind that the accountability of international organisations is only maximised by the simultaneous or successive use of various non-legal and judicial remedial mechanisms.

198

Courts and tribunals, both domestic and international, consider the arguments of the parties, appraise the evidence brought before them, establish the facts and declare the law that is applicable to them.[1] As this is the essence of the judicial function, the remedial potential of judicial remedies for states and non-state claimants is substantially more important than when they resort to non-legal mechanisms.

International administrative tribunals[2]

The UN internal system of justice: the 1995 proposals

A Report on the reform of the internal system of justice in the UN Secretariat was submitted by the then Secretary-General in September 1995, but the proposals were never put into effect.[3] With regard to the pre-litigation procedure, a series of measures proposed by the Secretary-General were designed to promote the early resolution of disputes before they reach the formal appeal stage.[4] Ombudsman panels would have been appointed to deal with disagreements, grievances and discrimination issues raised informally by staff members.[5] The review of administrative decisions would be conducted within the Office of the Under-Secretary-General for Administration and Management.[6]

The reform proposed by the Secretary-General in September 1995 provided for 'a new professionalised mechanism',[7] the main features of which may be summarised as follows.

(1) The Joint Appeals Board (JAB) would be replaced by an Arbitration Board that 'would be the best answer to the needs of the Organisation'.[8] The ten Arbitrators would be 'officials of the Organisation, not staff members subject to the authority of the

---

[1] *Effects of Awards of Compensation Made by the UN Administrative Tribunal*, Advisory Opinion of 13 July 1954, *ICJ Reports* (1954), p. 47, at p. 56.

[2] At the time of writing (spring 2000), the Joint Inspection Unit was preparing a report on the administration of justice in the UN Secretariat.

[3] A/C.5/50/2 of 27 September 1995. In its *Report on the Administration of Justice at the United Nations* the Joint Inspection Unit presented a brief overview of the attempts made during the last quarter of a century to improve the current system: A/55/57 of 7 March 2000, paras. 2–12. Many conclusions and recommendations contained in a 1986 Report of the JIU 'are endorsed, *mutatis mutandis,* in the present report' (*ibid.,* para. 7). The Report will be discussed during the 55th Session of the UN General Assembly under the item of the Review of the efficiency of the administrative and financial functioning of the United Nations.

[4] A/C. 5/50/2, p. 2, para. 4.   [5] *Ibid.*, p. 3, para. 10.   [6] *Ibid.*, p. 4, para. 14.

[7] *Ibid.*, p. 2, para. 4.   [8] *Ibid.*, p. 7, para. 26.

200 ALTERNATIVE REMEDIAL ACTION AND FUTURE OPTIONS

Secretary-General' and 'independent'.[9] They would be appointed by the Secretary-General after consultation with staff.[10]

(2) The Secretary-General would accept the unanimous recommendations of the proposed Arbitration Board, unless there was a compelling reason of law or policy not to do so.[11]

(3) In a first period, binding arbitration would be optional and it would only take place when each party specifically consented to it. Afterwards, binding arbitration would be introduced for 'defined classes of appeals, which could include, for example, appeals when the disputed issues are purely factual or do not involve more than a stated amount'.[12] Appeals to the UN Administrative Tribunal would be possible on the same grounds as at present after a decision taken subsequent to JAB advice.[13] Acting in a non-binding capacity, the Arbitration Board would make recommendations to the Secretary-General.[14]

(4) Acting in a binding capacity the Arbitration Board could not 'compel the Secretary-General to rescind a decision or compel the specific performance of an obligation'.[15] It 'must fix compensation in the event that the Secretary-General decides in the interest of the Organisation that an appellant should be compensated without further action being taken'.[16]

(5) Damages for actual loss could be recommended or awarded, to the exclusion of punitive or exemplary damages, as 'it would be inappropriate for public funds to be used to finance punitive awards'.[17]

(6) In the case of binding awards, appeal by either party to the UNAT would only be allowed on grounds of error of law, fundamental error of procedure or fact that has occasioned a miscarriage of justice.[18]

The 1995 proposals have been summarised here because they addressed issues of concern which continue to exist at present, as will become clear in the following pages.

The Joint Inspection Unit in its 2000 *Report on the Administration of Justice at the United Nations* has found the system at the UN to be 'slow, costly and cumbersome' and 'in several significant ways, far less effective than it could or should be'.[19] The JIU proposed the creation of an Office for the Settlement of Disputes and the Administration of Justice,

---

[9] *Ibid.*, p. 8, para. 28.   [10] *Ibid.*, p. 11, para. 41.   [11] *Ibid.*, p. 8, para. 30.

[12] *Ibid.*, p. 9, para. 32.   [13] *Ibid.*, p. 13, para. 52.   [14] *Ibid.*, p. 13, para. 52.

[15] *Ibid.*   [16] *Ibid.*   [17] *Ibid.*, p. 13, para. 50.

[18] *Ibid.*, p. 13, para. 52. The draft statute of the proposed Arbitration Board was contained in Annex II to the Report at pp. 37–45; corresponding revisions to the UNAT Statute were reproduced in Annex III at pp. 46–9.

[19] A/55/57, p. vii.

which should report directly to the Executive Office of the Secretary-General and which should encompass all units at present concerned with the administration of justice and the settlement of disputes in the organisation. This is in order to settle disputes between the organisation and staff members before they enter the formal litigation stage and to enhance the credibility of the units concerned.[20] The JIU strongly felt that the practice of accepting the unanimous recommendations of bodies such as the Joint Appeals Board – except in truly exceptional cases – should be revived.[21] With regard to the legal resources available to management and to staff there is a disparity between the 'phalanx of lawyers' at the disposal of the administration and the lack of sufficient proper legal advice and representation in what the Panel of Counsel in Disciplinary and Appeals Cases is capable of offering. At least a measure of parity should be brought about as soon as possible.[22]

As a matter of pre-remedial action, David Ruzié's suggestion that every decision (potentially) affecting an individual staff member should be reviewed by the organisation's Legal Office before the decision is actually taken, instead of only subsequently before the international administrative tribunal, should be welcomed.[23] With regard to the pre-litigation stage the UNAT has unequivocally condemned the practice of *marchandage*, where the organisation's administration is willing to make concessions in exchange for the staff member renouncing his right or legal remedy.[24] Attaching suspensory effect to the administrative review stage could provide the claimant with a substantially higher degree of protection in several respects, probably including preventing the occurrence of this kind of *marchandage*. Chris De Cooker rightly pointed out that, particularly in international organisations where prior informal conciliatory procedures exist, the procedural guarantees existing in the pre-litigation procedures of administrative review make them more

---

[20] *Ibid.*, paras. 108, 110 and 111. The function of the ombudsman would be included in this new Office: *ibid.*, para. 113.

[21] *Ibid.*, para. 124.   [22] *Ibid.*, paras. 136, 137, 141 and 143.

[23] Ruzié made the suggestion during a Conference on Proliferation of International Organisations: Legal Issues, held at Leyden, the Netherlands, on 18–20 November 1999: notes on file with the author. The Legal Service intervention during the pre-litigation stage is part of the process of complaints within the European Community (C. De Cooker, 'Pre-litigation Procedures in International Organisations' in C. De Cooker (ed.), *International Administration: Law and Management in International Organisations* (looseleaf publication) (The Hague: Kluwer Law International), contribution VI, pp. 1–23, at p. 13).

[24] Judgment No. 745 as referred to by D. Ruzié, 'Jurisprudence du Tribunal Administratif des Nations Unies', *AFDI* 42 (1996), 482–503, at 483.

formal and legalistic, resulting in a form of para-litigation. This is also because the relief sought and the grounds used in both procedures are closely linked.[25]

The jurisdiction of international administrative tribunals

For a variety of compelling reasons that have been explained earlier, all international organisations should either recognise the jurisdiction of existing international administrative tribunals or establish appropriate administrative and judicial mechanisms in order to provide their staff members with a legal remedy in the case of disputes arising from their service in that particular organisation.[26]

The jurisdiction of international administrative tribunals *ratione personae* should be widened so that access would also be possible for external candidates participating in an open competition for a particular vacant post, for example when they can base a claim on irregularities allegedly occurring in the course of the recruitment procedure.[27]

The Joint Inspection Unit proposed that the UNAT 'should have full powers to order the rescinding of a decision contested or the specific performance of the obligation invoked' and in alignment with the ILOAT the 'Tribunal alone should decide on the amount of compensation to be paid to the appellant'.[28]

With respect to the exercise of their judicial powers, international administrative tribunals should not adopt a too restrictive approach towards the sources of law at their disposal when dealing with disputes submitted to them; on the other hand, they should rigorously respect their statutory powers and not embark upon reforming the decision they are called upon eventually to annul.[29] International administrative tribunals should not continue, as is the case with the UNAT, to enter into a kind of dialogue with the Joint Appeals Board, while the

---

[25] De Cooker, 'Pre-litigation Procedures', p. 18.

[26] D. Ruzié, Working Paper No. 2, ILA Committee, pp. 1–2, paras. 7–9: on file with the author. See also above, p. 82, note 6.

[27] Ruzié, Working Paper No. 2, p. 1, para. 4 and Working Paper No. 1, ILA Committee, p. 2, paras. 5–11: on file with the author.

[28] A/55/57, paras. 116 and 117.

[29] Ruzié, Working Paper No. 1, ILA Committee, p. 1, para. 4 and p. 5, para. 30: on file with the author. The JIU noted the fact that the major international instruments on the protection of human rights are not incorporated in the UN internal regulations and rules: A/55/57, p. viii.

dispute is actually between the staff member and the organisation.[30] It would appear that the UNAT erroneously considers the Joint Appeals Board to constitute a jurisdiction of first instance while in fact it only has recommendatory powers.[31]

On the other hand, the interest of international administrative justice would be best served by international administrative tribunals not necessarily narrowly interpreting their jurisdiction and explicitly requiring in all cases an actual 'decision' rather than, when appropriate, resorting to the theory of 'implied decisions'.[32] However, if within the context of a pre-litigation administrative review a request is made to change the way a particular department is being organised, 'its explicit or implicit rejection would not seem to amount to acts that could adversely affect the official concerned'.[33]

Denial of justice

As for the remedial outcome, Michael Singer rightly observed that when conditions of employment are involved, the hearing before the international administrative tribunal can be considered to be adequate. This is in contrast to disputes involving claims of discrimination or arbitrary treatment.[34]

As for procedural rights, the UNAT (usually) and the ILOAT (more often than not) deny requests for oral proceedings to be held. Henry Schermers

[30] D. Ruzié, 'Jurisprudence du Tribunal Administratif des Nations Unies', *AFDI* 39 (1993), 610–26, at 611. See also Ruzié, 'Jurisprudence du Tribunal Administratif des Nations Unies' (1996), 491.

[31] D. Ruzié, 'Jurisprudence du Tribunal Administratif des Nations Unies', *AFDI* 44 (1998), 412–27, at 413.

[32] C. F. Amerasinghe, 'International Administrative Law in the 21st Century' in A. Anghie and G. Sturgess (eds.), *Legal Visions of the 21st Century: Essays in Honour of Judge Christof Weeramantry* (The Hague and London: Kluwer Law International, 1998), pp. 447–95, at p. 486.

On the basis of UNAT's judicial decisions the JIU described an 'administrative decision' within the meaning of Staff Regulation 11.1 – which is the basis of the administration of justice system at the UN – as 'a decision by the Administration concerning a staff member's terms of appointment, including all pertinent regulations and rules, which must be communicated to the staff member in writing and which must apply personally to him or her, thus causing imminent and actual effects on the staff member's terms of appointment': A/55/57, paras. 35 and 42.

[33] De Cooker, 'Pre-litigation Procedures', p. 10.

[34] M. Singer, 'Jurisdictional Immunity of International Organisations: Human Rights and Functional Necessity Concerns', *Virginia Journal of International Law* 36 (1995), 53–165, at 157–8.

and Niels Blokker have persuasively suggested that the inequality of the parties before an international administrative tribunal could be remedied somewhat if the organisation would renounce its right to make oral presentations in cases where the individual may not appear before it, and if the claimant's written statements could be included in the organisation's own written submissions.[35]

The denial of justice should also be avoided by preventing, as far as possible, contradictory trends amongst international administrative tribunals on the interpretation and application of the same rule of international administrative law. Structured exchange of information on judgments and orders and the ensuing mutual respect for each other's judicial decisions should be the first step towards enhancing the opportunities for claimants to enjoy similar remedial treatment.[36] The latter is also called into question when the UNAT gives the impression of acting sometimes more like a body of 'wise men' who do not have to legally justify their decisions as the ILOAT does.[37] Complementary to amending their financial status, changing the method of selecting UNAT judges by not leaving it entirely to the nominating states would constitute an important step in improving the quality of the judgments.[38] The JIU called 'upon Member states to spare no efforts to ensure that the individuals nominated' possessed 'high professional qualifications and experience in the judiciary'.[39]

An appeal procedure

Since the repeal of Article XI of UNAT's Statute by the General Assembly, the question of a general right to a second judicial instance has again been left wide open. Although the ILOAT's judgments may be reformed by way of binding Advisory Opinions rendered by the ICJ, it is difficult to see how individual claimants could also be able to trigger the procedure given the inherent limitations flowing from the ICJ's Statute, which will be discussed in the next chapter; moreover, the grounds that can be

---

[35] H. Schermers and N. Blokker, *International Institutional Law: Unity Within Diversity* (Dordrecht and London: Martinus Nijhoff Publishers, 1995), para. 607.

[36] Attempts to merge the international administrative tribunals of the UN common system have consistently been doomed to failure for historical and other reasons.

[37] Ruzié, 'Jurisprudence du Tribunal Administratif des Nations Unies' (1996), 485.

[38] D. Ruzié and P. Szasz in a written exchange of views: on file with the author.

[39] A/55/57, para. 119. A French proposal regarding the selection of UNAT judges has recently been submitted to the General Assembly's Fifth Committee and will be debated in the near future.

AMENDMENT OF EXISTING JUDICIAL REMEDIES 205

invoked before the ICJ should then be broadened so as to include errors in law as well.[40]

Divergent views are held on the need and scope of an appeals procedure. As was pointed out by the Joint Inspection Unit in its 1986 report, a 'system of two-stage judicial appeals is one of the basic principles of democratic law and is established in most countries. It is therefore natural that such a system should be desired by United Nations staff'; so although the principle of dual jurisdiction is not a fundamental right outside criminal legal proceedings, the ICJ's ruling on the promotion of justice for individuals seems to require an amelioration of the existing situation.[41] One of the alternatives would be to replace the existing Joint Appeals Board with a proper jurisdictional body of first instance, the UNAT then becoming a court of second instance as suggested by the Secretary-General in 1995.[42] Another alternative under consideration by the Legal Advisers of the UN system would be to have a body of three judges, one from the UNAT, one from the ILOAT and a neutral President, to deal with single staff member appeals.[43]

The Joint Inspection Unit is in favour of considering a revival of the role of the ICJ in the review of judgments 'aimed at ensuring full respect for the Charter in the application of administrative justice'.[44]

As to the scope of an appellate procedure, some are in favour of limiting it to reviewing the increasing number of judgments relating to large classes of staff members[45] involving normative decisions – the grounds for appeal obviously being limited to errors of law – while others are firmly in favour of opening up the appellate procedure to individual staff members for obvious reasons of fairness and due process of law.[46]

The establishment of a Permanent Appeals Tribunal for appeals from all international administrative tribunals and similar bodies could provide a third, and more far-reaching, alternative solution.[47]

Under any of these alternative possibilities a kind of filtering system along the lines of the ECHR model and the awarding of costs to the

[40] Ruzié, Working Paper No. 1, ILA Committee, p. 4, para. 18; on file with the author.
[41] *Ibid.*, p. 3, para. 14 and A/55/57, para. 164 referring to the Director-General of UNESCO who was citing the 1986 JIU report.
[42] Ruzié, Working Paper No. 1, ILA Committee, p. 3, note 13.
[43] Ruzié, Working Paper No. 2, ILA Committee, p. 4, para. 19 and P. Szasz in a written exchange of views with D. Ruzié: on file with the author.
[44] A/55/57, paras. 152 and 153.
[45] Szasz in a written exchange of views with Ruzié: on file with the author.
[46] Ruzié, Working Paper No. 2, ILA Committee, p. 4, paras. 19–20; on file with the author.
[47] Szasz in a written exchange of views with Ruzié: on file with the author.

206 ALTERNATIVE REMEDIAL ACTION AND FUTURE OPTIONS

respondent international organisation would have a restraining effect on individual appeals.[48]

Prospective and retrospective approaches

From a *prospective* remedial point of view the international administrative tribunals do not claim to supervise the conduct of the administration of an international organisation with a view to preventing the occurrence of a grievance, to restrain certain actions contemplated by the administration,[49] or to compel it to undertake a particular action. Wilfred Jenks rightfully observed that (*de lege lata*) they cannot grant anything in the nature of an interlocutory injunction,[50] but he immediately added that although any kind of preventive jurisdiction had to be considered premature (in 1962) the question whether there are any circumstances in which they should exercise such jurisdiction may arise at some time in the future.[51] The context of Jenks' observations makes it clear that he was thinking of individual cases, as he also recalled that there is no bar to interlocutory proceedings not inhibiting the freedom of executive action by the administration.[52]

One could fairly argue that at the beginning of this millennium the time may have arrived, now that the accountability of international organisations is being approached from a different perspective, for the question of preventive jurisdiction to be no longer limited to the potential exercise of such power by international administrative tribunals but by other judicial mechanisms as well; its potential scope should not be restricted to claims arising out of individual cases brought by staff members but could more broadly include non-staff members as well.

Much more far-reaching are those proposals to endow international administrative tribunals with extended jurisdiction over all disputes arising from contracts having an international organisation as a partner. Apart from providing an adequate alternative judicial remedial mechanism to the existing system of dispute settlement,[53] one of the

---

[48] Ruzié, Working Paper No. 2, ILA Committee, p. 5, para. 25; on file with the author.

[49] C. W. Jenks, *The Proper Law of International Organisations* (London and New York: Stevens, Dobbs Ferry and Oceana, 1962), p. 115.

[50] *Ibid.*   [51] *Ibid.*, p. 116.   [52] *Ibid.*

[53] On its inadequacies under the requirements of an equitable procedure see also P. Klein, *La Responsabilité des organisations internationales dans les ordres juridiques internes et en droit des gens* (Brussels: Editions Bruylant and Editions de l'Université Libre de Bruxelles, 1998), p. 272.

preconditions and advantages of such a change to the existing system would be the determination of the applicable law in the instrument endowing the tribunal with such jurisdiction. One should also be aware, however, that with such an innovation the relationship between the organisation and the individual claimant risks becoming one of subordination based on the regulatory nature of the organisation's prerogatives instead of remaining a contractual and thus egalitarian one,[54] alleviating to some extent the initial inequality in terms of power between the two contracting partners. Suffice it to observe that the innovation would not be such a major one because the ILOAT's jurisdiction has always included these kinds of disputes, although only one case has so far been decided.

The question may be raised whether the rationale of accountability and the remedial imperatives would not require the jurisdiction of international administrative tribunals *ratione personae* and *ratione materiae* to be widened so as to include *retrospective* claims from non-staff members *vis-à-vis* international organisations, for example for not having complied with internal operational guidelines and procedures. Such an action would be preceded by resorting to an inspection panel or similar mechanism, provided of course that no alternative mechanisms were available, for example before the domestic courts.

The possibility of such prospective/retrospective remedial action by third parties directly affected by the exercise of administrative powers had already been clearly discerned by Jenks back in 1962, because although the international public service may require a particular measure of executive discretion, it may 'be excessive in respect of the exercise of powers directly affecting third-party interests'.[55] Jenks' observation was made under the heading 'future dilemmas of international administrative law' and goes directly to the heart of the accountability debate.

Finally, one should not forget that there are a number of disputes, of an employment-related nature or otherwise, that cannot be submitted to domestic courts because of the jurisdictional immunity of the respondent international organisation, but which still cannot be submitted to international administrative tribunals either. This is one of the reasons why the potential role of domestic courts should be revisited.

---

[54] D. Meyer, 'Les Contrats de fournitures de biens et de services dans le cadre des opérations de maintien de la paix', *AFDI* 42 (1996) 79–119, at 115.

[55] Jenks, *Proper Law*, pp. 128–9.

The potential role of domestic courts

Having regard to the special features of claims against international organisations as they have become clear throughout this study, there is no reason in principle why, from a comprehensive remedial point of view, domestic courts should not play a significant role in dealing with such claims brought before them by non-state claimants. The function of domestic courts and their contribution to the interpretation, application and elaboration of both conventional and customary international law is extensively acknowledged and it gains importance every day. There are, in fact, no branches of international law where domestic courts are completely absent or where their contribution is irrelevant. In Part II of this study a great deal of attention was paid to the thorough analysis carried out by August Reinisch of the position of international organisations before domestic courts. It is now time to take a closer look at their potential role in the overall accountability regime of international organisations, complementary as such a role is and indeed should be to the remedial functions already being performed by international administrative tribunals and the inevitable role to be played by the International Court of Justice, which will be explored in the next chapter.

Waiver of immunity and the balance of interests

A first point to be noted concerns the *travaux préparatoires* of the General Convention on Privileges and Immunities and how the provision of Section 20 (which is of a preventive nature and operates before the invocation of jurisdictional immunity) evolved. Initially there was an obligation for the Secretary-General to waive immunity in every case where such a course is consistent with the interests of the UN since they constitute the *ratio legis* of the immunities. Later, the interests of the organisation became a condition qualifying and restricting the primary obligation to waive immunity in cases where this immunity would impede the course of justice:[56] from being the initial *raison d'être* for the granting of immunities, the interests of the international organisation became, without much substantial debate, limiting factors in practical terms exerting an influence upon the remedial system which, arguably, went beyond the exigencies emanating from them.

---

[56] *Report by the Executive Committee to the Preparatory Commission*, PC/EX/113/Rev. 1, 12 November 1945 and the *Report of the Preparatory Commission*, UN PC/20, 151 of 23 December 1945.

From a remedial point of view there is sufficient reason to argue that the interests of the international organisation as the *ratio legis* of the immunities granted should be subordinated to the promotion of good administration of justice. The potential remedial role of domestic courts would have been substantially greater from the outset if the margin of appreciation left to the Secretary-General had been restricted to the non-impediment of the course of justice.[57] A positive formulation of that discretion – to the extent that immunity should be waived if required by the promotion of the administration of justice – could contribute substantially to the implementation of an adequate accountability regime for international organisations. Alternatively, the UN Secretary-General should adopt a restrictive interpretation of the qualification as it now stands. It is worth noting in this regard that in deciding 'whether privileges and immunities exist and whether they should be waived the Secretary-General *may* take into account the views of the legislative body that appointed officials (other than Secretariat officials) or experts on mission':[58] an *obligation* to the same extent would have been more appropriate.

The obligation to provide alternative modes of settlement

Any assessment of the potential future role of domestic courts in the accountability regime for international organisations must also be firmly placed within the perspective of the obligation for the UN and other international organisations to make the necessary provisions for appropriate alternative modes of settlement, as has been duly recognised. It should be recalled that the 1945 ILO proposal providing, *inter alia*, for the establishment of an appropriate international tribunal for redress in certain cases (primarily of contractual and non-contractual liability) as the natural counterpart of immunities granted was of overall general application.[59] This ILO proposal was later reduced to appropriate modes of settlement as required under the General Convention.[60] It

---

[57] On the controversy surrounding the scope and modalities of the exercise of this power by the UN Secretary-General, see most recently the *Cumaraswamy* case before the International Court of Justice: *Difference Relating to Immunity from Legal Process of a Special Rapporteur of the Commission on Human Rights*, Advisory Opinion of 22 April 1999, *ICJ Reports* (1999), p. 62.

[58] A/54/695 of 29 December 1999, p. 9: emphasis added.

[59] C. W. Jenks, *International Immunities* (London and New York: Stevens & Sons and Oceana Publications, 1961), p. 43.

[60] *Ibid.*, pp. 43–4.

210   ALTERNATIVE REMEDIAL ACTION AND FUTURE OPTIONS

has been rightly pointed out that the Convention itself does not provide for any dispute settlement mechanism,[61] nor does it compel the organisations to resort to a specific method of settlement, such as the establishment of a tribunal, as it refers to multiple modes of settlement.[62] Although the Brussels Court of Appeal incorrectly ruled on other issues before it, its 1969 assessment concurring with the 1966 Court of First Instance judgment that there existed no jurisdiction before which an individual applicant could have brought his or her dispute with the organisation[63] is still as valid and as deplorable today as it was then. Given the lack of such an alternative remedial mechanism, the absence of a waiver of jurisdictional immunity before the domestic courts and the organisation not being bound by an arbitral *compromis*,[64] the balance that is sought by granting immunities can be seen to be disrupted,[65] as 'one cannot see where the UN could be sued, nor how, nor on what legal basis ... so long as it shelters behind its immunity from jurisdiction'.[66]

During the oral proceedings in the *Cumaraswamy* case, Judge Verechetin, referring to Section 23 of the General Convention, put the question to the UN Legal Counsel what, in the view of the Secretary-General, would be the legal remedies available to the private plaintiffs.[67] In his reply the UN Legal Counsel recalled the obligation in Article VIII to make remedies available to private parties who might otherwise be

---

[61] CR/98/16, p. 67, para. 123: oral proceedings in the *Cumaraswamy* case: Sir Eli Lauterpacht.

[62] R. Harpignies, 'Settlement of Disputes of a Private Law Character to which the United Nations is a Party: A Case in Point: The Arbitral Award of 24 September 1969 in Re Starways Ltd v. United Nations', *RBDI* 7 (1971), 451–68, at 457.

[63] *ILR* 45 (1972), at p. 451: Civil Tribunal of Brussels, 11 November 1966. Court of Appeal of Brussels, 15 September 1969, *Pasicrisie* (1969), 247–50, at 249.

[64] Even a formal, unilateral declaration made by the UN and binding in law, expressing the organisation's readiness to go to arbitration initiated by a private party, would be sufficient to meet the needs of Section 29, according to Sir Eli Lauterpacht during the oral proceedings in the *Cumaraswamy* case: CR/98/17, p. 52.

[65] I. Scobbie, 'International Organisations and International Relations' in R. J. Dupuy (ed.), *A Handbook of International Organisations* (The Hague, London and Boston: Kluwer Law International, 1998), pp. 833–67, at pp. 850–1 citing further *ILR* 94 (1994), 321 at 329, *AS v. Iran–United States Claims Tribunal*, Supreme Court of the Netherlands, 20 December 1985: 'On the one hand there is the interest of the international organisation having a guarantee that it will be able to perform its task independently and free from interference under all circumstances; on the other there is the interest of the other party in having its dispute with an international organisation dealt with and decided by an independent and impartial judicial body.'

[66] *Manderlier v. Organisation des Nations Unies and Etat Belge (Ministre des affaires étrangères)*, Court of First Instance of Brussels, 11 May 1966, *ILR* 45 (1972), at 455.

[67] CR/98/16, p. 69.

harmed by the immunity of the organisation and its agents. As Section 29 was intended to provide a complete system of remedies to private parties, the UN Legal Counsel subsequently reviewed the different alternative methods of settlement normally resorted to by the organisation.[68] Although the provisions of Section 29 were described by the Legal Counsel as 'intended to provide a complete remedy system to parties who alleged to have been harmed by actions of the UN or by its agents acting within the scope of their mandate',[69] the question of whether those remedial mechanisms have in fact been established and have been providing adequate alternative remedial protection should not have been left unanswered. The argument that the 'overwhelming majority of claims are settled through negotiations'[70] has already been addressed earlier in this study, and the different alternative mechanisms have in practice not always been functioning completely satisfactorily, as also pointed out by Pierre Klein.[71] The UN Legal Counsel then correctly pointed out that Article VIII of the General Convention does not require the establishment of a permanent or standing dispute resolution mechanism.[72] According to the UN Legal Counsel, the establishment of standing claims bodies is neither feasible, practical or economical, as other claims of a private nature could arise in any of the UN member states and out of innumerable factual situations. It would be financially burdensome and unjustified, given that the instances where the UN cannot otherwise settle the dispute are rare.[73]

Although under their constituent instruments and applicable internal rules sound financial management is one of the principles governing the actions and conduct of international organisations, the Report

---

[68] CR/98/17, pp. 9–11, paras. 8–13.

[69] *Ibid.*, p. 9, para. 6.   [70] *Ibid.*   [71] Klein, *La Responsabilité*, p. 277.

[72] CR/98/17, p. 21, para. 51. See also Harpignies recalling that the creation of a tribunal that would have jurisdiction over conflicts of a private-law nature between the organisation and third parties has never been contemplated: 'Settlement of Disputes', 455.

The Brussels Court of First Instance in the *Manderlier* case had observed that Section 29 would normally include setting up courts to decide such disputes (*ILR* 45 (1972), 451), concluding that the procedure followed in the settlement of the Congo claims was not an appropriate method of settlement within the meaning of Section 29 (*ibid.*, 447), because the claims had been examined by the respondent international organisation without any argument of any kind, resulting in a unilateral decision (*ibid.*, 452).

[73] CR/98/17, p. 10, para. 12 and p. 21, para. 51 (the argument of practicability had already been used by Clyde Eagleton in his 1950 Hague Academy Lectures: 'International Organisations and the Law of Responsibility', *RCADI* 76 (1950), 323–423, at 352 and 402).

of the Office of Internal Oversight Services on procurement-related arbitration and the costs involved[74] did provide one indication in favour of a standing dispute resolution system for the private claims envisaged here. It is obvious that member states have to pay the sometimes additional costs resulting from the organisation's desire for absolute jurisdictional immunity in disputes arising out of day-to-day contractual dealings.[75]

Three further observations have to be made at this juncture. First, the International Court of Justice in the *Effects of Awards* case made it clear that for 'expenditures [arising] out of obligations already incurred by the Organisation ... the General Assembly has no alternative but to honour these engagements'.[76] Moreover, financial constraints do not seem to have prevented a regional organisation such as the OAS, pursuant to the Headquarters Agreement with the United States, from establishing a permanent dispute resolution mechanism for small claims of a private-law nature (under (US) $2,000) arising from disputes for which jurisdiction would exist against a foreign government under section 1605(a)(2)–(6) of the FSIA.[77]

Secondly, one has to recall Jenks' remark made in 1961 in connection with Sections 22–3 of the General Convention that there is no 'corresponding right and duty' (to waive the immunity) in the case of the organisation itself being involved.[78] This study has shown that this is one of the areas where the main problems are to be found: Sections 22–3 should also be made applicable to disputes involving the organisations themselves.

Thirdly, it is particularly striking that the mechanism by which to settle disputes arising from innumerable factual situations arising in any of the UN member states has been permanent, at no extra costs for the UN budget and available in all of the organisation's member states – that is, in the domestic courts.

Given that the creation of a permanent settlement mechanism by the UN is unlikely in the medium term, there is, from a remedial perspective, even more reason today than ever before to explore the potential role of domestic courts, as the frequent reluctance of states to exercise

---

[74] See above, p. 157.   [75] Singer, 'Jurisdictional Immunity', 143.

[76] *Effects of Awards of Compensation Made by the UN Administrative Tribunal*, Advisory Opinion of 13 July 1954, *ICJ Reports* (1954), p. 47, at p. 59.

[77] Cited and referred to by Klein, *La Responsabilité*, pp. 253–4, and by A. Muller, *International Organisations and their Host-states: Aspects of their Legal Relationship* (The Hague and London: Kluwer Law International, 1995), p. 180.

[78] Jenks, *International Immunities*, p. 45.

their diplomatic protection of an injured individual probably greatly reduces the adequate level of fairness guaranteed by this other alternative mode of settlement.[79]

Domestic courts as an appropriate forum

Addressing the potential role of domestic courts, Jenks argued that the interpretation of the law defining the status and responsibilities of international organisations could not be safely left to domestic courts for two main reasons: the law itself was still rather underdeveloped and the future development of international organisations could be restricted by domestic judicial intervention.[80]

As to the first reason, it may be safely argued that over the last four decades the development of the law of international organisations, although still in progress and requiring consolidation as well as long overdue codification as indicated earlier, has reached a stage beyond which the domestic adjudication of disputes involving international organisations and subject to conditions to be reviewed below cannot cause serious or irreparable harm to its further development.

During the same period of time, the proliferation of international organisations and the unprecedented expansion of their activities cannot really be considered as being restricted or hampered in a substantial way by domestic courts asserting jurisdiction. To that extent the fear expressed by Jenks did not actually materialise.

The accountability regime currently being elaborated for international organisations and the vital role assigned in that context to remedial mechanisms of a judicial nature should be duly taken into account as overriding concerns with regard to each of the two reasons advanced by Jenks.

In discussing the question as to whether domestic courts provide an appropriate forum for disputes involving international organisations, the obligations incumbent upon the two main actors, states and international organisations, can correctly be identified as the source of mutually supporting and converging arguments in favour of a positive answer, subject, of course, to various modalities in matters of principle and fact. There is, indeed, not only an obligation for international organisations to prevent any abuse but also an obligation to make provisions for

---

[79] A. Reinisch, *International Organisations before National Courts* (Cambridge: Cambridge University Press, 2000), pp. 277–8.

[80] Jenks, *International Immunities*, p. 41.

appropriate methods of settlement under Section 29 of the General Convention, and for states there is an obligation under human rights instruments to provide access to a court in certain situations.[81] Singer has convincingly pointed out that although a member state cannot be directly responsible for human rights violations by an international organisation because it is beyond its jurisdictional reach, it may, however, violate its own human rights obligations by granting immunity to the international organisation in the absence of adequate alternative remedial mechanisms.[82]

The human rights imperative may lead to or even require a limitation or rejection by domestic courts of jurisdictional immunity claimed by international organisations, and the actual exercise of the courts' adjudicatory jurisdiction. There seems to be no reason whatsoever why the human rights imperative should operate in a different way towards organisational immunity compared with situations involving states.[83]

It is important not to overlook the fact that it is the forum state that is obliged to protect the individual's right of access to a court, and that the international organisation has an obligation to provide the potential claimant with adequate alternative dispute settlement mechanisms.[84] Consequently, a municipal court must first determine whether the concern for human rights demands that it take jurisdiction, regardless of the organisation's claim to immunity. Only when the answer is in the negative is there a requirement to consider whether to grant jurisdictional immunity.[85]

At the juncture of these two separate international obligations, however, the forum state will not only be entitled but will be obliged – in the case where the international organisation has not complied with its conventional obligation to provide adequate alternative settlement mechanisms – to deny jurisdictional immunity. Suspension of domestic litigation until, for instance, the General Convention's dispute settlement mechanisms have been exhausted would in turn almost certainly amount to another denial of justice, but this time by the domestic court.

---

[81] Reinisch, *National Courts*, p. 324. See also Singer, 'Jurisdictional Immunity', 91–5.

[82] Singer, 'Jurisdictional Immunity', 91–5. The human rights perspective would also require member states of an international organisation to ensure that acts, actions and omissions of the organisation are in conformity with general principles of human rights law, and thus to prevent violation by the organisation (*contra: ibid.*, 149, note 380).

[83] Reinisch, *National Courts*, p. 288.   [84] *Ibid.*, p. 289.

[85] Singer, 'Jurisdictional Immunity', 135.

A related but distinct issue arises from alleged human rights violations by international organisations *vis-à-vis* staff members or third parties. Here, the human rights imperative extends to the substantive compliance by international organisations with primary human rights standards, making the rationale for judicial involvement even more imperative at both the procedural and substantive level.

There is no reason why the elaboration of secondary, remedial rules *vis-à-vis* international organisations should not take place under the same conditions as those for putting into place and refining primary rules: namely, maintaining the delicate balance between preserving the necessary degree of autonomous decision-making for the international organisation and avoiding any gaps in their accountability from occurring (that is, not leaving states, staff members and third-party claimants in a position where they could (potentially) be adversely affected by the acts, actions or omissions of the organisations without proper and adequate remedial protection). From this perspective, a contractual or non-contractual claim brought before a domestic court would constitute tolerable interference, whereas direct efforts to influence the policy decisions of international organisations via domestic court orders would be an example of intolerable interference – for example, a party attempting to prohibit the UN by injunction from carrying out a particular peacekeeping mission,[86] a motion that has been qualified as a baseless action.[87]

It has also been duly acknowledged that the degree of legitimacy inherent in the interest of having their claim brought before domestic courts varies amongst the different groups of potential claimants, according to whether they are staff members, contractors or victims of tortious actions.[88]

The solution offered by Reinisch

Reinisch offers the view that by taking analogies from modern state immunity law and diplomatic law, the transfer of their underlying rationales – the protection of the internal exercise of authority and *ne impediatur officia* respectively – could lead to a result-oriented, appropriate

---

[86] Reinisch, *National Courts*, p. 325.

[87] McKinnon Wood as cited by P. Bekker, *The Legal Position of Intergovernmental Organisations: A Functional Necessity Analysis of their Legal Status and Immunities* (Boston and London: Martinus Nijhoff Publishers, 1994), p. 102.

[88] Reinisch, *National Courts*, pp. 326–7.

functional standard of immunity that protects the functioning of international organisations in that domestic courts concentrate 'on the (anticipated) consequences of denying immunity'.[89] At the same time, the granting of immunity should be made dependent on supervising not only the availability but more importantly the appropriateness and fairness of the alternative dispute resolution procedures offered by the respondent international organisation.[90]

A negative outcome of this evaluation would compel domestic courts to engage in vicarious dispute settlement to satisfy the legitimate interests of private claimants in a judicial forum,[91] as it can never be considered functionally necessary for international organisations to deprive private parties dealing with the organisation of all forms of judicial protection.[92]

A complementary solution may be found in replacing traditional immunity thinking with a lack-of-jurisdiction doctrine based on material reasons. This may result in the internal (that is, constitutional and administrative) law of the organisation being excluded from domestic jurisdiction because it is materially analogous to the same category of the law of states.[93] The organisation's operational procedures and guidelines would not be part of the applicable law before domestic courts to the

---

[89] Ibid., pp. 348–56, 359–63 and 365. Reinisch's conclusion is preceded by a critical review of the functional immunity standard in general and of the strict functional necessity concept in particular: ibid., pp. 330–44. For a critical analysis of the functional necessity doctrine, see also Singer, 'Jurisdictional Immunity', 101 et seq.

[90] Reinisch, National Courts, pp. 365–8. See also Singer, 'Jurisdictional Immunity', 101: his proposal is not only modest ('a sworn statement from a responsible official in an international organisation, reciting in detail that its settlement procedures meet certain specified standards, should be conclusive'), it obviously also has a rather low protective potential. As, indeed, the ECJ has recalled in Case 222/84, Johnston v. Chief Constable of the RUC [1986] ECR 1651, the principle of effective judicial control means that a certificate that claims to be conclusive, such as with regard to the privileges and immunities of an international organisation, could not allow the competent authority to deprive an individual of the possibility of asserting his rights by judicial process (as cited by J. Usher, General Principles of EC Law (London and New York: Longman, 1998), p. 86).

[91] Reinisch, National Courts, p. 369.

[92] Muller, International Organisations and their Host-states, p. 271. Muller has suggested a less far-reaching alternative for the domestic courts of host states: they would give a prima facie ruling, without involving themselves with the merits of the case, but it would nevertheless be binding on the international organisation to co-operate in the establishment of an arbitral tribunal actually to settle the case or to co-operate in the creation of a settlement procedure for non-contractual liability in clear cases of wilful disregard (ibid., pp. 181–2 and 184).

[93] Reinisch, National Courts, p. 377.

extent that they do not incorporate pre-existing legal rules. Any transgression – namely, the violation of applicable legal rules brought to light, for example, by any of the non-legal or quasi-judicial alternative remedial mechanisms reviewed earlier – may, of course, lead to domestic legal proceedings.

Differences between member states and organs should be considered to be constitutional issues. The more or less parallel application of a kind of political question doctrine implied in this approach should, in my view, give way in cases of a decision or an action of an international organisation violating fundamental human rights. That would be in line with, for instance, the 1997 decision of the Inter-American Commission on Human Rights in the *Gustavo Carranza* case.[94]

Issues governed by Staff Rules and Regulations are a good example of administrative law.[95] In this respect, Reinisch observes that the exclusivity of the jurisdiction of international administrative tribunals cannot be considered to constitute 'an inherently required necessity to guarantee the functioning of international organisations',[96] but is, rather, a matter of convenience.[97]

It should be added, however, that the view expressed by the UN Office of Legal Affairs in a memorandum to the UNRWA Legal Adviser (that the matter of immunity from suit 'should not be judged by domestic law except to the extent, of course, that it incorporates relevant international obligations') may find an inverted application to the effect that matters could be considered by domestic courts to the extent that the internal law of an international organisation incorporates international

---

[94] Report No. 30/97, Case 10.087, *Gustavo Carranza v. Argentina*, Annual Report of the Inter-American Commission on Human Rights, 1997, OEA/Ser.L/V/II.98, Doc. 7 rev. (1998) at 254 as referred to and reviewed by D. Shelton, *Remedies in International Human Rights Law* (Oxford: Oxford University Press, 1999), pp. 33–4.

[95] Reinisch, *National Courts*, pp. 378–9. The lack-of-jurisdiction approach was also clearly reflected in a detailed review of the provisions of the Convention on the Privileges and Immunities of Specialised Agencies in the 1947 *Becket Report* when dealing with Section 31(a): 'it was observed that this provision applied to contracts and other matters *incidental* to the performance by the agency of its main functions under its constitutional instrument and not to the central performance of its constitutional functions' (A/503 of 20 November 1947, Report of the Sixth Committee, A/C.6/191, para. 32: emphasis in the original).

[96] Reinisch, *National Courts*, p. 384.

[97] *Ibid.*, p. 392. It could be added that as a result of the international civil service not being subject to any domestic legal system, the administration of justice at the UN 'may fail to benefit from the most dynamic labour legislation developments', as was pointed out by the JIU: A/55/57, p. viii.

legal norms and rules.[98] Furthermore, there is no difficulty in accepting the argument that the immunity granted to an organisation covering its official activities does not extend to unlawful acts,[99] a position which in the area of sovereign immunity has already been attained in the combined application of the 1975 Foreign Sovereign Immunities Act and 1789 Alien Tort Claims Act in US case law.[100]

A proportionate functional immunity standard and a lack-of-jurisdiction approach, however, do not detract from the fact that 'a large number of ordinary *iure gestionis* acts performed by international organisations in their dealings with private parties hardly merit immunity from suit';[101] this is also due to the additional policy reason that enforcement of law should in normal circumstances be performed by the domestic courts of the state whose national legislation is applicable to the relationship or the situation giving rise to the dispute. Given that the UN, for instance, has for many years adapted the terms of its contractual arbitration clauses to local or regional conditions, Singer expects that it would not be appreciably more burdensome for them to submit themselves to domestic jurisdictions in such day-to-day matters, at least in headquarter/host states.[102]

The following areas should be considered.

In the absence of a regular employment relationship, disputes between an international organisation and individuals providing services are more likely to become subject to vicarious dispute settlement by domestic courts because the availability of alternative dispute settlement mechanisms may be low or non-existent.[103] Because contractual relationships with international organisations are governed by the law of a particular country, a domestic court will be perfectly capable of applying such a law according to its rules of private international law.[104]

Domestic courts seem to provide an appropriate forum for disputes arising out of claims for damages against international organisations, because of tortious behaviour, such as in the course of carrying out

---

[98] The UN Memorandum is cited in its original version by Reinisch, *National Courts*, p. 127, note 481.

[99] *Ibid.*, p. 207, note 208 referring to an applicant's argument before a UK court in *Mukoro v. EBRD and Others*, Employment Appeal Tribunal, 19 May 1994, ILR 107 (1997), 604–13.

[100] See, *inter alia*, M. Evans, 'International Wrongs and National Jurisdiction' in M. Evans (ed.), *Remedies in International Law: The Institutional Dilemma* (Oxford: Hart Publishing, 1998), pp. 173–90, at pp. 186–9.

[101] Reinisch, *National Courts*, p. 361.   [102] Singer, 'Jurisdictional Immunity', 85.

[103] Reinisch, *National Courts*, p. 385.   [104] *Ibid.*, p. 386.

official functions and activities,[105] and for which, as indicated earlier, the availability and functioning of adequate remedial mechanisms raises serious questions.

In both contractual and tort claims the absence of a proper contract and tort law of international organisations provides an additional reason to seize the remedial opportunity presented by domestic courts. The legitimate interest in those cases 'in having access to domestic courts may [however] not be regarded a fundamental right *de lege lata*'.[106]

The model proposed by Reinisch providing domestic courts as an appropriate forum for disputes involving international organisations, using a combination of a lack-of-jurisdiction approach in some areas and adjudication in ordinary private-law disputes, could eventually strike the delicate balance for which any remedial regime for international organisations has to search, provided that the future development of the practice of both international organisations and domestic courts corroborates Reinisch's premises. Indeed, the more controversial or political the functions and purposes of an international organisation are, the stronger is its need and claim for protective privileges and immunities,[107] and also the stronger are the requirements embedded in a well-functioning accountability regime.

If a domestic court does not grant immunity to the organisation and it decides to exercise its judicial powers to resolve the dispute brought before it by a non-state party, the resulting difference between the international organisation and the forum state should be settled according to the provisions of the General Convention or the Convention for Specialised Agencies.

The coherence required for a well-functioning remedial regime implies, in addition to the potential remedial role for domestic courts, that 'further development in international procedures of judicial redress may play a significant part in resolving some of the problems presented by international immunities', as observed by Jenks in 1961.[108] That is the focus of the final section of this chapter and of chapter 20.

The potential role of arbitration proceedings

International organisations may perform their obligation to make provision for appropriate settlement of disputes in various ways, as this study

---

[105] *Ibid.*, p. 387.   [106] *Ibid.*, p. 393.
[107] Bekker, *Legal Position*, p. 116.   [108] Jenks, *International Immunities*, p. 165.

demonstrates. One of the options available to them is the insertion in agreements and contracts of clauses providing for arbitration.

Arbitration between states and international organisations

States hosting the headquarters of an international organisation as a result enjoy a preferential standing, as indicated earlier in this study.[109] Headquarters Agreements normally provide for compulsory referral for final decision to arbitration in the case of any dispute that the parties have been unable to solve by using the other, non-legal dispute settlement mechanisms. Similar provisions have been inserted into agreements between international organisations and states hosting a diplomatic conference, states contributing troops to peacekeeping operations and other states that are, in one way or another, the beneficiaries of activities undertaken by an international organisation. In spite of the insertion of these clauses, apparently only a single arbitration proceeding was actually initiated in the mid-1980s under the aegis of the Permanent Court of Arbitration between the UNDP and Somalia, but it was terminated without an award in 1992.[110]

The remedial opportunity that arbitration between states and an international organisation may present is, of course, dependent upon the two parties being in a position and willing formally to enter into the dispute settlement procedure, as was clearly demonstrated in the *PLO Advisory Opinion* case: it brought to the fore the vulnerability of such compulsory arbitration clauses 'as the only legal remedy to solve the dispute'.[111] In a case where a state has a claim against an international organisation the respondent may similarly refrain from setting in motion the dispute settlement procedure provided for, leaving the claimant state with only political remedies; in such a situation a provision along the lines of Section 21(b) (enabling either party to ask the General Assembly to request an Advisory Opinion from the ICJ on any legal question arising in the course of arbitration) would then be

---

[109] See above, p. 36.

[110] P. Szasz, 'Granting International Organisations *Jus Standi* in the International Court of Justice' in A. Muller, D. Raic and J. Thuransky (eds.), *The International Court of Justice: Its Future Role After Fifty Years* (The Hague, Boston and London: Martinus Nijhoff Publishers, 1997), pp. 169–88, at p. 175, note 9.

[111] *Applicability of the Obligation to Arbitrate under Section 21 of the United Nations Headquarters Agreement of 26 June 1947, ICJ Reports* (1988), p. 12, at p. 20, para. 19 referring to the UN Secretary-General's view as it was confirmed and reiterated in General Assembly Resolution 42/230 (*ibid.*, p. 26, para. 30).

either inapplicable because of it being premature or alternatively of no avail.[112]

A wider use of arbitration for disputes between states and international organisations was proposed by the International Law Association as early as 1966 at its Fifty-second Conference.[113] A similar proposal explicitly urging the wider use of the Permanent Court of Arbitration was made within the context of the programme for the UN Decade of International Law (1992).[114]

A Steering Committee appointed by the Permanent Court of Arbitration's Secretary-General – pursuant to an authorisation given to him by the first ever Conference of Members of the PCA in 1993 – in 1994 identified the inclusion of international organisations as parties in the PCA dispute settlement proceedings as an area for immediate attention. According to the Steering Committee, 'International Organisations, and the States and other parties with whom they engage in transactions, lacked an effective forum for dispute resolution, and ... it was appropriate for the Permanent Court of Arbitration to take steps aimed at filling this gap.'[115]

Optional Rules for Arbitration involving International Organisations and States were drawn up along the lines of the PCA's 1992 Rules for Arbitrating Disputes between two states and they were patterned upon the UNCITRAL Arbitration Rules.[116] As to the scope *ratione personae* it has to be noted that the Rules would also apply to proceedings initiated by a state that is not a member state of the respondent international organisation.[117]

According to the introductory note by the PCA, the scope *ratione materiae* is intended to cover the widest possible range of potential disputes between states and international organisations.[118] They would include

---

[112] Eagleton rightly wondered 'which legal questions would be taken away from the tribunal and given to the Court for an advisory opinion ... [and to what extent] the arbitral tribunal is bound by the opinion of the Court': 'International Organisations', 420.

[113] J. Sztucki, 'International Organisations as Parties to Contentious Proceedings before the International Court of Justice?' in Muller, Raic and Thuransky (eds.), *International Court of Justice*, pp. 141–67, at p. 155.

[114] As reported by Sztucki, 'International Organisations', p. 155.

[115] Permanent Court of Arbitration, *Optional Rules for Arbitration between International Organisations and Private Parties*, 1996, pp. vi–vii.

[116] Permanent Court of Arbitration, *Optional Rules for Arbitration involving International Organisations and States*, 1996, p. vii. The Headquarters Agreement between the OPCW and the Netherlands provides for arbitration under the new PCA Optional Rules.

[117] Article 1(2)(b).   [118] PCA, *Optional Rules*, p. vii.

disputes as to membership rights and duties initiated by a member state when an international organisation has disregarded its own rules (such as rules of competence or rules of procedure).[119] This approach – admittedly presented in an introductory note and by way of example – clearly contrasts with the alleged desire within international organisations to withhold disputes of a constitutional nature from the compulsory jurisdiction of the ICJ[120] and from a potential role for domestic courts.[121]

The agreements governing special relationships in the framework of programmes for economic, financial and technical assistance, or those arising under Headquarters Agreements, were given by the PCA as the second example of a category of disputes for which states and international organisations may provide for compulsory arbitration to be governed by the PCA's Optional Rules.[122]

The third category of potential disputes consists of 'justiciable' relationships with third states, arising in fact from similar situations.[123] The qualification added appears to imply that because of pre-existing membership links, disputes between member states and international organisations are justiciable by nature. On the other hand, from a remedial perspective it is worth noting that the situation giving rise to the dispute between a state and an international organisation may, having regard to the wording used in the PCA's Introductory Note, be a 'dispute' without further qualification or 'justiciable *relationships*', and that in Article 33 of the Optional Rules agreements or relationships may both be of a contractual or of a tortious nature.[124]

With regard to the applicable law the arbitral tribunal 'shall apply the rules of the Organisation concerned and the law applicable to any agreement or relationship between the parties, and where appropriate, the general principles governing the law of International Organisations and the rules of general international law',[125] unless the parties agree to a settlement *ex aequo et bono*.[126]

Arbitration between non-state entities and international organisations

The remedial role of arbitration for non-state claimants who are not staff members has been referred to earlier; arbitration as a dispute settlement mechanism has been provided for and resorted to in the case of both contractual and non-contractual claims.

---

[119] *Ibid.*, p. vii, (a). [120] See below, p. 248. [121] See above, p. 216.
[122] PCA, *Optional Rules*, p. vii, (b). [123] *Ibid.*, p. vii, (c).
[124] PCA, *Optional Rules*, p. vii. [125] Article 33(1). [126] Article 33(2).

Staff members, in fact, have no alternative but to bring their claims against an international organisation before the competent international administrative tribunal after having exhausted the internal remedies provided by the organisation. At present, except for the ILOAT, an institutionalised form of appeal against the judgments of the UNAT is unavailable to them, unless they want to turn to their national state for the espousal of their claim in the exercise of diplomatic protection.

Optional Rules for Arbitration between International Organisations and Private Parties were drawn up by the Steering Committee and they, too, entered into effect on 1 July 1996. According to the PCA's Introductory Note, the Rules are intended to cover, *inter alia*, disputes between a private provider of goods and services, or employees and an international organisation;[127] as to the latter category, that remedial opportunity would affect the exclusive jurisdiction of the international administrative tribunals.

In contrast with the Optional Rules for Arbitration involving International Organisations and States, the arbitral tribunal dealing with the dispute involving private parties is not obliged to *apply* the rules of the international organisation and the applicable law but merely *to have regard to them*. The arbitral tribunal shall decide in accordance with the terms of the agreement and shall take into account the usages of the trade applicable to the transaction or relationship.[128]

Both sets of Optional Rules also provide for the possibility of interim measures of protection to be taken by the Arbitral Tribunal at the request of either party.[129]

At the time of writing (spring 2000) no cases using either of the Optional Rules have been instituted under the aegis of the Permanent Court of Arbitration.

[127] PCA, *Optional Rules*, p. vii.   [128] Article 33(3).   [129] Article 26.

20 An inevitable role for the International Court of Justice

The multiplicity and infinite variety of their acts, actions and omissions taking place on a multilevel scale may result in international organisations becoming involved in differences or disputes with a wide range of non-state entities such as staff members, national and international non-governmental organisations, private enterprises and individuals; and as described in Part I of this study this may occur on the three levels of accountability. In Parts II and III I reviewed the procedural aspects and the substantive outcome of remedial action that could be undertaken by non-state entities and this was followed in chapters 18 and 19 by taking a closer look at the available non-legal alternative remedial mechanisms and the possible improvements to existing judicial ones. The time has now come to pay attention once more to those main actors on the international scene who naturally and inevitably run a much greater risk of finding themselves opposed to an international organisation in a difference or a dispute because of their permanent dealings with international organisations through their membership links or otherwise, namely states.

Within a membership framework states have at their disposal a wide range of political and legal remedial actions to render operational the accountability of the international organisation, although decreasing circles of differential standing depending on their additional status – for instance, being a host state to an international organisation's headquarters or to one of its operational activities – have been identified.[1] The absence of membership links greatly reduces the number and changes the kind of available remedies on every level of accountability.

---

[1] See Part I, chapters 3, 4 and 6.

AN INEVITABLE ROLE FOR THE ICJ 225

In resorting to the remedial mechanisms, states may act to defend their own interests or rights or they may act on the initiative of or on behalf of one of their nationals, whether a staff member, representational non-governmental organisation, private enterprise or individual.

In order to resolve their differences or disputes with an international organisation, states can utilise any of the traditional dispute settlement mechanisms as referred to by the International Court of Justice in the *Reparations* case: 'Among these methods [for the establishment, the presentation and the settlement of claims] may be mentioned protest, request for an enquiry, negotiation, and request for submission to an arbitral tribunal or to the Court in so far as this may be authorised by the Statute.'[2]

As non-state claimants staff members, representational non-governmental organisations and private claimants are faced with a common procedural obstacle to their remedial potential because of the jurisdictional immunity of international organisations before domestic courts,[3] and in this respect this study has called for a reconsideration of the potential role of domestic courts.[4] The removal of this obstacle is a key element in an adequate implementation of the accountability regime for international organisations.

The principal judicial organ of the UN possesses what 'one might call the *"principal responsibility" for the* settlement *of disputes of a legal nature'.*[5] Turning to the remedial potential the ICJ may offer to states in differences or disputes with international organisations, it is clear that the limitation contained in Article 34(1) of the Court's Statute constitutes a procedural obstacle that is hard to overestimate, but the removal of which is just as pivotal in establishing a comprehensive and adequate accountability regime for international organisations as is overcoming their jurisdictional immunities before domestic courts.

It should be recalled that an adequate accountability regime can only be brought about by the various categories of claimants having multiple remedial mechanisms and opportunities at their disposal to which, simultaneously or consecutively, they can resort. States can obtain a judicial remedy for the tortious liability and/or organisational responsibility

---

[2] *Reparations for Injuries Suffered in the Service of the United Nations*, Advisory Opinion, *ICJ Reports* (1949), p. 174, at p. 177.

[3] See chapter 12. [4] See the second section of the previous chapter.

[5] President Bedjaoui in his address before the General Assembly's Sixth Committee, *Yearbook ICJ* 49 (1994–5), 216 (emphasis in original).

226   ALTERNATIVE REMEDIAL ACTION AND FUTURE OPTIONS

of an international organisation from the International Court of Justice in either a direct or an indirect way.

In the first two sections I will first pay attention to the indirect modalities whose remedial potential certainly should not be underestimated, as indicated earlier, before addressing the vital and complex question of direct remedial action in the third section.

Indirect remedial opportunity in an inter-state dispute before the Court

A first indirect remedial opportunity may arise when the tortious liability or legal responsibility of an international organisation as a result of one of its acts, actions or omissions is referred to during an inter-state dispute before the Court by any of the parties when they consider it to constitute an (important, relevant or subordinate) element of the subject-matter of the dispute between them. The legal validity, scope and interpretation of an act adopted by an organ of an international organisation could, for instance, easily play a decisive, major or more subordinate but actual role in the Court's determination of the respective rights and obligations of the state parties; this is demonstrated by pending cases.[6]

Parties may challenge an act of the international organisation; if their argument is upheld by the Court's majority they may thus obtain an indirect remedial ruling against the organisation, although the legal consequences of declared illegality will still have to emanate from further steps that must be taken by the competent organs in accordance with the organisation's applicable rules. Such a decision will occur in spite of the organisation not being a party to the dispute or the case, as the persuasive force of the Court's judgment on this legal issue extends beyond Article 59 of its Statute.

A second modality may present itself in relation to information that is relevant to an inter-state dispute and is to be provided by an

---

[6] *Questions of Interpretation and Application of the 1971 Montreal Convention arising from the Aerial Incident at Lockerbie (Libyan Jamahiriya v. United Kingdom); Questions of Interpretation and Application of the 1971 Montreal Convention arising from the Aerial Incident at Lockerbie (Libyan Jamahiriya v. United States of America); Application of the Convention on the Prevention and Punishment of the Crime of Genocide (Bosnia and Herzegovina v. Yugoslavia); Armed Activities on the Territory of the Congo (Democratic Republic of the Congo v. Burundi); Armed Activities on the Territory of the Congo (Democratic Republic of the Congo v. Rwanda); Armed Activities on the Territory of the Congo (Democratic Republic of the Congo v. Uganda); Application of the Convention on the Prevention and Punishment of the Crime of Genocide (Croatia v. Yugoslavia).*

international organisation upon the request of the International Court of Justice or on the organisation's own initiative, pursuant to Article 34(2) and (3) of the Statute.[7] In appropriate circumstances the information originating from the organisation's Chief Executive Officer may contain elements of a factual and/or legal nature, throwing light on the tortious liability and/or legal responsibility of the organisation supplying it. Although this possibility might be considered to be too remote, disputes on the use of force in the Great Lakes Region in Africa could be referred to as potentially being cases where the Secretary-General, in the exercise of his *amicus curiae* function, could perhaps act more as a quasi-defendant implicated in the inter-state dispute.

Parties will accordingly be able to use this to their advantage, as the information given by the organisation will be added to the records of the case. The degree of indirect remedial potential will, of course, depend on how crucial is the role played by the acts, actions or omissions in the subject-matter of the dispute as presented by the parties and/or as approached by the Court.

The remedial outcome could be less indirect if the Court were to request information of a quite specific and detailed nature that could potentially have a more substantial bearing on the case before it.

States appearing before the Court may also themselves create an indirect remedial opportunity under Article 51 of the Court's Statute when calling officials of an international organisation as witnesses to answer relevant questions put to them during the hearing not only by the parties under the control of the President, but also by the President and the other judges.[8] In appropriate circumstances – such as when the information that the official of the organisation would be able to supply is exceptionally confidential, or due to the organ's unique status (such as, for instance, the UNHCR or UNHCHR) – examination of the witnesses otherwise than before the Court itself can take place pursuant to Article 63(2) of the Rules of the Court. Overall protection would, of

---

[7] International organisations were thus given 'a status analogous to that enjoyed under the municipal law of many States by a public officer appearing as *amicus curiae* in proceedings relating to matters of public interest': C. W. Jenks, 'The Status of International Organisations in Relation to the International Court of Justice', *Transactions Grotius Society* 32 (1946), 1–41, at 2. On the special *amicus curiae* role of the Secretary-General in the advisory proceedings before the Court see, *inter alia*, S. Rosenne, 'The Secretary-General of the United Nations and the Advisory Proceedings of the International Court of Justice' in K. Wellens (ed.), *International Law: Theory and Practice: Essays in Honour of Eric Suy* (The Hague, Boston and London: Martinus Nijhoff Publishers, 1998), pp. 707–17.

[8] Article 65 of the Rules of the Court.

course, also become available, if circumstances so require, by the application of Article 46 of the Court's Statute and Article 59 of the Rules of the Court, which render the hearing not public in whole or in part; the cases on the use of force in the Great Lakes Region are again relevant here. The subsequent use by the Court, in reaching its decision in the inter-state dispute, of the information provided by an organisation's official appearing as a witness will determine whether any of the parties could derive an indirect remedial benefit from the initiatives they have taken under Article 51 of the Statute of the Court.

Similar observations apply when the Court decides that an inquiry should be carried out or an expert opinion be given pursuant to Article 50 of its Statute. In defining the subject of the inquiry or of the expert opinion under Article 67(1) of its Rules, the Court may very well touch upon issues and questions of operational activities undertaken by an international organisation that may eventually bring to the fore aspects of that organisation's non-contractual liability and/or responsibility.

The question whether the Court would – in the circumstances arising under Articles 34(2), 50 and 51 of its Statute and in the light of the testimony and results of an inquiry or expert opinion – apply the *Monetary Gold* case rule by analogy is a matter of a delicate and speculative nature. The problem could be circumvented by the use of alternative remedial solutions having a less indirect or direct character, which are envisaged in the following two sections.

(In)direct remedial opportunity by way of a (binding) Advisory Opinion

A member state which wants to raise the issue of the non-contractual liability and/or legal responsibility of an international organisation or of one of its organs, when it has allegedly occurred by an act, or in the course of a particular action (or omission), could of course try to convince a majority of the UN General Assembly or of the Security Council, other organs of the UN and Specialised Agencies, to request the International Court of Justice to deliver an Advisory Opinion on the relevant legal question, 'abstract or otherwise', although a serious attempt should be made to avoid questions too abstractly worded and unrelated to a 'defined issue or set of facts'.[9] The fact that the question

---

[9] As recommended by the Informal Inter-Allied Committee on the Future of the Permanent Court of Justice brought together in London (1943) by the British

'does not relate to a specific dispute should...not lead the Court to decline to give an opinion',[10] but that question, of course, should not relate to a legal question actually pending between two or more states.[11] So in a situation where the Court would not be able to render judgment in a contentious case between a (member) state and an international organisation, the Advisory Opinion may be used to obtain a remedy comparable to a declaratory judgment.[12] That is also borne out by the Advisory Opinion in the *Cumaraswamy* case: the Court could have been called upon to determine the appropriateness of the terms used by the Special Rapporteur or his assessment of the situation[13] and it did rule on the correctness of the Secretary-General's finding that the Special Rapporteur had been acting in the course of performing his mission.[14]

In establishing its jurisdiction to deliver such an Advisory Opinion, the Court considers the political motives behind the request to be of no relevance.[15] Although the Court included in the same pronouncement the political implications which the Opinion might have, it immediately qualified that statement as being of no relevance: the possibility that the requested Opinion could have the potential to undermine the progress already made or being made on a sensitive issue and could therefore be contrary to the interests of the UN could constitute a compelling reason for the Court to decline to deliver an Opinion.[16] Depending on circumstances such as its political power within the organisation, the situation giving rise to the legal issues and their perceived importance by other member states, the 'dissatisfied State'[17] will, of course, not always be successful in having a resolution containing such a request adopted. In

---

Government, cited by M. Pomerance, 'The Advisory Role of the International Court of Justice and its "Judicial" Character: Past and Future Prisms' in A. Muller, D. Raic and J. Thuransky (eds.), *The International Court of Justice: Its Future Role After Fifty Years* (The Hague, Boston and London: Martinus Nijhoff Publishers, 1997), pp. 271–323, at p. 321.

League Council requests did not contain broad abstract formulations, which could have entailed policy-setting rather than dispute settlement (*ibid.,* p. 278).

[10] *Legality of the Threat or Use of Nuclear Weapons,* Advisory Opinion, *ICJ Reports* (1996), p. 226, at p. 236.

[11] Article 102(2) of the Rules of the Court.

[12] C. Gray, *Judicial Remedies in International Law* (Oxford: Clarendon Press, 1987), p. 118.

[13] *Difference Relating to Immunity from Legal Process of a Special Rapporteur of the Commission on Human Rights,* Advisory Opinion of 22 April 1999, *ICJ Reports* (1999), p. 62, at p. 86, para. 56.

[14] *Ibid.*

[15] *Legality of the Threat or Use of Nuclear Weapons,* Advisory Opinion, *ICJ Reports* (1996), p. 226, at p. 234, para. 13.

[16] *Ibid.,* paras. 15 and 17.   [17] Gray, *Judicial Remedies,* pp. 111–12.

a situation the inverse of that which actually occurred, Malaysia would not, prior to the controversial interviews, have been able to convince the ECOSOC to request an Advisory Opinion on the way the Special Rapporteur had been carrying out the mandate with which he had been entrusted by the Commission on Human Rights.

From the point of view of contesting states in general it is to be noted that in 1956 at its Forty-seventh Conference the International Law Association adopted a motion with the aim of imposing upon the organs of the UN the obligation, under Article 96 of the Charter, to request from the International Court of Justice an Advisory Opinion concerning any situation in which a claim is made by a member state that the organ has exceeded its jurisdiction under the Charter.[18]

It has also been pointed out that, in spite of its non-binding nature, the remedial effect of an Advisory Opinion that has been exclusively requested pursuant to Article 96 of the UN Charter will normally extend beyond the member state which is involved in a difference or a dispute and which had been successful in triggering the request. Although the formal addressee of the Advisory Opinion may be the requesting organ, the real addressees will be the parties, the international organisation and public opinion.[19] The practical remedial consequences that would flow from the Advisory Opinion in terms of damages or otherwise would be a matter for the organisation to consider, although the principle of it being required to take such measures may have been included in both the request and the Opinion.

Non-contractual liability and the legal responsibility of an international organisation may also be at the heart of differences arising out of the interpretation or application of the 1946 General Convention on the Privileges and Immunities of the United Nations between the UN and a member state; a few points should be noted here from a remedial perspective.

Advisory Opinions under the 1946 General Convention: the right of initiative

The threshold for putting Article VIII, Section 30 of the General Convention into operation is unusual, as a full-scale dispute in the sense

---

[18] *ILA Report of the 47th Conference*, held at Dubrovnik, 26 August–1 September 1956 (London, 1957), p. 104.

[19] Pomerance, 'Advisory Role', p. 300, citing Judge Winiarski's Dissenting Opinion in the *Peace Treaties* case.

formulated by the ICJ – 'a disagreement on a point of law or fact, a conflict of legal views or of interests between two persons'[20] – is not required: a 'difference' would suffice, which thus lowers the access to the remedial mechanism, especially when using the French version of the text: 'toute contestation'. In the hypothesis under consideration in this study, the international organisation is the respondent 'party' to such a 'difference'; the lower threshold, however, is not matched by a corresponding wider access, as the request for an Advisory Opinion has to be made in accordance with Article 96 of the UN Charter – meaning that the organisation's organs have the right of initiative. The member state would thus seem to face the political obstacles inherent in the Article 96 triggering mechanism. The UN, and other organisations for that matter, are 'contested' in their interpretation and application of their privileges and immunities: allegedly they have caused harm and incurred legal responsibility in the process of doing so. There is reason to believe that international organisations may consider it a matter of self-interest to have these accusations tested and rejected by the UN's principal judicial organ at the earliest convenience. So although the initiative to start the remedial action is being withheld from the member state, and the international organisation has no discretion in this regard, the remedial potential for the member state is real and could include the whole range of remedial consequences that would normally flow from a ruling of the Court on the organisation's responsibility for non-compliance (that is, abuse) with the Convention, which has to be accepted as 'decisive' by both 'parties'.

However, on the first occasion that the Court received a request for an Advisory Opinion under Article VIII, Section 30 of the General Convention, the Court made it clear that such a difference does not change the advisory nature of the Court's function,[21] which has to be distinguished from 'the particular effects parties to an existing dispute

[20] PCIJ Series A, No. 2, *The Mavrommatis Palestine Concessions*, at p. 11. However, the International Court of Justice made it clear that 'it is not sufficient for one party to a contentious case to assert that a dispute exists with the other party. A mere assertion is not sufficient to prove the existence of a dispute any more than a mere denial of the existence of a dispute proves its non-existence. Nor is it adequate to show that the interests of the two parties to such a case are in conflict. It must be shown that the claim of one party is positively opposed by the other': *South West Africa Cases (Preliminary Objections) Ethiopia v. South Africa; Liberia v. South Africa*, Judgment of 21 December 1962, *ICJ Reports* (1962), p. 319, at p. 328.

[21] *Difference Relating to Immunity from Legal Process of a Special Rapporteur of the Commission on Human Rights*, Advisory Opinion of 22 April 1999, *ICJ Reports* (1999), p. 62, at pp. 76–7, para. 25.

232   ALTERNATIVE REMEDIAL ACTION AND FUTURE OPTIONS

may wish to attribute, in their mutual relations, to an advisory opinion of the Court'.[22]

The same so-called preventive approach may be found in Section 32 of the Convention on the Privileges and Immunities of the Specialised Agencies. This Convention stands out in several respects from a remedial perspective. In the first place, it provides that states parties may trigger the dispute settlement mechanism by voicing their concern that there has allegedly been an abuse of the privileges and immunities granted by the Convention in Section 24; this provision, which explicitly acknowledges the role of states as potential claimants, is absent from the General Convention. The consultations to be undertaken are not only aimed at establishing the facts but also, in the case of abuse, to provide a first remedy to the claimant state by including an attempt to ensure that no repetition will occur. And, finally, in the case of confirmation that an abuse has in fact taken place, the 'injured' state shall, according to Section 24, have the right to withhold from the Specialised Agency the benefits of the privilege and immunity so abused.

If, in the future, access to the International Court of Justice under Article 34 of its Statute is not widened so as to encompass a right of *locus standi* for international organisations, the modality of international organisations – despite being respondent parties to differences or disputes – being allowed or compelled to take the remedial initiative to request the Court to deliver a binding Advisory Opinion could usefully become more generalised beyond the area of privileges and immunities for all differences and disputes between states and international organisations concerning their non-contractual liability and/or legal responsibility. That would, of course, require that relevant agreements to that end become widespread in order to meet the constant *conditio sine qua non* set by the Court that the consent of the parties is essential for the advisory procedure to be used as a substitute for contentious proceedings.[23]

The procedure envisaged here could be triggered along the lines of the Specialised Agency Convention, including an attempt to ensure that the alleged violation does not reoccur. The possibility of a countermeasure by the state temporarily suspending the benefits at stake would, of course, only arise in particular circumstances. Moreover, the formulation of the question(s) to be submitted to the Court could very well

---

[22] *Ibid.*

[23] E. Lauterpacht, *Aspects of the Administration of International Justice* (Cambridge: Grotius Publications, 1991), p. 61.

include an indication by the Court of any remedial consequences in favour of the claimant state. The possibility that a Court pronouncement would clash with past decisions taken by the requesting organ[24] could be seen as another indication of the vulnerability of international organisations taking this preventive approach, but this possibility would not necessarily be any greater than in the case of a request by any two or more states acting in concert and affording them the opportunity to clarify their legal rights.[25]

Due attention has also to be paid to the procedural inequality of arms during the pre-request stage.[26] In its Opinion in the *Cumaraswamy* case, the Court pointed out that the formulation of the question to be submitted to the Court is in the hands of a particular organ without the member state concerned being able to control the drafting process, and it added that it was also not for the Secretary-General to formulate the terms of the question.[27] It should be noted that although, on the active side of accountability, the Secretary-General may be protecting the interests of the organisation, his role on the passive side seems to be reduced to a more instrumental one, as he lacks the personal capacity to request the Court to deliver an Advisory Opinion.

One of the circumstances in which it might be appropriate for the Secretary-General to be allowed to request an Advisory Opinion from the Court had already been referred to by Wilfred Jenks, namely if the Secretary-General were to be made responsible for the administration of a (UN) zone.[28] The several examples of UN Transitory Authorities mentioned earlier were cases that could have been dealt with in this way.[29]

---

[24] Referred to by Pomerance in connection with the League of Nations: 'Advisory Role', p. 284.

[25] Proposals of the Informal Inter-Allied Committee on the Future of the Permanent Court of Justice, as cited by Pomerance, *ibid.*, p. 286.

[26] In its 1956 ILOAT (UNESCO) Advisory Opinion the Court raised the question of whether, given certain procedural inequality between the UNESCO's Executive Board and its officials, it would be possible for the Court to remain faithful to the requirement of its judicial character: *Judgements of the Administrative Tribunal of the International Labour Organisation upon Complaints made against UNESCO*, Advisory Opinion of 23 October 1956, *ICJ Reports* (1956), p. 77, at pp. 85–6, as referred to by S. Rosenne, *The Law and Practice of the International Court 1920–1996* (The Hague, Boston and London: Martinus Nijhoff Publishers, 1997), p. 1017.

[27] *Difference Relating to Immunity from Legal Process of a Special Rapporteur of the Commission on Human Rights*, Advisory Opinion of 22 April 1999, *ICJ Reports* (1999), p. 62, at p. 81, para. 36.

[28] Jenks, 'Status of International Organisations', 13.   [29] See above, p. 20.

Remedial protection

Various factors and motives form an inevitable part of the process leading to the adoption of a resolution requesting an Advisory Opinion, including the debate (if one is actually taking place) on the precise wording of the request: they are decisive for the remedial outcome that the 'dissatisfied State' would have liked to occur. In appropriate circumstances the Court may feel the need to reformulate the question.

Given the remedial protection stemming from the invocation or *motu proprio* use of Article 103 of the Rules of the Court, 'the question of the effect of the pending request on the interim action of states and organs will generally [not] pose a major difficulty'.[30] Alternatively, the Court may be guided by Article 41 of its Statute to the extent that it recognises that provision to be applicable, either *proprio motu* or upon request by either of the 'parties'.

Furthermore, although currently applicable agreements provide for a decisive or binding force for, or acceptance by, the parties, nothing similar to Articles 59 and 60 of the Court's Statute is stated. This leaves open the possibility that in a subsequent inter-state contentious case the result of such an Advisory Opinion might be questioned;[31] this would, however, not include the specific remedial consequences contained in the Opinion, which are, *ex hypothesi*, to the benefit of the 'claimant' state. Christine Gray rightly observed that the issue should not be exaggerated and that the Court 'has to live with this problem'.[32]

In spite of the fact that Articles 59 and 60 of the Statute of the Court do not apply to binding Advisory Opinions, they do have persuasive force; this would call for a right of intervention for third states under Article 63 of the Statute,[33] although the utilisation of Article 66 of the Statute could have some supporting effect towards the claimant state.[34] Counsel for Malaysia in the *Cumaraswamy* case convincingly recalled that the procedure before the Court was in essence a contentious one.[35]

The preventive approach suggested earlier in the case of a dispute between a state and the UN on a matter of UN law would, of course,

---

[30] Pomerance, 'Advisory Role', pp. 284–5.

[31] L. Jully, 'Arbitration and Judicial Settlement: Recent Trends', *AJIL* 48 (1954), 380–407, at 390, note 43.

[32] Gray, *Judicial Remedies*, p. 137.

[33] Jully, 'Arbitration', 390, note 34 and R. Plender, 'Procedure in the European Courts: Comparisons and Prospects', *RCADI* 267 (1997), 1–343, at 238.

[34] On the potential role of representational non-governmental organisations before and during advisory proceedings, see above, p. 108.

[35] CR/98/17, p. 45.

remove the problem of the unwillingness of the organisation and the analogous application of the Eastern Carelia doctrine,[36] which is not so much relevant to the 'fear of introducing compulsory jurisdiction by the "advisory" back-door' [37] as to the Court's appreciation of the propriety of rendering the Opinion.[38] The Court may very well continue to 'emphasise the "organisational" aspects of the requests and correspondingly to minimise their "quasi-contentious" aspects',[39] but this does not detract from the fact that the international organisation will consider itself 'a quasi-defendant'[40] and that it may be tempted to act accordingly, with the organisation's Chief Administrative Officer and the member state concerned emerging as the main protagonists, both having 'a legitimate interest . . . in obtaining an opinion from the Court in respect of its own future action'.[41] From a remedial perspective then, 'the *calming effect of advisory proceedings* when, for whatever reason, the legal aspects of the dispute cannot be directly submitted to the Court as a contentious case'[42] may emerge in a less pronounced way.

The existence of a difference or of a dispute between an international organisation and a member state on the interpretation or application of a relevant international agreement does not necessarily in all circumstances result in the request for an Advisory Opinion having a retrospective character, as the subject-matter may also relate to prospective, future acts, actions or likely omissions by the organisation.

Moreover, states (potentially) particularly affected 'are always free to elicit, by consent, a declaratory judgment very much akin to an advisory opinion'.[43]

In spite of all the remedial potential associated with the mechanisms of binding Advisory Opinions of the Court, they 'are firmly rooted in the procedural incapacity' of international organisations[44] and they remain, as succinctly pointed out by Derek Bowett,[45] 'a device, the purpose of which is to alleviate, or compensate for, the lack of direct standing of

---

[36] See Rosenne on the traditional situation involving an unwilling state, *Law and Practice*, p. 1020.

[37] Pomerance, 'Advisory Role', p. 276.

[38] *Western Sahara*, Advisory Opinion, *ICJ Reports* (1975), p. 12, at p. 25, para. 33.

[39] Pomerance, 'Advisory Role', p. 299.   [40] *Ibid.*

[41] *Western Sahara*, Advisory Opinion, *ICJ Reports* (1975), p. 12, at p. 27, para. 41.

[42] President Bedjaoui's address, *Yearbook ICJ* 49 (1994–5), para. 21 (emphasis is original).

[43] Pomerance, 'Advisory Role', p. 323.   [44] Rosenne, *Law and Practice*, p. 1055.

[45] D. Bowett, 'The Court's Role in Relation to International Organisations' in V. Lowe and M. Fitzmaurice (eds.), *Fifty Years of the International Court of Justice: Essays in Honour of Sir Robert Jennings* (New York and Cambridge: Grotius Publications and Cambridge University Press, 1996), pp. 181–92, at p. 189.

international organisations before the Court'. From a strictly remedial perspective within the overall objective of an accountability regime for international organisations there is no reason for them to exercise 'political restraint' in the employment of the advisory jurisdiction.[46]

Direct remedial action by wider access to the Court: amending Article 34

The need for change

It is well known that during the United Nations Conference on International Organisation at San Francisco the desirability of permitting international organisations to be parties before the International Court of Justice was discussed in the Fourth Committee; some of the Committee Members were of the opinion that such cases might occur (New Zealand), while others were positively in favour of direct access for international organisations as applicants (Australia). The Committee's Chairman, who did not share this latter approach, ruled that if such an innovation was considered desirable, proposals should be presented.[47] Discussion on a Venezuelan proposal limited to jurisdictional disputes between international organisations and to appeals from judgments rendered by international administrative tribunals depending from the UN was postponed because of 'the complexity of the issues raised'.[48] One can only agree with Clyde Eagleton that 'the lack of vision shown in this discussion is regrettable'.[49]

At its Forty-seventh Conference, held in 1956, the International Law Association adopted a motion to the effect that the desirability of an amendment to give the UN and its Specialised Agencies direct access to the Court in contentious cases should be considered.[50] Several national branches had proposed amendments, but apparently not all were explicitly considering the situation of an international organisation being the respondent party in such contentious cases.[51]

---

[46] Pomerance, 'Advisory Role', p. 320.

[47] UNICIO, Documents of the UN Conference on International Organisation, San Francisco, 1945, vol. XIV, UN Committee of Jurists, at pp. 136 and 139.

[48] Ibid., Commission IV, Judicial Organisation, vol. XIII, at pp. 210 and 270.

[49] C. Eagleton, 'International Organisations and the Law of Responsibility', RCADI 76 (1950), 323–423, at 417.

[50] ILA Report of the 47th Conference, p. 104.

[51] See, however, the US, UK and Austrian proposals, pursuant to which access would also be open to non-governmental organisations that have Consultative Status A with the UN, individuals, international civil servants and others having contractual claims against international organisations: ibid., pp. 131–2.

In 1954 the Institut de Droit International declared that it was a matter of urgency to widen access to international organisations provided that at least a majority of the member states are members of the UN or parties to the Statute of the Court.[52] The wording of the initial proposal by Henri Rolin left no doubt as to international organisations also being a respondent.[53]

The positive response in 1970-1 by sixteen states on the same question has to be placed in perspective – the majority of states were apparently indifferent to the matter, as evidenced by the fact that about 100 of the then 130 parties to the Statute did not even reply to the questionnaire sent by the UN Secretary-General.[54] The positive replies to the question of wider access were, of course, not all unconditional, while some also provided suggestions as to how the acceptance of the Court's jurisdiction by international organisations could eventually be organised.[55]

From the 1976 Study of the US State Department on widening access, 'it was not clear whether the UN was seen as an applicant only...'.[56]

It is also interesting to note that when the International Law Commission was discussing Article 66 of what became the 1986 Vienna Convention on the Law of Treaties between States and International Organisations or between International Organisations, it decided not to propose giving *locus standi* to international organisations before the International Court of Justice; instead, it included a mechanism of compulsory conciliation, *inter alia* because that 'does not create any essential discrimination between States and International Organisations'.[57]

The 1997 proposals

In January 1997 the first detailed proposals on amending Article 34 of the Statute were tabled by Guatemala before the Special Committee on the Charter of the United Nations and on Strengthening the Role of the Organisation,[58] this initiative being followed in February of the same year by Costa Rica when it deposited a working document containing

---

[52] *Annuaire de l'Institut de Droit International* 45(2) (1954), 298, para. 6.

[53] As cited by P. Couvreur, 'Développements récents concernant l'accès des organisations intergouvernementales à la procédure contentieuse devant la Cour Internationale de Justice' in E. Yakpo and T. Boumedra (eds.), *Liber Amicorum Mohammed Bedjaoui* (The Hague, Boston and London: Kluwer Law International, 1999), pp. 293–323, at p. 297.

[54] J. Sztucki, 'International Organisations as Parties to Contentious Proceedings before the International Court of Justice?' in Muller, Raic and Thuransky (eds.), *International Court of Justice*, pp. 141–67, at p. 152.

[55] See Couvreur, 'Développements récents', pp. 299–300.

[56] Sztucki, 'International Organisations', p. 152.

[57] *Yearbook ILC* (1982), vol. II, Part II, p. 65, paras. 4 and 6.

[58] A/AC.182/L.95 and Rev. 1 of 28 January 1997.

238 ALTERNATIVE REMEDIAL ACTION AND FUTURE OPTIONS

alternative formulae to the text proposed by Guatemala.[59] In introducing its proposal, Guatemala referred to the ever-increasing role played by international organisations in international affairs and cited the conduct of extensive activities involving states and their governments as the main argument in favour of such a reform.[60] These proposals having hardly been discussed before the General Assembly's Sixth Committee in the autumn of 1997, the General Assembly in its Resolution 52/161 of 15 December 1997 – although asking the Special Committee to continue its analysis of the proposals on strengthening the role of the Court – also made it clear that any amendments of the Charter or the Statute could not be implied in measures aiming to remedy the impact of the increasing number of cases on the Court's functioning.[61] This position was confirmed in the General Assembly's subsequent Resolution 53/106, adopted on 8 December 1998.[62]

After some delegations during the 1999 session of the Special Committee had noted the lack of any practical need and political will or consensus within the Committee to proceed with the proposal, and also noting the prohibitive paragraphs in General Assembly Resolution 53/106,[63] on 4 April 1999 Guatemala withdrew its proposal, its recommendation on a proposed questionnaire and the consultation of the Court on the proposal:[64] 'its adoption in the foreseeable future [appearing] most unlikely'.[65]

Policy reasons

If the reasons as to why international organisations do not have *locus standi* before the International Court of Justice are more political than juridical, as stated by Philip Jessup in 1948,[66] then policy reasons could convincingly be put forward in favour of this long-overdue wider access to the International Court of Justice by amending Article 34(1) of its Statute. These policy reasons flow directly from the need for a comprehensive accountability regime for international organisations,

---

[59] A/AC.182/L.97 of 4 February 1997.   [60] A/52/33 of 2 April 1997, p. 29, para. 102.

[61] Paragraphs 3 and 4 of Resolution 52/161.   [62] Paragraph 4(e).

[63] A/54/33 of 12 May 1999, pp. 19–20, paras. 114–15.   [64] *Ibid.*, p. 20, para. 116.

[65] The Sixth Committee had discussed the *Report of the Special Committee on the Charter of the United Nations and on the Strengthening of the Organisation* during the General Assembly's 53rd and 54th sessions: A/C.6/53/SR, 5–8, 13, 16, 17, 28, 32 and 34; A/C.6/54/SR, 5–8, 17, 29, 30 and 34.

[66] P. Jessup, *A Modern Law of Nations: An Introduction* (New York: Macmillan, 1948), p. 25. See also Sztucki, 'International Organisations', p. 147: 'any answer to this question will probably be as good, or as bad, as any other'.

not only containing primary rules governing the conduct of these actors, but also providing for secondary rules as to the implementation of that accountability. Legal and political reasons in favour of giving international organisations *locus standi* can also be found in the fact that they are ultimately creatures of states,[67] that they do share with states the same systemic interests in abiding by obligations of the international legal system[68] and, to a far lesser extent in my view, that the Court would otherwise be unable to play a leading role in this area.[69]

Judicial remedial mechanisms should not only be open to staff members resorting to international administrative tribunals[70] and to private claimants making use of the potential role of domestic courts,[71] but also, in a direct way, to states as an alternative to the arbitral settlement of disputes with an international organisation[72] or to the binding Advisory Opinions route described in the previous subsection. Jerzy Sztucki's question whether, given the outcome in such cases so far, 'other or better results would have been achieved if these disputes could have been submitted to contentious rather than advisory jurisdiction of the Court'[73] is pertinent, but all the cases did involve the active side of accountability, namely the organisation acting as a quasi-applicant. From the other remedial perspective, namely the organisation becoming a quasi-defendant, the potential outcome of a contentious case is much more difficult to predict, if only because of the impact of the exercise of substantial procedural rights by both litigants and, of course, because of the Court's handling of this 'passive' category of disputes.

Disputes between international organisations could arise involving monetary or other issues in connection with the delivery of technical or other assistance to states, but the actual disputes have so far been 'settled more or less amicably', as arbitration clauses are rarely invoked.[74] Member states would consider administrative or political resolution to be superior to a judicial one for disputes between regional and universal organisations.[75]

---

[67] J. Charney, 'Is International Law Threatened by Multiple International Tribunals?', *RCADI* 271 (1998), 101–382, at 133, note 67.

[68] *Ibid.*, 367.   [69] *Ibid.*, 364–5.   [70] See above, p. 199.   [71] See above, p. 208.

[72] See above, p. 219.   [73] Sztucki, 'International Organisations', p. 149.

[74] P. Szasz, 'Granting International Organisations *Jus Standi* in the International Court of Justice' in Muller, Raic and Thuransky (eds.), *International Court of Justice*, pp. 169–88, at p. 172.

[75] *Ibid.*, p. 173. Unconvincingly on disputes between international organisations, see I. Seidl-Hohenveldern, 'Access of International Organisations to the International Court

240   ALTERNATIVE REMEDIAL ACTION AND FUTURE OPTIONS

According to Bowett there is 'little logic' in refusing access[76] to international organisations to the Court and thus compelling both parties to a difference or a dispute to use arbitration as an alternative.

This study has clearly demonstrated the need for such direct remedial action by states before the Court against a respondent international organisation. The second and third levels of accountability of international organisations (that is, non-contractual liability and organisational responsibility) have in the past and will undoubtedly also in the future give rise to a wide range of matters over which the jurisdiction of the International Court of Justice could be extended. A claimant state and a respondent organisation may find themselves rather unexpectedly in a situation where they both consider it necessary and desirable to refer their dispute to the Court. They may also have included special provisions in treaties and Conventions in force for matters to be decided by the Court in the future. Furthermore, legal disputes or differences may relate to the interpretation of a treaty or any question of international law and they may also concern the existence of any fact which if established would constitute a tortious act, but without having resulted in a breach of an international obligation by the organisation and/or concerning the existence of a fact which if established would constitute such a breach. Finally, legal disputes or differences could also concern the nature or the extent of the reparation to be made. Examples have been given in this study of all of these categories.

That 'there has not been any insistent demand from any international organisation for access to the contentious jurisdiction of the Court'[77] is hardly surprising given the comprehensive accountability regime which is in the process of being supplemented and also refined in its remedial aspects. The question of the substantive law to be applied in a case between an applicant state and a respondent organisation 'does not diminish the relevance or force of the identification of the need [for such a] procedural capacity of the organisation'.[78]

Jenks aptly observed that in the political climate of the spring and early summer of 1945 any suggestion to provide *locus standi in judicio* before the Court was premature. But he wisely added that 'the problem

---

of Justice' in Muller, Raic and Thuransky (eds.), *International Court of Justice*, pp. 189–216, at pp. 195–6.

[76] Bowett, 'The Court's Role', p. 189.   [77] Rosenne, *Law and Practice*, p. 653.

[78] Lauterpacht, *Administration of Justice*, p. 62, note 2 discussing the active *locus standi*.

remains and must some day receive an appropriate solution'.[79] Perhaps, almost six decades after the San Francisco Conference, it is now 'high time'.[80]

Having underlined the need for amending Article 34 of the Statute, I now turn to the modalities of wider access and the difficulties accompanying it. As always, substantive and procedural questions are interconnected, and thus the answers provided to some of them will inevitably co-determine the outcome of other issues. Attention will be exclusively on the aspect of organisations becoming respondent parties, although in the past the focus of doctrinal debates has been mainly, if not exclusively, on the question of organisations instituting proceedings against states. Any proposal and subsequent decision to amend Article 34 will obviously involve both aspects.[81]

Although the substantive and procedural questions are identical whether international organisations are granted *locus standi* as applicant or as respondent, the remedial perspective taken throughout this study will decisively influence the answers to be provided. The pertinent questions have also been raised during the debates within the Special Committee on the UN Charter and on the Strengthening of the Organisation.[82]

The amendment of the jurisdiction ratione personae: which international organisations should be granted locus standi?

Both proposals submitted in 1997 to the Special Committee on the UN Charter and on the Strengthening of the Organisation not only require

[79] Jenks, 'Status of International Organisations', 25, para. 35. He was joined by Eagleton in 1950, 'International Organisations', 415 and 418.

[80] Bowett, 'The Court's Role', p. 189. For a chronological reference to pleas from leading scholars see Sztucki, 'International Organisations', 153 and notes 41–6. The most thorough and authoritative analysis of the question of *locus standi* was carried out by P. Couvreur before his appointment as Registrar of the International Court of Justice: 'Développements récents'.

[81] On litigation by international organisations against states and the variety of subject-matters potentially involved see, *inter alia*, Szasz, 'Granting International Organisations', pp. 174–8.

[82] Couvreur, 'Développements récents', pp. 302–6. Accordingly, the argument merely referred to by Szasz ('Granting International Organisations', p. 182) that because states do not have the power to request Advisory Opinions, international organisations should be forced to make a choice between maintaining that privilege or accepting *locus standi*, becomes less relevant. The question whether states should be given the opportunity to request Advisory Opinions has been dealt with earlier (see above, p. 228).

the respondent to be an international organisation but impose additional conditions for the granting of procedural capacity before the ICJ which, because of the particular nature of international organisations, could be justified in order to meet the need for general legal security.[83]

The question of whether the capacity to appear before the Court should be granted to all international organisations or only to some was included in the draft questionnaire to be circulated to states and submitted by Guatemala in January 1998 during the session of the Working Group of the Special Committee.[84]

The draft texts submitted by Guatemala at first glance seemed to correspond to the obvious need that the *locus standi* as respondent should not be limited to particular categories of international organisations as they provided for 'any other international organisation'. The Court's Registrar has pointed out that international organisations or those which are based upon a purely bilateral treaty would then be excluded *a contrario*.[85] In Guatemala's revised version (1999) the qualification 'comprised of States' in the amended Article 34(1) has been deleted.[86]

In Costa Rica's proposal to amend Article 34, access would not be open to all international organisations: remedial action by states would only become possible against international organisations that have been explicitly authorised by their constituent instrument to appear before the Court. Although there is some value in the argument that a reference to the 'rules of the organisation' would leave the organisation with a larger degree of autonomy in the formulation of the envisaged authorisation, Philippe Couvreur immediately added that from the point of view of third parties the publicity of having such an authorisation inserted into the organisation's constituent instrument would present an advantage.[87] From a general remedial point of view that is certainly true. One could add that the concerns of general legal security and predictability would be more adequately met if the only source of the organisation's authorisation to procedural capacity were to be the constituent instrument, to the exclusion, that is, of the other rules of the organisation. If what

---

[83] Couvreur, 'Développements récents', p. 317. This study has earlier referred to the common and distinctive features of states and international organisations from a remedial perspective: see above, Part I, chapter 2, third section.

[84] A/AC.182/L.101 of 3 February 1998. The examination of the draft questionnaire was reported to the Special Committee's next session in 1999, during which Guatemala proposed to send out an abbreviated version of the questionnaire (A/54/33, p. 19, para. 113). The proposal was finally withdrawn by Guatemala.

[85] Couvreur, 'Développements récents', p. 316.

[86] A/54/33, para. 109.   [87] Couvreur, 'Développements récents', p. 317, note 65.

would appear to be a necessary condition has found its expression in a text, then these other rules, being subject to possible changes through a less cumbersome process than that of constitutional amendments, would be undesirable from the remedial point of view.

The difference from the Guatemalan proposal is striking and important as the latter draft encompasses *ratione personae* all international organisations, while restricting jurisdiction *ratione materiae*, whereas Costa Rica maintains *ratione materiae* the analogous application of the methods of acceptance by states, but has built into the condition *ratione personae* an explicit authorisation to be granted in the constituent instrument.

It has to be admitted that Costa Rica's proposal did not specify the nature of the constitutional authorisation required – that is, whether it would only be dealing with the procedural capacity as a matter of principle, or whether it could be further qualified by the addition of categories of disputes. The way in which Article 36 had been tentatively amended in Costa Rica's draft seems to indicate that only the former general kind of constitutional authorisation had been considered. Member states of an international organisation that had not been authorised along the lines of Costa Rica's proposal would thus lose their normal preferential standing from a remedial point of view; this loss of remedial advantage would have been partly compensated as a result of the new Article 96*bis* as proposed by Costa Rica and pursuant to which the UN and its Specialised Agencies could at any time be given such authorisation by the General Assembly.

Although 'relatively little has happened during the past half of a century in the development of the international personality of international organisations', the successive pleas to provide access to international organisations before the International Court of Justice 'stem from the recognition of their international personality'.[88] When the two countries drafted their proposals, possessing personality was rightfully not made an *a priori* condition for the granting of procedural capacity given, *inter alia*, the inevitably heterogeneous character of the substantive content of the personality of international organisations.[89]

As to the conditions attached to the procedural capacity, Costa Rica's proposed amendment to Article 35 of the Statute provided that access to the Court would be automatically available to an organisation duly authorised to that effect by its constituent instrument. Couvreur refers to

---

[88] Sztucki, 'International Organisations', pp. 146 and 142.
[89] Couvreur, 'Développements récents', p. 306.

244 ALTERNATIVE REMEDIAL ACTION AND FUTURE OPTIONS

the absence of any control or guarantee as regards these conditions.[90] From a remedial perspective it is important to note that those conditions would have to be included in the instrument not by the organisation itself but by the masters of the treaty, namely the member states who may subsequently become the applicants in proceedings instituted against the organisation.

The possibility raised by Paul Szasz[91] of an international organisation being unwilling to take the necessary measures to acquire *locus standi* before the Court is rather unlikely to occur because the advantages for the organisation emanating from such *locus standi* as a potential applicant would probably outweigh the anticipated disadvantages of becoming a respondent in a dispute with a state.

Although, without ruling it out altogether, international organisations should be enjoying the same freedom of limiting their acceptance of the Court's jurisdiction, they should be able 'to avoid litigating in the International Court of Justice by concluding agreements with actual or potential adversaries'[92] providing for alternative dispute settlement mechanisms. In this sense and to this extent international organisations cannot be compelled to accept the Court's jurisdiction,[93] the consensual basis of which should, even in the light of the remedial imperatives of the accountability regime, remain fully intact. Indeed also with regard to secondary rules the drafting of too rigid a system would not survive the complexities of international reality.[94]

Although a proper administration of international justice would certainly require that the relations between the Court and the entities subject to its jurisdiction, institutionally speaking, be as integrated as possible,[95] the compelling policy reasons advanced earlier in this study, which flow directly from the accountability regime for international organisations, seem to allow a minor departure from that requirement when this innovative procedural capacity is being devised. The essential position of equality between the parties before the Court would, in my view, best be achieved by the potential respondent international organisations becoming parties to the Statute, thereby depositing with the UN Secretary-General on the occasion of that accession a formal declaration

---

[90] *Ibid.*, p. 318.   [91] Szasz, 'Granting International Organisations', p. 183.

[92] *Ibid.*, p. 185.   [93] Unconvincingly *contra: ibid.*

[94] ILA Committee on Accountability of International Organisations, *Second Report*, submitted to the 69th ILA Conference (London, 2000), p. 4, para. 16.

[95] Couvreur, 'Développements récents', p. 318.

AN INEVITABLE ROLE FOR THE ICJ   245

that they will comply with the decisions of the Court in any case to which they are a party; the second paragraph of Article 94 of the Charter does not require a particular mirror provision. The contribution by international organisations towards the expenses of the Court could be fixed by the Court in each particular case.

In such a way, transparency and thus predictability could contribute to maximising the potential of remedial action for states, provided, of course, that the modalities of accepting the Court's jurisdiction *ratione materiae* are clothed with the same positive orientation.

The amendment of the jurisdiction ratione materiae

Guatemala's proposal

Under Guatemala's proposal the jurisdiction *ratione materiae* would have been determined in one of the following ways.[96]

(1) The constituent instrument may provide for one or various categories of disputes[97] to fall within the jurisdiction of the Court: accordingly, the dispute has to come within the limits thus contained in the organisation's basic document. In Guatemala's (1999) revised version, the reference to categories was replaced by 'and the dispute is one of those provided for in the relevant provisions of the instrument'.[98] Guatemala's text apparently does not consider the possibility of all disputes being included in the Court's jurisdiction by way of the organisation's constitutional provisions.

(2) In the case of an agreement between a/all member state/s and the organisation the same limitation to the Court's jurisdiction would occur, provided the organisation has, in a separate prior declaration, accepted the Court's jurisdiction *ratione materiae* conferred upon the Court by the agreement.[99] In the case of the United Nations such a

[96] Couvreur rightly noted the inappropriate location of these *ratione materiae* issues in the original version of the proposed Article on procedural capacity before the Court: *ibid.*, p. 317, note 65.

[97] Article 36A (1)(a) reads: 'The constituent instrument of the organisation confers competence on the court for such purpose and the dispute falls within the category or one of the categories of disputes provided for in the relevant provisions of the instrument . . .'.

[98] A/54/33, para. 109.

[99] Article 36A(1)(b) reads: 'A treaty to which all or a number of states members of the organisation are parties confers competence on the court for such purpose, the State party or the States parties to the dispute are parties to the treaty, the dispute falls within the category or one of the categories of disputes provided for in the relevant provisions of the treaty, and the organisation has, by means of a declaration, already accepted the competence conferred on the court by the treaty with respect to the dispute . . .'

246 ALTERNATIVE REMEDIAL ACTION AND FUTURE OPTIONS

declaration should take the form of a decision by the General Assembly.[100]

(3) In the case of a *compromis*, the Court's jurisdiction will, of course, be limited to the dispute as it has been described in the relevant instrument.[101] In its (1999) revised version of the proposal the two sub-paragraphs just referred to were replaced by one paragraph using *mutatis mutandis* Article 36(1) of the present Statute.[102]

From a remedial perspective the preferential standing of individual member states *vis-à-vis* the international organisation also becomes clear.

From the combination of Article 36A(1)(c) and Article 36B it becomes obvious that non-member states can only use the *compromis* as the exclusive method of accepting the Court's jurisdiction; this apparently seems to exclude acceptance of the Court's jurisdiction by way of pre-existing agreements such as Headquarters Agreements, which from a remedial point of view is not desirable and is hardly in accordance with existing practice.

Guatemala has made it clear that there was no link between the system of the prior declaration and the optional clause system.[103] More importantly from a remedial point of view, it is difficult to see why this declaration has to be additional to the acceptance already contained in the agreement between a state and an international organisation.[104] In its (1999) revised version Guatemala in a new Article 36B made the conferral of the necessary competence on the Court dependent upon the organisation's declaration accepting the Court's jurisdiction, such declaration to be deposited with the Court's Registrar, and to contain an undertaking to comply in good faith with the decisions of the Court.[105] As far as declarations analogous to the ones under Article 36(2) of the

---

[100] Article 36A(3) reads: 'In the case of the United Nations, the prior acceptance of the competence of the Court provided for in paragraph 1(b) above shall take the form of a General Assembly decision.'

[101] Article 36A(1)(c) reads: 'The State party or States parties to the dispute, on the one hand, and the organisation, on the other, have decided, by special agreement, that the dispute shall be referred to the Court.'

[102] Article 36(A)(2) reads: 'The competence of the Court shall extend to all disputes between a State or a number of States, on the one hand, and a public international organisation, on the other, which are referred to it by the parties. It shall also encompass, with respect to such disputes, all matters specifically provided for in treaties to which one or a number of States and a public international organisation are parties.'

[103] A/AC.182/L.103, p. 3, para. 17.

[104] Couvreur, 'Développements récents', p. 319, note 72.

[105] A/54/33, p. 19, point D.

present Statute are concerned, there is, because of the principle of 'organisational equality' in law between international organisations, no cogent reason[106] why the international organisations should be authorised by the UN General Assembly to make such declarations as had been proposed by the 1956 ILA Resolution.[107]

From a remedial perspective there was no particular reason why member states should not be able to rely on compromissory clauses inserted into agreements they have concluded with organisations in their membership capacity (for example, as troop-contributing countries) or with international organisations with whom they do not have membership links (for example, to provide them with headquarters or facilities to enable the organisation to organise a conference or operational activities of a particular or emergency nature).

The apparent discrimination between member and non-member states to an extent beyond that which the preferential standing of member states seems to require or justify under the accountability regime for international organisations was removed by means of the oral revision introduced by Guatemala in 1998 and by determining that bilateral treaties between states and an international organisation are included within the envisaged scope of application of Article 36A(1)(b).[108]

Costa Rica's proposal

Costa Rica's proposal provided for an analogous application of the existing provisions of Article 36, adding the necessary changes with regard to international organisations and reaffirming that the jurisdiction *ratione personae* will depend on the constitutional attribution of the required procedural capacity. The combination of both conditions substantially reduces the range of international organisations that would be allowed to act as a respondent in a dispute which has arisen with a state party to the Statute.[109]

---

[106] Contra: Szasz, 'Granting International Organisations', p. 183.

[107] Part I(c) of the Resolution as cited by Sztucki, 'International Organisations', p. 153.

[108] A/53/33, p. 24, para. 129.

[109] Relevant parts of Article 36 read:

'1. The jurisdiction of the Court comprises all cases which the parties *or which public international organisations, so authorised by their constituent instrument,* refer to it and all matters specially provided for in the Charter of the United Nations or in treaties and conventions in force.

2. The States parties to the present Statute *and public international organisations, so authorised to do so by their constituent instrument,* may at any

The overall approach followed by Costa Rica not only has the advantage of greater transparency and predictability for the potential claimant state(s), but it would also provide *in limine* more guarantees between the prospective applicant and respondent; it maintains the balance between the normal degree of freedom in accepting the Court's jurisdiction by its current clientele, and it preserves the remedial advantages for applicant states attached to the reciprocity aspect of the methods of acceptance becoming available to international organisations.[110]

Freedom of exclusion

The freedom for an international organisation, under both proposals, to exclude particular categories of disputes from the Court's jurisdiction *ratione materiae* could, for instance, result in the organisation's 'constitutional differences or disputes to be withheld from the Court's judicial control'.[111] It is undoubtedly true that from a political point of view international organisations and member states might be reluctant to open up their constitutional dispute to the Court's judicial control,[112]

time declare that they recognise *ipso facto* and without special agreement, in relation to any other state accepting the same obligation, the jurisdiction of the Court in all legal disputes concerning:
  (a) The interpretation of a treaty;
  (b) Any question of international law;
  (c) The existence of any fact which, if established, would constitute a breach of an international obligation;
  (d) The nature or extent of the reparation to be made for the breach of an international obligation.
  3. The declarations referred to above may be made unconditionally or on condition of reciprocity on the part of several or certain States **or public international organisations**, or for a certain time.
  Such declarations shall be deposited with the Secretary-General of the United Nations, who shall transmit copies thereof to the parties to the Statute, **to the public international organisations that had previously deposited such declaration** and to the Registrar of the Court.'

[110] It is not quite clear why the difficulties allegedly attached to reciprocity under an optional clause system were invoked by Switzerland in its 1970–1 reply, while a constitutionally based acceptance clause would involve reciprocity (extracts from the Swiss reply cited by Couvreur, 'Développements récents', pp. 299–300). Sweden and Austria were in favour of an optional clause system (*ibid.*, note 22).

[111] *Ibid.*, p. 322, note 80.

[112] *Ibid.*, p. 320. Bowett would prefer disputes relating to the internal functioning of the organisation to be excluded, the jurisdiction *ratione materiae* concentrating on claims connected with its external functions: 'The Court's Role', p. 189. Couvreur has convincingly argued that such a distinction 'quelque légitime qu'elle puisse être en théorie, semble peu pertinente aux fins de déterminer les bases de compétence ratione materiae qui devraient permettre à la Cour d'exercer son office': 'Développements récents', p. 319.

AN INEVITABLE ROLE FOR THE ICJ   249

but the remedial component of the accountability regime for international organisations provides a persuasive counter-argument to the benefit of potential claimant states, acting individually or in concert. Although it is accepted that the Court should not seek to interfere in an organisation's exercise of its political discretion, such an exercise 'does not take place outside [a] legal framework', as pointed out by Danesh Sarooshi;[113] this observation applies both to advisory and contentious proceedings. Constitutional review of their acts by the Court was excluded or limited by the exclusion clause in the agreements concluded between the UN and the Specialised Agencies.[114] Whether a judicial review of acts of international organisations would also imply control over the true existence of the facts leading to the decision has always been a controversial issue.[115] Under both the principles of good governance and due process of law, a decision must not only be reasoned, but also reasonable, namely based on correct findings of fact, and, in my view, the scrutiny thereof would come within the scope of judicial review.

Although as pointed out by Eagleton an international organisation is indeed 'no more bound to compulsory jurisdiction than is any State',[116] the accountability imperatives would seem to make it impossible for the freedom envisaged to lead to such an exclusion, particularly so as, when discussing the potential role of domestic courts, the 'contentieux constitutionel' for the right reasons became eligible for not being subject to domestic judicial interference, let alone a judicial review. Moreover, constitutional issues can arise and have arisen within the context of 'normal' inter-state contentious cases,[117] as indicated earlier. Whether

[113] D. Sarooshi, *The UN and the Development of Collective Security: The Delegation by the UN Security Council of its Chapter VII Powers* (Oxford: Clarendon Press, 1999), pp. 141–67, at p. 47.
[114] Sztucki, 'International Organisations', p. 159.
[115] See, for instance, A. Gross, 'Redress against Decisions of International Organisations', *Transactions Grotius Society* 36 (1951), 30–48, at 36 and 38–9, 42 and 46.
[116] Sztucki, 'International Organisations', p. 410.
[117] As is demonstrated by the pending cases:
Questions of Interpretation and Application of the 1971 Montreal Convention arising from the Aerial Incident at Lockerbie (Libyan Jamahiriya v. United Kingdom);
Questions of Interpretation and Application of the 1971 Montreal Convention arising from the Aerial Incident at Lockerbie (Libyan Jamahiriya v. United States of America);
Legality of Use of Force (Federal Republic of Yugoslavia v. Belgium);
Legality of Use of Force (Federal Republic of Yugoslavia v. Canada);
Legality of Use of Force (Federal Republic of Yugoslavia v. France);
Legality of Use of Force (Federal Republic of Yugoslavia v. Germany);
Legality of Use of Force (Federal Republic of Yugoslavia v. Italy);
Legality of Use of Force (Federal Republic of Yugoslavia v. The Netherlands);

250 ALTERNATIVE REMEDIAL ACTION AND FUTURE OPTIONS

the subject-matter of a dispute unilaterally brought by a state against an international organisation would fall completely within the respondent's competences would, of course, be decided by the Court.[118]

Some procedural aspects and rights

Although as a result of Guatemala's withdrawal of its proposal in the spring of 1999 another window of opportunity may have been lost, attention could still be paid to a few procedural aspects and rights during State v. International Organisation litigation before the Court; there is no need at the present stage of the debate, however, to discuss all the necessary amendments to the corresponding provisions of the Charter and the Court's Rules.

On the second and third levels of accountability, international organisations bear non-contractual liability and organisational responsibility for all the acts, actions and omissions performed, conducted or caused by all its constituent organs – primary, principal, subordinate or subsidiary – and by its officials, agents and experts on mission: therefore the respondent in any claim brought before the Court is the organisation as such and not any of these organs, nor any of its officials, agents or experts. As succinctly pointed out by Szasz, an international organisation 'has only a single legal personality and thus its organs, no matter how senior, could not appear as independent legal subjects before the Court'.[119] Accordingly, it will be the Chief Administrative Officer who will be called upon to defend the interests of the organisation, in the same way as he/she would do if the organisation was the applicant. The Chief Administrative Officer, or his/her Representative, will thus appear before the Court and be responsible for submitting the Counter-Memorial, including raising preliminary objections to jurisdiction and admissibility,[120] and the eventual Rejoinder, and he/she will take part in

Legality of Use of Force (Federal Republic of Yugoslavia v. Portugal);
Legality of Use of Force (Federal Republic of Yugoslavia v. United Kingdom);
Application of the Convention on the Prevention and Punishment of the Crime of Genocide (Bosnia and Herzegovina v. Yugoslavia);
Armed Activities on the Territory of the Congo (Democratic Republic of the Congo v. Burundi);
Armed Activities on the Territory of the Congo (Democratic Republic of the Congo v. Rwanda);
Armed Activities on the Territory of the Congo (Democratic Republic of the Congo v. Uganda);
Application of the Convention on the Prevention and Punishment of the Crime of Genocide (Croatia v. Yugoslavia).

[118] Couvreur, 'Développements récents', pp. 316–17.

[119] Szasz, 'Granting International Organisations', p. 171.

[120] Sztucki, 'International Organisations', p. 163. In this latter respect, remedial

AN INEVITABLE ROLE FOR THE ICJ   251

the oral proceedings. The authorisation (not to accept the jurisdiction of the Court but actually to take part in the proceedings),[121] as well as the determination of the litigation strategy, would have to come from the organisation's most representative and principal political organ. Acceptance of the Court's jurisdiction 'should be honoured notwithstanding any resentment by some of its Member States'.[122] The Secretariat may obviously have a direct interest in the outcome of the proceedings; the UN Secretary-General's special *amicus curiae* role may therefore acquire 'a deeper significance in the future development of international judicial techniques'.[123]

'The cornerstone of any judicial proceedings is the cardinal principle of equality of the parties; it is this principle that underlies all the procedural provisions of the Court's Statute and Rules.'[124] There is no reason to depart from this principle in contentious proceedings involving international organisations.

Although Guatemala's first proposal only seemed to exclude the possibility, its (1999) revised version did actually specifically exclude, for both the state and the international organisation, the appointment of

considerations also seem to require the applicant state to exhaust judicial or other remedies if provided for by or in the respondent's constituent instrument: Seidl-Hohenveldern, 'Access of International Organisations', p. 192.

It should be noted that the Court's case law in advisory proceedings has made it clear, for instance, that negotiations between a member state and an organisation do not necessarily have to be protracted in cases where a deadlock occurs at an early stage: 'Negotiations do not of necessity always presuppose a more or less lengthy series of notes and despatches; it may suffice that a discussion should have been commenced, and the discussion may have been very short; this will be the case if a deadlock is reached, or if finally a point is reached at which one of the Parties definitely declares himself unable, or refuses, to give way, and there can therefore be no doubt that the *dispute cannot be settled by diplomatic negotiation*': *Applicability of the Obligation to Arbitrate under Section 21 of the United Nations Headquarters Agreement of 26 June 1947*, Advisory Opinion, *ICJ Reports* (1988), p. 12, at p. 34, para. 56 referring to an *obiter dictum* in the *Mavrommatis* case (emphasis in the original). The negotiations should be conducted by both parties in accordance with the principles and guidelines for international negotiations as contained in General Assembly Resolution 53/101, adopted on 8 December 1998.

[121] The occurrence of the circumstances governed by Article 53 of the Statute should be considered as rather unlikely, although the 1999 revised version of Guatemala's proposal explicitly referred to it (A/54/33, p. 19, point F).

[122] Seidl-Hohenveldern, 'Access of International Organisations', p. 194.

[123] Rosenne, *Law and Practice*, p. 1748.

[124] President Bedjaoui's address, *Yearbook ICJ* 49 (1994–5), 214. At the time of writing (spring 2000), the Court's Rules Committee was in the process of preparing proposals to the Court on, *inter alia*, witness evidence, counterclaims and preliminary objections (according to President Guillaume's Press Conference in February 2000).

252 ALTERNATIVE REMEDIAL ACTION AND FUTURE OPTIONS

a judge ad hoc,[125] thus preventing the application of the principle of equality of the parties before the Court that could provide the basis for such a possibility.[126] Such a judge ad hoc could, however, provide substantial assistance to the Court in clarifying rules and practices of the organisation.[127]

Provisional measures of protection

The respondent international organisation should also have the right to request the Court to indicate provisional measures pursuant to Article 41 of the Statute. The only observation to be made in this context is that the collective interests also of a financial nature represented and being protected by the organisation might actually play a (prominent) role in the Court's consideration of whether the circumstances would require it to exercise its power. Interim measures of protection would help to mitigate the effects of delays in the settlement of international claims by a partially interlocutory injunction.[128]

The potential urgency of the issues to be decided may lead to the parties requesting the application of the summary procedure provided for in Article 29 of the Court's Statute.

In cases of the application of Articles 29 or 41 of the Court's Statute, the burden of justification for the continuance of the activity challenged should for reasons of fairness be on the respondent international organisation.[129]

Intervention

With regard to intervention, other states should be allowed to request intervention in the proceedings,[130] for instance because they have

---

[125] A/54/33, p. 19, point E, although Guatemala was 'not completely convinced that this exclusion ... is justified' (A/AC.182/L. 103, p. 3, para. 14).

[126] Couvreur, 'Développements récents', p. 320.

[127] *Ibid.*, p. 321. See also in favour but for different reasons, Seidl-Hohenveldern, 'Access of International Organisations', p. 199. Within the same context, resorting to the use of technical assessors under the Court's Rules should be encouraged; see also Article 289 UNCLOS.

[128] Gray, *Judicial Remedies*, p. 70.

[129] James N. Paul, 'Law and Development in the 1990s: Using International Law to Impose Accountability to People on International Development Actors', *Third World Legal Studies* (1992), 1–16, at 11.

[130] In passing it may be noted, for instance, that under the present Statute the procedural rights of intervening third states are broader than in the context of WTO Panel Proceedings, although there seems to be a continuous convergent trend: N. Covelli, 'Public International Law and Third Party Participation in WTO Panel Proceedings', *JWTL* 33 (1999), 125–39, at 125–6.

concluded similar agreements with the same (or another) international organisation. The state requesting intervention may have allowed the respondent organisation to conduct operational activities on its territory which are of the same kind as the ones in the case before the Court and which posed the same hazardous risks. The would-be intervener may, of course, be a party to the Convention that is in question before the Court, giving it the right to intervene: Conventions on privileges and immunities of international organisations would be relevant examples.[131]

The remedial potential of a request for the right to intervene has been mentioned earlier in this study. It is sufficient for present purposes to recall that the remedial advantage for the state(s) may consist of the Court – at the merits stage of the case between another state and an international organisation – acting upon data provided by the state during the pleadings even when the request turns out to be unsuccessful.[132]

Other international organisations could also have an interest of a legal nature that could be affected by the Court's decision in a case between a state and another international organisation. Guatemala's proposal provided for international organisations to be able to request intervention in such proceedings;[133] Costa Rica's proposal was silent on the matter. The subject-matter of the dispute could, for instance, be the interpretation and application of a Convention (almost) identical to agreements concluded between the organisation requesting the intervention and other states, or the organisation may be involved in operational activities similar to the ones conducted by the respondent organisation that gave rise to the claim for non-contractual liability. In cases where other international organisations are also parties to the Convention the construction of which is in question before the Court, they should be able to exercise their right to intervene, as provided for in the 1999 revised version of Guatemala's proposal.[134]

As with regard to requests for the indication of provisional measures, the Court may give more weight in these situations to the fact that

---

[131] *Contra*: Seidl-Hohenveldern, 'Access of International Organisations', pp. 200–1: his argument that the difficulties inherent in such interpretation interventions would be multiplied seems to be going too far given the limited number of states taking the opportunity to present their views during advisory proceedings on similar matters. The high number (28) of written statements submitted to the Court in the *Legality of the Use of Nuclear Weapons* case is an exception, probably caused by the particular subject-matter of the request.

[132] I. Brownlie, *The Rule of Law in International Affairs at the Fiftieth Anniversary of the United Nations* (The Hague and London: Martinus Nijhoff Publishers, 1998), p. 124.

[133] A/54/33, p. 19. Seidl-Hohenveldern's fears in this regard (see note 131, above) may be considered to be going too far: Couvreur, 'Développements récents', p. 321, note 76.

[134] A/AC.182/L.103, p. 2, para. 13.

collective interests are being represented by the international organisation requesting the intervention.

In both cases – a request for intervention and a request for the indication of provisional measures – the Court may thus, to a larger degree than it has been doing up until now in inter-state proceedings, 'balance the interests involved, to consider whether the harm likely to result from failure to award [the request]...would be greater than that from their award'.[135]

It should be duly noted that the same argument could also be put forward in favour of allowing representational non-governmental organisations that have special consultative status with the respondent organisation to request intervention to protect collective interests of a legal nature that may be affected: such intervention would not necessarily be in support of the position of either the applicant or the respondent.

Amicus curiae

A third state or a third organisation may wish to remain outside the dispute but it may be willing to assist the Court in the capacity of *amicus curiae*. With that aim in mind, Article 34(2) and (3) of the ICJ's Statute should be amended accordingly so as to include states with regard to contentious proceedings between a state and an international organisation. Neither Guatemala's nor Costa Rica's proposal contained any suggestions in this respect. In the absence of relevant clauses in the Court's Statute and Rules the Court has in practice – with the agreement of the two parties, of course – allowed a third state to participate as *amicus curiae* in inter-state proceedings, as was demonstrated in the *Corfu Channel* case.[136]

The protection of the (potentially affected) legal interests of third states and the Court's concern that 'full light be thrown on the facts alleged'[137] will have to be balanced by the Court against the prejudice potentially caused to the disputing state(s) and international organisation. However, a simultaneous exercise by different actors of both the rights of an intervener and indirect participation as *amicus curiae* may, from a remedial perspective, very well tilt the balance unfavourably for the disputing state(s) and international organisation.

---

[135] Gray, *Judicial Remedies*, p. 141 discussing the ECJ's approach to interim measures.

[136] See Covelli, 'Public International Law', 136–7 (*Corfu Channel* case: *UK v. Albania*).

[137] *ICJ Reports* (1949), p. 17, as cited by Covelli at p. 137.

Locus standi *for non-state entities: representational non-governmental organisations and individuals?*

Possible access for individuals to the Permanent Court of International Justice was a question at the centre of the debates within the Advisory Committee of Jurists entrusted with the task of drafting a Statute for the PCIJ. The Committee based itself on the qualification 'international' in order to reject any such possibility.[138] This approach was not seriously doubted when the Statute of the present Court was drafted.[139] In current conditions and irrespective of the lack of *locus standi* for individuals, the needs of good administration of international justice render questionable the practice of the Court not envisaging legal representatives of an individual being allowed perhaps as *amicus curiae* to present his/her own views.[140]

As to different categories of individuals and the remedial opportunities available to them before the Court, Shabtai Rosenne has pointed to the incongruity that the exercise by a state of its right of diplomatic protection enables an individual to have his/her international claim decided by the Court whereas an international official is deprived of that possibility, even in the course of advisory proceedings directly concerning him/her.[141]

Starting from the assessment that individuals do not have political control and are frequently looking for mechanisms to have political and juridical decisions overturned, and taking into account the example of Europe's regional international courts, Mark Janis recently proposed granting direct access to individuals, along the lines of Protocol 11 to the 1950 European Convention on Human Rights. In Janis' proposal, *locus standi* for individuals would make it possible for them to bring suits against both states and international organisations.[142] A new paragraph would be added to Article 35 – namely paragraph 4, pursuant to which the Court may receive petitions 'from any person, non-governmental organisation, or group of individuals claiming to be the victim of a violation of international law by one of the States parties to the Court

---

[138] Couvreur, 'Développements récents', p. 294, note 2. On the earlier antecedents of the states-only presumption, as he called it, see M. Janis, 'Individuals and the International Court' in Muller, Raic and Thuransky (eds.), *International Court of Justice*, pp. 205–16, at pp. 206–7.

[139] Couvreur, 'Développements récents', p. 295.

[140] Rosenne, *Law and Practice,* pp. 608 and 654.   [141] *Ibid.,* p. 1744, note 61.

[142] Janis, 'Individuals and the International Court', pp. 209–12: one of his arguments drawn from the under-utilisation of the Court seems less relevant within the concerns of accountability of international organisations.

or by an international organisation ...'[143] – provided that the respondent state or international organisation has by declaration, along the lines of the optional clause system under the 1950 European Convention on Human Rights,[144] accepted the Court's jurisdiction to that end. Article 36(1) would be amended accordingly.[145]

Janis' proposal is wide-ranging *ratione personae*, as it would not only provide access to a single individual, but also to a group of individuals (echoing, as it were, the eligibility conditions for requests to the World Bank Inspection Panel) and to non-governmental organisations without specifying whether the NGOs should be nationally or internationally based. From a remedial perspective it is worth noting that the Court's jurisdiction *ratione materiae* would be limited to alleged violations of international law, thus excluding claims that are merely non-contractual claims.

Janis is right when he expresses the 'probably' realistic expectation that it would take 'several, indeed many, lean years while we wait for states and the United Nations to accept the option of individual applications to the International Court of Justice'.[146]

How can the necessary changes be brought about?

Bringing about the innovative *locus standi* before the International Court of Justice for international organisations both as applicants and as respondents will, of course, depend on the political willingness of the main actors on the international scene. The procedural aspects of any innovative amendments to the Court's Statute are governed by Article 69 of the Statute referring to Article 108 of the UN Charter. Attempts to circumvent these requirements by way of drafting additional Protocols or otherwise are doomed to fail for both legal and political reasons.

It is, of course, equally important that the innovation be welcomed and supported by the principal judicial organ of the United Nations. In its 1990 reply to an inquiry by the UN Secretary-General, the ICJ may have alluded to the possibility of granting *locus standi* to international organisations before it when it stated that disputes 'will ever more

---

[143] *Ibid.*, p. 214.   [144] *Ibid.*, pp. 210 and 214–15.

[145] *Ibid.*, p. 215: 'The jurisdiction of the Court comprises all cases which the parties refer to it, all matters specially provided for in the Charter of the United Nations or in treaties or conventions in force, and all individual applications referred to it pursuant to Article 35(4).'

[146] *Ibid.*

frequently involve groups of States and international organisations, as well as States individually'.[147] In 1999 Guatemala recommended that the Court be consulted on its proposal, a recommendation that was later withdrawn together with its revised draft proposals.[148]

While fully recognising the difficulties accompanying the elaboration of such proposals, President Bedjaoui, during his term in office, on several occasions before the main political and legal organs of the United Nations,[149] during debates held by learned societies and in his scholarly writings, firmly acknowledged the need for such an innovation, which he unreservedly favours and which would include a system of judicial review of acts of international organisations. Similar views have also been expressed by other members of the Court on various occasions.

Recalling Article 70 of the Statute empowering the Court to propose amendments it may deem necessary through written communications to the Secretary-General, Jenks convincingly stated that a unanimous recommendation by the Court in favour of granting *locus standi* to international organisations 'would carry great weight'.[150]

The lukewarm reaction to the proposals submitted by Guatemala and Costa Rica and their subsequent withdrawal does not seem promising for this long overdue innovation to be accepted by the international community of states. However, this does not detract from the fact that they have provided the very first detailed basis for discussion.[151]

The possibility of any proposal aimed at granting *locus standi* to international organisations being accepted will also depend on whether it involves amending only the Court's Statute or both the Charter and the Statute, which was one of the questions contained in the draft questionnaire submitted by Guatemala.[152] It is worth noting that Guatemala reserved its right '[to] reintroduce [its proposal] once more auspicious prospects for [its] adoption arise'.[153]

Four elements should not be forgotten in the debate concerning widening access in favour of international organisations.

---

[147] Cited by Sztucki, 'International Organisations', p. 142.
[148] A/54/33, p. 19, paras. 113 and 116.
[149] Couvreur, 'Développements récents', pp. 300–2.
[150] Jenks, 'Status of International Organisations', 37, para. 53.
[151] Couvreur, 'Développements récents', p. 322.
[152] In Guatemala's own view, 'the adoption of the new proposed amendments to the Statute of the Court would not require an amendment to the Charter of the United Nations itself because disputes between the United Nations and States, whether or not they are Members, can be referred to the Court': A/AC.182/L.103, p. 2, para. 10.
[153] A/54/33, p. 20, para. 116.

(1) In the first place, even if international organisations have been granted direct access to the International Court of Justice, such an innovation 'shall not deprive [them] ... of their right to obtain *bona fide* advisory opinions of the International Court of Justice'.[154]

(2) In the debate over the Guatemalan proposal the argument was used that, as a result of the innovations, cases of insufficient importance would nevertheless be brought before the Court.[155] This also applies to inter-state disputes, and the possibility of the Court rejecting abusive claims[156] is also inherent in contentious proceedings instituted by a state against an international organisation. Following the example set by the Inter-American Court of Human Rights, the case would not be closed until the respondent organisation has fully complied with all remedial orders and awards.[157]

(3) There is no compelling reason why, in the same way as international human rights law has been creative,[158] the establishment and refinement of an accountability regime for international organisations would not develop innovative procedures to allow state and non-state entities (potentially) affected in their interests or rights by acts, actions or omissions of an international organisation to bring complaints directly against the organisation concerned.

(4) The Court not only 'takes its decisions on the basis of law, following a most meticulous examination of each case, without failing to take account of the meta-juridical factors, the expectations of the Parties and the imperative requirements of justice and peace',[159] but 'many a smaller or weaker State has obtained through the Court what it would no doubt have been unable to secure by other means'.[160]

Part IV of this study has been dedicated to alternative remedies and options for the future, as most constituent instruments of international organisations contain no provisions authorising any of their principal organs to adjudicate disputes between third parties and the organisation, and jurisdictional immunities before domestic courts are secured.[161] A rather balanced and adequate picture seems to emerge, providing equivalent (legal) protection for both states and non-state

---

[154] Seidl-Hohenveldern, 'Access of International Organisations', p. 202.

[155] A/52/33, p. 30, para. 108.   [156] Gray, *Judicial Remedies*, p. 160, note 7.

[157] D. Shelton, *Remedies in International Human Rights Law* (Oxford: Oxford University Press, 1999), p. 191.

[158] *Ibid.*, p. 93.   [159] President Bedjaoui's address, *Yearbook ICJ* 49 (1994–5), 212.

[160] *Ibid.*

[161] See also P. Bekker, *The Legal Position of Intergovernmental Organisations: A Functional Necessity Analysis of their Legal Status and Immunities* (Boston and London: Martinus Nijhoff Publishers, 1994), p. 195.

entities. They can resort to a complementary variety of judicial and non-judicial mechanisms, the mere availability of which could very well also operate as an incentive for international organisations to take the necessary pre-remedial action at multiple levels. It would be feasible, for instance, to leave provisional measures of protection and other procedural remedies to be taken by inspection panels, while entrusting the decision on the merits of the difference or dispute to domestic courts. International organisations should afford 'judicial or arbitral remed(ies) to third parties for the settlement of any disputes which may arise', as such a course of establishing remedial opportunities would be 'consistent with the expressed aims' of international organisations 'to promote freedom and justice for individuals'.[162] Consequently, international organisations must be considered to have the implied powers to establish both judicial and non-judicial subsidiary organs and bodies to establish appropriate mechanisms for redress.[163] From this same perspective, 'individuals and companies concerned may be given the right to sue the organisation before ... internal courts'.[164]

Although true judicial protection can only result from a direct appeal against an act,[165] it is also good to bear in mind that 'any proposal to extend the use of judicial settlement to new areas ... must take account of the limitations of judicial remedies'.[166] The role of judicial remedies is necessarily restricted because the extent to which they can modify the status quo is limited, they are a product of a bilateral process and they are dependent on a finding of (organisational) responsibility.[167] As depicted in this Part IV, the remedies, however, do not have to be 'almost invariably retrospective'.[168]

When called upon by states and non-state entities to solve differences and disputes arising from claims against international organisations, both domestic and international courts and tribunals by definition have to interpret the organisation's constituent instrument, 'which is

---

[162] *Effects of Awards of Compensation Made by the UN Administrative Tribunal*, Advisory Opinion of 13 July 1954, *ICJ Reports* (1954), p. 47, at p. 57.

[163] *Ibid.*, pp. 57 and 61.

[164] F. Seyersted, 'Settlement of Internal Disputes of Intergovernmental Organisations by Internal and External Courts', *ZAÖRV* 24 (1964), 1–121, at 41, referring in note 129 to the 'semi-judicial Eligibility Review Board of the International Refugee Organisation [that] was to hear and determine appeals from individual refugees against administrative decisions by the International Organisation denying them status of refugees eligible for assistance'. The Board was never established.

[165] Gross, 'Redress', 31.   [166] Gray, *Judicial Remedies*, p. 210.   [167] *Ibid.*   [168] *Ibid.*

conventional and at the same time institutional'.[169] In carrying out this exercise of interpretation, judges will have to pay special attention to 'the very nature of the organisation created, the objectives which have been assigned to it by its founders, the imperatives associated with the effective performance of its functions, as well as its own practice'.[170]

An observation made by Chittharanjan Amerasinghe in connection with international administrative law deserves more general application from a remedial perspective. He noted that the written internal law of an international organisation is normally subordinated to general principles of law of a fundamental nature, but that precedence may have to be removed in cases where a more advantageous situation for the affected party would result from a general practice of that particular organisation.[171]

The development of alternatives may be hampered by the fact that it is difficult to exclude judicial remedies,[172] but it has to be recalled that from the perspective of a well-functioning and comprehensive accountability regime for international organisations the remedial potential should be maximised for all potential claimants by consecutively or simultaneously resorting to a combination of both non-legal and judicial mechanisms, provided that the circumstances and admissibility conditions permit them to do so. An extraordinary example of this was reported in the media in January 2000: two Rwandan women who had been testifying before the Commission of Inquiry planned to commence legal proceedings against the UN because the UN Blue Helmets abandoned their families during the genocide in spite of having the mandate to protect them. This clearly corroborates the point that certain remedial mechanisms such as national and international Commissions of Inquiry may bring to light cases of political/legal accountability that may become relevant in subsequent domestic or international judicial proceedings concerning the alleged liability and/or responsibility of the organisation and its officials, emanating either from action or inaction.

The remedy sought and the remedial mechanism resorted to should, as indicated earlier, be adequate and tailored to the level of

---

[169] *Legality of the Use by a State of Nuclear Weapons in Armed Conflict*, ICJ Reports (1996), p. 66, at p. 75.

[170] *Ibid.*

[171] C. F. Amerasinghe, *Principles of the Institutional Law of International Organisations* (Cambridge: Cambridge University Press, 1996), p. 352.

[172] C. Harlow, 'Access to Justice as a Human Right: The European Court of Justice and the European Union' in P. Alston (ed.), *The European Union and Human Rights* (Oxford: Oxford University Press, 2000), pp. 187–213, at p. 207.

accountability at issue. Accordingly, disputes involving conflicting views on the effects of a course of conduct proposed by an international organisation may be more suited to an inquisitorial mechanism such as an inspection panel than an adversarial process implied in contentious judicial proceedings before an international court or tribunal. It also has to be acknowledged that the least intrusive of all remedies, namely the declaratory judgment, could also be used as an anticipatory, preventive device *vis-à-vis* institutional acts or operational activities allegedly potentially affecting the interests or rights of states or non-state entities. The line between a declaratory judgment and an order to take action or an injunction to abstain from doing so certainly becomes blurred in such an anticipatory approach;[173] the relief sought should not necessarily be limited in that way.

As to the remedial fora themselves, it would be helpful if the International Court of Justice, in the exercise of its extra-judicial function, channelled through to the relevant international organisations – that is to the extent that they are the targeted addressees – applications brought before it by non-state entities such as individuals and non-governmental organisations. The same applies in the sphere of human rights to petitions, communications or complaints before competent Committees, Commissions or Courts; they are in fact addressed to international organisations and they are therefore declared inadmissible for that reason.[174]

As a result of this voluntary co-operation between judicial or quasi-judicial and political fora, the international organisations themselves could, in turn, be led to request the International Court of Justice for an Advisory Opinion on any legal question (within the scope of their activities) if a consistent pattern of petitions and claims – that can also originate from the ombudsman, inspection panel or Commissions of Inquiry – would make it reasonable and wise to do so. Such an initiative would enable them, acting upon the Court's Advisory Opinion, to 'remedy' the acts, actions or omissions that have been challenged, or to take the necessary pre-remedial action required. The accountability regime for international organisations could only benefit from such an approach.

---

[173] Shelton, *Remedies*, p. 129.

[174] An alternative solution would obviously consist of extending the jurisdiction of these human rights bodies so as to include petitions, communications and complaints *vis-à-vis* international organisations submitted by staff members and third parties.

Conclusion

The purpose of this study has been to explore the existence of, access to and the outcome of political and legal remedial mechanisms, both of which a comprehensive accountability regime for international organisations would require. In mapping this territory I have looked at the general features of remedies against international organisations as compared to remedies in international law in general and contrasted them with remedies against the main actors on the international scene. The various remedies had to be tailored to the different levels of accountability and to the wide range of potential claimants, both states and non-state entities. The remedial opportunities, both in terms of access and forum, and the remedial potential were found to vary according to the differential standing of the claimant.

The differential remedial regime that was found to exist for those who are allegedly affected in their interests or rights by acts, actions or omissions of an international organisation was also reflected in the procedural difficulties and issues each separate category faces when actually resorting to remedial action. Additionally, the category of non-state claimants is still encountering the common procedural obstacle of jurisdictional immunity before the domestic courts, which is normally claimed by and frequently granted to international organisations. The substantive outcome of their remedial action could be described as fundamentally different within that same category of non-state claimants.

Given the present state of the remedial regime *vis-à-vis* international organisations, the need was felt to explore alternative remedial opportunities and mechanisms for states and non-state entities in cases where the pre-remedial action to be taken by the organisation has not proved to be entirely successful. Different models of non-legal alternative remedies were explored, and in relation to the second and third

264   CONCLUSION

levels of accountability possible changes to existing judicial remedial mechanisms were reviewed. The time has now come after having conducted the analysis in the preceding Parts of this study, and before making some final observations, to return to the basic questions that were identified at the beginning.[1]

With regard to the entitlement to remedies, the range of potential claimants extends to all those whose interests or rights have been or are likely to be affected in the course of their contractual or incidental dealings with organisations by acts, actions or omissions of international organisations, at any of the multiple levels on which the institutional and operational activities are conducted. Both in theory and in practical terms the remedial regime has to accommodate an almost unlimited constituency of potential claimants.

The different levels and forms of accountability make it necessary and inevitable that the availability of and the access to remedial mechanisms are designed and organised somewhat differently depending upon whether the act, event or situation giving rise to the claim is of an individual or of a collective nature. The dual role of states has to be duly acknowledged: in raising the accountability of an international organisation they are looking for remedial opportunities, both legal and non-legal, to assert and protect not only their own interests and rights, as *parens patriae*, but also, in the exercise of their diplomatic protection, of individuals the claims of whom they have decided to espouse. Staff members and private claimants will normally only be given access to remedies in order to protect their individual interests and rights. A separate and independent standing for representational non-governmental organisations that would allow them to assert and protect collective interests and rights has been shown to be virtually non-existent at present.

Interaction between the remedial functions that have been identified could potentially result in a continuum of non-legal and legal mechanisms aimed at the protection of both individual and collective interests and rights. The remedial force of the functioning of an ombudsman, an inspection panel and a Commission of Inquiry will normally extend beyond the individual or group of individuals that originally set in motion any of these non-legal remedial mechanisms.

The same combined individual/collective remedial effect will normally emerge when legal mechanisms have been resorted to by individual states or individual claimants, in spite of the legally binding force of the *res judicata* formally being limited to the parties to the difference

---

[1] See above, p. 27.

CONCLUSION   265

or the dispute. This phenomenon does not extend to case law brought about by domestic courts, mainly because of the inherent diversity of the applicable law, at least until international organisations have elaborated and consolidated a uniform body of contractual and tort law.

As to the nature of the remedial outcome, the particulars of the case law of the international administrative tribunals have been noted, while the award of monetary compensation for damages, once contractual or tortious liability has been established, is the normal remedy awarded to other categories of non-state claimants. Apart from when they negotiate a lump-sum agreement on behalf of their nationals, non-monetary remedies seem, at present, to be paramount for states by means of the mechanism of declaratory judgments, interlocutory orders and decisions or otherwise. André Gross has rightly observed that the preference for 'preventive judicial review would answer the point of compensation in some measure'.[2]

The immature state of development of a remedial regime, especially for non-state claimants other than staff members, makes it almost impossible at present to discern a pattern of criteria that are being applied to determine the amount of compensation and methods of payment: even in the decisions of international administrative tribunals no real consistency in the calculation of the amount of the compensation could be found. For the same reason, the answer to the question of what part the gravity of the acts, actions or omissions should play in the remedies afforded has to remain speculative.

The immature state of development of a remedial regime is, of course, embedded in the evolving process of elaboration and consolidation of the overall accountability regime for international organisations.

Remedial justice requires the prosecution and punishment of those responsible for the acts, actions or omissions that gave rise to the remedial action in the first place. International organisations in practice take disciplinary measures against individual staff members once their individual 'contribution' has been clearly established[3] and they seek the

---

[2] A. Gross, 'Redress against Decisions of International Organisations', *Transactions Grotius Society* 36 (1951), 30–48, at 44.

[3] See also in this regard General Assembly Resolution 53/217 of 7 April 1999 on procurement-related arbitration in which the General Assembly requested the Secretary-General to report, *inter alia*, on 'disciplinary action taken against staff members responsible for wrongdoing that resulted in arbitration'. The UN Secretary-General reported that disciplinary action had been taken in 'the case of one arbitration involving suspected fraud by a contractor and a UNDP staff member': A/54/458 of 14 October 1999, para. 24. It is worth noting that the Office of Internal Oversight Services does not participate in or take administrative action and neither

266   CONCLUSION

reimbursement of financial losses suffered by the organisation as a result of negligence or violation of regulations or instructions,[4] ultimately by instituting proceedings before domestic courts. The same recuperatory initiatives are available to international organisations *vis-à-vis* defaulting contractors and sub-contractors in the absence of insurance agreements being invoked.

Having due regard to the way in which international organisations implement this particular aspect of remedial justice, the fundamental objection 'to the permanent exemption of substantial numbers of international officials from any jurisdictional control of their official acts'[5] will continue. It is indeed, as Wilfred Jenks pointed out in 1943, 'essential to the maintenance of a proper sense of public responsibility that international civil servants should be legally accountable for their official acts':[6] no such legal remedial mechanism exists at the moment, neither for states nor for non-state claimants, the former also being prevented by Article 100 of the UN Charter and similar provisions from taking indirect remedial action of a political nature, leaving them with only the political sanction of not renewing the appointments of the highest officials of the organisation.

In a natural combination with the absence of a system of judicial review of the acts in most international organisations, this lack of legal accountability is one of the most serious deficiencies in the present remedial regime *vis-à-vis* international organisations. The jurisdiction of the World Administrative Tribunal proposed by Jenks would have included cases in which official acts performed on behalf of an international organisation were alleged to have violated a private right.[7]

The absence of any kind of legal remedial action at the national or international level for all categories of potential claimants with respect to responsible individual officials is a direct consequence of the privileges and immunities granted to officials for all acts undertaken in the course

does it initiate disciplinary action, although its findings may very well trigger such an outcome. 'Representatives of the OIOS usually appear before the Joint Disciplinary Committee to present evidence and other testimony as to the cases they have investigated': A/55/57, para. 57.

[4] F. Seyersted, 'Settlement of Internal Disputes of Intergovernmental Organisations by Internal and External Courts', *ZAÖRV* 24 (1964), 1–121, at 25.

[5] C. W. Jenks, 'Some Problems of an International Civil Service', *Public Administration Review* 3(2) (1943), 93–105, at 103.

[6] *Ibid.*, 103–4.

[7] *Ibid.*, 104: other areas of jurisdiction were cases where international organisations were involved in legal relationships governed by municipal law, disputes relating to real estate, buildings, contracts, etc.

CONCLUSION 267

of their official activities. Coupled with the jurisdictional immunity of the international organisations themselves mirroring the protection of their officials, this leaves claimants without remedies. International law may be moving 'towards a universally applicable system of administrative jurisprudence covering the conduct and protection of UN personnel wherever in the world their mission may take them'[8] and the slow but gradual setting in place, for instance, of a proper code of conduct to govern practices and procedures of officials and experts on mission by the UN Secretary-General[9] is to be welcomed as a first step towards providing the necessary yardsticks for accountability, but it does not reach the required remedial level.

From an international legal responsibility perspective, states and international organisations are in fact ironically giving rise to the same kind of dilemma. Malcolm Evans has persuasively argued that the efficiency of international law may be undermined if the individual becomes the focus of attention to the exclusion of the state in cases where individual and state responsibility coexist under international law.[10] There is no intrinsic reason why this caveat should not be applicable to the relationship between an international organisation and its officials, agents and experts on mission.

Also bearing in mind the potential role of domestic courts, there is little prospect of the international organisation being held liable before domestic courts for acts that are in violation of primary rules and give rise to an individual staff member's liability.[11]

This dilemma is bound to arise. The finding of an individual staff member's responsibility usually presupposes a similar finding on the organisation's part.[12] Waiving an official's immunity to enable a domestic court to exercise its jurisdiction over official acts undertaken in the name and

---

[8] *Difference Relating to Immunity from Legal Process of a Special Rapporteur of the Commission on Human Rights*, Advisory Opinion of 22 April 1999, *ICJ Reports* (1999), Separate Opinion of Judge Weeramantry, p. 94.

[9] The need for such a code for the latter category has been underlined by and during the *Cumaraswamy* case (CR/98/16, p. 20, para. 18; p. 24, para. 18) and unsurprisingly also by Jenks 'as they are not subject to the same measure of administrative discipline as either governmental representatives or officials of international organisations': C. W. Jenks, *International Immunities* (London and New York: Stevens & Sons and Oceana Publications, 1961), pp. 140–1.

[10] M. Evans, 'International Wrongs and National Jurisdiction' in M. Evans (ed.), *Remedies in International Law: The Institutional Dilemma* (Oxford: Hart Publishing, 1998), pp. 173–90, at p. 173.

[11] *Ibid.*, p. 188, but in relation to states.

[12] *Ibid.*, p. 189, but in relation to states.

268   CONCLUSION

on behalf of the organisation would entail the risk of the organisation being sheltered from its responsibility. It is important not to lose sight of the fact that both the international organisation and the individual staff member may be in breach of primary rules and that they cannot be treated as each other's alter ego within the international system.[13]

A solution has to be found in a combination of judicial review of acts of international organisations at the international level and the creation of a remedial mechanism for establishing the individual staff member's responsibility for the act, action or omission having affected the interest or rights of non-state claimants. The findings of the Commission of Inquiry into the events in Rwanda amply demonstrate the obvious need for remedial innovation to permit litigation in the public interest. The whole issue is undoubtedly of a delicate nature and involves complex political and legal aspects,[14] which in turn can be approached differently from a functionalist or constitutionalist perspective, as indicated at the beginning of this study.

Once the necessary remedial mechanisms, both political and legal, are put in place, one final factor has to be carefully monitored. Occasionally, in very cautious terms, and mostly in connection with judicial fora, a fear has been expressed that both the UNAT and the ILOAT have been paying too much attention to the interests of international organisations as such[15] and that the International Court of Justice is guided by the rule of effectiveness when the authority of an international organisation is in question.[16] Such an approach would be based on a 'virtual presumption'[17] that the international organisation and its administration are using their extensive powers in an acceptable way.[18]

Although Chittharanjan Amerasinghe's observations have been formulated within the context of the organisation/staff member relationship, they can be potentially extrapolated to other relations with states and

[13] *Ibid.*, p. 186, but in relation to states.

[14] See, for instance, I. Seidl-Hohenveldern, 'Les Organisations internationales et les actes illicites des fonctionnaires' in his *Collected Essays on International Investment and on International Organisations* (The Hague and London: Kluwer Law International, 1998), pp. 37–44.

[15] C. F. Amerasinghe, 'International Administrative Law in the 21st Century' in A. Anghie and G. Sturgess (eds.), *Legal Visions of the 21st Century: Essays in Honour of Judge Christof Weeramantry* (The Hague and London: Kluwer Law International, 1998), pp. 447–95, at p. 493.

[16] J. Charney, 'Is International Law Threatened by Multiple International Tribunals?', *RCADI* 271 (1998), 101–382, at 140–1 referring to Maurice Mendelson when discussing the interpretation of treaties.

[17] Amerasinghe, 'International Administrative Law', p. 493.   [18] *Ibid.*

CONCLUSION 269

other non-state entities. To prove the wrongdoing of an international organisation would invariably be more difficult if it became something of a trend to hold that international organisations are acting within their rights in acting as they do. According to Amerasinghe, the judiciary may be responding to the needs of international organisations to conduct their business efficiently, and the trend to be 'too pro-organisation' has to be checked in the future.[19]

The plausible reasons for contributing to or guaranteeing the well-functioning of international organisations echoes the intolerable interference argument frequently invoked by international organisations on various occasions, thus exacerbating the pre-existing inequality of power between the international organisation and non-state entities, which manifests itself in a less pronounced way *vis-à-vis* some (categories) of its member states. Due caution towards political and legal remedial mechanisms is called for in order to ensure that in the delicate balancing the necessary degree of autonomy in the decision-making process of the international organisations is not being preserved at a price that is not reconcilable with the demands of a well-functioning accountability regime leaving no loopholes.

The *internal* accountability of an international organisation built along the hierarchy of its organisational structure is currently in the process of reform within the UN; the interaction with *external* accountability towards third parties should also be reflected in the remedial sphere. For instance, if a court or tribunal finds that an act, action or omission by a competent organ of an international organisation or taking place under its authority is completely or partially in conflict with primary rules incumbent upon that organisation, and if the organisation's internal law only allows partial reparation to be made for the consequences of these acts, actions or omissions, then the judicial decision should, if necessary, afford just satisfaction to the injured party.[20]

It seems pointless to envisage a comprehensive set of primary rules governing the conduct of international organisations without putting into place, both at the domestic and international levels, appropriate remedial mechanisms for their enforcement.

Given the three levels of accountability and its different forms, a remedial regime will always and inevitably consist of a combination

[19] *Ibid.*
[20] Analogous to Article 41 of the European Convention on Human Rights.

of power-oriented mechanisms (first level of accountability) and of rule-oriented procedures (second and third levels of accountability).

This study has demonstrated that there is, at present, a lack of a reasonable level of coherence in the (emerging) law of remedies against international organisations.[21]

Today, the position of both a state and a non-state claimant against an international organisation and their right to an effective remedy in the light of the applicable rules has still not found a satisfactory solution. Maybe some day there will also be, as a legal matter, direct accountability on the part of both the international organisations and their officials towards the interested beneficiaries of their operational activities.

There is probably no more appropriate way to conclude this study than by citing one final time the visionary Wilfred Jenks, to whom the development of international (institutional) law owes so much: 'The extent to which executive authority should be subject to judicial control may prove to be both the most difficult and the most important of all the outstanding dilemmas.'[22]

---

[21] This is no different from the situation of human rights protection against states: D. Shelton, *Remedies in International Human Rights Law* (Oxford: Oxford University Press, 1999), p. 361.

[22] C. W. Jenks, *The Proper Law of International Organisations* (London and New York: Stevens, Dobbs Ferry and Oceana, 1962), p. 129.

Bibliography

Amerasinghe, C. F., *Local Remedies in International Law*, Cambridge: Grotius Publications, 1990.

Amerasinghe, C. F., 'Evidence before Administrative Tribunals' in R. Lillich (ed.), *Fact-finding Before International Tribunals, Eleventh Sokol Colloquium*, Ardsley-on-Hudson and New York: Transnational Publishers, 1992, pp. 205–33.

Amerasinghe, C. F., *The Law of the International Civil Service: As Applied by International Administrative Tribunals*, Oxford: Clarendon Press, 2 vols., 2nd revised edn, 1994.

Amerasinghe, C. F., 'The Future of International Administrative Law', *ICLQ* 45 (1996), 773–95.

Amerasinghe, C. F., 'International Court of Justice Cases relating to Employment in International Organisations' in V. Lowe and M. Fitzmaurice (eds.), *Fifty Years of the International Court of Justice: Essays in Honour of Sir Robert Jennings*, New York and Cambridge: Grotius Publications and Cambridge University Press, 1996, pp. 193–209.

Amerasinghe, C. F., *Principles of the Institutional Law of International Organisations*, Cambridge: Cambridge University Press, 1996.

Amerasinghe, C. F., 'International Administrative Law in the 21st Century' in A. Anghie and G. Sturgess (eds.), *Legal Visions of the 21st Century: Essays in Honour of Judge Christof Weeramantry*, The Hague and London: Kluwer Law International, 1998, pp. 447–95.

Anderson, D., 'Negotiation and Dispute Settlement' in M. Evans (ed.), *Remedies in International Law: The Institutional Dilemma*, Oxford: Hart Publishing, 1998, pp. 111–21.

Arsanjani, M., 'Claims against International Organisations: Quis Custodiet Ipsos Custodes?', *Yale Journal of World Public Order* 7 (1980–1), 131–76.

Bekker, P., 'The Work of the International Law Commission on Relations between States and International Organisations Discontinued: An Assessment', *LJIL* 6 (1993), 3–16.

BIBLIOGRAPHY

Bekker, P., *The Legal Position of Intergovernmental Organisations: A Functional Necessity Analysis of their Legal Status and Immunities*, Boston and London: Martinus Nijhoff Publishers, 1994.

Bellmann, C. and R. Gerster, 'Accountability in the World Trade Organisation', *JWTL* 30 (1996), 31–74.

Bissell, R., 'Recent Practice of the Inspection Panel of the World Bank', *AJIL* 91 (1997), 741–4.

Bissell, R., in a 'Panel on the Accountability of International Organisations to Non-state Actors', *ASIL Proceedings* 92 (1998), 359–73.

Blum, Y., *Eroding the Charter*, Dordrecht and London: Martinus Nijhoff Publishers, 1993.

Bowett, D., *UN Forces: A Legal Study of United Nations Practice*, London: Stevens, 1964.

Bowett, D., 'The Court's Role in Relation to International Organisations' in V. Lowe and M. Fitzmaurice (eds.), *Fifty Years of the International Court of Justice: Essays in Honour of Sir Robert Jennings*, New York and Cambridge: Grotius Publications and Cambridge University Press, 1996, pp. 181–92.

Bradlow, D. and S. Schlemmer-Schulte, 'The World Bank's New Inspection Panel: A Constructive Step in the Transformation of the International Legal Order', *ZAÖRV* 54 (1994), 392–415.

Bradlow, D., during the 'Panel on Accountability of International Organisations to Non-state Actors', *ASIL Proceedings* 92 (1998), 359–73.

Brownlie, I., *The Rule of Law in International Affairs at the Fiftieth Anniversary of the United Nations*, The Hague and London: Martinus Nijhoff Publishers, 1998.

Burdeau, G., 'Les Organisations internationales entre gestion publique et gestion privée' in J. Makarczyk (ed.), *Theory of International Law at the Threshold of the 21st Century: Essays in Honour of K. Skubiszewsky*, The Hague, London and Boston: Kluwer Law International, 1996, pp. 611–24.

Cançado Trinidade, A., 'Exhaustion of Local Remedies in International Law Experiments Ganting Procedural Status to Individuals in the First Half of the Twentieth Century', *NILR* 57 (1977), 373–92.

Charney, J., 'Is International Law Threatened by Multiple International Tribunals?', *RCADI* 271 (1998), 101–382.

Childers, E. and Urquhart, B., *Renewing the UN System*, Uppsala, Sweden: D. Hammarskjold Foundation, 1994.

Chinkin, C., *Third Parties in International Law*, Oxford: Clarendon Press, 1993.

Colin, J. P., 'Les Relations contractuelles des organisations internationales avec les personnes privées', *Revue de Droit International et de Droit Comparé* (1992), 6–43.

Couvreur, P., 'Développements récents concernant l'accès des organisations intergouvernementales à la procédure contentieuse devant la Cour Internationale de Justice' in E. Yakpo and T. Boumedra (eds.), *Liber Amicorum Mohammed Bedjaoui*, The Hague, Boston and London: Kluwer Law International, 1999, pp. 293–323.

Covelli, N., 'Public International Law and Third Party Participation in WTO Panel Proceedings', *JWTL* 33 (1999), 125–39.

De Cooker, C., 'Pre-litigation Procedures in International Organisations' in C. De Cooker (ed.), *International Administration: Law and Management in International Organisations* (looseleaf publication), The Hague: Kluwer Law International, contribution VI pp. 1–23.

De Visscher, P., 'Observations sur le fondement et la mise-en-oeuvre du principe de la responsabilité de l'organisation des Nations Unies', *Revue de Droit International et de Droit Comparé* 40 (1963), 165–73.

Eagleton, C., 'International Organisations and the Law of Responsibility', *RCADI* 76 (1950), 323–423.

Evans, M. (ed.), *Remedies in International Law: The Institutional Dilemma*, Oxford: Hart Publishing, 1998.

Evans, M., 'International Wrongs and National Jurisdiction' in M. Evans (ed.), *Remedies in International Law: The Institutional Dilemma*, Oxford: Hart Publishing, 1998, pp. 173–90.

Gerster, R., 'Accountability of Executive Directors in the Bretton Woods Institutions', *JWTL* 27 (1993), 87–116.

Gilbert, G., 'Rights, Legitimate Expectations, Needs and Responsibilities: UNHCR and the New World Order', *International Journal of Refugee Law* 10 (1998), 349–88.

Gray, C., *Judicial Remedies in International Law*, Oxford: Clarendon Press, 1987.

Gross, A., 'Redress against Decisions of International Organisations', *Transactions Grotius Society* 36 (1951), 30–48.

Guillaume, M., 'La Réparation des dommages causés par les contingents français en Ex-Yougoslavie et en Albanie', *AFDI* 43 (1997), 151–66.

Haasdijk, S., 'The Lack of Uniformity in Terminology of the International Law of Remedies', *LJIL* 5 (1992), 245–63.

Harlow, C., 'Access to Justice as a Human Right: The European Court of Justice and the European Union' in P. Alston (ed.), *The European Union and Human Rights*, Oxford: Oxford University Press, 2000, pp. 187–213.

Harpignies, R., 'Settlement of Disputes of a Private Law Character to which the United Nations is a Party: A Case in Point: The Arbitral Award of 24 September 1969 in Re Starways Ltd v. United Nations', *RBDI* 7 (1971), 451–68.

Harris, D., M. O'Boyle and C. Warbrick, *Law of the European Convention on Human Rights*, London: Butterworths, 1995.

Hartwig, M., *Die Haftung der Mitgliedstaaten für Internationale Organisationen*, Berlin, Heidelberg and New York: Springer, 1993.

Heukels, T. and A. McDonnell (eds.), *The Action for Damages in Community Law*, The Hague and London: Kluwer Law International, 1997.

Higgins, R., *UN Peacekeeping 1946–1967: Documents and Commentary*, vol. II, *Asia*, London: Oxford University Press, 1970.

Higgins, R., 'The Legal Consequences for Member States of the Non-fulfilment by International Organisations of their Obligations toward Third Parties', *Annuaire de l'Institut de Droit International* 66(1) (1995), 251–469 and 66(2) (1995), 233–320.

Higgins, R., 'Remedies and the International Court of Justice: An Introduction' in M. Evans (ed.), *Remedies in International Law: The Institutional Dilemma*, Oxford: Hart Publishing, 1998, pp. 1–10.

Hirsch, M., *The Responsibility of International Organisations Towards Third Parties: Some Basic Principles*, Dordrecht, Boston and London: Martinus Nijhoff Publishers, 1995.

Hobe, S., 'Der Rechtsstatus der Nichtregierungsorganisationen nach Gegenwärtigen Völkerrecht', *Archiv des Völkerrechts* 37 (1999), 152–76.

International Law Association, *Report of the 68th Conference*, London, 1999.

International Law Association Committee on Accountability of International Organisations, *First Report*, London, 1998.

International Law Association Committee on Accountability of International Organisations, *Second Report*, London, 2000.

Janis, M., 'Individuals and the International Court' in A. Muller, D. Raic and J. Thuransky (eds.), *The International Court of Justice: Its Future Role After Fifty Years*, The Hague, Boston and London: Martinus Nijhoff Publishers, 1997, pp. 205–16.

Jenks, C. W., 'Some Problems of an International Civil Service', *Public Administration Review* 3(2) (1943), 93–105.

Jenks, C. W., 'The Status of International Organisations in Relation to the International Court of Justice', *Transactions Grotius Society* 32 (1946), 1–41.

Jenks, C. W., *International Immunities*, London and New York: Stevens & Sons and Oceana Publications, 1961.

Jenks, C. W., *The Proper Law of International Organisations*, London and New York: Stevens, Dobbs Ferry and Oceana, 1962.

Jessup, P., *A Modern Law of Nations: An Introduction*, New York: Macmillan, 1948.

Jully, L., 'Arbitration and Judicial Settlement: Recent Trends', *AJIL* 48 (1954), 380–407.

Klein, P., *La Responsabilité des organisations internationales dans les ordres juridiques internes et en droit des gens*, Brussels: Editions Bruylant and Editions de l'Université Libre de Bruxelles, 1998.

Kokott, J., Interim Report in the *First Report of the ILA Committee on Diplomatic Protection of Persons and Property*, London, 2000, pp. 3–27.

Lauterpacht, E., *Aspects of the Administration of International Justice*, Cambridge: Grotius Publications, 1991.

Linda, R. (ed.), *The International Ombudsman Anthology: Selected Writings from the International Ombudsman Institute*, The Hague, London and Boston: Kluwer Law International, 1999.

Lonbay, J. and A. Briondi (eds.), *Remedies for Breach of EC Law*, Chichester: John Wiley and Sons, 1997.

Martha, R., 'Representation of Parties in World Trade Disputes', *JWTL* 31 (1997), 84–96.

Merrills, J., 'Reflections on the Incidental Jurisdiction of the International Court of Justice' in M. Evans (ed.), *Remedies in International Law: The Institutional Dilemma*, Oxford: Hart Publishing, 1998, pp. 51–70.

Meyer, D., 'Les Contrats de fournitures de biens et de services dans le cadre des opérations de maintien de la paix', *AFDI* 42 (1996), 79–119.

Minear, L., 'Introduction to Case-studies' in N. Azimi (ed.), *Humanitarian Action and Peacekeeping Operations: Debriefing and Lessons, Report of the 1997 Singapore Conference*, The Hague: Kluwer Law International, 1997, pp. 43–66.

Muller, A., *International Organisations and their Host-states: Aspects of their Legal Relationship*, The Hague and London: Kluwer Law International, 1995.

Nehl, H., *Principles of Administrative Procedure in EC Law*, Oxford: Hart Publishing, 1999.

Okawa, P., 'Environmental Dispute Settlement: Some Reflections on Recent Developments' in M. Evans (ed.), *Remedies in International Law: The Institutional Dilemma*, Oxford: Hart Publishing, 1998, pp. 157–72.

Paul, James N., 'Law and Development in the 1990s: Using International Law to Impose Accountability to People on International Development Actors', *Third World Legal Studies* (1992), 1–16.

Plender, R., 'Procedure in the European Courts: Comparisons and Prospects', *RCADI* 267 (1997), 1–343.

Pomerance, M., 'The Advisory Role of the International Court of Justice and its "Judicial" Character: Past and Future Prisms' in A. Muller, D. Raic and J. Thuransky (eds.), *The International Court of Justice: Its Future Role After Fifty Years*, The Hague, Boston and London: Martinus Nijhoff Publishers, 1997, pp. 271–323.

Prechal, S., 'EC Requirements for an Effective Remedy' in J. Lonbay and A. Briondi (eds.), *Remedies for Breach of EC Law*, Chichester: John Wiley and Sons, 1997, pp. 3–13.

Qureshi, A., 'Extraterritorial Shrimps, Non-governmental Organisations and the WTO Appellate Body', *ICLQ* 48 (1999), 199–206.

Ravillon, L., 'Les Organisations internationales de télécommunications par satellite: vers une privatisation?', *AFDI* 44 (1998), 533–51.

Reinisch, A., *International Organisations before National Courts*, Cambridge: Cambridge University Press, 2000.

Rensmann, T., 'Internationale Organisationen im Privatrechtsverkehr', *Archiv des Völkerrechts* 36 (1998), 305–44.

Reuter, P., 'Le Droit au secret et les institutions internationales', *AFDI* 2 (1956), 46–65.

Ritter, J. P., 'La Protection diplomatique à l'égard d'une organisation internationale', *AFDI* 8 (1962), 427–56.

Rosenne, S., *The Law and Practice of the International Court 1920–1996*, The Hague,
Boston and London: Martinus Nijhoff Publishers, 1997.

Rosenne, S., 'The Secretary-General of the United Nations and the Advisory
Proceedings of the International Court of Justice' in K. Wellens (ed.),
International Law: Theory and Practice: Essays in Honour of Eric Suy,
The Hague, Boston and London: Martinus Nijhoff Publishers, 1998,
pp. 707–17.

Ruzié, D., 'Jurisprudence du Tribunal Administratif des Nations Unies', *AFDI* 39
(1993), 610–26.

Ruzié, D., 'Jurisprudence du Tribunal Administratif des Nations Unies', *AFDI* 42
(1996), 482–503.

Ruzié, D., 'Jurisprudence du Tribunal Administratif des Nations Unies', *AFDI* 43
(1997), 430–44.

Ruzié, D., 'Jurisprudence du Tribunal Administratif de l'Organisation Internationale du Travail', *AFDI* 43 (1997), 445–61.

Ruzié, D., 'Jurisprudence du Tribunal Administratif des Nations Unies', *AFDI* 44
(1998), 412–27.

Salmon, J., 'Les Accords Spaak–U Thant du 20 février 1965', *AFDI* 11 (1965),
469–97.

Sarooshi, D., 'The Legal Framework Governing United Nations Subsidiary Organs',
BYIL 67 (1996), 413–78.

Sarooshi, D., *The UN and the Development of Collective Security: The Delegation by
the UN Security Council of its Chapter VII Powers*, Oxford: Clarendon Press,
1999.

Sarooshi, D., 'The Powers of the United Nations International Criminal
Tribunals', *Max Planck Yearbook of UN Law* 2 (1999), 141–67.

Schermers, H. and N. Blokker, *International Institutional Law: Unity Within Diversity*,
Dordrecht and London: Martinus Nijhoff Publishers, 1995.

Schlemmer-Schulte, S., 'Panel on the Accountability of International Organisations to Non-state Actors', *ASIL Proceedings* 92 (1998), 359–73.

Schlemmer-Schulte, S., 'The World Bank Inspection Panel: Its Creation, Functioning, Case Record and its Two Reviews', *Zeitschrift für Europarechtliche Studien*
1 (1998), 347–70.

Schlemmer-Schulte, S., 'The World Bank's Experience with its Inspection Panel',
ZAÖRV 58 (1998), 353–88.

Schlemmer-Schulte, S., 'The World Bank, its Operations and its Inspection Panel',
Recht der Internationale Wirtschaft 45 (1999), 175–81.

Schlemmer-Schulte, S., 'Introductory Note to the Conclusions of the Second
Review of the World Bank Inspection Panel', *ILM* 39 (2000), 243–8.

Schmidt-Assmann, E. and L. Harrings, 'Access to Justice and Fundamental Rights',
European Review of Public Law 9 (1997), 529–49.

Scobbie, I., 'International Organisations and International Relations' in R. J. Dupuy (ed.), *A Handbook of International Organisations*, The Hague, London and Boston: Kluwer Law International, 1998, pp. 831–96.

Seidl-Hohenveldern, I., 'Access of International Organisations to the International Court of Justice' in A. Muller, D. Raic and J. Thuransky (eds.), *The International Court of Justice: Its Future Role After Fifty Years*, The Hague, Boston and London: Kluwer Law International, 1997, pp. 189–216.

Seidl-Hohenveldern, I., 'Les Organisations internationales et les actes illicites des fonctionnaires' in *Collected Essays on International Investment and on International Organisations*, The Hague and London: Kluwer Law International, 1998, pp. 37–44.

Seyersted, F., 'United Nations Forces: Some Legal Problems', *BYIL* 37 (1961), 351–475.

Seyersted, F., 'Settlement of Internal Disputes of Intergovernmental Organisations by Internal and External Courts', *ZAÖRV* 24 (1964), 1–121.

Shelton, D., 'The Participation of Non-governmental Organisations in International Judicial Proceedings', *AJIL* 88 (1994), 611–42.

Shelton, D., *Remedies in International Human Rights Law*, Oxford: Oxford University Press, 1999.

Shihata, I., *The World Bank Inspection Panel*, Oxford: Oxford University Press, 1994.

Shihata, I., *The World Bank Inspection Panel in Practice*, Washington, DC: Oxford University Press, 2nd edn, 2000.

Shraga, D., 'UN Peacekeeping Operations: Applicability of International Humanitarian Law and Responsibility for Operations-related Damage', *AJIL* 94 (2000), 406–12.

Siekmann, R., 'The Fall of Srebrenica and the Attitude of Dutchbat from an International Legal Perspective', *Yearbook of International Humanitarian Law* 1 (1998), 301–12.

Singer, M., 'Jurisdictional Immunity of International Organisations: Human Rights and Functional Necessity Concerns', *Virginia Journal of International Law* 36 (1995), 53–165.

Stephens, B. and M. Ratner, *International Human Rights Litigation in US Courts*, Irvington-on-Hudson and New York: Transnational Publishers, 1996.

Szasz, P., 'Granting International Organisations *Jus Standi* in the International Court of Justice' in A. Muller, D. Raic and J. Thuransky (eds.), *The International Court of Justice: Its Future Role After Fifty Years*, The Hague, Boston and London: Martinus Nijhoff Publishers, 1997, pp. 169–88.

Szasz, P., 'Adjudicating IGO Staff Challenges to Legislative Decisions' in G. Hafner et al. (eds.), *Liber Amicorum Professor Ignaz Seidl-Hohenveldern in Honour of his 80th Birthday*, The Hague and London: Kluwer Law International, 1998, pp. 699–720.

Szasz, P., 'The Complexification of the United Nations System', *Max Planck Yearbook of UN Law* 3 (1999), 1–57.

Sztucki, J., 'International Organisations as Parties to Contentious Proceedings before the International Court of Justice?' in A. Muller, D. Raic, and J. Thuransky (eds.), *The International Court of Justice: Its Future Role After Fifty Years*, The Hague, Boston and London: Martinus Nijhoff Publishers, 1997, pp. 141–67.

Usher, J., *General Principles of EC Law*, London, New York: Longman, 1998.

Wenckstern, M., 'Die Haftung der Mitgliedstaaten für Internationale Organisationen', *Rabels Zeitschrift* 61(1) (1997), 93–114.

Wirth, D., during the 'Panel on Accountability of International Organisations to Non-state Actors', *ASIL Proceedings* 92 (1998), 359–73.

Zacklin, R., 'Responsabilité des Organisations internationales' in Société Française de Droit International: Colloque du Mans, *La Responsabilité dans le système international*, Paris: Pedone, 1990, pp. 91–100.

Index

Access to remedies,
accountability levels, 264
contractual claims, 41, 90–1, 115
contractual standings, 38
human rights, 214
immunities *see* Immunities
individuals, 39, 198, 264
institutional standings, 36–8
internal remedial mechanisms, 42
international administrative tribunals,
41, 84
judicial remedies, 40–3, 77
member states, 36, 38, 39–40, 65, 224–5
non-governmental organisations (NGOs),
39, 107–8
non-member states, 37, 38
non-state entities, 38, 39, 225
officials and staff, 38, 42, 84
operational standing, 37–8
penultimate ranking, 38
political remedial mechanisms, 39–40
preferential standing, 36–9, 41, 44
preliminary issues, 18
privileged institutional standing, 36–7
privileged operational standing, 37
scope *ratione fori*, 39–40
scope *ratione personae*, 36–9
Accountability,
autonomy, 2, 25, 49
components, 8
constituencies, 22, 27
continuous process, 7
conventions, rules, 75
efficacy, 13
European Community, 3, 11
financial management, 88–9

forms, 8, 12
forum, 22
general/individual interest, 79
immunities, 120
individuals, 7
inter-organisational accountability, 3, 36
internal accountability, 36, 269
judicial remedies, 34
officials and staff, 129
ombudsman, 170, 178, 181
overarching nature, 26
parliaments, 32
prerequisite, 27
primary rules, 7, 17, 26, 58
protection function, 11
representational NGOs, 106
secondary rules, 8, 17
states, 7, 22
World Bank, 185–7
Accountability levels,
access to remedies, 264
administrative/financial, 8, 31
commissions of inquiry, 191
comprehensive regime, 14
first level, 29–32, 57–9, 119, 173
legal, 8–9
member states, 29–33
political, 8, 17, 29, 31
privileged operational standing, 37
scope *ratione materiae*, 28–35
second level, 14, 32–3, 198
supervision/monitoring, 28
third level, 14, 32–3, 198
tortious liability, 28, 64
Accountability regimes,
accountability levels, 14, 29

280   INDEX

Accountability regimes, (cont.)
  comprehensive regimes, 14, 120
  disarmament, 11
  environment, 11
  financial managemnet, 88, 139
  general features, 7–9, 26–7, 131
  international societal interests, 141
  remedial outcomes, 13, 135, 137, 138,
    139, 225
Advisory Committee of Jurists, 255
Advisory Opinions,
  General Convention (1946), 56, 230–3
  Headquarters Agreements, 56
  Inter-American Court of Human Rights
    (IACHR), 55–6, 110
  International Court of Justice (ICJ), 55,
    56, 69, 86, 140, 204, 220, 228–36, 239
Affirmative action, 58
Alternative remedial action,
  arbitration *see* Arbitration
  commissions *see* Commissions of inquiry
  domestic courts, 209–13
  future options, 169–70
  immunities, 40
  inspections *see* Inspection panels
  International Labour Organisation
    (ILO), 209
  non-legal *see* Non-legal remedial action
  ombudsman *see* Ombudsman
  pre-remedial *see* Pre-remedial action
  voluntary submission, 18
Amerasinghe, Chittharanjan, 76, 128, 260,
  268–9
Amicus curiae,
  International Court of Justice (ICJ), 56,
    109, 110, 112–13, 227, 251, 254
  non-governmental organisations (NGOs),
    109, 110, 112
  UN Secretary-General, 251
Appeals,
  international administrative tribunals,
    204–6, 223
  International Court of Justice (ICJ), 86,
    204–5
  JAB *see* Joint Appeals Board
  officials and staff, 82
  review procedure eliminated, 86
  UN Administrative Tribunal (UNAT),
    84, 223
Arbitration,
  Arbitral Tribunal, 156, 158

Arbitration Board proposed, 199–200
  contractual claims, 18, 91, 93–5,
    156–60
  Headquarters Agreements, 220, 222
  human rights, 18
  immunities, 91
  non-state entities, 22–3
  officials and staff, 83, 84
  Optional Rules, 222, 223
  peacekeeping/enforcement operations,
    157, 160
  Permanent Court of Arbitration (PCA),
    220–3
  potential role, 219–23
  procurement-related cases, 157–60
  scope *ratione materiae*, 221
  scope *ratione personae*, 221
  states/international organisations, 220–2
  UNCITRAL Rules, 221
  United Nations, 67, 84, 93, 94, 157–60,
    199–200
  waiver of immunities, 91, 93
Arsanjani, Mahnoush, 69, 93, 97, 98, 121
Asian Development Bank, 182
Australia, 236
Autonomy,
  see also Immunities
  accountability, 2, 25, 49
  functional autonomy, 25, 118
  remedies, 23
  states, 23

Banks,
  Asian Development Bank, 182
  European Bank for Reconstruction and
    Development (EBRD), 180
  Inter-American Development Bank, 182
  International Bank for Reconstruction
    and Development (IBRD), 93, 180
  World Bank, 182–90, 256
Bekker, Peter, 75, 173
Belgium,
  Bosnian war, 53
  Brussels Court of Appeal, 210
  League for the Defence of Human
    Rights, 165, 174
  ONUC operation, 77
  Rwanda, 100, 193, 196
Blokker, Niels, 204
Bosnia and Herzegovina, 53, 194, 195
Bowett, Derek W., 14, 17, 98, 235, 240

INDEX 281

Brownlie, Ian, 54
Budgets,
  see also Finance
  contributions refused, 31
  liabilities, compensation/damages,
    49, 139
  voluntary contributions, 31, 34, 164, 165

Calvo clause, 74
Canada, 53
Cançado Trinidade, Antonio, 78
Childers, Erskine, 181
Chinkin, Christine, 36
Claims,
  claimant's approach, 44–6
  claims commissions, 72, 73, 77, 99,
    103–5, 164
  contractual see Contractual claims
  illustrative examples, 12–13
  non-contractual, 8, 41, 43, 44
  peacekeeping/enforcement operations,
    53, 72–3, 77, 162–6
  private law, 50
  procedural aspects see Procedure
  public interest, 170
  remedies against states, 44–5
  remedies against whom, 44–53
  requests/applications, 50
  respondents, selection, 45–6
  state responsibility, 44
  torts see Tortious liability
  United Nations, 14, 136
Cold War, 2
Commissions of inquiry,
  accountability levels, 191
  declaratory judgments, 190
  fact-finding, 190–1
  humanitarian aid, 32
  individuals, 198
  International Court of Justice (ICJ), 192
  non-legal remedial action, 170, 190–7
  parliaments, 31–2
  peacekeeping/enforcement operations,
    20, 32, 192, 193–7, 260
  potential remedial effect, 190–7, 265
  pre-remedial action, 65
  recommendations, 191
  Rwanda, 127, 143, 190, 191, 192, 193–6,
    260, 268
  Security Council, 165–6, 192, 194,
    195, 196

  Somalia, 20
  Srebrenica, 143, 192, 193–6
Committee on Applications for Review of
  Administrative Judgments, 79
Compensation,
  see also Damages
  Advisory Board for Compensation
    Claims, 84
  budgets, liabilities, 49, 139
  ex gratia payments, 142, 161, 165–6
  holding-harmless clause, 71
  international administrative tribunals,
    151–3, 202
  lump-sum agreements, 73, 162
  moral injury, 152, 153, 162
  tortious liability, 163, 164
Complaints,
  investigation, 17–18, 64
  maladministration, 179
  ombudsman see Ombudsman
Conciliation,
  contractual claims, 94
  UNCITRAL Rules, 67, 94, 156
Confidential information,
  archives, 127, 129
  injunctive relief, 58
  international administrative tribunals,
    128
  international criminal tribunals, 130–1
  professional secrets, 127
Congo, 73, 77, 97–9
Constitutional obligation, conventional
  requirements, 13–14
Contracts,
  claims see Contractual claims
  contracting-out, 24
  contractual liabilities, 41, 46, 74, 89–95,
    156–60, 173
  international organisations, 47, 48–9, 75
  iure gestionis/iure imperii, 90
  officials and staff, 75, 81
  peacekeeping/enforcement operations,
    24, 90, 92, 94
  tenders, 90
  third parties, 48–9
  UN General Conditions, 157
Contractual claims,
  access to remedies, 41, 90–1, 115
  accountability, 64, 75
  arbitration, 18, 91, 93–5, 156–60
  conciliation, 94

282 INDEX

Contractual claims, (cont.)
contract law absent, 65
negotiations, 156
officials and staff, 81, 91
overall picture, 89–92
private claimants, 89–95, 115
remedial outcomes, 137, 156–60
sub-contracting, 92–3
third parties, 44
Conventions,
accountability, rules, 75
constitutional obligation, 13–14
human rights, 15, 255, 256
immunities *see* General Convention on
Privileges and Immunities (1946)
NGOs, legal personality, 107
supervision/monitoring, 15
Vienna Convention (1986), 237
Corporate veil,
legal personality, 44
member states, 46
Costa Rica, 237, 242, 247–8, 253, 254,
257
Costs,
international administrative tribunals,
154–5
remedial outcomes, 145–6, 154–5
restitutio in integrum, 146
Council of Europe, 84, 107
Counterclaims,
private claimants, 91
tortious liability, 162
Courts,
Brussels Court of Appeal, 210
Court of First Instance (CFI), 179
European Court of Human Rights
(ECHR), 67, 163, 205
European Court of Justice (ECJ), 84, 110,
140–1, 179
ICJ *see* International Court of Justice
Inter-American Court of Human Rights
(IACHR), 55–6, 110, 138
national *see* Domestic courts
Permanent Court of Arbitration (PCA),
220–3
Permanent Court of International
Justice (PCIJ), 255
Couvreur, Philippe, 242, 243
Criminal tribunals *see* International
criminal tribunals
Customary international law,
see also International law

immunities, 114
rights, remedies, 17
rules/norms, 1
Cyprus, 73, 98

Damage,
legal acts, 2
non-contractual liability, 8
operational activities, 8
peacekeeping/enforcement operations,
72, 77, 99, 102
tortious liability, 28, 64, 79
Damages,
see also Compensation
human rights, 141
injury to reputation, 141–2
international administrative tribunals,
147
International Court of Justice (ICJ), 55
lex loci, 141
moral damages, 152, 153, 161, 162
punitive damages, 144–5, 161
remedial outcomes, 55, 137, 139, 141–2,
144–5
De Cooker, Chris, 83, 201
Decisions,
annulment, 147, 151
individual representations, 172
internal remedial mechanisms, 39
legislative decisions challenged, 84–6
non-state entities, 29
operational decisions, 58
political decision-making, 44
rules/norms, 172
secondary organs, 58
treaty compatibility, 29
Declaratory judgments,
bilateral claims, 108
commissions of inquiry, 190
European Court of Justice (ECJ), 140–1
International Court of Justice (ICJ), 54–5,
140–1
remedial state action, 79
Denial of justice,
immunities, 114, 120, 214
internal remedial mechanisms, 75
international administrative tribunals,
203–4
Development assistance,
non-governmental organisations (NGOs),
107
sub-contracting, 24, 93

INDEX 283

Diplomatic protection,
discretion, 75
exhaustion of local remedies, 76–8
holding-harmless clause, 75
member states, 65, 73–8, 213
United Nations, 75, 78–9
vis-à-vis international organisations,
73–6
Disarmament, accountability regimes, 11
Dispute settlement mechanisms,
basic provisions, 173
lacking under General Convention, 210,
211
Organisation of America States (OAS),
212
World Trade Organisation (WTO), 10, 111
Dispute Settlement Understanding,
non-governmental organisations
(NGOs), 111
Dissolution, political remedial
mechanisms, 33
Domestic courts,
alternative remedial action, 209–13
forum, 213–15
immunities *see* Immunities
international organisations, 116–17
judicial abstention, 117–21
judicial activism, 121–5
judicial remedies, 116–25
potential role, 208–19

Eagleton, Clyde, 12, 96, 145, 236, 249
Economic and Social Council (ECOSOC),
111, 230
Egypt, 92
Energy-related operations, 24
Environment,
accountability regimes, 11
protection treaties, 112
Eritrea, 20
Estoppel, concurrent/subsidiary liability,
49
European Bank for Reconstruction and
Development (EBRD), 180
European Co-ordinated International
Organisations, 84, 86
European Commission on Human
Rights, 18
European Community,
institutionalised accountability, 3, 11
integration, 179, 180
ombudsman, 178–80

European Convention on Human Rights
(1950), 255, 256
European Court of Human Rights (ECHR),
exhaustion of local remedies, 67
filtering system, 205
non-economic loss, 163
European Court of Justice (ECJ),
Court of First Instance (CFI), 179
declaratory judgments, 140–1
judicial role, 179
non-governmental organisations (NGOs),
110
officials and staff, 84
European Parliament,
Committee on Petitions, 179
ombudsman, 179
Evans, Malcolm, 11, 267
Ex gratia payments, 142, 161, 165–6
Exhaustion of local remedies,
diplomatic protection, 76–8
European Court of Human Rights
(ECHR), 67
Headquarters Agreements, 68, 76
individuals, 78
internal remedial mechanisms, 18, 43,
66–8, 76–9
international law, 67
officials and staff, 79, 82
peacekeeping/enforcement operations,
67
Expressio unius est exclusio alterius, 37

Finance,
see also Banks; Budgets
accountability, 8, 13, 88–9, 139
financial liabilities, 102
financial management, 88–9, 139
international financial organisations,
121
First-level remedies, potential outcomes,
57–9, 119
Forum,
accountability, 22
domestic courts, 213–15
international administrative
tribunals, 85
selection, 44

General Convention on Privileges and
Immunities (1946),
absolute immunity, 122
Advisory Opinions, 56, 230–3

284 INDEX

General Convention (cont.)
  archives and documents, 129
  code of conduct, 175
  differences, 68–9, 219
  immunity invoked, 120
  no dispute settlement procedure,
    210, 211
  non-contractual liability, 230
  preventive approach, 231–2
  settlement procedures, 88, 103, 209–10,
    214
  waiver of immunities, 89, 124,
    208, 212
Germany, 53
Gilbert, Geoff, 52, 101
Governing Commission of the Saar
  Territory, 109
Governmental authority,
  peacekeeping/enforcement
  operations, 16, 20
Gray, Christine, 10, 108, 136, 138, 139,
  163, 234
Greece, 162
Greenpeace, 110
Gross, André, 265
Guatemala, 237, 238, 242, 243, 245–7, 250,
  251, 253, 254, 257

Harpignies, R. H., 14
Headquarters Agreements,
  Advisory Opinions, 56
  arbitration, 220, 222
  constitutional obligation, 14
  disputes, 68
  exhaustion of local remedies, 68, 76
  individuals, 76
  International Court of Justice (ICJ), 246
  liabilities, claims, 41
  OAS/United States, 41, 212
  organisational responsibility, 174
  privileged institutional standing, 36–7
  termination, 14, 34
  UN/United States, 68, 160–1
Higgins, Rosalyn (Judge), 46, 109, 128
Hobe, Stephan, 113
Holding-harmless clause, 70–3, 75
Host states,
  see also Member states
  agreements *see* Headquarters
    Agreements
  expulsion, officials and staff, 33

judicial remedies, 37
peacekeeping/enforcement operations,
  77
Human rights,
  access to remedies, 214
  arbitration, 18
  Belgian League for the Defence of
    Human Rights, 165, 174
  collective action, 138
  Commission on Human Rights (CHR),
    194, 230
  conventions, 15, 255, 256
  damages, 141
  European Convention, 255, 256
  European Court of Human Rights
    (ECHR), 67, 163, 205
  Human Rights Committee, 101
  immunities, 116, 139, 214
  imperative, 214, 215
  Inter-American Commission on Human
    Rights, 217
  Inter-American Court of Human Rights
    (IACHR), 55–6, 110, 138
  internal remedial mechanisms, 76–7
  international protection, 11, 14–16, 22
  multinational corporations, 15
  non-governmental organisations (NGOs),
    15, 112
  ombudsman, 181
  operational guidelines/directives, 15
  peacekeeping/enforcement operations,
    101, 102, 181
  personal safety, 130
  primary rules, 14, 15
  remedies against states, 22, 27, 80,
    93, 138
  secondary rules, 14
  United Nations, 15, 101
  Universal Declaration on Human Rights,
    153
  violations, 27, 139, 215
Humanitarian aid,
  commissions of inquiry, 32
  non-governmental organisations (NGOs),
    107
  sub-contracting, 24, 93

Illegal acts, 2, 38, 136
Immunities,
  see also General Convention on Privileges
    and Immunities (1946)

INDEX   285

accountability, 120
acta iure gestionis/acta iure imperii, 122,
    123,125
alternative remedial action, 40
arbitration, 91
conventions, 14, 56, 68–9, 88, 89, 103,
    120, 122, 124, 129, 175, 208
customary international law, 114
denial of immunity, 121
denial of justice, 114, 120, 214
derivative, 92, 93
differences over privileges and
    immunities, 68–70, 115, 219
functional, 25, 118, 122–3, 215–19
human rights, 116, 139, 214
in limine litis, 115
international administrative tribunals,
    42, 155, 207
international financial organisations,
    121
jurisdictional immunity, 22, 25, 37, 40,
    42, 50, 89, 91, 92, 93, 103, 114–25,
    207, 214
legal personality, 119
loss of immunity, 120
ne impediatur officia, 123, 215
official capacity, 123
peacekeeping/enforcement operations,
    98, 103
protection, 22
ratio legis, 208, 209
reciprocity, 119
restrictive, 122, 124
Special Convention on the Privileges and
    Immunities of Specialised
Agencies, 68, 88, 219, 232
states, 22, 37
sub-contracting, 92–3
tortious liability, 122
United Nations, 50, 56, 69–70, 88, 89, 92,
    93, 120–1, 129, 210–11, 217–18
United States, 37, 122
unwarranted suits prevented, 118
waiver *see* Waiver of immunities
Indemnities, tortious liability, 161
Individuals,
    access to remedies, 39, 198, 264
    accountability, 7
    commissions of inquiry, 198
    exhaustion of local remedies, 78
    Headquarters Agreements, 76

institutional acts, 29
legal redress, states, 16
staff *see* Officials and staff
Information,
    confidential *see* Confidentioal
        information
    disclosure, 125–9
Injunctive relief,
    confidential information, 58
    International Court of Justice (ICJ),
        54, 128
    pre-emptive remedy, 26
    remedial outcomes, 137
    remedial state action, 79
    structural injunctions, 139
Inspection panels,
    alternative remedial action, 170,
        181–90
    models, 187–90
    ratione materiae, 183
    ratione remedii, 184
    World Bank, 182–90, 256
Institut de Droit International, 46, 48, 49,
    95, 237
Institutional acts,
    challenged, 42
    controls, 29
    individuals, 29
    judicial review, 66
    operational activities distinguished,
        28–9
    restitutio in integrum, 136
Insurance,
    tortious liability, 96–7, 161
    United Nations, 96, 161
Inter-American Commission on Human
        Rights, 217
Inter-American Court of Human Rights
        (IACHR),
    Advisory Opinions, 55–6, 110
    collective actions, 138
Inter-American Development Bank, 182
Inter-organisational accountability, 3
Inter-state disputes,
    contentious proceedings, 66
    International Court of Justice (ICJ), 56,
        226–8
    judicial equality, 67
Internal remedial mechanisms,
    access to remedies, 42
    administrative decisions, 39

286 INDEX

Internal remedial mechanisms, (cont.)
  exhaustion *see* Exhaustion of local
    remedies
  human rights, 76–7
  internal accountability, 36, 269
  jurisdiction, 51, 90
  lack, denial of justice, 75
  nemo judex in causa sua, 66
  United Nations, 69
International administrative tribunals,
  access to remedies, 41, 84
  annulment, decisions, 147, 151
  appeals, 204–6, 223
  compensation, 151–3, 202
  compulsory jurisdiction, 120
  confidential information, 128
  costs, 154–5
  Council of Europe, 84
  damages, 147
  denial of justice, 203–4
  European Co-ordinated International
    Organisations, 84, 86
  exclusive jurisdiction, 38, 42
  forum shopping, 85
  ILOAT *see* International Labour
    Organisation Administrative
    Tribunal
  immunities, 42, 155, 207
  independence questioned, 83
  injury to reputation, 141
  jurisdiction, 38, 42, 120, 202–3
  legislative decisions challenged,
    84–6
  NATO, 84
  OECD, 84
  officials and staff, 82, 84–6, 147–55
  oral hearings refused, 83, 203
  prospective/retrospective approaches,
    206–7
  ratione materiae, 147, 148, 207
  ratione personae, 147, 202, 207
  ratione remedii, 139
  reform, 199–207
  remedial outcomes, 149–55
  reparative orders, 138
  stare decisis rules, 85
  statutes, 10, 64
  tortious liability, 160
  UNAT *see* UN Administrative Tribunal
    (UNAT)
  variety of remedies, 149–51

International Bank for Reconstruction and
    Development (IBRD), 93, 180
International Civil Aviation Organisation
    (ICAO), 91, 180
International civil servants *see* Officials and
    staff
International Civil Service Commission, 85
International Commission of the Civil
    Service, 148
International Committee of the Red Cross
    (ICRC), 101, 129, 131
International Court of Justice (ICJ),
  1997 proposals, 237–8
  Advisory Opinions, 55, 56, 69, 86, 140,
    204, 220, 228–36, 239
  amicus curiae, 56, 109, 110, 112–13, 227,
    251, 254
  appeals, 86, 204–5
  commissions of inquiry, 192
  compromis, 246
  compulsory jurisdiction, 222
  damages, 55
  declaratory judgments, 54–5, 140–1
  direct remedial action, 236–61
  disclosure, 128
  Eastern Carelia doctrine, 235
  effectiveness rule, 268
  freedom of exclusion, 248–50
  Headquarters Agreements, 246
  indirect remedial opportunity, 226–36
  inevitable role, 224–61
  injunctive relief, 54, 128
  inter-state disputes, 56, 226–8
  interim measures, 56–7
  intervention, 252–4
  locus standi, 241–5, 255–6
  need for change, 236–7, 256–61
  non-governmental organisations (NGOs),
    108–10, 255–6
  potential outcome of remedies, 54–5
  procedural aspects and rights, 250
  provisional measures of protection, 252
  public policy, 238–41
  ratione materiae, 243, 245–50, 256
  ratione personae, 241–5
  remedial protection, 234–5
  remedies against states, 138
  restitutio in integrum, 55
  Rules of Court, 128, 227, 228, 234,
    250, 251
  specific performance, 54

INDEX 287

Statute, 42. 55, 56, 57, 108–9, 110, 204,
225, 227, 228, 234, 237, 238, 243,
251, 252, 255, 257
tortious liability, 161, 225–6
UN Charter, 14, 108, 230, 231, 237
International criminal tribunals,
confidential information, 130–1
evidence, 129–32
Former Yugoslavia (ICTY), 101, 129
peacekeeping/enforcement operations,
131
rules of procedure, 130
waiver of immunities, 131
witnesses, 129, 130
International financial organisations,
banks *see* Banks
immunities, 121
International Labour Organisation (ILO),
alternative remedial action, 209
arbitration, 95
non-government organisations (NGOs),
106, 112
trade unions, 106
International Labour Organisation
Administrative Tribunal (ILOAT),
compensation, 151–3, 202
contracts, 95
costs, 154, 155
denial of justice, 203, 204
interests of organisations, 268
jurisdiction, 207
oral hearings, 83, 203
pre-litigation procedure, 83
remedial outcomes, 149–55
respondents, 85
review system, 86
specific performance, 150, 151
unsuccessful candidates, 79
variety of remedies, 149–51
International law,
common code of good conduct,
27
customary *see* Customary international
law
exhaustion of local remedies, 67
judicial remedies, 10
non-state entities, 30
remedies, 10–12
rules/norms, 1, 30, 47
states, competences, 21
International Law Association (ILA),

access to ICJ, 236
Advisory Opinions, 230
arbitration, 221
Committee on Accountability of
International Organisations,
establishment, ix
First Report, 8, 25, 28
Second Report, 7, 57, 173
immunities, 117
International Law Commission,
diplomatic protection, 74
state responsibility, 10
International League for the Rights of
Man, 109
Intervention, ICJ, 252–4
Iraq, 101
Italy, 20, 37, 162

Janis, Mark, 255, 256
Jenks, Wilfred, 20, 41, 70, 95, 108, 178,
206, 207, 212, 213, 233, 240, 257,
266, 270
Jessup, Philip, 238
Joint Appeals Board (JAB),
jurisdiction, 202–3, 205
replacement proposed, 199
unanimous recommendations, 201
Judicial remedies,
access, preliminary issues, 18
access to remedies, 40–3, 77
accountability, 34
amendment of existing remedies,
198–224
availability, 40–1
damages *see* Damages
declaratory judgments, 54–5, 79, 140–1
equality of arms, 40
host states, 37
immunities *see* Immunities
injunctions *see* Injunctive relief
international law, 10
member states, 32–3
national courts *see* Domestic courts
non-governmental organisations (NGOs),
108–17
permanent machinery absent, 41
post-adjudicatory stage, 45
potential outcomes, 54–7
predictability, 41
remedies against states, 22
restitution *see* Restitutio in integrum

288 INDEX

Judicial remedies, (cont.)
specific performance, 54, 137–40, 150, 151
waiver, 18
Judicial review,
absence, 66
sufficient scope, 40
United Nations, 16–17
Jurisdiction,
exclusive jurisdiction, 38, 42
extended jurisdiction, 19–20, 51
immunity *see* Immunities
inherent jurisdiction, 19, 20
internal remedial mechanisms, 51, 90
international administrative tribunals, 38, 42, 120, 202–3
Joint Appeals Board (JAB), 202–3, 205
lack of jurisdictional connection, 77
tortious liability, 160
Justice, denial *see* Denial of justice

Klein, Pierre, 88, 136, 137
Korea, 53

Lauterpacht, Elihu, 55
Lauterpacht, Hirsch, 126
Law of war, 102
League of Nations, 109, 149
Legal personality,
contractual claims, 91
corporate veil, 44
immunities, 119
liabilities, 46, 119
non-governmental organisations (NGOs), 107, 129
peacekeeping/enforcement operations, 92
Legal remedies *see* Judicial remedies
Lessons-Learned Units, 59, 188
Liabilities,
abuse of rights, 47
acquiescence, 47
concurrent/subsidiary, 46, 47, 48, 49, 50
contractual, 41, 46, 74, 79, 89–95, 156–60, 173
default, 17
financial, 49, 102
legal personality, 46, 119
member states, 45, 46, 47, 48, 49
non-contractual *see* Non-contractual liability

non-liability clauses, 47, 49
primary obligations, non-compliance, 45
primary rules, 74
state of the law, 46–50
torts *see* Tortious liability
undertakings, 47
Libya, 20
Locus standi see Access to remedies
Lump-sum agreements, 73, 162
Luxembourg, 162

Malaysia, 69, 161, 234
Martha, Rutsel, 110
Member states,
see also States
access to remedies, 36, 38, 39–40, 65, 224–5
accountability levels, 29–33
applicants, 34
budgetary contributions, 31
co-operation suspended, 31
control and power, 1–2
corporate veil, 46
diplomatic protection, 65, 73–8, 213
hosts *see* Host states
judicial remedies, 32–3
liabilities, 45, 46, 47, 48, 49
participation, 40
permanent withdrawal, 31
political decision-making, 44
procedure, 66–80
supervision/monitoring, 8, 29–30
temporary withdrawal, 31
Merrills, John, 56
Meyer, Dorothée, 156
Monitoring *see* Supervision/monitoring
Multinational corporations, human rights, 15

Namibia, 20
Nauru, 22
Negligence,
remedial outcomes, 137, 143, 163
tortious liability, 97, 163
Negotiations,
contractual claims, 156
non-state entities, 63
Netherlands, 53, 101
New Zealand, 236
Non-contractual liability,
see also *Liabilities*

INDEX   289

claims, 8, 41, 43
damage, 8
General Convention (1946), 230
governing law, 173
remedial outcomes, 137
Non-governmental oraganisations (NGOs),
   access to remedies, 39, 107–8
   amicus curiae, 109, 110, 112
   consultative status, 38, 108, 112
   development assistance, 107
   Dispute Settlement Understanding,
      111
   European Court of Justice (ECJ), 110
   human rights, 15, 112
   humanitarian aid, 107
   International Court of Justice (ICJ),
      108–10, 255–6
   International Labour Organisation (ILO),
      106, 112
   international organisations,
      relationships, 106–7
   judicial remedies, 108–17
   legal personality, 107, 129
   locus standi lacking, 107–8, 255–6
   procedural obstacles, 106–13
   remedial outcomes, 135
   representational NGOs, 106–13, 135
   United Nations, 106, 108
Non-legal remedial action,
   alternative remedial action, 177–97
   commissions of inquiry, 170
   inspections *see* Inspection panels
   ombudsman *see* Ombudsman
Non-member states,
   access to remedies, 37
   applicant states, 34
   primary rules, 33
Non-state entities,
   access to remedies, 38, 39, 225
   arbitration, 22–3
   archives, access, 127, 129
   burden of proof, 125, 126
   claimants, 114–32
   decisions, 29
   disclosure, 125–9
   evidence, 125–32
   international law, 30
   negotiations, 63
   procedural obstacles, 114–32
   third parties, 33–4, 38
North Atlantic Treaty Organisation (NATO),

Bosnian war, 194
international administrative
   tribunals, 84
peacekeeping/enforcement
   operations, 53

Office for Administration and
   Management, 199
Office of Internal Oversight Services
   (OIOS), 157, 158, 160, 181
Office of Legal Affairs (UN), 93, 94, 96, 162
Officials and staff,
   access to remedies, 38, 42, 84
   accountability, 129
   arbitration, 83, 84
   consultative committees, 148
   contractual claims, 81, 91
   disciplinary measures, 143, 144
   disputes, 12, 78–80, 147
   employment,
      applications, 79
      contracts, 75, 81, 91
      dispute procedure, 81–2, 119, 122
   European Court of Justice (ECJ), 84
   exhaustion of local remedies, 79, 82
   expulsion, 33
   international administrative tribunals,
      82, 84–6, 147–55
   joint appeals boards, 82
   legislative decisions challenged, 84–6
   loyalty/discretion, 129
   marchandage, 201
   official capacity, 123
   organisational responsibility, 24
   performance of duty, 26
   political remedial mechanisms, 30
   pre-litigation procedures, 82–3, 147, 201
   procedure, 81–7
   protection system, 81–4
   reappointment withheld, 30
   remedial outcomes, 147–55
   special service agreements, 83
   staff regulations, 82
   third-party claims, 51
   United Nations, 69–70, 78–9, 81, 84, 85 ,
      86, 91, 129
Ombudsman,
   accountability, 170, 178, 181
   alternative remedial action, 178–81, 264
   European Community, 178–80
   human rights, 181

290   INDEX

Ombudsman, (cont.)
  recommendations, 178
  United Nations, 81, 181
Operational activities,
  challenged, 42
  controls, 29
  damage, 8
  implementation, 58
  institutional acts distinguished,
    28–9
  judicial review, 66
  tortious liability, 97
Opérations des Nations Unies au Congo
    (ONUC), 77, 97–9, 162, 166
Opinions, Advisory see Advisory Opinions
Organisation for Economic Co-operation
    and Development (OECD), 84
Organisation of American States (OAS),
    41, 212

Parliaments,
  accountability, 32
  commissions of inquiry, 31–2
Peacekeeping/enforcement operations,
  Advisory Board for Compensation
    Claims, 84
  arbitration, 157, 160
  claims, 53, 72–3, 77, 162–6
  claims commissions, 72, 73, 77, 99,
    103–5, 164
  combat-related activities, 102
  commissions of inquiry, 20, 32, 192,
    193–7, 260
  contracts, 24, 90, 92, 94
  damage, 72, 77, 99, 102
  Department of Peacekeeping Operations
    (DPKO), 159, 193, 194, 195
  Dutchbat operation, 100, 101, 193
  ex gratia payments, 165–6
  exhaustion of local remedies, 67
  financial liabilities, 102
  governmental authority, 16, 20
  holding-harmless clause, 71–3
  host states, 77
  human rights, 101, 102, 181
  immunities, 98, 103
  Implementation Force, 165
  international criminal tribunals, 131
  legal personality, 92
  lump-sum agreements, 73, 162
  mandates, 102

Memorandum of Understanding,
    71, 72
military necessity, 102
North Atlantic Treaty Organisation
    (NATO), 53
ONUC operation, 77, 97–9, 162, 166
Operation Silver Back, 100
Operation Turquoise, 193
operational command and control, 52,
    99–101
operational necessity, 102, 103
Rwanda, 100, 127, 143, 190, 191, 192,
    193–7
Security Council see UN Security Council
Special Committee on Peacekeeping
    Operations, 105
Srebrenica, 100, 101, 143, 192, 193,
    194, 196
Stabilisation Force, 165
Status of Forces Agreement (SOFA), 72–3,
    77, 84, 98, 99, 102–5, 164, 165
sub-contracting, 24, 93
third-party liabilities, 102–3
tortious liability, 77, 97–105, 115,
    162–6
UN Secretary-General, 52, 101, 103,
    165, 192
UNAMIR, 193, 194, 195, 196
UNEF, 73, 98
UNFICYP, 73, 98
United Kingdom, 53
United Nations, 52–3, 71–3, 77, 97–105,
    157, 162–6, 190–7
UNOSOM II, 20, 165–6, 193
UNPROFOR, 195
Permanent Court of Arbitration (PCA),
    220–3
Permanent Court of International Justice
    (PCIJ), 255
Philippines, 108
Political remedial mechanisms,
  access to remedies, 39–40
  dissolution, 33
  officials and staff, 30
  potential outcomes, 57
Portugal, 53
Pre-remedial action,
  alternative remedial action, 172–6
  commissions of inquiry, 65
  pre-litigation procedures, 64, 82–3,
    147, 201

INDEX 291

primary rules, 26
Primary rules,
  accountability, 7, 17, 26, 58
  compliance, 17, 65
  development/refinement, 11, 21
  human rights, 14, 15
  infringement, 3
  liabilities, 74
  limitation, 21
  non-member states, 33
  pre-remedial action, 26
  remedies against states, 21
Private claimants,
  see also Non-state entities
  contractual claims, 89–95, 115
  counterclaims, 91
  individuals *see* Individuals
  NGOs *see* Non-governmental
    organisations (NGOs)
  procedure, 88–105
  remedial outcomes, 156–66
  tortious liability, 89, 96–105,
    160–6
Privatisation, 24
Procedure,
  action against international
    organisations, 63–5
  claimants, 50–2
  complaints, investigation, 64
  member states, 66–80
  obstacles,
    non-governmental organisations
      (NGOs), 106–13
    non-state entities, 114–32
  officials and staff, 81–7
  pre-litigation procedures, 64, 82–3,
    14, 201
  private claimants, 88–105
  procedural justice, 63
  substantive justice, 63

Rabel, E., 163
Ratione fori, 39–40
Ratione materiae,
  inspection panels, 183
  international administrative tribunals,
    147, 148, 207
  International Court of Justice (ICJ), 243,
    245–50, 256
  scope, 20, 22, 28–35, 82, 131, 221
Ratione personae,

international administrative tribunals,
  147, 202, 207
International Court of Justice (ICJ),
  241–5
respondenti, 44–53
scope, 20, 22, 36–9, 111, 221
Ratione remedii,
  inspection panels, 184
  international administrative
    tribunals, 139
  scope, 54–9
Reinisch, August, 37, 96, 116, 117, 118,
  121, 125, 155, 161, 208, 215–19
Remedial outcomes,
  apologies, 142–3
  compensation *see* Compensation
  contractual claims, 137, 156–60
  costs/fees, 145–6, 154–5
  damages *see* Damages
  disciplinary action, 143, 144
  ex gratia payments, 142, 161, 165–6
  first-level remedies, 57–9, 119
  general features, 135–46
  guarantees, 143
  International Court of Justice (ICJ), 54–5
  memorials, 143
  negligence, 137, 143, 163
  non-contractual liability, 137
  non-governmental organisations
    (NGOs), 135
  non-monetary, 138, 139
  officials and staff, 147–55
  potential outcomes, 54–9, 119
  private claimants, 156–66
  tortious liability, 160–6
Remedies,
  access *see* Access to remedies
  accountability *see* Accountability
  affirmative orders, 26
  against whom, 44–53
  alternative *see* Alternative remedial
    action
  autonomy, 23
  common features, 23–5
  corporate approach, 51
  corporate character, 22
  customary international law, 17
  distinctive features, 19–23
  equality, 40, 67, 244
  implied powers, 25–6
  inequality, 23–4, 25–6, 103

292　INDEX

Remedies, (cont.)
  internal *see* Internal remedial
    mechanisms
  international law, 10–12
  jurisdiction *see* Jurisdiction
  legal *see* Judicial remedies
  need for, 12–19
  political *see* Political remedial
    mechanisms
  pre-emptive/prospective, 26
  pre-remedial *see* Pre-remedial action
  reciprocity, 23
  scope *ratione see* Scope
Remedies against states,
  accountability, 7, 22
  claims, 44–5
Remedies against states, (cont.)
  comparison, 19–25, 42
  consortium of states, 22
  extended jurisdiction, 20
  human rights, 22, 27, 80, 93, 138
  individuals, legal redress, 16
  International Court of Justice (ICJ),
    138
  judicial remedies, 22
  primary rules, 21
  reciprocity, 23
Restitutio in integrum,
  costs/fees, 146
  institutional acts, 136
  International Court of Justice (ICJ),
    55
  legal, 136
  material, 136
Reuter, Paul, 126, 127
Ritter, Jean-Pierre, 74, 170
Rolin, Henri, 237
Rosenne, Shabtai, 55, 109, 110, 255
Rules/norms,
  customary international law, 1
  decisions, 172
  international law, 1, 30, 47
  rule of law, 16
  violation, 8, 65
Ruzié, David, 201
Rwanda,
  Belgium, 100, 193, 196
  commissions of inquiry, 127, 143, 190,
    191, 192, 193–6, 260, 268
  UNAMIR, 193, 194, 195, 196
  UNAMIR II, 193

Salmon, Jean, 77, 99
San Francisco Declaration, 192
Sarooshi, Danesh, 50, 129, 131, 249
Schermers, Henry, 203
Scope,
  ratione fori, 39–40
  ratione materiae, 20, 22, 28–35, 82,
    131, 221
  ratione personae, 20, 22, 36–9, 111,
    221
  ratione personae respondenti, 44–53
  ratione remedii, 54–9
Secondary rules,
  accountability, 8, 17
  compliance, 65
  human rights, 14
Set-offs, 162
Seyersted, Finn, 19, 51, 52, 114
Shaw, Malcolm, 57
Shelton, Dinah, 11, 17, 80, 127, 136, 138,
    145, 146
Singer, Michael, 118
Somalia, 20, 165–6, 193, 220
Sovereignty, states, 21, 24
Spain, 53
Special Convention on the Privileges and
    Immunities of Specialised Agencies
    68, 88, 219, 232
Special rapporteurs, mandates, 30, 230
Specific performance, 54, 137–40, 150, 151
Staff *see* Officials and staff
States,
  see also Member states
  arbitration, international organisations,
    220–2
  autonomy, 23
  competences, 21
  diplomatic relations, 29
  jurisdictional immunity, 22, 37
  non-members *see* Non-member states
  remedies *see* Remedies against states
  sovereignty, 21, 24
Status of Forces Agreement (SOFA), 72–3,
    77, 84, 98, 99, 102–5, 164, 165
Sub-contracting,
  contractual claims, 92–3
  development assistance, 24, 93
  humanitarian aid, 24, 93
  immunities, 92–3
  peacekeeping/enforcement operations,
    24, 93

INDEX 293

Subsidiary organs, delegated powers, 30–1
Supervision/monitoring,
  accountability, 28
  conventions, 15
  member states, 8, 29–30
  purposes, 29–30
Switzerland, 107–8, 162
Szasz, Paul, 70, 71, 85, 87, 164, 244, 250
Sztucki, Jerzy, 239

Telecommunications, 24
Tortious liability,
  accountability levels, 28, 64
  compensation, 163, 164
  counterclaims, 162
  damage, 28, 64, 79
  immunities, 122
  indemnities, 161
  insurance/self-insurance, 96–7, 161
  international administrative
    tribunals, 160
  International Court of Justice (ICJ), 161,
    225–6
  jurisdiction, 160
  lex loci delicti commissi, 160
  negligence, 97, 163
  non-economic loss, 163
  operational activities, 97
  peacekeeping/enforcement operations,
    77, 97–105, 162–6
  primary rules, 74
  private claimants, 89, 96–105, 115,
    160–6
  remedial outcomes, 160–6
  remedial state action, 79
  standard of proof, 126
  third parties, 47, 74, 102–3
  United States, 122
  waiver of immunities, 161
Treaties
  decisions, compatibility, 29
  environmental protection, 112
  good faith, 1
  international organisations, 47
  Vienna Convention (1986), 237
Tribunals,
  administrative *see* International
    administrative tribunals
  Arbitral Tribunal, 156, 158
  criminal *see* International criminal
    tribunals

ILOAT *see* International Labour
  Organisation Administrative
  Tribunal
UNAT *see* UN Administrative Tribunal
United Nations *see* UN tribunals
World Administrative Tribunal
  proposed, 266

UN *see* United Nations
UN Administrative Tribunal (UNAT),
  appeals, 84, 223
  compensation, 151–3
  costs, 154, 155
  denial of justice, 203, 204
  interests of organisations, 268
  jurisdiction, 202, 203
  marchandage, 201
  oral hearings, 83, 203
  remedial outcomes, 149–55
  respondents, 85
  review system, 86, 87
  specific performance, 150, 151
  unsuccessful applicants, 79
  variety of outcomes, 149–51
UN Assistance Mission for Rwanda
  (UNAMIR), 193, 194, 195, 196
UN Children's Fund (UNICEF), 180
UN Conference on International
  Organisation, 236, 241
UN Decade of International Law (1992), 221
UN Development Programme (UNDP),
  159, 220
UN Emergency Force (UNEF), 73, 98
UN General Assembly,
  appeal review procedure, 86
  arbitration cases, 157, 159
  awards, 212
  condemnation, 143–4
  ICJ powers, 238
  insurance, 96
  legality, resolutions, 148
  legislative decisions challenged, 85
  member states, 88
  officials and staff, 81, 85, 86
  pre-remedial action, 175
  preferential standing, 37–8
  procurement-related claims, 94
  remedies, compliance, 139
  third-party liabilities, 102
  tortious liability, 160–1, 163
  transitory administrations, 20–1, 233

294   INDEX

UN High Commission for Refugees
   (UNHCR),
   Model Co-operation Agreement, 71
   operational activities, 101
UN Operation in Somalia (UNOSOM II), 20,
   165–6, 193
UN Peacekeeping Force in Cyprus
   (UNFICYP), 73, 98
UN Protection Force (UNPROFOR),
   195
UN Relief and Works Agency for
   Palestinian Refugees in the Near
   East
(UNRWA), 217
UN Secretary-General,
   amicus curiae, 251
   arbitration cases, 157, 159–60
   Bosnian war, 194
   Bulletins, 97, 101
   claims commissions, 103–5
   code of conduct, 175, 267
   Executive Office, 201
   immunities,
      criminal evidence, 129
      differences, 69–70
      waiver, 50, 89, 103, 124, 208–9
   internal justice, 81, 199–201, 205,
      210
   litigation discouraged, 84, 88
   lobbying, 79
   margin of appreciation, 209
   member states, 88
   Office for Administration and
      Management, 199
   peacekeeping/enforcement operations,
      52, 101, 103, 165, 192, 195
   pre-remedial action, 175
   Rwanda, 195, 196
   Secretariat, 50, 81, 96, 130, 131, 175,
      194, 196, 199
   Under-Secretary-General, 72, 199
spreadlong1pc
UN Security Council,
   see also Peacekeeping/enforcement
      operations
   commissions of inquiry, 165–6, 192, 194,
      195, 196
   Military Staff Committee, 100
   operational oversight, 101
   political direction, 52
   sanctions committees, 37

states, preferential standing, 37
strategic direction, 100
UN Special Commission on Iraq
   (UNSCOM), 101
UN Temporary Executive Authority
   (UNTEA), 20
UN tribunals,
   common-system tribunals, 85, 86
   judicial powers, 20
   UNAT *see* UN Administrative Tribunal
UNCITRAL,
   Arbitration Rules, 221
   Conciliation Rules, 67, 94, 156
United Kingdom, 53
United Nations,
   Advisory Board for Compensation
      Claims, 84
   Advisory Committee on Administrative
      and Budgetary Questions, 175
   arbitration, 67, 84, 93, 94, 157–60,
      199–200
   Charter, 14, 37, 52, 78, 79, 86, 100, 108,
      111, 121, 123, 153, 175, 230, 231,
      237, 250, 266
   civil responsibility law, 174
   claims against, 14, 136
   Commission on Human Rights (CHR),
      194, 230
   contracts, tenders, 90
   diplomatic protection, 75, 78–9
   Economic and Social Council (ECOSOC),
      111, 230
   General Conditions of Contract, 157
   Headquarters Agreement, 68, 160–1
   human rights, 15, 101
   Human Rights Committee, 101
   immunities, 50, 56, 69–70, 88, 89, 92,
      93, 120–1, 129, 210–11, 217–18
   insurance, 96, 161
   internal remedial mechanisms, 69
   JAB *see* Joint Appeals Board
   Joint Inspection Unit (JIU), 181, 200–1,
      202, 204, 205
   Joint Staff Pension Board, 85
   judicial review, 16–17
   Legal Counsel, 69, 70, 210–11
   Military Staff Committee, 100
   non-governmental organisations (NGOs),
      106, 108
   Office of Internal Oversight Services
      (OIOS), 157, 158, 160, 181, 212

Office of Legal Affairs, 93, 94, 96, 162, 201, 217
officials and staff, 69–70, 78–9, 81, 84, 85, 86, 91, 129
ombudsman, 81, 181
Panel of Counsel, 154, 155, 201
peacekeeping *see* Peacekeeping/ enforcement operations
practice, 3
preferential standing, 37–8
sanctions committees, 37
Special Committee, 237, 238, 241, 242
subsidiary organs, 50–1
Tort Claims Board, 96
trusteeship agreements, 20
United States,
Headquarters Agreements,
OAS, 41, 212
UN, 68, 160–1
immunities, 37, 122
peace-enforcement operations, 53
State Department, 237
tortious liability, 122
Universal Declaration on Human Rights, 153
Urquhart, Brian, 181

Venezuela, 236

Waiver, judicial remedies, 18
Waiver of immunities,

see also Immunities
arbitration, 91, 93
balance of interest, 208–9
conditional, 131
General Convention (1946), 89, 124, 208, 212
international criminal tribunals, 131
judicial interpretation, 121, 124
risks, 267–8
tortious liability, 161
UN Secretary-General, 50, 89, 103, 124, 208–9
Wenckstern, Manfred, 45, 50
West New Guinea, 20
World Administrative Tribunal, 266
World Bank,
accountability, 185–7
Clarifications (1996), 183, 184–5
inspection panels, 182–90, 256
World Health Organisation (WHO), 180
World Trade Organisation (WTO), dispute settlement mechanisms, 10, 111

Yugoslavia, 22, 53
Bosnia and Herzegovina, 53, 194, 195
Srebrenica, 100, 101, 143, 192, 193, 194, 196

Zacklin, Ralph, 153
Zaslawski, Emil, 55

CAMBRIDGE STUDIES IN INTERNATIONAL AND COMPARATIVE LAW

Books in the series

Principles of the Institutional Law of International Organisations
C. F. Amerasinghe

Fragmentation and the International Relations of Micro-states
Jorri Duursma

The Polar Regions and the Development of International Law
Donald R. Rothwell

Sovereignty over Natural Resources
Nico Schrijver

Ethics and Authority in International Law
Alfred P. Rubin

Religious Liberty and International Law in Europe
Malcolm D. Evans

Unjust Enrichment
Hanoch Dagan

Trade and the Environment
Damien Geradin

The Changing International Law of High Seas Fisheries
Francisco Orrego Vicuña

International Organisations before National Courts
August Reinisch

The Right to Property in Commonwealth Constitutions
Tom Allen

Trusts: A Comparative Study
Maurizio Lupoi

On Civil Procedure
J. A. Jolowicz

Good Faith in European Contract Law
Reinhard Zimmermann and Simon Whittaker

Money Laundering
Guy Stessens

International Law in Antiquity
David J. Bederman

The Enforceability of Promises in European Contract Law
James Gordley

International Commercial Arbitration and African States
Amazu A. Asouzu

The Law of Internal Armed Conflict
Lindsay Moir

Diversity and Self-determination in International Law
Karen Knop

Remedies against International Organisations
Karel Wellens

International Human Rights and Humanitarian Law
René Provost